THE

Penguin History

of

AMERICAN
LIFE

THE
IRISH
WAY

ALSO BY JAMES R. BARRETT

Work and Community in the Jungle:
Chicago's Packinghouse Workers, 1894–1922

William Z. Foster and the Tragedy of American Radicalism

THE
IRISH
WAY

BECOMING AMERICAN
IN THE MULTIETHNIC CITY

JAMES R. BARRETT

THE PENGUIN PRESS

New York | *2012*

THE PENGUIN PRESS
Published by the Penguin Group
Penguin Group (USA) Inc., 375 Hudson Street,
New York, New York 10014, U.S.A. • Penguin Group (Canada), 90 Eglinton Avenue East, Suite 700,
Toronto, Ontario, Canada M4P 2Y3 (a division of Pearson Penguin Canada Inc.) • Penguin Books Ltd,
80 Strand, London WC2R 0RL, England • Penguin Ireland, 25 St. Stephen's Green, Dublin 2,
Ireland (a division of Penguin Books Ltd) • Penguin Books Australia Ltd, 250 Camberwell Road,
Camberwell, Victoria 3124, Australia (a division of Pearson Australia Group Pty Ltd) •
Penguin Books India Pvt Ltd, 11 Community Centre, Panchsheel Park, New Delhi – 110 017,
India • Penguin Group (NZ), 67 Apollo Drive, Rosedale, Auckland 0632, New Zealand
(a division of Pearson New Zealand Ltd) • Penguin Books (South Africa) (Pty)
Ltd, 24 Sturdee Avenue, Rosebank, Johannesburg 2196, South Africa

Penguin Books Ltd, Registered Offices: 80 Strand, London WC2R 0RL, England

First published in 2012 by The Penguin Press, a member of Penguin Group (USA) Inc.

Photograph credits appear on pages 367–369.

LIBRARY OF CONGRESS CATALOGING-IN-PUBLICATION DATA
Barrett, James R.,———.
The Irish way : becoming American in the multiethnic city / James R. Barrett.
p. cm.
Includes bibliographical references and index.
ISBN 978-1-59420-325-1
1. Irish—United States—History—19th century.   2. Irish—United States—History—20th century.
3. National characteristics, Irish.   4. City and town life—United States—History—19th century.
5. City and town life—United States—History—20th century.   6. Cultural pluralism—United States.
7. Ireland—Emigration and immigration.   8. United States—Emigration and immigration.   I. Title.
E184.I6B273 2012
305.891'62073—dc23   2011040105

Printed in the United States of America
1   3   5   7   9   10   8   6   4   2

DESIGNED BY NICOLE LAROCHE

FOR JENNY BARRETT

and

CATHERINE MARIE ELLIS BARRETT

(1913–2005)

CONTENTS

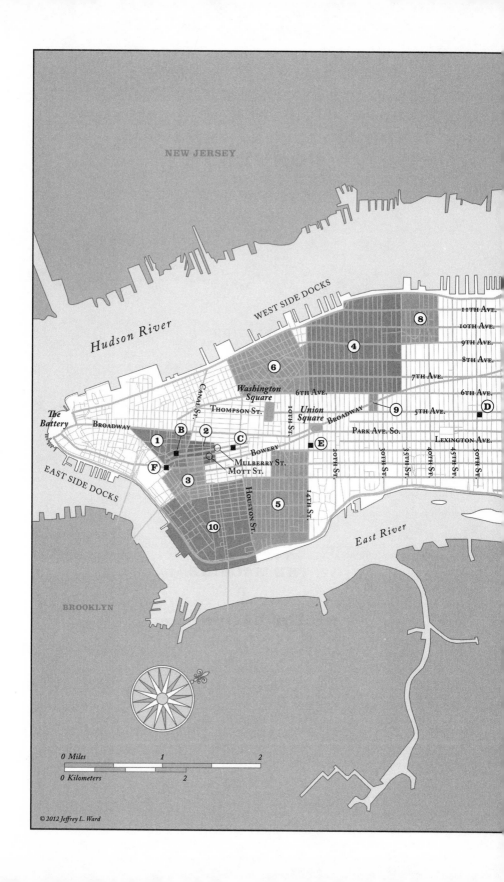

NEW JERSEY

WEST SIDE DOCKS

Hudson River

The
Battery

EAST SIDE DOCKS

BROADWAY

CANAL ST.

Washington
Square

THOMPSON ST.

Union
Square

BROADWAY

PARK AVE. SO.

11TH AVE.
10TH AVE.
9TH AVE.
8TH AVE.
7TH AVE.
6TH AVE.
5TH AVE.

LEXINGTON AVE.

6TH AVE.

10TH ST.

20TH ST.

30TH ST.

35TH ST.

40TH ST.

45TH ST.

50TH ST.

Bowery

MULBERRY ST.
MOTT ST.

HOUSTON ST.

14TH ST.

East River

BROOKLYN

0 Miles   1   2

0 Kilometers   2

© 2012 Jeffrey L. Ward

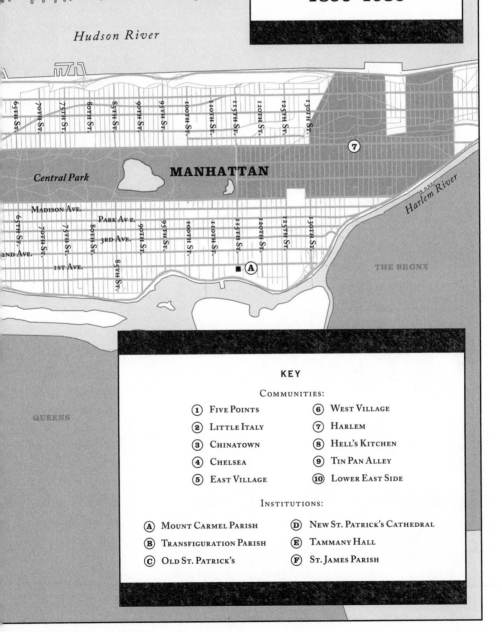

IRISH AMERICAN
AND OTHER
ETHNIC COMMUNITIES
OF
NEW YORK CITY
1890–1930

Hudson River

Central Park

MANHATTAN

Madison Ave.

Park Ave.

3rd Ave.

1st Ave.

2nd Ave.

Harlem River

THE BRONX

QUEENS

65TH ST. 70TH ST. 75TH ST. 80TH ST. 85TH ST. 90TH ST. 95TH ST. 100TH ST. 110TH ST. 115TH ST. 120TH ST. 125TH ST. 130TH ST.

8TH ST.

KEY

COMMUNITIES:

1. FIVE POINTS
2. LITTLE ITALY
3. CHINATOWN
4. CHELSEA
5. EAST VILLAGE

6. WEST VILLAGE
7. HARLEM
8. HELL'S KITCHEN
9. TIN PAN ALLEY
10. LOWER EAST SIDE

INSTITUTIONS:

A. MOUNT CARMEL PARISH
B. TRANSFIGURATION PARISH
C. OLD ST. PATRICK'S

D. NEW ST. PATRICK'S CATHEDRAL
E. TAMMANY HALL
F. ST. JAMES PARISH

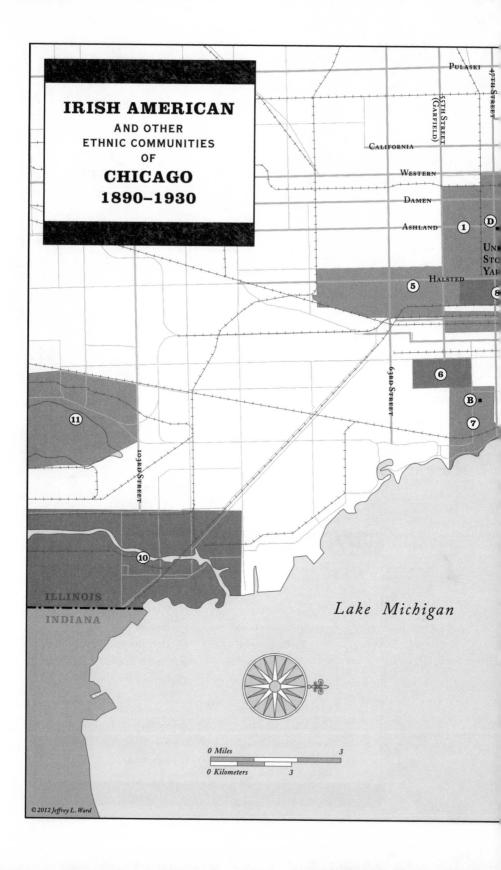

IRISH AMERICAN
AND OTHER
ETHNIC COMMUNITIES
OF
CHICAGO
1890–1930

PULASKI

47TH STREET

55TH STREET
(GARFIELD)

CALIFORNIA

WESTERN

DAMEN

ASHLAND ① Ⓓ

UNI...
STO...
YAR...

⑤ HALSTED ⑧

63RD STREET

⑥

Ⓑ ∎

⑦

⑪

103RD STREET

⑩

ILLINOIS
INDIANA

Lake Michigan

0 Miles   3

0 Kilometers   3

© 2012 Jeffrey L. Ward

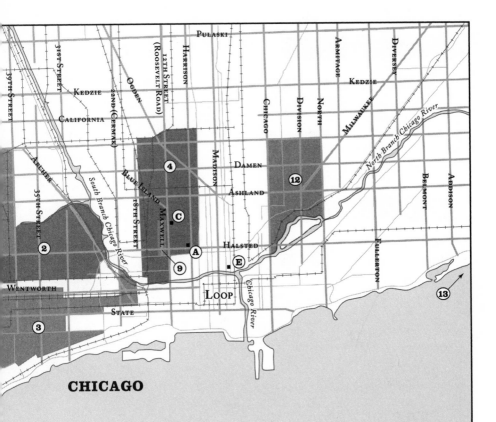

CHICAGO

KEY

COMMUNITIES:

1. BACK OF THE YARDS
2. BRIDGEPORT
3. BLACK BELT
4. LITTLE ITALY
5. ENGLEWOOD
6. WASHINGTON PARK
7. HYDE PARK
8. CANARYVILLE
9. MAXWELL STREET DISTRICT/ JEWISH GHETTO
10. SOUTH CHICAGO STEEL DISTRICT
11. PULLMAN
12. "POLONIA" (POLISH DISTRICT)
13. EVANSTON, ILLINOIS

INSTITUTIONS:

A. HULL HOUSE
B. UNIVERSITY OF CHICAGO
C. HOLY FAMILY PARISH
D. UNIVERSITY OF CHICAGO SETTLEMENT HOUSE
E. OLD ST. PATRICK'S CHURCH

INTRODUCTION

T hough surrounded by Poles and Italians," the Jewish writer Harry Golden recalled of his Lower East Side neighborhood, "it was the Irish and the Irish alone we Jews admired . . . we identified the Irishman not only with the English language but also with the image of what an American looked like. The Irish were the cops and the firemen and the ballplayers. Although the immigrant Jew and the Irish poor did not get along well, these Irish were still the figures Jewish immigrants wanted to emulate."[1]

Immigrants who arrived in American cities around the turn of the century found it difficult to avoid the Irish. Between 1840 and 1890, more than three million Irish immigrants had entered the United States, and by 1900, an estimated five million of their first and second generations were settled in. There were more Irish in Brooklyn and Manhattan than in Dublin, and more in the United States than in the nation of Ireland. But then the sources of immigration shifted, and between 1890 and 1920, eighteen million "new immigrants," largely from eastern and southeastern Europe, came to the United States.[2] When they arrived in the American city, they found the Irish.

Whether they wanted to save their souls, get a drink, find a job, or walk around the corner, the newcomers often had to deal with entrenched Irish Americans. They might get a job through an Italian *padrone*, but the foremen, union officers, and shop stewards were likely to be Irish; they might worship at a Polish church, but the bishop who governed the spiritual realm of urban life was likely to be Irish too. The Irish saloonkeeper, priest, cop, and ward heeler have become caricatures, but each really did interact with the new immigrants every day, as did the Irish nun, public schoolteacher, and street tough. As the reformer Emily Balch observed in 1910, "The newcomers, encountering Irish policemen, Irish politicians, Irish bureaucrats, Irish saloon keepers, Irish contractors, and Irish teachers could be excused for thinking that 'Irish' equaled 'American.'"[3] In these spheres and many others, the Irish played a significant role in the newcomers' "Americanization"; as a result, the multiethnic American city of the early twentieth century assumed a peculiarly Hibernian cast.

Even in cities with large ethnic enclaves and vast arrays of voluntary organizations, newer immigrants navigated a world dominated by the Irish. Between the 1890s and the 1930s, when Ireland was emerging as a modern nation and the United States became a major economic and political power, they seemed to be everywhere.[4]

This book is a study of Irish Catholic Americans, particularly of the second and third generations—those who were shaped not in the Irish countryside but in the streets of America's largest cities—and of later Irish immigrants who arrived between the 1880s and 1920s. It is also an interethnic history, tracking their relations with other ethnic and racial groups with whom they shared neighborhoods, workplaces, churches, and other urban institutions. Identity in the United States, as we will see, emerged from dynamic relationships *among* ethnic groups, as well as from particular groups' own distinct history and traditions, and it can be understood only in the context of these interactions.[5] As the literary scholar Henry Louis Gates, Jr., has written of American culture, "Mixing and hybridity are the rule, not the exception."[6]

Here we view the Irish American community from the bottom up, focusing our attention on common people—parish priests, street gangsters, ward heelers, and union activists. Certainly the elite was important in the development of the Irish American community, but we can best view the engagement of the Irish with other peoples, and appreciate their impact on the new multiethnic urban culture, at street level.

Individual ethnic cultures were enduring and influential. The newer ethnic groups were not *assimilated* in the sense that they were completely absorbed into some sort of cultural mainstream: in the effort to settle in, their own cultures offered them their most important resources. But a gradual *acculturation*, by which newer immigrants acquired knowledge and skills that allowed them to deal with their new city worlds, was central to their experience. This Americanization was partly a coercive process that occurred in settlement houses, night school classes, and corporate programs, where middle-class elites pressed WASP values on working-class immigrants. But most immigrants came to understand their new world less through such formal programs than through informal contacts with the Irish and other experienced working-class Americans of diverse ethnic backgrounds in streets, churches, and theaters. Understanding that is a key to understanding the multiethnic American city.[7]

AMERICA'S FIRST ETHNIC GROUP

The Irish were America's first ethnic group, and their deepest roots lay in rural Ireland. They saw themselves as a diasporic people—exiled from their homes by cruel fate and brutish English colonizers. The Great Famine of 1845–52 haunted their communities for decades—it cost Ireland more than half of its population through disease, starvation, and migration. The human dimensions of this searing catastrophe account for the grim determination with which the Irish went about carving out a place in American society. By the time they reached American shores, the Irish had experienced not only the systematic destruction of much of their traditional culture, but also a devastating natural disaster and the willful British neglect of their suffering that expressed itself in thousands of individual tragedies. The Famine cast its shadow over millions of Irish Americans as a result of the community's vibrant oral traditions.[8] Their struggles, both in Ireland and in the American city, produced a culture that mixed aggressiveness, a sentiment of grievance, a sensitivity to slights and, above all, a strong instinct to survive. For all the nostalgia of later years, most Irish had no desire to return to their native soil; they wished only to thrive where they had landed.[9]

Nativist hostility toward the Irish created a defensiveness in their relations with later waves of migrant peoples. In the 1830s and 1840s, Protestant gangs invaded Irish Catholic neighborhoods in Philadelphia, Boston, and New York, burning homes, convents, and churches.[10] In 1855, the anti-immigrant Know-Nothing Party briefly won control of Chicago's city government by appealing to xenophobia, pro-temperance sentiment, and anti-Catholicism. German immigrants poured into the city too, but the poorer Irish bore the brunt of the reaction. "Who does not know," mayoral candidate Levi Boone thundered in the election that year, "that the most depraved, debased, worthless and irredeemable drunkards and sots which curse the community are Irish Catholics?"[11] Excluded from much of the city's public life, the Irish immigrants fell back upon their own communities and institutions.

Mid-nineteenth-century nativists began referring to a "Celtic mind," an "Irish nature," and something they termed "Irishism"—a depravity characteristic of the immigrants and perhaps also of their children.[12] Citizens of Rhode Island debated whether the Irish should be excluded from the provisions of the Fifteenth Amendment, as they appeared to be a distinctly different race from both African Americans and the "white" mainstream.[13] Since they generally arrived with fewer skills and resources than the Germans, the Irish competed for low-wage work with African Americans. Comparisons between African and Native Americans and the "savage Irish" were common. Even if the Irish did not labor alongside African Americans, their tasks so closely resembled those performed by free and enslaved blacks that they were often called "nigger Irish," while African Americans were sometimes referred to as "smoked Irish." Black workers constituted only a tiny part of the nineteenth-century labor force in northern cities, and Irish workers succeeded in driving them from many unskilled jobs. These early confrontations, and later ones with African American strikebreakers, enhanced Irish American racism, as they insisted on distinguishing themselves as "white" workers.[14]

Nativist attacks also forced the Irish to organize. Adversity shaped the way they forged their identities as "white" and "American" and coped with the exigencies of urban industrial life. The timing of their arrival, the hostile reception they faced, and their efforts to build organizations and develop defensive strategies made Irish Catholics stand out as different. Arriving in extremely large numbers, and clustering in distinct city enclaves, they retained strong ties to Ireland and to their religious traditions. "The Irish seemed to understand," folklorist William Williams noted, "that they had to succeed as a people, not just as individuals." Only if they could construct an identity as both Irish and American would they thrive.[15] In the years ahead, many new ethnic groups would follow the same road.

When later immigrants settled into New York, Chicago, and Boston, it was often in close proximity to Irish Americans. To the extent that the newcomers learned from watching their neighbors, it was most often from observing the Irish. Jewish labor leader Abraham Bisno remembered that his Irish neighbors in Chicago's West Side ghetto were not much better off than the Jewish immigrants, and "the only point to their advantage was that they were older immigrants and knew more about America." After World War I, as New York's Greenwich Village gradually transformed from an Irish to an Italian neighborhood, the Irish remained all around the Italians, in the same streets and work sites, sometimes even occupying the same houses. In this sense the Irish community represented the "America" to which the immigrant Italians had to adapt. For the Italians, Irish ways were American ways. When immigrants distinguished English speakers from their own people, they often referred not to mainstream WASPs but to the Irish. When immigrant actors or musicians invoked "American" characters and characteristics, the Irish usually were the models.[16]

IRISH AMERICANISM

Yet if the Irish American community spoke to the new immigrants, it was seldom with one voice. A class distinction separated the "shanty" Irish poor from the upwardly mobile "lace curtain" element; regional origins also divided the community, as county and clan organizations provided ready sources for socialization. Only in the American city did many Irish develop a coherent national identity. The emergence of this identity was less an impediment to their acculturation than a prerequisite for it. Like the Italians, Polish, and others who would follow, most of the Irish who came before World War I arrived with a local identity based on kinship networks in rural villages. By the immigration boom of the early twentieth century, nationalist agitation, nativist attacks, and political self-interest had induced them largely to abandon these regional distinctions and become self-consciously "Irish."[17] Their achievement of such cohesion gave them an advantage over more recent arrivals: it facilitated the networking and social organization required to exert social, political, and economic influence.

The mass nationalist movement, which had matured by the time similar movements among African Americans and eastern European immigrants reached their zenith in the World War I era, provided a model of sorts for these later movements. "Physical force" activists, who advocated armed struggle against the British, vied with constitutionalists for the movement's leadership.[18] Likewise, Socialist and syndicalist radicals like "Mother" Jones, Elizabeth Gurley Flynn, and William Z. Foster vied with conservative American Federation of Labor (AFL) craft union leaders—disproportionately Irish American—whose much narrower vision of "labor" often excluded women, the unskilled, and racial minorities.[19] Progressive clerics and bishops advocated social welfare measures and Americanization of the church, while their conservative adversaries opposed social reform and argued for a unique Catholicism distinct from American culture.[20] The Irish "rebel girl" Margaret Sanger gave advice to immigrant women on sexuality and birth control very different from that of the church patriarchy.[21]

In other words, "Irishness" had not one but many versions, and like "Americanism," it was a contested identity, with groups and individuals projecting very different understandings. Americanized Irish passed on no single coherent set of ideas and values as a legacy to later migrant peoples.[22] But several major influences shaped what it meant to be Irish American, and the multiethnic urban culture that the Irish fashioned provided the framework for migrant peoples who followed them into the American city.

Above all, a particularly formal and intense Catholicism had fused with a modern Irish identity as it emerged on both sides of the Atlantic. Tempered by repression and discrimination, first under British colonialism and then in the face of American nativism, Catholicism pervaded daily life in Irish American communities, as it did that of many later immigrants, especially Italians and Poles.[23] Anticlericalism flourished in some wings of the Irish nationalist movement, but the overwhelming majority of immigrants and their children were devout. The Catholicism of the urban parish often lent the community a parochial mentality and instilled a strong attachment to neighborhood turf.

In politics, the primary Irish American tendency was instrumental: to get and exercise power, in one's own interest or in the community's. They perfected this approach in the urban machine and passed it on to later immigrants. But their sense of nationalist grievance and their links to working-class communities and organizations also opened them to the possibility of social reform and, occasionally, to social transformation. An abiding attachment to the nation—to Ireland as well as the American Republic—shaped ethnic relations, sometimes lending their politics an idealism. They often embraced a hyperbolic brand of American patriotism, as if wrapping themselves in the flag might finally bring them acceptance.

Still, their Irish identity persisted. "The awareness of being Irish came to us as small children through plaintive song and heroic story," labor radical Elizabeth Gurley Flynn recalled. "We drew in a burning hatred of

British rule with our mother's milk." Irish identity was reinforced in the
pages of the Irish American press, in the celebration of St. Patrick's Day
and other festivals, in voluntary organizations, and in everyday popular
culture.[24] Attachment to the Irish nation might have dissipated, but events
on both sides of the Atlantic repeatedly reinforced it. In Ireland, the 1880s
Land War pitted impoverished peasants against Anglo-Irish landlords;
the Home Rule movement pressed for local control; and the 1916 Easter
Rising erupted and was brutally suppressed by the British. In the United
States, the strong anti-Catholicism of the 1890s was aimed primarily at
the Irish; and in the early 1920s the Ku Klux Klan resurged.

Finally, a belligerent if narrow class consciousness pervaded many Irish
American communities, meeting each call for social mobility with skepticism. Even the rising "lace curtain" class, desperately craving respectability, seemed burdened with a profound ambivalence bordering on guilt
about leaving the old neighborhood behind. Among Irish American
workers, class consciousness often extended only to the limits of their own
communities. Their most common impulse was to exclude: to bar more
recent immigrants, women, and people of color from jobs and unions; to
discriminate against women and minorities; and to fight more radical
groups in the labor movement.

THE IRISH AND SOCIAL DIFFERENCE

Traditional Irish attitudes make such exclusionary tendencies difficult to
understand. In some respects, for example, Irish and African Americans
were unlikely foes. The Irish exhibited considerable sympathy for the slave
and opposition to slavery. In nationalist discourse, comparisons between
the oppressed Irish and black slaves were common, and abolitionist sentiment could fuse with nationalist agitation. Daniel O'Connell (1745–1847),
the leading voice for Irish rights in the United Kingdom, and Father
Theobald Mathew (1790–1856), the island's most influential cleric, both
endorsed the antislavery cause. For four months in 1845–46, the former
slave and African American abolitionist Frederick Douglass lectured to

fifty overflow crowds throughout Ireland. "I go on stage coaches, omni-
buses, steamboats, into first cabins, and in the public houses," Douglass
wondered, "without seeing the slightest manifestation of that hateful and
vulgar feeling against me." But abolitionism was never a mass movement
in Ireland, while in American cities, competition for jobs, neighborhoods,
and resources, abolitionist nativism, and the Catholic Church's ambivalence toward slavery all accentuated a deep animosity between Irish and
African Americans.[25]

Some aging immigrants stressed Ireland's homogeneity and insisted
that it was only in the new world that they had discovered racial and ethnic difference. A favorite story in Irish oral histories and memoirs is the
immigrant's first encounter with an African American. When Bertha
Devlin arrived as a teenager in 1923, hoping for work as a domestic servant,
she wondered at the bewildering range of ethnic groups she encountered in the immigrant throngs at Ellis Island. "There were Italians, . . .
Portuguese, . . . every type of people," each group in native dress. But it
was the black workers unloading and carting goods who made the greatest impression: "You know, you never see no colored people in Ireland."
She feared these workers a bit because the devils in Irish folklore were
all dark.[26] Particularly immigrants coming from the Gaelic-speaking far
west or the islands off the west coast may have been racially and ethnically
naïve.[27] Immigrants who arrived between the 1880s and the early 1900s
often came from these more remote areas.

But the Irish *did* have an understanding of race, and social difference
was acknowledged along several lines. Many Irish men had served in the
British Army in colonial settings or spent time working in London, with
its substantial nonwhite population. The Catholic/Protestant distinction
was fundamental to Irish society: Irish people framed their strong sense
of grievance and their identity as an oppressed people in opposition to
their Protestant neighbors. The Irish also developed a strong prejudice
against "travelers," migratory folk of lower status and education whose
cultural life and identity were quite separate from those of deeply rooted
country people. Anti-Semitism might be found in late-nineteenth-century

Irish cities, when it was common in Russia and eastern Europe. But Jews generally considered Ireland tolerant compared to most other European societies.[28]

Irish social tolerance certainly has a mixed history, then, but the particular strands of racism and anti-Semitism that characterized many Irish American neighborhoods were the products of life in the American city more than of any old country experience. Daniel O'Connell insisted that the immigrants had not learned the cruelty of racism in Ireland, and Frederick Douglass found the Irish "warm-hearted, generous, and sympathizing with the oppressed everywhere." It was in the American city that they learned "to hate and despise the colored people . . . to believe that we eat the bread which of right belongs to them . . . that our adversity is essential to their prosperity."[29]

Irish Americans interacted with recent immigrants, black migrants, and other people of color more than most native-born people did. Due to their religious background, their political allegiances, and their memories of oppression at the hands of the British, they could show strong sympathy for racial minorities and subject colonial peoples. Irish American attitudes about race and other social forms of social difference were often complex, then, and their behavior uneven. At times, they clearly conveyed racist, anti-Semitic, and other intolerant attitudes; at others, more tolerant and progressive views; but they clearly shaped the racial attitudes, language, and behavior of later immigrants among whom they lived, loved, worked, and played.

IRISH AMERICANIZATION

Acculturation was the gradual learning process by which immigrants and their families came to terms with their new environment, absorbing ideas and lessons from many sources. Mastering the English language and gaining an understanding of politics and government were crucial to this process, as was coping with daily challenges. A vigorous campaign of Americanization targeted immigrants and their children, particularly in the early twentieth century, when it became a sort of crusade. Settlement house reformers, government officials and professional patriots, corporate executives and managers set up programs in public schools, factories, churches, and elsewhere not only to teach the English language but also to convey a coherent version of Americanism reflecting the values of the native-born middle class.[30]

Theodore Roosevelt urged a muscular version of Americanization. "The men who do not become Americans and nothing else, are hyphenated Americans," he declared before a largely Irish Catholic Knights of Columbus gathering in New York on Columbus Day in 1915, "and there ought not to be room for them in this country."[31] Roosevelt was confident in his understanding of what it meant to be an American, an understanding modeled on his own upper-class Protestant background and experience.

But there were clearly alternative notions of American culture and alternative paths to Americanization. Most immigrants did their learning less in government programs than on street corners and in vaudeville houses, workplaces, saloons, and union locals. More important, the whole notion of Americanism and the question of how one became an American were highly contested. Immigrants played vital roles in creating many Americanisms.[32] When they were gradually integrated into the new society, it was less into a hostile WASP mainstream than into an emerging multiethnic working-class milieu that they themselves had pioneered.

This book considers the city spaces in which the Irish operated as Americanizers: in congested streets and parks; in the Catholic church, workplaces, labor organizations, and the urban political machine; on the stage and in popular literature and music; and through social and political movements. The chapter titles are metaphors for these spaces: thus "The Street" probes other public spaces besides the city street, while "The Stage" explores not only musical theater and vaudeville but also comic strips, urban realist literature, and films.

My object is not to advance a universal theory of Irish Americanization.

The size and location of their communities varied: they left a deeper mark in New York, with its huge Irish population, than in, say, Milwaukee. But in Chicago, New York, Boston, and other cities where established Irish American populations encountered more recent immigrants and migrant peoples of color, they played a vital role in creating a new interethnic culture.[33]

A legacy of real and imagined slights shaped Irish Catholic consciousness and their defensive urban culture. They told themselves and others that their success was hard-won, that they must stick together and take care of their own. At its best, this mind-set led Irish Americans to support integration and reform for other oppressed migrant peoples; at its worst, it became an excuse for racial and ethnic intolerance such as the Irish themselves had faced. An abiding tension between inclusiveness and exclusiveness, between cosmopolitanism and parochialism, lies at the heart of Irish American relations with other groups. This story turns on the dynamic between these impulses.

ONE

THE STREET

In the summer of 1918, on his first Sunday in Chicago, a teenage Langston Hughes, future playwright, poet, and writer, took a walk. The city's South Side "Black Belt" was already taking on the character of what African American sociologists came to call "Black Metropolis"—a city in itself. Separated from white Chicago by a series of invisible lines, it was filling with thousands of migrants from the Deep South, and State Street was buzzing with theaters, restaurants, dance halls, cabarets. "Midnight," Hughes recalled, "was like day." Accustomed to the more subtle racism of Lawrence, Kansas, the young man unwittingly crossed what the Chicago cops called a "deadline" along Wentworth Avenue, which separated the Black Belt from the old Irish American neighborhood of Bridgeport. A gang of white boys quickly set upon Hughes and beat him up, explaining simply that "they didn't allow niggers in that neighborhood."[1]

Langston Hughes survived to become a major figure in American literature and an astute observer of race and race relations. Charles Mallory, a young black man living on the city's divided South Side a few years later, was not as lucky. Crossing into the largely Irish American Canaryville neighborhood, which one sociologist called "a moral lesion in the life of the city," Mallory encountered Joseph Gilmartin and Edward Kelly. They demanded to know "what he was doing in their neighborhood," then beat him to death.[2]

The summer after Hughes's visit, American cities exploded in racial violence. In Chicago, the 1919 race riot claimed the lives of twenty-three African Americans and fifteen whites and injured hundreds more on both sides of the color line. Assessing the riot's causes, the Chicago Commission on Race Relations emphasized severe overcrowding, a lack of recreational facilities, and competition for jobs and political influence, but investigators also observed the peculiarly important role played by Irish American social athletic clubs, what we would recognize today as street gangs. "But for them," the commission concluded, "it is doubtful if the riot would have gone beyond the first clash."[3]

"MOVING DAY":

as white neighbors watch, an African American family moves out of an integrated neighborhood on Chicago's South Side in the wake of the summer 1919 race riot.

Scholars think about urban space in abstract theoretical terms, but city youth and others navigating its complexities every day experienced it in visceral ways. In the early twentieth century, the Irish, with their strong sense of turf, taught later migrants the social significance of these dividing lines. In the process, they shaped the ethnic realities of city life.

IRISH EVERYWHERE

The urban ubiquity of Irish Americans stemmed in part from their sheer volume and the timing of their arrival. In New York, they came in large numbers as early as the 1820s and 1830s, settling into the slums and laboring jobs of Lower Manhattan. By the time thousands of Famine migrants arrived in the late 1840s and early 1850s, the earlier generation had already created a network of institutions and organizations that facilitated their gradual rise.[4] In Chicago in the 1830s and 1840s, thousands of immigrants crowded into the little settlement of Bridgeport, taking construction jobs on a giant public works project, the Illinois and Michigan Canal. They then fanned out along the banks of the river and the burgeoning railroad system, laying and maintaining track or working in meatpacking plants, steel mills, and building construction sites.[5] By the eve of the Civil War, more than 260,000 Irish-born lived in Manhattan and Brooklyn; in Chicago ten years later, the figure was about forty thousand, about one-quarter of the city's population.[6] In these and other cities, vicious street battles between Catholics and Protestants paralleled the political storms gathering between competing political machines.

Many later immigrant sojourners returned to their native lands after making a stake in America, but for the Irish there was no turning back. In Chicago, New York, and other cities, they dug in, struggling to make a place for themselves. And they kept coming. Of the two million who left Ireland between 1850 and 1900, about 70 percent left after 1870.[7] Some Irish were neither urban nor Catholic, but the great majority were both.[8] As city people, they came into close contact with later immigrants and migrant peoples of color. In many regions of the East and Midwest, the German American population was actually larger, but the Irish were far more concentrated in the cities—about 90 percent by 1920—and were certainly more visible. "In a single generation," the Irish American writer Peter Quinn observes, "the Irish went from the most rural people in Western Europe to the most urbanized in North America."[9]

More than other immigrants, the Irish scattered throughout the inner city. Areas known as Irish neighborhoods were never homogeneous: in general, the Irish tended to spread out. In 1900, they were the most widely dispersed of Chicago's ten major ethnic groups; a generation later, Irish parishes remained sprinkled through the city's length and breadth.[10] In late-nineteenth-century New York, they roamed from Battery Park to Washington Heights and increasingly to Brooklyn and the Bronx. The 1880 census estimated that 1,854,571 people of Irish heritage were living in New York's boroughs, but only two of Manhattan's wards, Tribeca and the Battery, had small Irish majorities; elsewhere, they lived amid other ethnic groups.[11] The overwhelming majority of Philadelphia's Irish lived in neighborhoods where they constituted a minority; as a result, they interacted more extensively with the recent immigrants than did the Germans. Indeed, they seemed to be everywhere.[12]

In the early twentieth century, as the completion of subway and elevated lines brought other parts of the city within reach, many Irish moved farther out—in New York, to Queens, the Bronx, and deeper into Brooklyn; in Chicago, to new parishes up and down the city's length. The same sort of outward movement was occurring elsewhere. But even newer "Irish" neighborhoods included many Italians, Jews, and others, while more recent Irish immigrants revitalized some older ethnic enclaves. Continuing migration from Ireland sustained the huge urban communities. They were often poverty-stricken but were also well organized and intensely clannish.[13] Having arrived early on, with a facility in English and strong parish-based organizations and political connections, the Irish turned their cultural proclivities to their distinct advantage in unions, the Democratic Party, and the Catholic Church, and assumed a proprietary attitude toward many city neighborhoods.

ETHNIC AND RACIAL TERRITORIALITY

One of the earliest lessons that many black and immigrant youth learned was that urban neighborhoods were exclusive: their city worlds were carved into distinct ethnic spaces, and it was generally advisable to keep to one's own. By the 1890s, the Irish had been relegated to city slums for a generation or more and had "turned their association with city streets from a slight into a strength." "In the city," writes Peter Quinn, "whoever the streets belong to gets to define what it takes to belong."[14] In New York and Chicago, many of these streets belonged to the Irish before other European immigrants and Mexican and black migrants arrived. As they went about the city, the newcomers devised imaginary maps showing neighborhood boundaries.

In the early twentieth century, Chicago's Wentworth Avenue was a vital site for racial conflict. The black American Communist Claude Lightfoot remembered standing with other African American boys at the top of a railroad embankment along Wentworth, pelting his adversaries with "Irish confetti"—paving stones or bricks.[15] Deadlines could be quite precise. "Remember it's the Ragen's Colts you're dealing with," a gang of Irish youth bragged to a trespasser. "We have two thousand members between Halsted and Cottage Grove, and Forty-third and Sixty-third streets. We intend to run this district. Look out."[16] Thinking back to his South Side neighborhood in the 1930s, Chicago's postal commissioner Henry McGee, Sr., remembered its very precise dimensions. They "ended abruptly at the Rock Island railroad tracks," he recalled, "a half block west of my house . . . There was a sense of great danger in walking beyond the tracks. I grew up with a consciousness that Chicago was not safe outside of the black areas."[17]

Such boundaries involved more than childhood skirmishes. The term *deadline* was an Irish American invention, though its precise origins are obscure. Many attribute it to Thomas F. Byrnes (1842–1910), the pioneer of modern urban detective work. Arriving from Ireland as an infant, Byrnes grew up along the Hudson River in Lower Manhattan. After serving in a volunteer fire brigade and in the Civil War, he rose quickly through the ranks of the New York Police Department, in part through astute self-promotion. He was named chief of detectives in 1880 and superintendent in 1892. Byrnes is also given credit for coming up with the terms *third degree*, a particularly intense form of criminal interrogation, and *rogues' gallery*, a collection of photographs maintained in police headquarters for criminal identification. When pickpockets and robbers repeatedly victimized messengers and business people in the city's financial district, Byrnes drew a "deadline" at Fulton and Liberty streets and declared the area below that line off-limits to criminals. Officers arrested on sight not only pickpockets but also the many homeless people and itinerant workers who slept in the Battery.[18]

But the term had even earlier roots. Large numbers of the Union army prisoners at Andersonville Confederate prison were Irish immigrants from New York and Chicago. Guards warned them that if they crossed a "deadline" in the prison yard, they would shoot them immediately. Civil War veterans likely carried the term back to their city neighborhoods.[19]

In other cities, too, boundaries based on race and ethnicity, although imaginary, were difficult to breach. In the 1890s the future Communist leader William Z. Foster (1881–1961) joined the Bulldogs, a largely Irish Catholic gang of about five hundred in Skittereen, part of Philadelphia's old West End. Nearby blacks, he recalled, were "deadlined at Lombard Street . . . and strictly forbidden to cross over into white, Bulldog territory. The Negro man or boy who ventured across these rigid deadlines was unmercifully slugged."[20]

In Greenwich Village, Irish violence toward blacks dated back at least to the 1860s, when the two groups competed for spots on the docks and as domestics in middle-class homes. African Americans had lived in the Village since the days of Dutch colonial rule, and by the time the Irish arrived in large numbers, one part of Greenwich Village was termed "Little Africa." During the 1863 Draft Riots, a small black community on Thompson Street was torched. Confrontations between Irish and African American youth continued into the early twentieth century, both in the Village and in Harlem, where many blacks had moved.[21]

Rosanna Weston, a young African American woman who grew up near the border of black and Irish neighborhoods on the Lower West Side of Manhattan during the 1920s, recalled, "My parents said they called this neighborhood San Juan Hill because there was so much fightin' going on . . . on this side lived all the black people, and on that side lived all the Irish. That was forbidden territory." Language often ignited the confrontations. "The Irish would call 'em bad names, niggers . . . and they'd be out there fightin.'"[22] "My brother couldn't go past Eighth Avenue to play," Anna Murphy, another West Side resident, recalled, "because he was black and that was Irish. . . . One Saturday the Irish would run, and then the next Saturday the blacks would run across that street. It was almost a ritual."[23] For European immigrants and black migrants alike, deadlines underlined social difference.

Conflict between African Americans and Irish had not in any sense been preordained. In the mid-nineteenth century, the two groups shared Five Points, that quintessential Irish neighborhood celebrated by Martin Scorsese in *Gangs of New York* (2002). Visiting the slum in the 1840s, Charles Dickens found it inhabited by gangs, pigs, and poverty, but home

"MIDSUMMER IN THE FIVE POINTS":
*an engraving of the old Irish neighborhood on
New York City's Lower East Side, 1873.*

as well to a lively interracial culture, especially in saloons and dance halls; intermarriage was not unusual. But by 1860, when many Irish were developing a more distinct identity as "white," most African Americans had been pushed out of the quarter. Still, intermarriage among Irish, blacks, Chinese, and others had been so common by that point that an observer wondered how the census investigators could ever classify its residents.[24] These intermarriages further stigmatized the despised Irish in the eyes of the Protestant middle class.

The early fraternization between Irish and African Americans has sometimes been taken as an indication of intergroup solidarity, but the Irish, struggling for jobs, urban space, and some measure of acceptance, soon distanced themselves from African Americans, driving them from docks and other workplaces—and from neighborhoods like Five Points.[25] In the late nineteenth century, the Irish took on a besieged mentality, resenting any lost territory. First the Chinese had moved in, an Irish priest recalled of his beloved Transfiguration parish in 1897; "then came the Jews, who not satisfied with Baxter street, settled in Mott, Hester, Bayard, and Chrystie streets. Then came the Italians and they drove the Irish from Mulberry and Park Streets and took full possession of the 'Bend' . . . so that at the end of twenty years we have in our parish limits scarcely eight hundred English-speaking people."[26]

Most interethnic violence sprang spontaneously from such perceived encroachment. Gangs, often the teenage boys of a particular block, defended their territory against comparable groups from other blocks. Reformer Mary Kingsbury Simkhovitch (1867–1951) described the phenomenon during the early twentieth century, as Italians moved into streets near her settlement house in Greenwich Village: "The Street had a gang of boys known as the Jones Street Gang. Other streets had their own gangs . . . defenders of their own territory, and battle ensued whenever a boy from outside the street ventured onto foreign soil. . . . All outsiders, in fact, were looked on with suspicion." In Chicago, too, gangs tended to develop locally and spontaneously from play groups and then eventually link up to control their "turf." Indeed, it was only in opposition to "invad-

GREENWICH VILLAGE:
a scene from Thompson Street, New York City, 1905.

ing" groups that such gangs developed firm identities and some level of organization.[27]

Radical bohemianism did not emerge in Greenwich Village until the 1910s. At the turn of the century, Italians were packed into the crowded streets of the South Village, African Americans in a small enclave south and west of Washington Square, the Protestant gentry on the blocks around and north of the square, and the Irish in the West Village to the docks. In Minetta Lane, a prominent vice district, "racial mixing was the order of the day." The saloons were all Irish owned, and an Irish gang, the Hudson Dusters, controlled the turf, though the establishments welcomed a mixed clientele of Irish, Italians, African Americans, and middle-class reformer types. Such mixing was the exception to the rule, however; much of the complex geography of the Village was carved up along ethnic lines.[28]

African Americans could expect trouble entering most white ethnic neighborhoods, but Irish gangs had the worst reputations. Any ethnic group encroaching on what they viewed as their territory was likely to encounter hostility. As Caroline Ware observed of Greenwich Village in the 1920s, "The Italian boy knew which streets it was good for him to walk on and he also knew the consequence of walking on the other side of the park which the Irish had set apart for themselves."[29] In his autobiographical novel *A Diving Rock on the Hudson*, the Jewish proletarian author Henry Roth recounts the trauma he incurred when his parents uprooted him in 1914 from the Lower East Side, where they had settled among other Jewish immigrants in 1909, to Harlem, where he was surrounded by the Irish. He never really settled there at all. The persistent themes of exile and displacement in Roth's writing stem in part at least from losing, at a formative age, the community he had known and loved.[30]

As others moved into their neighborhoods, the Irish displayed a special interest in and talent for street fighting. "Among the Irish," wrote Frederic Thrasher, a University of Chicago sociologist who studied gangs in the 1920s, "fighting has been described as a sort of national habit." They defined their enemies in both territorial and ethnic terms. Most gangs, Thrasher observed, were defensive, but Irish gangs "seem[ed] to look for trouble."[31] In many cities, Italian, Jewish, and other youth made it a point to avoid Irish enclaves, traveling on the back streets to work or play.[32]

From the 1920s on, Irish gangs increasingly integrated other ethnic groups, but some boundaries remained starkly drawn. "There seems to be a 'deadline' near 69th and Robey for the pure Italians," a University of Chicago student wrote in the early 1930s, referring to a portion of Englewood on the South Side. "It is never safe for an individual Italian to wander near this district." The group identity here was based less on nationality than on gang identity. The Gimlets, the largely Irish gang who enforced the deadline, included some products of marriages between Germans and Irish, but not Italians. The Gimlets lived to fight. "If they appear in the playground," the student warned, "get your gang as there will be trouble."[33]

Gang turfs were often clearly demarcated, but trouble could also start on ostensibly common ground like crowded streetcars, playgrounds, parks, church carnivals, or other social events that drew gang members from one neighborhood into another. Even when Irish kids encountered children from other ethnic groups in school, their peers and parents pressured them to "stay with their own kind."[34] Ethnic boundaries established by the Irish to maintain their control of strategic areas in Boston's North End were remarkably rigid and endured long after Italians constituted a majority in the area.[35]

The limits of interethnic mixing were apparent in what the *Chicago Tribune* in 1910 called "the Wickedest District in the World." The Maxwell Street area on Chicago's old West Side boasted the second-highest crime rate of any police court in the nation, most of it due to juvenile delinquency. "Murderers, robbers and thieves of the worst kind are here born, reared and grow to maturity in numbers that far exceed the record of any similar district anywhere on the face of the globe," the *Tribune* claimed. Much of the violence was territorial, and gangs gradually incorporated members of newer ethnic groups as they settled in. But Irish gangs also terrorized Germans, Italians, Jews, and others until the turn of the century—long after they had become a minority in the neighborhood.[36]

Some of the conflict in neighborhoods like Chicago's "Bloody Maxwell" and New York's Lower East Side had roots in anti-Semitism. Ironically, old-world Ireland had experienced little anti-Semitic conflict, in part because its Jewish population never exceeded a few thousand, mostly concentrated in Dublin. As late as 1904, Limerick experienced a boycott of Jewish businesses and what was characterized as a pogrom, but such hostility was rare and seldom involved violence. As in many societies, the degree of acceptance often depended upon the degree of assimilation. To the extent that he maintains a distinct Jewish identity, Leopold Bloom in James Joyce's *Ulysses* is a marginal man. On the other hand, Emanuel Steen, the son of a Jewish scrap dealer, grew up in the slums of Dublin and attended a Catholic secondary school. He spoke a bit of the Irish language and English with a heavy brogue, but no Yiddish. "We were just ordinary Irish kids. We didn't feel any different . . . I was Irish, nothing else." Only after he arrived in Harlem in the 1920s did Steen rediscover his Jewish identity.[37]

Ignorance of Jews was more common than hostility toward them, but Irish cities featured important Jewish businessmen and elected officials, and as the Irish encountered them, some degree of affinity between the two groups unmistakably developed. Ireland's small Jewish population was not only accepted but often admired. Irish nationalists would frequently compare their own nation's plight with that of the Jews. When anti-Semitism did rear its head, someone like the radical Michael Davitt (1845–1906) was often there to denounce it.[38] In the American city, some Irish spoke out against the scourge of anti-Semitism. Chicago's elite Irish Fellowship Club protested the Russian trial of a Jew under the old "blood libel" for killing a Christian child, and priests and New York's Tammany Hall politicians took part in protest meetings against attacks on Jews.[39]

The situation in the streets, however, was often quite different. Holy Family, one of Chicago's earliest Irish parishes, was located near the old Jewish ghetto and the garment factories and clothing markets—the proximity brought considerable petty violence tinged with anti-Semitism.[40] In the early 1880s, when the Jewish labor leader Abraham Bisno's family arrived in the ghetto, "the entire neighborhood seldom went three or four blocks out of their familiar ways . . . In our immediate neighborhood, the population was Irish . . . Parents would not allow their children out of sight. Occasionally children were beaten up by children of our neighbors. Jews with whiskers were continually assaulted as they went along." Families who moved a bit west or south beyond the ghetto were attacked, and confrontations between Jewish and Irish youth were common. "When the Irish won, it wasn't safe to show your face on the street for almost a week."[41]

On New York's Lower East Side, where a progressive Jewish working-class culture had taken hold by 1900, radical Jews found it much easier to deal with Germans than Irish. One reason was practical, as the Yiddish of the Jewish working class was close enough to German to facilitate communication; another reason was political, as some German workers also embraced the cause of socialism. By comparison, the aggressive Irish, with their strong ties to the church and to Tammany, must have seemed distant at best and often rather threatening.[42]

In areas where Irish Catholic neighborhoods bordered those of Jews, anti-Semitism continued to be a source of conflict. Ron Michaels recalled growing up Jewish on the Far West Side of Chicago in the interwar years: "My neighborhood was very diverse, but it was predominantly Irish Catholic along with some Jewish, Greek and Polish families. There were unwritten boundaries and my problem was that my route to public school went past Resurrection Parish. Some of the older Catholic kids would stop me on a regular basis." His father refused to give him the money his tormentors demanded and ordered him to defend himself, which he did successfully.[43]

Not surprisingly, many Jews developed negative impressions of the Irish. An intensive study of one predominantly Irish block in turn-of-the-century Harlem found that Jews considered their Irish neighbors "drunken," "thriftless," and "careless."[44] Such attitudes were common enough that "Irish jokes" circulated among Jews, and a derogatory Yiddish word, *betzemer*, developed to refer to Irish Americans.[45]

Not all prejudice originated with the Irish, of course. Poles and other eastern European immigrants brought anti-Semitic attitudes with them from the old world. Polish confrontations with Jews in American cities likely fed on such antagonism. Similarly, northern Italians often despised Sicilians; Lithuanians held a grudge against Poles; and Poles resented Germans. But in the United States, the newcomers faced a striking range of ethnic and racial groups. Ethnic and racial geography became increasingly complex, and newer immigrant groups learned its boundaries of necessity. As the Italians of New York moved west into East Harlem, for example, they gradually displaced older Irish enclaves—and encountered terrific resistance. Welcome in neither the Tammany Hall established clubs nor in the neighborhood churches, they built up a deep resentment of the Irish.

Over time, as the complexion of the population shifted, so did ethnic territoriality. "We didn't have to worry about blacks in those days," Peter Pascale, a second-generation Italian, said of the 1920s. "We worried about the Irish. . . . We took a lot of beatin's from them, but then we were the majority and we beat the shit outta them."[46] "I passed through the league of nations on my way to school every day!" Bill Phelan recalled of growing up in Chicago's Englewood during the interwar years. "Many days I would have to fight my way back and forth with my brothers and my sister. I had to take care of them too. It was quite a job on some days."[47]

IRISH AMERICAN MASCULINITY

Despite all this hostility, newcomers could also display a grudging respect for Irish fighting prowess. The Irish record in sports underscores their influence in realms of everyday life that defined masculinity. Social athletic clubs grew out of nineteenth-century organizations that aimed to maintain a Gaelic culture through sports, though eventually many of the groups fielded immigrant and African American athletes under their Gaelic banners. In baseball, which many immigrant boys viewed as the essence of American urban culture, an estimated one-third of all major league players were Irish in the 1890s, while eleven of sixteen managers in the 1920s were of Irish descent.[48]

Irish success in bare-knuckle boxing, then in organized prizefighting, undoubtedly enhanced their reputation for toughness. These fighting skills originated in the nineteenth-century Irish countryside, where extended clans and large gangs of peasants and farmers had engaged in more or less organized "faction fights," using sticks, at fairs and markets. Donnybrook, a fair on the southern outskirts of Dublin, was home to particularly fractious fights; hence the nickname. Often based on family grudges, class tensions, or even politics, the fights had a dimension of recreational violence to them, and a boisterous bachelor culture bred an admiration for physical prowess and courage. The fighting tradition became part of the rough culture of mid-nineteenth-century Irish laborers on American canal construction sites, where organized groups fought for control of jobs.[49]

Irish Americans dominated early bare-knuckle prizefighting, and "Boston Strongboy" John L. Sullivan (1858–1918), the son of an immigrant hod carrier, emerged in 1889 as heavyweight champion of the world. After a decade of fighting in theaters, music halls, and saloons, Sullivan defeated Jake Kilrain for the title after seventy-five rounds in the last major bare-knuckle championship bout. A brawler and drinker who was frequently in trouble with the authorities wherever he toured, Sullivan identified closely with the Irish American community and his working-class roots. In turn, they loved him for his brusque confidence, a commodity many Irish Americans craved. "My name is John L. Sullivan," he told the world, "and I can lick any son-of-a-bitch alive." It was, as sports historian Elliot Gorn notes, "a defiant cry for a down-trodden people who, in their first full post-immigrant generation, sought a fairer share of America's opportunities." Later immigrants would share that craving. Sullivan retired to a career of acting, bartending, and occasional short boxing bouts, but the Irish boxers kept coming.[50]

In the early twentieth century, prizefighting was increasingly diverse, and boxers were often identified by race and ethnicity. As thousands of immigrant boys searched for tough role models, Irish American boxers dominated the sport. Nine world champions between 1870 and 1920 were of Irish descent. Ethnic boxers carried with them the pride of their often-despised communities. Street gangs embraced the sport, and immigrant kids were drawn to it both as a way to establish their masculinity and as a route to social success. In the twentieth century, professional boxing became a path to both notoriety and upward mobility for one generation of black and immigrant fighters after another.[51]

The rise of the African American boxer Jack Johnson (1878–1946) challenged not only Irish dominance but also notions of white male supremacy. In 1908, Johnson secured the world heavyweight title, and a year later, after defeating a series of "great white hopes," including several Irish

JACK JOHNSON (1878–1946):
black World Boxing champion and threat to
white supremacist notion of masculinity, 1915.

American boxers, he settled into Chicago's burgeoning black community. He became a great hero to African Americans and notorious among whites for ostentatious displays of wealth, for dating and marrying white women, for taunting his opponents and critics, and for generally flouting racial conventions. In 1910, "Boilermaker" Jim Jeffries (1875–1953) challenged him to a fight: Jeffries had returned from retirement, he said, "for the sole purpose of proving that a white man is better than a Negro." He lost that "fight of the century." Black communities across the country celebrated, while in some cities spontaneous race riots erupted. Johnson then opened Café de Champion, an integrated club just over the

Wentworth Avenue deadline, and later another one in Harlem. But he was hung in effigy from trolley lines and light poles in Chicago neighborhoods, and taunts followed him around the city. His taste for celebrity drew the deep hatred of many whites, part of the ongoing confrontation between Irish and African Americans.[52]

Jewish, Italian, and other ethnic boxers tended to take Irish professional names—an obvious example of Irish influence in the sport. They did so in deference to the pugnacious reputation of the Irish as well as to minimize ethnic discrimination. "A majority of the Prize-fighters in New York," journalist Burton Hendrick noted in 1913, "are really Jews who operate under Irish names." In Chicago, too, Jewish and Polish "pugs" took on Irish names as they entered the trade. The Lithuanian boxer Josef Paul Zukauskas became "Jack Sharkey," even as he explained to a *Chicago Tribune* reporter that "the Jews and the Italians are the best fighters today."[53]

Italian, Jewish, and Polish gangsters in New York and Chicago also took on Irish monikers. Al Capone's bodyguard "Machine Gun" Jack McGurn was formerly known as James Gebardi, alias James DeMora. In New York, Richie Fitzpatrick, who ran part of the Lower East Side, was a Russian Jew, and Paolo Vacarelli, who muscled the Irish gangs out of the Five Points, was known as Paul Kelly. Kelly chose a familiar route to success—boxing, social athletic club organizer, saloonkeeper, muscle man for a Lower East Side politician, and dock union racketeer.[54]

Elsewhere a broader Americanizing of immigrant names was happening, as Irish foremen and immigration officials simply renamed incoming immigrants. Italian building laborers, Slovak factory workers, and Polish miners became Tim O'Sullivan or Pat Murphy.[55] While such renaming was undoubtedly motivated by the wish to avoid discrimination, its symbolic significance—the exchange of a foreign identity for a perceived "American" one—could not have been lost on these immigrant workers or their descendants.

This name-changing phenomenon illustrates how later immigrants modeled their behavior on Irish Americans and their notions of masculinity. Gangs established their reputations through their fighting prowess.

Beliefs about white racial and Irish ethnic superiority; a combative, protective orientation to urban turf; and an embattled communal solidarity were elements of this notion of masculinity. To have honor or "heart" was to successfully defend one's own community from interlopers.[56]

The combative habits of the Irish extended even to some clergy. New York's "fighting priest," Father Philip "Mac" Magrath (1877–1936), roamed his waterfront parish with a prayer book in one hand and a rubber hose in the other to combat the largely Irish "Dusters," a waterfront gang that robbed seamen. If the prayer book didn't discourage them, a whack with the hose would. Magrath seemed to seek out confrontations. A sign in his Catholic Seamen's Mission read, "If you want to know who's boss, START SOMETHING."[57] Second-generation immigrant youth from many ethnic backgrounds embraced such toughness. "Jewish, Italian, and Polish youth highly esteemed this ability," writes sports historian Steven Reiss. "It was a sign of manliness and a useful skill because of the frequency of interethnic gang fights at public parks and playgrounds and other border areas separating rival groups."[58]

Contemporary sociologists and reformers attributed Irish bellicosity to national character, but the traditions of faction fighting and territoriality, imported from Ireland's rural south and west, did shape life in American cities.[59] Long before they defended their neighborhoods against Italians, Poles, and Jews, Irish gangs fought blacks, native-born whites, and one another. As early as 1836, parishioners armed with muskets and paving stones defended Old St. Patrick's in the Five Points against a large Protestant mob, and from that day forward, the Irish jealously guarded their parish turf. By the time of the new immigration, the Irish had controlled much of the inner city's residential and scarce recreational facilities for decades, and they resented incursions by the new arrivals.

In the mid-nineteenth century, Irish gangs often established clear lines of demarcation between turfs and fought for control among themselves and with native-born Protestant gangs. The modern urban street gang dedicated to protecting its turf grew from antebellum gangs and volunteer fire companies along the Bowery and in the Five Points, in South Philadelphia, in Boston's North End, in Chicago's South Side, and elsewhere.[60] The prominence of Irish Americans on many metropolitan police forces from the mid-nineteenth century on also helped them control urban territory.

In the early twentieth century, when Irish Americans lived increasingly alongside more recent immigrants, they continued to see these neighborhoods as theirs. Having won a modest place for themselves by driving out blacks or Chinese, as in Lower Manhattan, they were prepared to defend their territory.[61] This siege mentality was undoubtedly accentuated during the heavy in-migration of black migrants of the World War I era. In Harlem and parts of Chicago's South Side, black migrants entered neighborhoods that the Irish considered to be their own. The Irish developed a special reputation for excluding blacks. "If the [legal] restriction of the district can't keep them out," a Congregational minister said of the residential covenant on his South Side neighborhood, "the Irish will."[62]

THE LANGUAGE OF THE STREET

However much trouble they made for newer groups, Irish Americans contributed mightily to the city's distinctive language. Immigrants traditionally absorbed the language of their new society through night school English and civics classes and from their own children, who often spoke the old-world language at home; but a distinctively urban English became the language of the public space—the crowded street, the neighborhood stoop, the city park, and the school. Immigrant workers and their children were far more likely to speak that language than that of the respectable WASP home.[63] Part of Americans' fascination with the vocabulary and accents of our cities lies in their polyglot origins among diverse ethnic populations. The modern American idiom was shaped by languages from around the world.

A black migrant working in the hide cellar at Chicago's Armour meatpacking plant could pick up some Lithuanian from his workmates, even as they absorbed some Mississippi-inflected English vocabulary from him. The language one absorbed depended a lot upon where one did the learning. The actor Jimmy Cagney learned Yiddish from the Jewish immigrant kids in the New York building where he grew up. If a Yiddish word sounded good and conveyed an urbane style, young people from other ethnic groups might start using it.[64] City language was also inflected by class. The term *scab*, first applied to traitors within an ethnic community and later to strikebreakers, came into use among Irish laborers in Chicago during the labor upheavals of the 1880s, then spread to other ethnic groups.[65]

Many factors, regardless of ethnic group, facilitate English acquisition: literacy in the first language, length of time in the United States, social class—and residence in ethnically mixed neighborhoods. This last variable is particularly significant for our story. People in ethnically homogeneous neighborhoods could get by with very little English, but those in more diverse communities had to acquire English quickly. Immigrant neighborhoods were far more ethnically mixed than historians once thought, so many immigrants, whatever their background, surely picked up English on city streets.[66]

Many immigrants arrived with at least some knowledge of Irish Gaelic, a language that British authorities had systematically repressed and that by the nineteenth century was in decline. But some early immigrant communities were primarily Gaelic speaking, and in the 1880s with the arrival of thousands of poverty-stricken immigrants from the west of Ireland, the language enjoyed a resurgence. New York in the 1890s was home to perhaps as many as eighty thousand Irish Gaelic speakers.[67]

In the long run, however, Irish Gaelic never had much chance as a popular language in the United States. "The 'broken English' which many western emigrants spoke," historian Kerby Miller writes, and the Irish brogue of the English speakers, "remained objects of ridicule among native Americans . . . associated with poverty and shame."[68] Concentrating on fitting Irish youth with the tools they would need to get ahead in a middle-class Protestant society, even Catholic institutions of higher education made little effort to preserve Gaelic. "In their rapid movement from Irish to English," linguist Daniel Cassidy concludes, "Irish speakers, and their children and grandchildren, had lost the Irish language completely . . . without a whisper or a trace."[69]

But something strange occurred in the course of all this concerted forgetting. Language itself, in stories and jokes, in political speeches and street corner banter, remained vital to the emerging Irish American culture, and some of its roots went back in bits and pieces to the despised and repressed language of an earlier generation. Corruptions of the Irish Gaelic language survived in the memories of old-timers and were refreshed by more recent immigrants. Irish words, phrases, accents, and pronunciations seeped into the English of working-class neighborhoods. When young immigrants who were eager to blend in acquired urban lexicon, it was often sprinkled with Irishisms.

By naming everyday urban phenomenas, Irish slang became a vital form of urban communication. Successfully living and operating in streets and alleys, the Irish provided snappy labels for many institutions and phenomena: *speakeasy, slugger, dude, square* (as in honest). They measured their city turf in *blocks*. They disdained all *suckers, stool pigeons, squealers, phonies,* and *swells* (the last a term laden with deep class resentment). Irish Americans provided a vocabulary that urban dwellers from many ethnic backgrounds used to describe their new world.[70]

"It was from these crossroads dockside neighborhoods," Daniel Cassidy writes, ". . . that the banished, penalized tongue of the Irish was scattered across North America and became a key strand in the slang of back alleys and slums, a demotic dialect of the dispossessed Irish-American vernacular."[71] Along with German and Yiddish, Irish Gaelic is the origin of numerous city words and phrases.

The newer immigrants and their children encountered Irishisms and pronunciations in jokes, popular songs, comic strips, vaudeville, and musical hall acts. Elements of Gaelic merged "into the lingo of street gangs and the police forces created to control them, into hobo camps and circus trains, into folk songs of east and west."[72] Nineteenth-century Irish gamblers, moving up the Mississippi River from New Orleans, brought with them *taro, racketeer,* and *scam.* Such slang echoed through American city streets with an "onomatopoeic resonance" similar to that of the other great urban wellspring, Yiddish.[73] The new urban language took on German, Italian, and other accents as well. The resulting dialect in other parts of the country was different from that of New York and Brooklyn, partly because of regional and ethnic differences in populations, and partly because of borrowings from Irish Gaelic.

Three aspects of Irish American slang made it particularly useful to those in the nation's industrial slums. First, it was an oppositional language, providing an alternative to formal, respectable English.[74] Second, it emerged from Irish youth on the streets and was popularized in gangster and Broadway musical films, in comic strips, and on the vaudeville stage, which made it particularly accessible to immigrant youth. Indeed, many popular culture terms were originally denoted by Irish slang, like the word *jazz.* That music itself, of course, had African roots and was refined in African American communities, first in the South and in northern industrial cities, and it became the soundtrack for the Americanization of young immigrants. But the name *jazz* was likely coined by an Irish American journalist.[75]

Although this hybrid language facilitated communication and interaction, it could also play a negative role in marking and stigmatizing social difference. Once recent immigrants, or more often their children, observed racial distinctions among myriad groups inhabiting the city, and began to grasp their significance, they used labels to distinguish them. Even young children could pick up racial slurs in school or in the streets. Some elementary school immigrant children acquired a racialized vocabulary and images along with nursery rhymes and games. In the early 1930s, a University of Chicago sociology student recorded the following rhymes that young children jumping rope on the South Side were chanting:[76]

Eena, meena, mina, moe, Catch the negro by the toe.
If he hollers, let him go, Eena, meena, mina, moe.

Red, white and blue. Your father is a Jew.
Your mother is a curly head. And so are you.

My name is on the window, my name is on the door.
My name is Shinnie Dago and I own a candy store.

These lyrics and the prejudice they conveyed were passed on by Americanized children to others. "Irish Americans, so often the teachers and arbiters of race," historian David Roediger observes, "could make Italians
'Guineas' and Jews 'Kikes.'"[77]

PLAYING IN THE STREET

In the early twentieth century, black and immigrant youth crowding into
working-class neighborhoods made use of recreational spaces that often
brought ethnic groups together.[78] Parks, playgrounds, swimming pools,
and beaches offered not only refuges from overcrowded tenement apartments and nagging parents but also common ground for recreational activities and relations between the sexes; in some cases, they were the only
place to take a bath.[79]

But public recreational spaces and facilities were few in number. In
their absence, children organized their games in city streets and alleys, in
abandoned lots and industrial sites—wherever they found space. With the
exception of a few irregular spots below Fourteenth Street, social worker
Pauline Goldmark reported in 1914, "the entire West Side of Manhattan
from Seventy-second Street to the Battery is arid, desolate . . . smoke
stained." In Hell's Kitchen, a densely populated stretch of residential
blocks hemmed in by docks, slaughterhouses, soap and glue factories,
warehouses, and stables, "the blocks swarm with children who have no
other playground." Young second-generation Irish and Germans, and
smaller numbers of Italians and African Americans, saw the streets as their
"natural playground." "They are the most constant and vivid part of [a
boy's] life. They provide companionship, invite [him] to recklessness, and

THE COP SETTLES A DISPUTE IN A FRIENDLY WAY:
*a beat cop intervenes between boys on the streets of the Lower
West Side of Manhattan, 1915. Lewis W. Hine.*

offer concealment." Most of the street play Goldmark observed was tech-
nically illegal, which brought the boys into conflict with shopkeepers and
police. Hatred of the police became a sort of neighborhood tradition.[80]

Like many Manhattan youth, Al Smith (1873–1944), a future governor
of New York, grew up swimming in the East River, climbing the rigging
and masts of ships along the South Street port, and playing in the shadow
of the Brooklyn Bridge. For him, the occasional trip to Central Park or
Coney Island was a source of great excitement.[81] During the summers, the
few city swimming pools were thronged. Adjacent to the pools, municipal
baths gave residents of neighborhoods where hot running water was scarce
a chance to bathe. In 1910, an outdoor pool opened in the heart of Chicago's old Jewish ghetto—and thousands of children from the surrounding neighborhoods poured in each day, more than 48,000 in one summer
month and 4,700 on one particularly hot day in July 1913.[82] Young African

Americans used city pools in Chicago, New York, and elsewhere, though racial clashes were common.[83]

At Chicago's West Side Park no. 2, many groups celebrated holidays, both ethnic and American, and disputes were unusual, leading the *Tribune* to call the park a melting pot where immigrant youth were molded into good citizens. "The parks had a role in holding neighborhoods together," Alderman Ed Kelly remembered of his boyhood experience on the Near North Side of Chicago in the interwar years. "We had our softball games there, and we played basketball, cards and dice . . . the park was what kept us together . . . where you hung out." Where there was no park, kids spent their days out on the streets and in the alleys.[84]

But in the stifling summer months, scarce recreational venues could also become contested terrain. City youth who poured into the streets and fled to the beaches often found, once they got there, that the Irish and, later, other gangs had already staked out their turf, as they had in Brooklyn's Borough Hall and along the docks in Red Hook. Jewish, Italian, and Lithuanian immigrants seeking relief at South Boston beaches encountered hostile Irish boys who considered them "theirs." Trouble might break out at any moment, but gangs were more active and violence more common during summer. Not coincidentally, the great Chicago race riot of 1919 had its roots in a confrontation over informal racial boundaries at a South Side beach.[85]

For these same reasons, Chicago's Washington Park became the venue for frequent clashes as the surrounding area changed from largely Irish to more ethnically mixed and then African American. In James T. Farrell's *Studs Lonigan,* a saga of Irish working-class life, Studs's father, Patrick, recalls that when he bought their building, "Wabash Avenue had been a nice, decent, respectable street for a self-respecting man to live with his family. But now, well, niggers and kikes were getting in."[86] In the 1920s, the neighborhood's black population grew from 15 to 92 percent.[87] By World War II, the deadlines had shifted farther south and remained precise and well recognized. In the 1940s, "the safe boundaries for us were as far north as Twenty-Second Street and as far south as Sixtieth Street," the black entrepreneur Dempsey Travis recalled, "but south of Washington Park was a dangerous area."[88] Smaller playgrounds were also often protected turf. In New York, when Italian or Jewish kids got together to play ball in Harlem playgrounds, Irish gangs frequently drove them off.[89]

IRISH AMERICAN PAROCHIALISM

In some ways, the late-nineteenth-century Irish neighborhoods of Lower Manhattan were cosmopolitan, linked as they were to the international market through the busy port of New York and surrounded by diverse groups of immigrants. Mixed crews of sailors from around the globe lived in rooming houses near the docks. Irish longshoremen handled commodities from foreign ports and occasionally took items home for their families' own use. Gangs of boys dove into the East River for bananas

NEW YORK WATERFRONT:
Manhattan's docks, Lower East Side, viewed from Brooklyn, 1926.

dropped from ships arriving from South America; they acquired monkeys, parrots, or goats brought by sailors from Africa or the West Indies.

In other respects, however, these communities were quite closed. Irish longshoremen clung desperately to the inward-looking slum neighborhoods they had created for themselves on the West Side.[90] They developed an unusually strong attachment to their dockside neighborhoods and an antipathy to interlopers, from whatever ethnic background. As labor historian David Montgomery has observed, "Sedentary communities of extended families developed around the piers and persisted for decades, even generations." As late as the 1940s, sustaining a sense of "Irishness" facilitated the control of good jobs and union offices on the New York docks.[91]

Irish neighborhoods had a distinctive communal quality, reinforced by a tightly knit parish life but also intertwined with politics, work, unionism, and sometimes crime. For every isolated enclave like Chelsea, however, there were many more city neighborhoods where the Irish lived among other ethnic groups. Longshoreman, policeman, and future mayor William O'Dwyer (1890–1964) called the Brooklyn waterfront "a sea of every racial stock," and most early-twentieth-century New York neighborhoods were quite mixed.[92] Robert Woods, who studied Boston at the turn of the century, drew a stark contrast between two neighborhoods in this regard. In the extremely diverse South End, he found, schools were quite mixed, and the "process of assimilation has advanced a step" through social intercourse between older and more recent immigrants. In the North End, by contrast, more recent Italian and Jewish immigrants poured in, and the Irish population was dominated by the first and second generations, including more than six thousand recent immigrants. Here "isolation was still possible . . . parts of the district are still solidly Irish."[93]

Even where they mingled daily with other ethnic groups, the Irish achieved a distinctive and highly organized social and cultural life. Indeed, Irish and other ethnic enclaves often resembled self-contained villages, to the point that Chicago historian Dominic Pacyga aptly describes them as "spatially integrated, but socially segregated."[94] The very presence of peoples from around the world seemed to accentuate Irish Americans' attachment to their particular piece of earth—and the institutions they had built there. Novelist James T. Farrell recalled that his Chicago neighborhoods "possessed something of the character of a small town. They were little worlds of their own."[95] Such communal relationships provided the basis for numerous voluntary organizations, labor unions, and political parties. They explain how even Irish Americans who grew up amid great ethnic diversity could recall much later that in their neighborhoods "everybody was Irish."[96]

In the face of massive immigration and black migration, however, such tightly knit cultures often took on a decidedly aggressive quality. Outsiders were perceived as threats, and gangs protected the communal turf. Long after Italians moved into Boston's North End, as sociologist William F. Whyte noted, Irish gangs continued to look upon strategic points there as their personal property.[97] Residing in some of the most cosmopolitan cities in the world, then, Irish Americans could exhibit strikingly parochial worldviews. Partly because of this parochial conception of urban space, Catholics from a variety of ethnic backgrounds later opposed neighborhood racial integration.[98]

In the late nineteenth century, many Irish left congested inner-city neighborhoods to construct new parish communities in outlying areas. A generation later, newer immigrants did the same, and once again they found the Irish there before them. After World War II, as ethnic working-class neighborhoods became more diverse and parishes served more ethnically mixed clienteles, this outward migration provided the geographic basis for broader identities based on religion and race, a process sociologists have termed "spatial assimilation."[99] Ethnic concentrations and culture continued to thrive in such neighborhoods, and a "white ethnic" identity began to emerge, but these communities remained racially segregated.

Many later-arriving immigrants observed that anti-Semitism, racism, and hostility toward newcomers seemed to be stronger among the Irish than other settled ethnic groups. "The Irish in America were never friendly towards us," a Polish National Catholic paper observed, "and they never will be. They consider themselves a higher and more privileged group here and look upon us with contempt."[100] Marie Cutaia, an Italian New Yorker, remembered the battles in Hell's Kitchen. "They used to call us guineas . . . or wops or meatballs . . . to say they were better Americans than us. But we were born here, too."[101] The Irish reputation for racism was strong enough to drive erstwhile enemies like the Italians and Jews together for mutual protection. "To the Irish," Lee Silver recalled of his Manhattan neighborhood in the 1920s, "the Italians were guineas and the Jews were kikes, and they were antagonistic and aggressive, so the Italians and the Jewish kids would coalesce against the Irish."[102]

One of New York's largest ethnic confrontations took place in 1902, when young Irish and German workers in a printing plant attacked the funeral procession of the region's most important Orthodox rabbi, throwing bolts and screws at the mourners. According to Jewish witnesses, responding police attacked the crowd of mourners rather than their assailants; the police superintendent later admitted that the factory had been the source of previous anti-Semitic attacks. The broader context for the confrontation was significant. Jewish voters had recently bolted Tammany for a reform ticket, and in the electoral campaign, the main issue was police corruption. The riot resulted in mass meetings, recollections of Russian pogroms, and the formation of a Vigilance League in the Jewish community. Though some responsibility for the riot certainly rested with Irish Americans, Tammany politicians took an active role in suppressing the conflict.[103]

ORGANIZED CRIME AND THE OLD NEIGHBORHOOD

Organized criminal gangs perpetrated some of this violence and famously carved the city up into fiefdoms. Although criminal gangs are commonly associated with Italian immigrants, their origins lay in older Irish communities. New York's Irish neighborhoods produced some notorious street gangs, whose alumni graduated into serious crime, running the rackets and other illicit activities during Prohibition.[104] Informal street gangs sometimes overlapped with more serious criminal elements. Chicago's Canaryville blurred casual violence and organized crime: the neighborhood was a "pretty tough hole," according to one Irish cop, because of the proliferation of "athletic clubs" (often a euphemism for gangs) among second- and third-generation Irish youth. The social athletic club, which likely grew from Gaelic sports groups among the early immigrant Irish, thrived on a masculine youth culture that put a premium on physical aggression and territorial solidarity. In this environment, a hard-core criminal element, the "Canaryville School of Gunmen," blended with the ubiquitous athletic clubs to make the neighborhood a forbidding place for outsiders.[105]

No group exemplified this transformation from neighborhood gang to organized crime (or the connections between crime and politics) better than Ragen's Colts, one of many social athletic clubs, with a combined membership of about seven thousand. The group thrived under the patronage of Frank Ragen, who rose to be a county commissioner. From 1908 until the gang's disbanding in August 1927 (due primarily to a split in the Democratic Party), the Colts remained deeply involved in politics, violence, and crime on Chicago's South Side. Originating in Canaryville, they gradually integrated a few gangsters from other ethnic backgrounds. They differed from nineteenth-century Irish gangs in their size, their organization, and the range of their operations.[106]

Recruited from among the toughest sons of Irish stockyard workers, the Colts' motto was "Hit me and you hit two thousand." At their peak in the 1910s, they actually had a membership of close to three thousand. In the 1920s, they ran a substantial clubhouse equipped with parlors, a pool room, and athletic equipment—where shootings occurred frequently. A fairly broad subgroup acted as the military arm of the local Democratic Party, supporting John "Dingbat" Oberta and other party stalwarts in the stockyards region, and they were implicated in serious election-day crime. A smaller, hard-core element provided muscle for organized crime on the South and West Sides, especially during the 1920s "Beer Wars," when the city's gangs fought for control of the illicit trade in alcohol. After one shoot-out inside the clubhouse, police found shotguns, pistols, ammunition, and dynamite in an open safe. Al Capone's gang raked the Colts' headquarters with machine guns, killing one member and wounding another. (Later some members signed on with Capone against other Irish gangsters.)[107]

The prototypical criminal within the Colts was Hugh "Stubby" McGovern, who was indicted several times (but never convicted) for kidnapping, murder, gambling, and racketeering. Arrested in 1923 for slugging a policeman and later on various bootlegging charges, McGovern was implicated in at least four murders. It is impossible to establish the reason for his acquittals, but he and other Colts were clearly well connected politically. He and an associate were eventually killed at the end of 1928 in a wild shoot-out inside a South Side speakeasy. More than one hundred patrons and several waiters were in the club during the shooting, but apparently no one saw anything.[108]

McGovern's female counterpart was May Duigan (1873–1929), the infamous "Chicago May," whom the Irish feminist author Nuala O'Faolain has celebrated. Born into the beautiful tedium of a largely abandoned Irish village at the end of the 1870s, facing the same dismal prospects as many of her contemporaries, May stole her boat fare from her parents and arrived in Chicago in 1892 at the age of nineteen. She employed her good looks as a ticket into a tough world. Submerging herself in Chicago's and later New York's underworlds, she built a career based on a series of cons that entrapped men and relieved them of their wallets, using prostitution as a cover for robbery.[109]

May followed a trajectory outside communal loyalty, responsibility, and hard work; but other young Irish women immigrated to find not just economic opportunity but also escape from social and sexual repression. Most Irish immigrant women reconstituted the world they left behind or built female-centered communities in convents, parish societies, women's unions, or similar institutions. Others, like May, rebelled, living beyond the strictures of the church or the patriarchal household, on the fringes of American urban society.

The Irish street gang embraced not just violence and crime but also legitimate aims and functions, although the lines between the two were often blurred. Commissioner Frank Ragen himself conceded that "there was a rough element among them [the Colts], but they were also a force for good in the stockyards district."[110] They helped to rig elections, but they also held Christmas parties for the neighborhood children and had a good reputation for helping the poor. They fielded strong-arm men, bootleggers, and political fixers but also produced talented runners, football players, wrestlers, and boxers. As late as October 1917, the Colts played a series of exhibition games against the American Giants of the Negro League. The trophies lining their clubhouse shelves testified to their athletic success. Thousands attended their dances and Fourth of July picnics. Ostentatiously patriotic, they claimed that 1,100 members, nearly half the organization, volunteered for service in World War I.[111]

Most Americanized Irish had little to do with Hugh McGovern's kind of violence, but many undoubtedly saw the Colts—and the Colts saw themselves—as protectors of their community. When a mother feared that her young daughter was being pursued by a predator, she would approach members of the gang for protection. When an anti-Catholic speaker was advertised, the Colts showed up in force and even before the program began pelted the stage with bricks, rotten vegetables, and folding chairs.[112] Gangsters, as one contemporary criminologist stressed, were genuinely popular, "homegrown in the neighborhood gang, idealized in the morality of the neighborhood."[113] The Colts' strong sense of turf and loyalty to community ties, their masculinist bravado, and their sports, politics, and rackets all touched the heart of the Irish American community. Most important, the Colts and groups like them provided a model for later street gangs. The concept of the social athletic club, under the sponsorship of neighborhood notables, spread to later immigrant groups, especially the Italians, as a site for socializing and group sports—then a basis for gangs and, later, for organized crime.[114]

Neighborhoods like Canaryville contributed a disproportionate number of *both* gangsters *and* policemen and politicians. When strong-arm robber Patrick O'Grady was arrested for shooting a taxi driver, his brother was the detective lieutenant in charge of the case, and another brother intervened as a member of the state legislature. Allegations of collusion between Irish cops and Irish gangs were common. In 1918, when white taxi drivers and a group of "sluggers" attacked blacks near the boundary between Bridgeport and the Black Belt, Irish policemen simply ignored calls for help. The Chicago Commission on Race Relations concluded that such collusion enabled the Colts and other Bridgeport and Canaryville gangs to attack African Americans with impunity during the Chicago race riot of 1919. The Colts "are allowed to operate free from police interference," the *Chicago Defender,* Chicago's black daily, observed. In Chicago and New York, claims of police brutality inflicted on African Americans and Mexican migrants frequently noted that the policemen were Irish.[115]

In the early 1900s, when hostile Irish audiences attacked actors in plays that they found offensive, sympathetic Irish cops often failed to intervene. At a particularly delicate moment during the Irish War for Independence, Manhattan's elite Union Club raised the Union Jack. Across Fifth Avenue, at St. Patrick's Cathedral, five thousand supporters of the radical nationalist group Sinn Fein departing from a memorial Mass spied it. The crowd attacked and severely damaged the Union Club building. "No clubbing," officers cautioned the policemen charged with clearing the avenue. Only four people were arrested that day, two of them by Jewish and German American officers. A fourth person, the scion of a wealthy family, armed himself with a sword and swore to help Lieutenant McCarthy—who immediately arrested him. Some riots, it seemed, were deemed less dangerous to the public safety than others.[116]

The Irish cop might also serve as a social worker of sorts. Before the advent of organized social work, juvenile courts, and "child-saving" institutions, the neighborhood cop was often all that stood between a delinquent child and a life of crime. On Chicago's dangerous West Side, Daniel J. Talbot intervened for minor offenders at court, collected food and clothing for them from neighborhood merchants, marched them to church and synagogue, and eventually helped to establish a neighborhood refuge for them, complete with dormitory, dining hall, and school.[117]

Still, not much love was lost between Irish gangsters and cops. Many of Chicago's South Park police came from Sherman and Fuller Park, two areas with the greatest gang activity. The Irish cops who ran gangs out of the parks took pride in the rougher part of their work.[118] The feeling was mutual. When asked for a two-dollar contribution toward the burial of a policeman, Chicago's late-nineteenth-century gambling and political kingpin Michael Cassius McDonald (1839–1907) was alleged to have responded, "Here's ten bucks, bury five of 'em."[119] According to historian Kerby Miller, the Irish American community's typical attitude toward policemen was ambivalent—"admiration for their status mingling with contempt for their social apostasy."[120]

Investigators also found connections between Irish gangsters and unions, especially in the building trades. During the open shop campaign of the early 1920s, when the unions were struggling to maintain their grip on the construction industry's labor market, Ragen's Colts and other gangs supplied labor sluggers and bombers. The common link between labor leaders, politicians, policemen, and gangsters was the old Irish neighborhood. Notwithstanding the close association of the Capone organization with Italians, the Irish continued to dominate both the unions and the Chicago underworld into the 1920s, with frequent neighborhood and kinship ties between the two.[121] Similar connections could be found between gangs like the Dusters and the Gophers, the corrupt International Longshoremen's Association, and the Tammany machine on Manhattan's West Side.[122]

As new immigrants poured into the cities, Jewish and Italian gangsters entered the old Irish gangs as enforcers and assassins, then began to muscle the Irish out of the immigrant neighborhoods and the red-light districts altogether. Some older Irish criminals retired, leaving the trade to the newcomers, but many of the younger ones, now often members of ethnically diverse gangs, decided to fight it out, leading to bloody urban wars. As late as the 1930s, a Chicago sociologist's long list of "Who's Who in Gangland" included diverse nationalities, but most of the names were Irish. Similar Irish American underworlds thrived in Boston and New York, where an interethnic "Combine" under Irish leadership controlled much of the illicit beer trade during Prohibition.[123]

Having begun his career as a labor slugger during a Chicago newspaper strike, Dean O'Banion (1892–1924) built a criminal empire on the city's North Side, integrating Poles and Jews, but few Italians, into his gang. When Al Capone sought to expand onto the North Side, O'Banion declared a war that took his own life; then at the infamous St. Valentine's Day Massacre, Capone's henchmen posed as police and gunned down several of the late O'Banion's henchmen. In New York, the Irish Catholics "Legs" Diamond and "Mad Dog" Coll fought a similar war with "Dutch" Schultz, a leader in the emerging Jewish mob. The Irish lost all these conflicts, but the gangs that replaced them after World War II were neither exclusively Italian nor Jewish but were often multiethnic and included the remaining Irish gangsters. On the West Side of Manhattan and the South Side of Chicago, Irish American hitmen continued to work for largely Italian criminal organizations into the 1970s.[124]

RACE RIOT

Ragen's Colts and other Irish social athletic clubs helped enforce the racial boundaries on the South Side, and they were responsible for much of the violence in Chicago's bloody 1919 race riot. Most recent immigrants, seeing the conflict as one between white and black Americans, had decided to sit it out. But the Colts, with powerful political connections as a kind of military arm to the local Democratic machine, tried to draw eastern European immigrants into it. A few days into the riot, a huge fire broke out, destroying forty-nine homes in the heavily Polish and Lithuanian neighborhood Back of the Yards; rumors spread that blacks were responsible.

That fire, like most of the violence perpetrated against African Americans in the riot, originated with the Colts and other Irish gangs, as a grand jury, the Chicago Commission on Race Relations, and settlement house reformer Mary McDowell all agreed. They had blackened their faces in order to mislead the fire victims, hoping they would join in the racial violence.[125] "It was evident during the riot," McDowell observed, "that our Polish neighbors were not the element that committed the violence; it was committed by the second and third generation young men from the 'athletic clubs.'"[126]

On one level, by trying to draw Poles and Lithuanians into a white alliance across ethnic lines, the Colts exercised a kind of inclusion. But the newcomers would have to fit into an implied racial hierarchy: the fire betrayed the cynical contempt that some Irish American youth felt for the impoverished Polish and Lithuanian immigrants whose homes they burned.[127]

The Colts continued to try to enforce racial boundaries for years afterward. Hugh McGovern spent much of his energy enforcing the deadline. In March 1926, McGovern was part of a group who lured James Thomas, an African American restaurant porter, to the back of the Colts' clubhouse with an offer of drinks. There they beat Thomas, shot him twice, stabbed him several times, and dumped him on the street for dead. The police found Thomas alive, however, and he survived long enough to identify McGovern and David "Yiddles" Miller as his assailants.[128]

Even as they attacked blacks, the Colts also posed as protectors of the broader Catholic immigrant community. In September 1921, they led a demonstration of three thousand against the Ku Klux Klan, hanging a hooded figure in effigy. This street theater also aimed to unite Catholic immigrants behind Irish American leaders. At that time, Chicago's Irish American politicians were campaigning to brand Mayor "Big Bill" Thompson's Republican machine an Anglo-Saxon anti-Catholic conspiracy and a racial threat because of his strong base in the city's burgeoning black community. When Thompson ran for another term in 1927, on a motto of "America First," Irish American politicians interpreted it to actually mean "Africa First" and made an explicit appeal to the Italian community. Italian immigrants hardly embraced the Irish as brothers, and

Irish and Italian hostility remained thereafter, but in that 1927 election, the heavily Italian First Ward voted overwhelmingly for the Irish American Democratic mayoral candidate.[129]

Still, new immigrant communities reacted ambivalently to such racist appeals. During Chicago's 1919 race riot, the reactionary Polish newspaper *Narod Polski* editorialized that the blacks were partly responsible for the violence that had befallen them, but other Polish community leaders warned their community against succumbing to the contagion of race hatred. Father Louis Grudzinski, one of Chicago Polonia's most influential clerics, urged his flock to hold back from racial violence. Even after Polish homes were burned in the conflict, Grudzinski reminded his parishioners of their long-standing conflicts with the neighboring Irish. He insisted, in words they were sure to understand, that his parishioners refrain from taking revenge: "We must not be moved by agitators and then be condemned for having caused the black *pogrom*."[130]

Apparently the advice worked in the stockyards neighborhood. Julia Goryl remembered one black family in the heart of the Polish community that remained untouched throughout the riot.[131] Polish immigrants in Buffalo during the 1920s (interviewed by sociologist Niles Carpenter) sometimes demonstrated antipathy toward traditional enemies like the Jews and Lithuanians, or toward the Irish and other native-born workers and foremen who were antagonistic toward them, but they showed little hostility toward African Americans.[132]

The evidence regarding race prejudice among second- and third-generation Poles is mixed at best. As late as 1928, about one-third of Carpenter's Buffalo sample supported the statement "The Negro should be permitted all the privileges and rights accorded to the whites," while another third remained indifferent. But that support was considerably less than among the immigrant generation.[133] Likewise, Chicago's huge Polish community showed little tension or conflict with blacks in the early twentieth century, but after World War II Poles and other second- and third-generation Slavic groups were much more involved in race riots.[134]

Gangs often incubated racist attitudes, language, and behavior, but they could also create solidarity across racial lines. "Far more than we realize," J. Adams Puffer observed in 1912, "the boys' gang is helping out the public school in the great problem of assimilating the diverse races in the United States."[135] The gang often brought immigrant youth into contact with other ethnic groups, a transgression that could produce fruitful investigation or bitter conflict.[136] "I never ask what nationality he is," declared a thirteen-year-old Lithuanian gang leader. "A Jew or a nigger can be a pal of mine if he's a good fellow."[137] Jacob Riis saw New York's turn-of-the-century gangs as products not of any particular ethnic group but rather of the mixing of the races in the city itself. The gangs were "made up of the American-born sons of English, Irish, and German parents . . . The 'assimilation' of Europe's oppressed hordes . . . is perfect. The product is our own."[138]

WHITE ETHNIC GANGS

During the interwar years, street gangs and social athletic clubs proliferated, made up increasingly of a burgeoning new generation of immigrant youth. In the early 1930s, crowds of young men thronged the street corners and storefronts in Polish and Italian neighborhoods. In 1935, in a six-by-nine-block neighborhood in Chicago's "Little Sicily," a sociology student counted twenty gangs representing nearly one thousand boys. Around the same time, another Italian neighborhood on the Northwest Side hosted seventy-five distinct gangs. Italian, Polish, and other social athletic clubs mixed sports, politics, music, and dance with neighborhood violence and, often, criminal activity. Many ethnic gangs originated in young men's struggle to defend themselves, their friends, and their ethnic turf against outsiders. So many gangs emerged in Polish neighborhoods that in the minds of reformers and the public, the ethnic group became closely associated with juvenile delinquency.[139]

Almost half of the gangs in sociologist Frederic Thrasher's sample were predominantly of one nationality. But 40 percent of them were of mixed white nationalities, a growing trend. (A small number of gangs mixed African Americans and ethnic whites, often second-generation Jews.) The gradual ethnic integration of gangs opened the way for acculturation across ethnic lines. As early as the 1920s, African Americans showed up as gang members, but their numbers were still small and they were less likely to organize gangs than second- and third-generation European immigrants. After World War II, in the wake of massive African American and Latino migrations, street gangs spread widely to communities of color.[140]

While later immigrant groups certainly brought their own criminal traditions with them, like the Sicilian Mafia and the Black Hand societies, the Irish passed on many gang trappings to the later groups. Long after the Irish lost their majority status in a neighborhood, Irish gang names and deadlines were passed on and retained: "Fuller Park is an old Irish community which lies south and east of the Stockyards," University of Chicago researchers wrote in the 1930s. "While Italians, Mexicans and Poles have invaded the area, the patterns of the old Irish gangs are still prevalent, and the boys still meet in basement and storefront clubrooms."[141]

Later immigrants, initially unaware of American racial conventions, emulated Irish American patterns of conflict with African Americans. Violence against blacks was rare in eastern European communities before the 1920s, but the Murderers, a gang of second-generation Poles in Back of the Yards, trumpeted their role in the 1919 Chicago race riot and continued to attack black packinghouse workers in the early 1920s. They recognized that such actions reflected white supremacist conventional wisdom among the Irish and other more Americanized youth.[142]

In the 1920s, when Mexican immigrants entered the stockyards and the South Chicago steel mill district in large numbers, Polish street gangs chased them out of playgrounds and off neighborhood streets. As with Irish gang violence, these confrontations often arose over issues of interracial sexual contact. "For the Poles and other new immigrant groups around the Back of the Yards and elsewhere in the city," Andrew Diamond writes, "the Irish athletic clubs of the 1910s and 1920s were standard bearers of Americanization, and their actions against both blacks and new ethnic groups provided vivid demonstrations of the meaning and power of whiteness and Americanism on the city streets."[143] In New York as in Chicago, the Irish passed on not only gang names and deadlines but also a strong sense of territoriality. "Every block had a gang," Tony Arrigo recalled of his East Side Manhattan neighborhood in the 1920s and 1930s. "If a kid from another block came down our street, we questioned him. First of all, you wanted to know what he was doin' on 30th Street."[144]

Most conflict between Chicago gangs was organized on a territorial rather than on a strictly racial or ethnic basis. In the early 1900s, the Irish gangs the Shielders and the Dukies fought for control of the old Irish neighborhood of Bridgeport, separated by the deadline of an abandoned streetcar track along Fortieth Street. In such conflicts, spatial separation helped create what urban historian Robin Bachin calls "one's sense of one's place in the urban landscape."[145] Before, during, and long after the 1919 race riot, the "Mickies" terrorized African Americans in territorial conflicts: the Mickies normally attacked blacks who ventured across the Wentworth deadline. That and other boundaries became racialized in the context of heavy black migration in the 1910s and 1920s. As newer ethnic groups settled into Bridgeport, Italians, Poles, and other ethnic groups became Mickies. These panethnic white gangs, often led by Irish Americans, enforced segregation in housing, parks and recreational facilities, and public spaces within Bridgeport—just as the homogeneous Irish gangs had done before them. Once they perceived a racial threat, the warring "white" gangs embraced racial solidarity. In areas where race was not the main concern, ethnically mixed gangs fought one another. African Americans called all the Bridgeport white gangs Mickies, regardless of their ethnic composition.[146]

White gangs, then, were one way recent immigrants absorbed from the Irish a racialized map of the city, attitudes about African Americans, and a language of racial exclusion. Still, some immigrants at first showed a marked indifference to American racial conventions, identifying more with their own ethnic group or even a particular old-world local identity than with any notion of "whiteness."[147] And during the interwar years, many white ethnic young people showed a readiness to cross ethnic and racial lines.

AMERICANIZATION BY DANCE HALL AND MOVIE THEATER

Immigrants' children found their own way in the new urban culture, as historian David Nasaw wrote of New York, "effectively 'Americanizing' themselves on the streets and in the city's amusement centers." Despite racial segregation in many venues and the persistence of ethnic subcultures, a degree of mixing clearly took place in theaters, nightclubs, dance halls, and other urban venues.[148] During World War I, an estimated eighty-six thousand Chicagoans went dancing nightly. Reformers succeeded in closing many of these dance halls, but in the early 1920s they were reopening as dance schools. "Even in ethnically segregated neighborhoods, such as those in Chicago's stockyard district," Nasaw observed, "the jazz and jazz dancing popular in the downtown nightclubs and ballrooms had displaced the once popular 'Polish hop.'"[149] Large, fancy clubs like Chicago's White City and Dreamland, and Manhattan's Roseland and Grand Central Palace, drew patrons from around the city and beyond; small neighborhood halls provided common ground for young people from various ethnic communities. Reformers and immigrant elders railed against the dance hall's influence, but it persisted in one form or another through the Great Depression.[150]

Around the turn of the century, the Irish social athletic clubs established Gaelic Park, a dance pavilion on Chicago's Southwest Side; in the 1920s, it welcomed Polish and Lithuanian girls but remained dangerous territory for young men from other ethnic groups. A chasm was opening between old world cultures and Americanizing immigrant youth: Sundays found one side of Gaelic Park devoted to traditional Irish jigs and reels, based on the fiddle and accordion, while the large pavilion was reserved for jazz and "American dancing." Chicago's Polonia Park, in Back of the Yards, was mostly frequented by young Poles and Lithuanians, although some Polish girls traveled to Gaelic Park to seek out Irish American boys. "For a great many people the dance hall provides a means of sexual experience beyond the control of primary groups to which the individuals belong," sociology student Paul Cressey observed in the early 1920s. A few young Irish women from Bridgeport attended dance halls, but they were jealously guarded by the Irish gangs. "The general atmosphere of the place toward an outsider is one of hostility," another student reported.[151]

Dance halls and pavilions, because they often served as common ground, opened the prospect of sexual contact across ethnic and racial lines, as well as the great taboo, intermarriage. Neighborhood patrolling by established white ethnic gangs often aimed to discourage interethnic romances involving newcomers. When Filipinos or Chinese first "invaded" a white dance hall, a near riot developed with resident Italian, Polish, or other gangs.[152]

But by the early 1920s, if not earlier, the very Irish American gang members who once enforced such boundaries regularly transgressed them.[153] The "Red Light" and "Bright Light" districts, in between African American and Irish neighborhoods, had nightclubs and cafés that often attracted Irish American youth looking for music, shows, and the thrill of interracial sex.[154] James T. Farrell's character Studs Lonigan and his boys had railed against the influx of Jews and blacks into their South Side neighborhood, but then in the early 1920s they were strongly attracted to the bright lights, jazz, and excitement of the city's racially mixed clubs. Conflicted Irish American anxieties over race persisted as young men seemed at once repelled by and strongly attracted to the lifestyles of African Americans.[155] The Colts' gunman Hugh McGovern met his own death at the hands of another Irish American gangster in a racially mixed café in the burgeoning Black Belt.

In the following two decades, jazz clubs, dance halls, brothels, and strip joints spread interracial contacts to the second generation of Poles and Italians, young women as well as young men. During the Depression, ethnic youth, faced with challenges in school, in the streets, and in the job queue, found the exploding commercial culture extremely attractive. The new interethnic youth culture was reflected in the era's street gangs.[156]

The Irish American street gang was a kind of coercive Americanization. By carving up the city into distinct ethnic turfs and relentlessly defending their own, Irish gangs developed a strong sense of territoriality that they transmitted to later immigrants. Even as they fought newer immigrant youth and, later, gradually integrated them into their gangs, the Irish conveyed a racialized vision of the city, in which racial distinctions were embedded in neighborhood geography. The gangs became what one sociologist called "racial sentinels," guarding the deadlines of the racially divided city.[157] More recent immigrants—Italians and Jews—learned this lesson in urban geography well and formed comparable gangs. Having arrived in the United States with little awareness of American racial conventions, they absorbed Irish hostility toward African Americans. Thereafter black and Latino migrants often met violent resistance from entrenched Polish, Italian, and ethnically mixed "white" gangs.

TWO

THE PARISH

In May 1915, two distinct generations of Catholics gathered on the Lower East Side to celebrate the centennial of Old St. Patrick's Cathedral on Mulberry Street, the original seat of the New York diocese. Long a bastion of the city's Irish community, the modest church now symbolized how far the Irish had come since the "Famine ships" had brought them to New York Harbor. Surrounded by a high stone wall, the modest church had been besieged by nativist crowds and protected by armed parishioners in the 1830s and again in the 1840s. It was a focal point for early St. Patrick's Day parades and a source of great pride. If the Irish considered their neighborhood turfs almost sacred, it was in places like Old St. Pat's that they developed and fostered this belief.

By 1915, however, the parish was changing. The aging cathedral's communicants were now heavily Italian, and the narrow streets were filled with Chinese, Russian, and eastern European Jewish immigrants. The huge and far more elegant St. Patrick's Cathedral on Fifth Avenue had replaced it as the diocesan seat. The new cathedral, whose windows and altars were designed by Tiffany and Company and by artists in France and Britain, had taken more than two decades to construct and was dedicated in 1879 in a fashionable part of Midtown Manhattan.

The 1915 gathering at Old St. Pat's graphically represented a transformation that was occurring in cities throughout the nation: a more diverse

OLD ST. PAT'S, MOTT STREET (ESTABLISHED 1815):
*focal point for the old Irish neighborhood on the
Lower East Side, Manhattan, circa 1870.*

Catholic community was emerging. John Murphy Cardinal Farley and the "cathedral Irish"—the clergy, Midtown politicians and dignitaries, businessmen and professionals, middle-class matrons, and their well-dressed children—returned to the old neighborhood for the celebration, filling the altar and the front pews. But most of the cathedral was occupied by its newer parishioners: Italian workers and their families, the men in flannel shirts, the women in frayed black shawls.[1] As the celebration unfolded, tension between these two generations sizzled.

The Irish shared more than their streets with the recent immigrants; they also shared their church. Since the 1880s, the Irish Catholic clergy, laity, and hierarchy had been watching new immigrants transform the church's complexion. But the church also provided the newcomers (as it had done for the Irish) with an institutional structure and resources, as well as extensive social networks that could be mobilized in the interests of the poor. This story of Catholic Americanization remains largely untold.

Like most working-class urban institutions, the Catholic Church was ethnically segmented. Immigrants had a strong tendency to settle in enclaves around their distinct national parishes, and the territorial quality of Catholic parish culture reinforced ethnic and racial division in the next generation. Within one square mile in Chicago's stockyards neighborhood, immigrant families erected eleven separate parishes based on distinct ethnic cultures. Ethnic Catholics could map out the industrial city in physical and cultural terms.[2] In the 1880s, the opening of Chicago's St. Bernard's parish signaled the successful Irish invasion of the largely WASP Englewood neighborhood; Father Bernard Murray imported five thousand marchers from South Side parishes to parade.[3] Because of the relationship between parish and neighborhood, ethnic Catholics thought of city space in parish terms.

But the parish turf was also sacred. "The church steeple towering over bungalows reminded people of God's presence; the sound of the church bells was another reminder of the divine," Catholic historian Jay Dolan notes. "The parish permeated the neighborhood with a religious quality that was uniquely Catholic."[4] On holy days, large processions—including thousands of schoolchildren, priests, nuns, and laity—wound their way through densely populated streets, "claiming both the parish and its inhabitants as sacred ground" and demonstrating the strength and pervasiveness of Catholicism in city life.[5] The parish was a focus for their social lives and a rallying point for politics: here, as well as in urban political machines, immigrants honed their political skills.[6]

Priests and nuns who followed their flocks from the old country founded ethnically based religious orders, schools, hospitals, and other institutions in immigrant communities. The ethnic parish school, which taught mostly in the immigrant vernacular at least until World War I, was the key institution by which first-generation immigrants passed on their culture and language, as well as religious beliefs, to the second. More than any other institution, the ethnic parish allowed new immigrants to

MAY PROCESSION:
Catholic school children from Holy Redeemer parish parade through the streets
of east Boston on their way to crown the Blessed Virgin, early 1920s.

reconstruct their old-world cultures. Filled with familiar sights, sounds, and smells, resounding with well-known religious language, ritual, and symbolism, the parish church provided immigrant Catholics with a moment of beauty and the divine in the workaday world. Here immigrant workers and their families escaped, however briefly, the industrial slums.

But they could not always escape the Irish.

IRISH CATHOLICISM

In the wake of the Great Famine, Irish immigrants had steeped themselves in a "Devotional Revolution," a movement that emphasized formal, prescribed worship practices; the status and central role of the parish priest; and the authority of the church hierarchy. This new devotionalism, as well as the trauma of the Famine, gave rise to a flood of priests and nuns: between 1840 and 1900, when the Irish population was reduced by nearly half, the ratio of priests to the general population fell from 1:3000 to 1:900, and the ratio of nuns, from 1:6500 to 1:400. Many of them dispersed across the earth as missionaries, ensuring that Irish influence on the church was truly transnational; thousands followed the immigrants into the cities of the United States. As upwardly mobile Irish strove for respectability, older Irish folk practices were consciously suppressed, and the demands for a stern, formal Catholicism were reinforced.[7]

Unlike their secularized European counterparts and unlike some other ethnic groups in the United States, the working-class Irish exhibited a fierce devotion to the church, forged amid famine and disease, repression and forced relocation. It helped fuse Catholicism with Irish national identity and greatly reinforced the Irish character of the American church. Most Irish identified overwhelmingly with their neighborhood parish and attended Mass at least weekly. Over 90 percent of turn-of-the-century New York Irish claimed to be Catholic, and of them 90 percent claimed membership in a particular parish. In 1900, a visitor to Manhattan's rough West Side waterfront neighborhoods would encounter a church every three or four streets, their steeples forming a familiar part of the urban skyline.[8]

Underlying the public face of Irish American Catholicism lay a rich religious life in the two- and three-room apartments and rambling wooden tenements in American cities and industrial towns. Irish Americans held the home as a sacred space and adorned it accordingly. This habit began in nineteenth-century Ireland but, like Irish Catholicism generally, was transformed by the Famine, emigration, and gradual upward mobility in the American city. Mid-nineteenth-century cottages in rural Ireland had displayed little religious ornamentation besides the traditional St. Brigid's cross of blessed palms.[9]

But after the Famine, in a strengthened economy, Irish clergy made a concerted effort to ignite popular religious participation and encouraged Irish women to mark their homes with more ornate signs of their spiritual lives. Catholic publications urged families to dedicate a space specifically for religious devotions. Candles, statues, holy pictures, and other religious goods transformed a humble cottage into a sacred space.[10]

In the United States, even the poorest Irish homes featured religious prints and statues, while rising Irish families took particular pride in giving their homes the proper appearance. In a three-room West Side tenement apartment occupied by an Irish American couple and their six children, Barnard College sociologists found a family shrine consisting of a print and two statues of the Blessed Virgin; pictures of Anthony, Benedict, and other saints; a rosary and a family Bible; two crucifixes; newspaper photos of popes Leo XIII and Pius X; photos of the family and a relative's tombstone in Ireland; and vases of artificial flowers. Inexpensive mass-produced religious articles made it possible for even the poorest families to show their piety, religious historian Colleen McDannell writes, "while infusing color and individuality into their drab surroundings."[11]

Well into the twentieth century, the Irish remained more firmly attached to the church than other ethnic groups, with the possible exception of the Poles. In 1900, in the midst of the new immigration from Italy and eastern Europe, Irish Americans still represented almost one out of every two American Catholics. The religion resided at the center of many immigrant working-class cultures, but none more than the Irish.[12] Throughout most of the twentieth century, Irish Americans participated disproportionately in religious practice. They were more apt than other groups to attend weekly Mass, send their children to parochial schools, and remain observant into the second and third generations.[13] In the first half of the twentieth century, the Catholic Church was more than an important institution in Irish American communities: it was, in many respects, the center of their world.

THE IRISH ADVANTAGE

By the 1880s, and earlier in some places, the Irish dominated American Catholicism to the point that critics often referred to it as the "One Holy, *Irish*, and Apostolic" Catholic Church. By the time other immigrants began arriving in large numbers, the church was not simply American but Irish American, steeped in Irish ways. In an institution famous for its

complex organization and hierarchical authority structure, the Irish commanded the high ground.[14]

By 1875, in Boston and some other cities, Irish Americans held a "near-
monopoly" on the diocesan priesthood. In every census from 1880 on,
while Boston's population became increasingly diverse, nearly 80 percent
of its priests were still first- or second-generation Irish. (The comparable figure for New York City was 70 percent.) As late as World War II,
priests' ethnic origins had not significantly changed. Boston was extreme
in this regard: by the early twentieth century, Polish in other cities were
either importing or educating their own priests and nuns. But the Italians
continued to deal with Irish religious, some trained in new immigrant
languages.[15]

Whatever their ethnic background, most of these priests and nuns were
subject to Irish American bishops. In the early twentieth century, the Irish
controlled the important dioceses of New York, Boston, Philadelphia,
Chicago, and Baltimore. By 1920, two-thirds of all Catholic bishops (three-
fourths in New England) were of Irish birth or descent. Even in St. Louis,
where German American clergy clearly outnumbered them, the Irish accounted for eleven of twelve priests promoted to the episcopacy between
1854 and 1922. The newer immigrant groups, representing a huge proportion of the laity, were effectively frozen out. "Other immigrant groups
resented such Irish domination," Jay Dolan notes, "and before long the
Irish became the common enemy."[16]

Some of the conflicts occurred *within* the Irish community, as the Irish
tried to maintain control of the hierarchy through higher-level administrative appointments while Irish Americans tried to work their way into
it. In 1901, the conflict reached the boiling point when an American, Peter
Muldoon, was elevated to auxiliary bishop of Chicago and a member of
the old "Irish cabal" was excommunicated for his resistance.[17]

German immigrants clashed with the Irish repeatedly over issues
of governance. In 1891, German American leader Peter Paul Cahensly
proposed an organization of the American church along ethnic rather
than geographic lines, allowing much greater autonomy and episcopal

representation for each ethnic group. He received considerable support from other foreign-born Catholics—and strenuous opposition from the Irish American hierarchy. The church's traditions and hierarchical character favored the Irish—and the pope rejected the concept.

Irish American bishops opposing such demands certainly had their own interests in mind, but they also worried about the church's status in American society. Anti-Catholicism surged in the 1890s: members of the American Protective Association pledged to not hire, work with, vote for, or strike with a Roman Catholic. The hierarchy was at pains to refute claims that theirs was a "foreign" institution. "The prejudice is unjust," New York archbishop Michael Corrigan agreed, "but nevertheless . . . we are continually obliged to show that we Catholics are not opposed to the institutions of this country; that we are not subjects of a foreign potentate; and we are sincerely attracted to the land of our birth and adoption."[18] Nonetheless the issue of ethnic autonomy persisted, especially among the Poles, in Chicago, Detroit, and the anthracite coal towns—wherever more recent immigrants sought greater control over their religious lives.

Irish control did not produce a unified ideology on social questions or even on the place of the church in American society. During the 1890s "Americanist" controversy, Irish bishops were found on both sides. Conservatives like Archbishop Corrigan, suspicious of social reform, insisted that a separate and unique American Catholicism should maintain its distinct identity and values in a hostile, materialistic society; and that all Catholic children must attend parish schools. But the majority liberals, led by Baltimore archbishop James Gibbons and St. Paul archbishop John Ireland, celebrated American republican ideology, encouraged cooperation with other denominations and with the U.S. government, and favored the assimilation of Catholics into the broader society, even as they maintained allegiance to an Americanized church. "I need not tell you of course," Chicago archbishop George Mundelein wrote to Theodore Roosevelt, ". . . that there is hardly any institution here in the country that does so much to bring about a sure, safe, and sane Americanization of immigrant people as do our parish schools." The children who passed through them were and would continue to be "every bit as good American citizens as they are Catholics."[19]

Pope Leo XIII dealt a severe blow to the "Americanist" faction with an 1899 encyclical condemning the idea that there could ever be a distinctively "American" Catholic Church. There was only one universal church, he wrote, under direct control of the Vatican and characterized by traditional Catholic values and teaching. In 1907, in another encyclical, Pope Pius X condemned "modernism" and unleashed what Father Thomas Shelley called "a witch hunt against heretical 'moles' that recalled the worst days of the Inquisition." No one was burned at the stake in Brooklyn, but the crackdown inhibited creative Catholic efforts in theology and philosophy.[20]

The popes' encyclicals did not put an end to Irish efforts to Americanize the new immigrants—and all Irish American bishops fought vociferously the Anglo-American nativist vision of Americanization. Even the most ardent liberals tolerated the persistence of ethnic culture and emphasized religious over any political solidarity. The rampant anti-Catholicism encouraged them to stress Catholic solidarity in a diverse church. Above all, they feared that the immigrants, unless they were gathered under the watchful eye of the Irish American clergy and hierarchy, would fall prey to Protestant urban missionaries.

The "Americanist" debate reinforced earlier conflicts over ethnic representation in the church leadership and autonomous ethnic parishes. On this point, Irish American bishops, both liberals and conservatives, closed ranks, opposing ethnic representation and maintaining a remarkable hold on power. A papal compromise allowed for the persistence of national parishes, but the controversy continued to divide the Irish American liberal majority of bishops from the growing bulk of immigrant Catholics. They did not want their church to become an "instrument of Americanization," Chicago's Polish priests wrote to the Vatican in 1920. But the clergy and hierarchy's American church spoke with a decidedly Irish accent.[21]

The Catholicism of the newer immigrants had a different character from that of Irish Catholicism. "The result," historian Oscar Handlin concluded, "was a struggle, parish by parish, between the old Catholics and the new, a struggle that involved the nationality of the priest, the language to be used, the saints' days to be observed, and even the name of the church . . . The centralization, the discipline, and the order of the Catholic Church, its long experience in reconciling national difference, and its international tradition, all were inadequate to contain the peasants' urge to reconstitute their religious life in America exactly as it had been at home in the village."[22]

The "Irish advantage" in such confrontations went far beyond language facility. Not only had they organized most of the earliest parishes and church institutions, but their sons and daughters poured into religious orders and diocesan seminaries out of all proportion to their size in the population. So many Irish entered clergy ranks that religious orders that had originally been formed by French or German priests and nuns became largely Irish American.[23] From the mid-nineteenth century on, major Catholic institutions of higher learning began to flourish—and they were staffed overwhelmingly by the Irish, as were the major English-language Catholic newspapers and periodicals. When children from newer ethnic communities did rise in the church, it was often Irish Americans who trained and mentored them. Their dominance encouraged Irish Americans to see themselves as spokespeople for the church, and their perspectives permeated the institution.[24]

THE ITALIAN AND POLISH "PROBLEMS"

Early-twentieth-century pastors and bishops were preoccupied with what came to be called the "Italian problem."[25] From the perspective of Irish American clergy, it consisted of two fairly distinct challenges. On the one hand, Italians—particularly the small educated and professional class—exhibited a pronounced anticlericalism. Italians therefore made a sharp distinction between religion, which came from the people, and the institutional church, which they tended to view with considerable cynicism. In Ireland and Poland, religion and national identity tended to reinforce each other, but Italian nationalism had emerged in direct opposition to the church. As historian Rudolph Vecoli concludes, "It was difficult to be both an Italian patriot and a faithful Catholic." First in Italy and then in the United States, Italian anticlericalism spread to workers (along with socialism and anarchism). Amid mass immigration, *mangiapreti*, literally "priest eaters," were an everyday part of most large Italian communities. In immigrant communities, Irish control over the church and the authoritarian bent of some bishops enhanced Italian anticlericalism. Some Italian immigrants lionized the sixteenth-century friar Giordano Bruno, who had been burned at the stake by church authorities, as a great hero of free thought, and they celebrated yearly the republican patriot Giuseppe Garibaldi's march on Rome and his confrontation with the pope. Such spectacles "scandalized the American Irish, who were distinguished by reverence and respect for their priests."[26]

Their strong anticlericalism brought Italians into conflict with Irish American clerics, bishops, and laity. The confrontation was particularly fierce in Chicago just after the turn of the century. Here Edmund M. Dunne emerged as an important spokesman for the church's duty to Americanize the immigrants. An ambitious Italian-speaking Irishman, he took control of an Italian parish and declared war on the forces of Italian free thought.

When the Italians wanted to name a predominantly Italian public school for Garibaldi, Dunne blocked it, leading *Tribuna Italiana* to complain of the "ignorant intolerant fanaticism of the Irish." Organized into the Circolo Giordano Bruno, the intelligentsia fought a running battle with Dunne. The conflict only sharpened when he was elevated to chancellor, the top administrative position in the archdiocese. When an anarchist shot a Denver priest on the altar as he administered Communion, Dunne called the Circolo "an evil thing that the city police would do well to kill." Jane Addams, the country's most prominent settlement house reformer and a neighbor of the anticlericals, tried to make a distinction between anticlericalism and anarchism; Dunne labeled her "the patron saint of anti-Catholic bigotry in the city." For its part, *La Parola dei socialisti* considered the priest a "vile liar."[27] Dunne left little room for free thinking among Italian Americans: he put the church in charge of their lives and Irish Americans in charge of the church.

Confrontations with the *mangiapreti* were not unique to Chicago—radicals and anticlericals also fought church influence in New York's Italian community. In eastern European immigrant communities, "clericals," who followed the church's lead in most matters, waged running battles with rationalist "freethinkers," who fought the church's influence in their communities. Freethinkers erected elaborate social, cultural, and political networks paralleling those of the Catholic parishes, though their influence varied greatly from one community to another. They were clearly a majority among Chicago's Czechs, who established their own cemetery to make certain they would *not* be buried in consecrated ground; and they were weakest among the Poles, for whom the church ruled supreme. Freethinkers and anticlericals were an influential minority in the Lithuanian enclave.[28] An immigrant barber, a reader of the socialist paper *Naujienos*, explained that the Lithuanian freethinking Raymond Chapel was "something like a church, only you don't have to believe in anything." The local priest would not hear the confession of anyone reading *Naujienos* and would not bury freethinkers in the Catholic cemetery. "But now we don't care," the barber said, "we have our own cemetery now. The people don't care what the priest says any more."[29]

By far the more common "Italian problem," however, was the persistence of *campanilismo*, the intensely local folk form of Catholicism that peasants and workers brought with them from the Mezzogiorno (Sicily and the hill towns of southern Italy). In the United States, their church attendance was irregular, particularly among men; they did not send their children to parish schools and failed to provide sufficient financial support to the hierarchy. Even among devout Italians, the priest occupied a less lofty position in Italian parishes than in other communities. The *festa*, an ancient celebration of the community's patron saint, was the center of the peasant's religious life, and it remained under the control of lay societies, beyond the reach of clerics. "The saint belonged to the people," immigrants explained to Jacob Riis, "not to the church."[30] In his description of a South Side *festa*, a University of Chicago sociology student reported that "the church and the priest are *not* the center of the various rites." Everyone got dressed up and the whole neighborhood mobilized, marching through the streets past gaily decorated houses and stalls filled with foods and religious objects.[31]

A *FESTA*:
the feast of San Rocco on the streets of Little Italy, Lower Manhattan, 1932.

This communal brand of Catholicism was practiced as much in city streets as in the pews of a church. So Chicago's West Side Irish—and their counterparts in other neighborhoods that mixed large numbers of Irish and Italians, such as Greenwich Village, Harlem, and the North End of Boston—constantly witnessed the spectacle of an "alien" form of Catholicism in their streets. "Besides being an embarrassment," folklorist and historian Robert Orsi writes, "*feste* challenged the authority of official Catholicism over the religious lives of the immigrants."[32]

As with the Irish, Poles' national identity was fused with their Catholicism. Poles were fiercely devoted to their pastors and to their parish churches.[33] A shining example was St. Stanislaus Kostka, on Chicago's North Side. In the early twentieth century, St. Stan's, with its forty-five thousand parishioners, was thought to be the largest Catholic parish on earth. The level of church influence in Chicago Polonia's everyday life reminded one observer of a peasant village in the Middle Ages. Poles saw themselves as deprived of the status and resources that the enormous size of their community and its commitment to the church justified. At first, ambitious clergy who tried to guard the interests of their congregations in an Irish-dominated institution often had little choice but to cultivate ties with the Irish American hierarchy. Such efforts yielded results for the Resurrectionists, a Polish religious order, and others, but also set off bitter conflicts throughout Polonia. Eventually, their very devotion led Poles into conflicts with the Americanization-minded Irish hierarchy, and they saw Polish priests who collaborated with the Irish as turncoats. The poet Stanislaw Dangiel condemned the Polish accomplices of the Irish church bosses who, in their pursuit of financial resources, raised the banner of "the harp, the snake, and the three leaf clover."[34]

So large and healthy was Polish Catholicism that it finally generated demands for a distinctive Polish church—Polish parishes, Polish priests and bishops, and the maintenance of Polish language and ritual. These demands ran "head-on into the aggressive Americanization position by the Catholic hierarchy."[35] The result was two rare schisms in the church. In Detroit in 1885, Bishop Caspar Borgess dismissed the charismatic Father Dominic Kolasinski as pastor of St. Albertus parish for alleged financial mismanagement and sexual improprieties. But most parishioners were outraged at the Irish American bishop's interference in parish business, and the affair quickly escalated into a confrontation, riots, and eventually the excommunication of Kolasinski and his entire flock; they were later reinstated.[36]

Then in the 1890s in Scranton, Pennsylvania, the particularly devout but class-conscious Polish anthracite coal miners clashed with the Irish Catholic hierarchy over control of parish policy and funds. "The aim of the Irish Roman Church," according to their leader, the Reverend Franciszek Hodur (1866–1953), was "to keep people in submissiveness, not to educate, redeem or make them noble." The American church, Hodur wrote, "was devised by Irish prelates and is inimical to us." The result, in 1897, was a schism and the creation of the Polish National Catholic Church with Hodur as its first bishop. The movement went on to actively compete with the Roman Catholic Church in several large Polish communities.[37]

As one Polish American author has concluded, Polish Catholics often saw Irish Americans and Protestant Anglo-Saxons as "two prongs of the same nativist fork."[38] These tensions persisted well into the second half of the twentieth century, along with a strong element of class resentment.

The most effective manager for Americanization in Chicago was George Mundelein (1872–1939), the child of German immigrants. Raised and educated in New York among Irish Catholics, he was named Archbishop of Chicago in 1915. There he was surrounded by Irish and Irish American clergy, whom he enlisted in his campaign to build a cohesive American church in the heart of a particularly diverse city. His efforts brought him appointment as a cardinal in 1924, but they also brought him into conflict with recent immigrant communities and especially with the large organization of Polish priests. By the 1910s, Mundelein observed, diverse cities were in a "state of transition," as immigrant children were "rapidly Americanizing and perhaps deserting too quickly the language and traditions of the parents to become thoroughly American in everything but perhaps name."[39]

Chicago's Polish priests complained to Polish diplomats at the Vatican, asking them to intervene with the pope to help them save their distinctive Polish American Catholicism, provide them with more recognition, and appoint a Polish auxiliary bishop in Chicago. The Polish American petition wounded the Americanizers' sense of hierarchy and American nationalism. It enraged them that Chicago's Polish priests had gone outside not only the church but the American nation to enlist the authority of the Polish government in their demands. The Americanizers struck back: with Mundelein in the lead, a committee of American bishops issued a strongly worded response.[40]

The bishops, largely Irish American, favored a natural process of Americanization within the church involving a gradual acculturation of the second generation. Mundelein insisted that the bishops were not trying to Americanize the immigrants' existing national parishes or to force them to abandon their cultures. He accepted their distinctiveness in his conversations with Rome but insisted on the gradual evolution of an interethnic American church: "To interfere in any way in what is a perfectly natural change here in the United States by emphasizing a spirit of foreign nationalism would cost the loss of many souls and effect really nothing in the end."[41] Mundelein and the other Americanizing bishops saw resolving this issue as critical to retaining the church's influence in American society. The various ethnic groups, he argued, must come together and assert their identity as Catholics: "We must then be one great family, all working together."[42]

Archbishop Mundelein carefully cultivated the national parishes: he sponsored special collections to support the destitute in Poland and other countries; he ensured that all Polish American clergy received instruction in Polish language and culture; and he admonished immigrant youth to be proud of their ethnic heritage. The massive collections he raised for Poland in the wake of World War I and for Ireland in the wake of its revolution (1919–21) were particularly successful—not just in raising large donations but in drawing the city's various Catholic groups together in support of a large project across ethnic lines. "I need only remind the pastors of the Polish-speaking parishes," Mundelein wrote in his April 1921 pastoral letter on Irish relief, "that when an appeal was made a few years ago for the war sufferers in Poland, those churches whose membership was made up almost entirely of Americans of Irish descent were first and foremost in giving." The same held good when he appealed to them later for the starving German and Austrian children.[43]

But Archbishop Mundelein also strove to encourage the acculturation of the second generation and resisted efforts to isolate the various Catholic ethnic groups from one another. He was particularly concerned that the cultivation of distinct ethnic cultures and the establishment of national parishes would cut immigrants off from the rest of American society, to the disadvantage of these communities and the church. He strongly resisted appointing an auxiliary bishop specifically for Poles, fearing that every ethnic group would also demand one. Mundelein precipitated a major crisis in 1921 by choosing Edward Hoban, an Irish American, to replace Paul Rhode, a Polish American auxiliary bishop, as vicar general (second in administrative command to the bishop) of the Chicago archdiocese. Instead of rising to bishop's status in Chicago, Rhode had been appointed bishop of Green Bay, Wisconsin, in 1915. Chicago Poles had been demanding a bishop of their own at least since 1891 and the loss of Rhode to Green Bay and the elevation of yet another Irish American to power embittered many.[44]

In 1917, Mundelein announced he would establish no new national parishes, even though the Poles and other burgeoning ethnic communities were clamoring for them. He tried to mix ethnic groups by assigning Polish-speaking priests to non-Polish territorial parishes, and at the diocesan seminary, he standardized the curriculum, aiming to make it "an engine of Americanization." But the various "ethnic leagues" and especially the Polish constituency were strong enough that many of these plans failed. Polish American lobbying and the city's exploding Polish population forced Mundelein to reassign Polish clergy from territorial to national parishes. In the 1920s, he held to the letter of his decision by designating as territorial a number of new parishes that were, in practice, Polish national parishes.[45]

Other Americanization innovations had more lasting effects. In 1916, soon after his elevation as archbishop, Mundelein reorganized the archdiocesan schools, appointing a reliable central school board and demanding a standard curriculum and texts in the English language, with the exception of reading and religion, which continued to be taught in each parish's vernacular.[46] *The New York Times* called the move "a radical departure in the education in parochial schools . . . which in substance means Americanization."[47] Many early high schools were attached to national parishes, but Mundelein gradually handed them over to religious orders of teaching nuns, brothers, and priests, often Irish American, whom the archdiocese could more easily control.[48]

While Mundelein was forced to tread warily with the Poles, in subsequent decades he gave smaller ethnic communities less consideration.

During the 1920s, when Mexican immigrants began to arrive in larger numbers, certain territorial parishes became, in effect, Mexican, but the now-cardinal chartered no national parishes for the new migrants.[49] In the long run, that policy undermined the integrity of distinct ethnic cultures and led to the decline of immigrant languages. Mundelein remained adamant: "It is of the utmost importance to our American nation that the nationalities gathered in the United States should gradually amalgamate and fuse into one homogeneous people and, without losing the best traits of their race, become imbued with the one harmonious national thought, sentiment, and spirit, which is to be the very soul of the nation. This is the idea of Americanization."[50]

The perpetuation of strict ethnic divisions and separate cultures, Mundelein feared, would seriously retard assimilation for the long run. He also may have feared that in an era of heightened American xenophobia, a church comprised overwhelmingly of distinct ethnic groups could easily be labeled anti-American. Edward Kantowicz, his biographer, observes that "Mundelein's German ancestry also made it imperative for him to overcompensate with outspoken Americanism." During World War I, the church, like so many other institutions in the United States, took on a heightened sense of nationalism. Mundelein insisted that every pastor purchase a minimum of $100 in Liberty Bonds from parish funds, even if they had to borrow it, and he bought $10,000 worth himself.[51]

THE IRISH MODEL IN A DIVERSE CITY

The Irish model for Americanization was the robust, highly institutionalized form of Catholicism that had been born in the wake of the Great Famine; it found the *festa* and other Italian folk rituals barbaric. "In short," Catholic historian Mary Elizabeth Brown concludes, "the real 'Italian Problem' was the clash between *mezzogiorno* and Irish-American Catholicism."[52] "The Italians are not a sensitive people like our own," an Irish priest reported. "The Italians are callous as regards religion."[53]

The Irish particularly resented the Italians' neglect of the church's formal teachings. It was not simply that they ignored prescribed prayers like the Apostles' Creed, the journalist Bernard Lynch complained; they were ignorant of the church's most "elementary truths . . . such as the Trinity, the Incarnation, and the Redemption."[54] "Americans, Protestants and Catholics alike," Vecoli writes, "came to regard the Italians as little better than pagans and idolaters."[55] Italians "were always looked upon as though we were doing something wrong," a lifelong Italian Harlem resident recalled regarding the *festa* of Our Lady of Mount Carmel. Irish disapproval of Italian religious life also reflected deep-seated conflicts in the streets and workplaces. This hostility left deep wounds. As late as the 1930s, relations between Irish and Italians in heavily Catholic neighborhoods remained bitter.[56]

The same characteristics that made Italians bad Catholics, Lynch argued, made them unfit to be good Americans: they were largely devoid of "personal independence and manliness." This equation of Catholicism and American citizenship came up often in Irish American discourse during the era of mass immigration. During the 1920s, Mexican migrants, who like the Italians had strong indigenous religious traditions and a substantial group of radical anticlericals, poured into Chicago, where they found an Irish American clergy that "not only wanted to transform the Mexicans into good citizens, . . . they also wanted to make Mexican Catholics into American Catholics."[57] Irish American priests and bishops spoke of democratic values, then, but their lessons for Italians and Mexicans entailed order, respectability, and hierarchy.

Only a generation or so earlier, ironically, this tension between formal devotionalism and folk practices had gripped Ireland itself. Late-nineteenth-century Irish immigrants sprang disproportionately from the island's Irish-speaking rural west, where some folk practices persisted despite the Irish church's efforts to formalize religious devotions; some immigrants had brought these folk devotions with them to Irish American communities. The conflict between such "greenhorn" practices and the Victorian respectability of the "lace curtain" middle class lingered even as the Irish went about Americanizing their new immigrant brethren. In general, however, later Irish immigrants brought with them the more formal and cleric-centered Catholicism of the Devotional Revolution. The gradual emergence of an Irish American bourgeoisie reinforced such devotional characteristics. Their desire for respectability shaped the twentieth-century urban church and brought Irish clerics and hierarchy into conflict with Italians and other more recent immigrants.[58]

With their "proletarianized" church a largely working-class body, the Irish pioneered social and religious institutions to serve the poor—schools, orphanages, hospitals, social settlements, youth groups, charity organizations, and homes for unwed mothers. In the process, they set up an institutional framework and system of socialization that later Catholic immigrants encountered as they settled into the city. The Irish response to urban problems was brick-and-mortar Catholicism—the construction of huge institutions that paralleled those of the state and, more important, elaborate social networks that facilitated Irish influence within and well beyond the church. The crucial question was how such institutions would accommodate the new immigration and the great migration of African Americans. These enormous parishes slowly—and often reluctantly—integrated newcomers. St. James in Manhattan's Lower East Side, which claimed sixteen thousand communicants and the largest parochial school in late-nineteenth-century New York, emerged by the 1920s as a multiethnic parish, reflecting the community's mixture of Catholic groups.[59]

In most large cities, the Jesuits and the Irish Christian Brothers established boys' high schools explicitly to serve the children of the poor; by 1900, they were producing a new elite who ran city halls and county boards, police and fire departments, law firms and labor unions. The vital networks forged in these institutions helped produce the Irish American middle class. As the cities' populations changed, the schools continued to perform their same functions but with more diverse student bodies. New immigrant families with modest goals sent their sons to the parish high school if one was available, but ethnic youth with loftier aims went on to the Christian Brothers' De La Salle Institutes (in Lower Manhattan and on Chicago's South Side) or to Jesuit institutions like Xavier (founded in

1847 in Chelsea) or St. Ignatius (founded in 1870 on Chicago's old West Side). Long after student bodies shifted from overwhelmingly Irish to Polish, Mexican, and African American, they continued to be taught and mentored largely by Irish and Irish American priests and brothers.[60]

Comparable institutions arose for young Irish American women. The premier teaching orders were the Sisters of Mercy, established in Dublin in 1827 by Catherine Elizabeth McAuley; and the Sisters of Charity of the Blessed Virgin Mary, established by Mary Frances Clarke in Dublin in 1831. Both orders followed impoverished Irish immigrant workers into American cities and opened schools to teach their children. In New York, they also created an elaborate system of facilities for the poor, the sick, abandoned women, and young children. The first school chartered in Chicago in 1846 was a convent school for young women. Even as Irish American working-class families placed great emphasis on the education of their daughters, they established institutions that would continue to serve young women from immigrant and minority backgrounds in the next generations.[61]

The upsurge in vocations in nineteenth-century Ireland sent Irish nuns across the globe as missionaries, teachers, and nurses, spreading the rather distinctive Irish Catholicism wherever they went. But they went disproportionately to the United States, where a burgeoning urban population of Irish poor needed schools, orphanages, and other Catholic institutions.[62] Though they were subject to priests and bishops, nuns ran most Catholic charities, hospitals, and schools. Working on their own, apart from men, they provided an important example to the young women whom they trained. Nuns encouraged girls to continue their educations and to consider those professions that were open to them. Whereas Polish and German parochial schools aimed to sustain the ethnic culture and language, the curriculum in schools taught by Irish nuns resembled that of the public schools, though it also included Catholic religious instruction. Irish nuns were responsible not only for the upward mobility of many Irish women, historian Sarah Deutsch writes, "but also, in the long run, for Americanizing them."[63]

Irish nuns were activists. From the mid-nineteenth century on, they worked in the everyday world, confronting poverty, unemployment, illness, and alcoholism, helping widows, deserted wives, and orphans.[64] In New York, when middle-class Protestant women reformers set out to aid the immigrant poor by establishing institutions reflecting their own perspectives and values, they found an extensive network of Irish nuns already in place, working closely with ward and city politicians, and the usual array of voluntary organizations. Though the middle-class reformers have captured the imagination of historians, they lost the actual battle in the streets. By the 1880s, nuns were rearing more than 80 percent of New York City's dependent children. Jewish groups nurtured another 10 percent, leaving only 10 percent for disappointed Protestant reformers.[65]

The situation was more striking in Chicago, where Irish Catholic institutions constituted major sinews of the new urban society. Arriving amid a torrent of poor peasants who were in desperate need, nuns established and staffed the city's major public institutions. Their broad impact is evident in the accomplishments of one Irish order in one American city.

Catherine McAuley's Sisters of Mercy embraced Paul's admonition to "go into the middle of a perverse world": they ventured first into the slums of Dublin and then those of Chicago, where they arrived in 1846. The working lives of these "walking nuns" were far distant from those of most Victorian-age women. Led by Agatha O'Brien, who was one of seventeen children of a County Carlow barrel maker, they established the city's first permanent hospital, first orphanage, first adult education program, first home for "wayward girls," first women's academy, and first nurses' training program. During the cholera epidemics of 1849 and 1857 and in the wake of the great Chicago Fire of 1871, the Sisters of Mercy developed a reputation for remaining with the sick, injured, and destitute. Many of them died in the process. While O'Brien proudly described the Sisters as representing a "mixture of nations," the recruits came largely from Chicago's working-class Irish parishes. In 1896, the order reached 225 nuns, by which point they had established five elementary schools and several women's high schools, at a time when such institutions were rare.[66]

The Sisters of Mercy were only one of dozens of orders in the nation. By 1920, ninety thousand nuns worked in schools and other Catholic institutions throughout the United States. They came from many ethnic groups, but second-generation Irish American women comprised by far the largest proportion. Working apart from men, nuns became important role models for the young women whom they trained for leadership in the Irish community. They organized separate retreats for factory girls and telephone operators, as well as for teachers, businesswomen, and secretaries. In a religious culture where one's choice of patron saint said it all, the nuns tended to identify with women saints and the Blessed Virgin.[67]

In the wake of the great migration of African Americans in the World War I years and the 1920s, Irish American nuns played a vital role in their education. Katharine Drexel, the founder of the Sisters of the Blessed Sacrament for Indians and Colored People, was the daughter of an old, wealthy Philadelphia family, but she had been raised largely by Irish immigrant domestics. Her nuns came largely from Irish working-class homes and dedicated themselves to the service of African Americans in and outside the church. Orders of mostly Irish Franciscan and Loreto nuns took up the same work on Chicago's South Side, while German, Polish, and other orders followed in their wake. Long before the civil rights movement of the 1960s, these nuns quietly provided African American youth with quality education. All nuns resided in parish convents or the institutions they had established themselves, so these sisters were rare among white people in that they lived and worked in black neighborhoods.[68]

For some Irish Americans, then, being a Catholic entailed not only having a degree of tolerance but also dedicating oneself to performing public service. In an increasingly diverse society, Catholicism generated tensions and conflicts, but it also taught social justice and especially racial and ethnic tolerance. Given the longtime Irish American hostility toward African Americans, the Irish Catholic reaction to black Catholics in their midst was far more mixed than one might expect.

Father Thomas Farrell was the pastor of St. Joseph's, the original and premier Irish parish in Greenwich Village, around the time of the Civil

War. An ardent abolitionist, he set aside $5,000 in his will to establish New York's first African American parish. Wary that conservative John Cardinal McCloskey would not follow through, Farrell enlisted two of his protégés, Richard Burtsell, another strong abolitionist, and Father Edward McGlynn, the original labor priest and pastor of St. Stephen's, to make sure he did. After Farrell died in 1880, Burtsell, who came from a wealthy New York family, took full responsibility for establishing the new parish, providing a down payment from his own savings. St. Stephen's and other Irish parishes contributed substantial amounts to the project.[69]

The new parish St. Benedict the Moor, established in 1883 on Bleecker Street in a former Universalist church, became the first black Catholic church north of the Mason-Dixon line. St. Joseph's pastor complained that many of his own Irish parishioners attended Mass at the black church, making St. Benedict's one of the few integrated congregations in nineteenth-century Manhattan; whites were required to occupy the gallery. In 1898, as New York's black population moved north, St. Benedict's moved to the Tenderloin on the West Side, where it was shepherded by a succession of Irish American priests. St. Benedict's famous lyceum became what the black radical Hubert Harrison called the "intellectual center of the New York Negro." The old parish building was bequeathed to the Village's most recent Catholic arrivals, the Italians. Irish societies continued to raise funds for the black parish at least through World War I.[70]

This was the period of great expansion in brick-and-mortar Catholicism, but building construction could never keep pace with the huge wave of immigrants entering American cities. Between 1890 and 1906, while the number of church buildings increased by 35 percent, communicants increased by 93 percent. This meant that many immigrants had to share church space with existing Irish congregations. As late as 1906, almost two-thirds of American Catholics worshiped in English-language parishes, while another 20 percent attended parishes where services were in English and one or more other languages. The result was considerable friction between established parishioners and the newcomers. In Chicago,

Irish ushers turned away Italian immigrant families who arrived at Mass in ragged clothes and without the customary pew rent.[71] The earliest arrangements for Italian Catholics in late-nineteenth-century New York were "annex parishes" in the basements of older Irish churches. Bishop Giovanni Battista Scalabrini had established a ministry for Italian immigrants as early as 1885, but the city claimed few Italian parishes until the early twentieth century, and many Italians and other ethnic groups remained in the basements under Irish clerical control.[72]

The message could not have been lost on the Italians in a religious tradition where the parish church symbolized the very soul of the community, where ethnic enclaves competed with one another for the grandest structures in the urban skyline, where towering Gothic and Romanesque steeples rose above the slums of immigrant working-class neighborhoods. The Irish reminded the Italians and other later immigrants daily that they were on top, and they often did so by physically relegating their congregations to the bottom layer of their hierarchical church.

As neighborhoods changed their ethnic complexions, the "parochial" territoriality enforced by street gangs also emerged in the discourse of Catholic clergy and laity. In early 1920s New York, Patrick Joseph Cardinal Hayes appointed an Italian priest as pastor at the formerly Irish Holy Rosary parish in Harlem. Irish American parishioners felt sold out and abandoned by one of their own—even though the newcomers were fellow Catholics. Edwin Fay complained of having to hand his parish over to "a foreign element," and Ida Collins of being "turned out of the House of God we helped to build."[73] In the 1910s in Chicago, when the giant wave of Polish immigration threatened to swamp St. John Berchmans's "American" population, Pastor Julius DeVos wrote to Cardinal Mundelein in a distinctly military vein, demanding a reorganization of the parish boundaries: "To maintain this territory as American we should have some more American ground to the west and south. Our eastern ground is largely Polish . . . We need some western territory to counterbalance their number . . . The Belgians alone cannot stem the advance of the Poles here.

NEW ST. PATRICK'S CATHEDRAL:
a magnificent edifice dedicated in 1879 and constructed uptown on Fifth
Avenue, some of the most expensive real estate in New York City, circa 1870.

The Americans can and should be helped by having their share of territory
to maintain here the five nationalities now represented: Belgians, Polish,
Irish, German and Italian."[74]

This visceral Catholic sense that a parish's physical dimensions should
correspond to the community of souls it served was nowhere more evident than in the narrow streets of Greenwich Village. Here at the end of
the nineteenth century, Irish-born Father Denis Paul O'Flynn (1847–1906)
presided over the giant parish of St. Joseph's, a community of some ten
thousand. As its ethnic and religious composition shifted from Irish to
Italian, Flynn fought every effort to establish a new congregation that
might "steal" his parishioners. In 1900, Greenwich Village was probably
about 90 percent Catholic and increasingly dense, but Flynn resented ef-

forts by Italians to make a place for themselves within his own congregation. Greenwich Village was Catholic, and for him, Catholic meant Irish. Contemplating the construction of an impressive new school in 1896, he worried to Archbishop Michael Corrigan that "the Jews, the Italians and others are encroaching on us."[75]

From 1913 to 1927, the New York diocese maintained an Italian Bureau, which supervised and provided a forum for clerics who served Italian congregations. The bureau was headed by an Irish American, with an active Italian priest as his aide.[76] Father O'Flynn's worries about the Italians flooding Lower Manhattan, diluting Irish dominance, and undermining the territorial integrity of St. Joseph's had some basis in reality. Irish longshoremen and their families regularly attended Mass at the Italian church St. Anthony's, presumably because of its proximity to the West Side docks. Irish American clergy in Chicago observed similar mixing.[77] In the streets of Greenwich Village and Harlem, as Italians arrived in ever greater numbers, St. Joseph's Day contended with St. Patrick's Day as the communities' most important religious observation.

The turbulent situation at Transfiguration parish, on the Lower East Side, illustrates the tensions that set in when a parish changed its ethnic complexion. Here, as in many other locations, a growing Italian population was "annexed" to a dwindling Irish congregation. Thomas Lynch, the parish's Irish-born rector, felt besieged. "Where do all these dark-eyed, olive-tinted men and women come from?" he asked. The key, Lynch concluded, was that an American style of Catholicism must instill American values. "What Catholics these people would become if they only had the qualities fitting them to be good Americans!" By all means bring in Italian priests, he agreed, but only under the watchful eyes of Irish American clerics. Above all, he warned, keep the Italian priests and nuns away from the younger generation, who must be Americanized by the resident clergy. In the meantime, the newcomers could continue to worship down in the basement. "Italians as a body," he concluded, "are not humiliated by humiliation."[78]

In fact, the Italians complained bitterly about their banishment to the lower depths. By 1900, their massive influx into Lower Manhattan had mostly displaced the old Irish parishioners at Transfiguration. An English-language Mass remained for remnants of the once-large Irish congregation, but the parish was turned over to a group of Italian priests in 1902.[79] At Harlem's Mount Carmel in 1891, the Reverend Michael Carmody sent a newly installed order of Italian nuns on an extended retreat, then changed the locks on the convent doors. When they complained to Carmody, he sent them to the archbishop, refusing to work with them any longer.[80]

In June 1898, John Murphy Farley (1842–1918), vicar general and later cardinal of the New York Archdiocese, observed that the cause was lost: there were already about three hundred thousand Italians in the city. Some rectors, he complained, "seem to feel that they are not responsible for the Italians." On the contrary, Farley argued, rectors had responsibilities "to *all* the souls in their parish."[81]

THE IRISH AMERICAN HIERARCHY:
*John Murphy Farley (1842–1918), the Irish-born archbishop
and later cardinal of New York, 1914.*

Irish Americans could not marginalize the newcomers indefinitely. If nothing else, maintaining their power and influence depended to some degree on being able integrate newcomers into the church, the Democratic Party, and other popular institutions. As a result, in the church's official discourse to an increasingly diverse flock, they employed a kind of Catholic cosmopolitanism to demonstrate the church's global reach. Chicago archbishop Patrick Feehan's 1890 Silver Jubilee involved eight thousand schoolchildren who sang not only "The Star-Spangled Banner" and "The Red, White, and Blue" but also the Polish, Italian, German, and French national anthems. Speakers delivered the main address in German, Italian, Bohemian, French, Polish, and Irish Gaelic as well as in English.[82]

By the 1920s, some Irish clerics were celebrating the church's multicultural character. Speaking at the laying of a cornerstone at St. Martin of Tours African American church in Manhattan, Father James Lynch concluded, "The trowel used in the ceremony was given by a Protestant friend; the cellar was dug by an Irish contractor who employed Italian laborers; and the earth, which was carted away by negro drivers, was used to fill in a Jewish cemetery."[83]

To the Italians, however, what the Irish presented as Americanized Catholicism had a pronounced Hibernian personality. Many Irish priests were ill suited to the task of leading overwhelmingly Italian parishes, but they persisted. While the Poles quickly established their own national parishes and recruited priests and nuns from the old country and from among their own second generation, Italians were far less likely to do so, remaining longer in Irish-dominated mixed parishes. The Italians certainly produced their own priests and nuns and imported others from Italy, but their numbers were far fewer than the Irish, and as a consequence, they often had to rely upon Italian-speaking Irish men and women. The result was an ongoing battle between two very different conceptions of Catholicism.[84]

THE OTHER SETTLEMENT HOUSES

The social and economic turbulence at the end of the nineteenth century moved the church to address the problems facing its working-class families in its own way. This tendency toward separatism was particularly strong in places like Boston, where the Catholic poor had good reason to feel excluded.[85]

The settlement house has long symbolized the project of Americanization, bridging the chasm between the native-born middle class and the immigrant poor and bringing mainstream Protestant values to the ethnic enclaves of American cities.[86] Chicago's Hull House, established in 1889 by Jane Addams, became the great example of this crusade, but scores of similar institutions were operating by the early 1900s. Yet the movement also had a Catholic dimension: Catholic reformers established dozens of settlement houses in the very heart of the immigrant communities. German American women played vital roles in them, but most settlements were established, staffed, and directed largely by Irish clergy and laity. The Irish American Holy Family parish, immediately adjacent to Hull House and the West Side's burgeoning Italian population, projected a strong sense of "American" Catholic culture, a counterweight to the values conveyed at neighboring Hull House.[87]

Aiming to Americanize the Catholic immigrant poor—and to keep them away from Protestant reformers—Catholic settlement houses were one more way the Irish tried to shape the new immigrants in their own image. Madonna House in South Philadelphia had an overwhelmingly Italian clientele, yet St. Patrick's Day was a major event there: its clubrooms were "decorated in emerald hue and the entertainment included songs, recitations, monologues and stories relating to Ireland and Irish subjects." At the same time, Italian immigrant thespians were rehearsing for a production of *Robert Emmet,* a play about the Irish patriot.[88] In Greenwich Village, amid the ongoing Italian immigrant "invasion," St. Anthony's parish drama society staged that same play and another, *The*

Case Against Casey.[89] Irish theatrical traditions flourished in mixed immigrant neighborhoods. Al Smith, the future governor of New York and the nation's first Catholic presidential candidate, worked days at the Fulton Street Fish Market, but he developed his theatrical talents in the St. James parish drama society, where he shared the stage with future lawyers, judges, notable politicians, and Jimmy Walker, a future mayor of New York.[90]

Chicago's Catholic Women's League, like its mainstream contemporaries, offered middle-class and professional women a creative outlet for their reform impulses, while providing the city's poor with vital services through such institutions as Guardian Angel Mission and the Madonna House settlement. Catholic activists engaged in many of the same efforts as their Protestant contemporaries, but theirs were different in several respects. While Protestant missions tried to convert West Side Italians, Irish American reformers tried to address the broader economic, cultural, social, and spiritual needs of immigrant workers and their families. They conceived of their work as "charity" rather than reform, making fewer distinctions than Protestant institutions did between "deserving" and "undeserving" poor. While middle-class Irish Americans often looked down on their charges as "beloved but dependent children" and felt obliged to convey to impoverished Italians their own notions of Catholic womanhood, they also recognized a fundamental bond with their charges. Moreover, while the mainstream settlement movement's ties with organized labor were institutional or pragmatic, the Catholic movement's ties were often personal. Chicago Federation of Labor president John Fitzpatrick's wife, a member of the Chicago Federation of Teachers, was active in the settlement movement, as were glove maker–activist Agnes Nestor and the two leading figures in the teachers' union, Margaret Haley and Catherine Goggin.[91] Such close ties shaped the movement's policies on issues of class.

In New York City's Italian immigrant communities, the children were increasingly influenced by the church's Irish American character. The Irish clergy's worst nightmare was that the "loose" religious habits of the Italians would render their children prey for Protestant missionaries—worries that had some basis in reality.[92] To insulate Italian and other immigrant Catholic youth from the predations of the cagey Protestants, Irish priests established a whole range of social institutions. On the Lower East Side, Father William Walsh established parish-based settlement houses and a program of youth activities to complete directly with middle-class Protestant programs. Barat House, one of the earliest Catholic settlements, provided vocational classes, cultural events, a kindergarten, and day care facilities on the Bowery. Walsh offered a summer camp, dances, sports programs, a theater group, and outdoor movies.[93] By 1915, twenty-seven Catholic settlements operated nationwide.[94]

Many of these programs were eventually taken over by Italian and other immigrant priests, who aimed to bridge the yawning gap between old-world parents and their Americanized offspring—a goal for Jane Addams and other Protestant settlement house reformers as well. They attracted the youth with baseball leagues, bowling alleys, and country outings, but they infused these activities with Catholic values and tried also to maintain the Italian language.[95] In these and other ways, the inner-city ethnic parish, so often considered a bulwark against acculturation, played a vital role in Americanizing immigrant youth.

By far the most ambitious of the church's programs for young people was the Catholic Youth Organization (CYO), formed in Chicago in 1930. It was the brainchild of Bishop Bernard J. Sheil, who would go on to play an important role in the interethnic labor organizing of the late 1930s. Explicitly designed to combat juvenile delinquency and to Americanize immigrant youth, the CYO fought Depression conditions with social services and youth programs. Its greatest success was a large, racially integrated sports program that eventually included the world's largest basketball league and a boxing tournament that produced a long string of champions. In many American cities, CYO gyms provided vital life experience for black and immigrant youth, mixing these young people in relative equality. Success in a CYO sport could mitigate the effects of racism and even bring black athletes access to the Irish Catholic networks that controlled cities like Chicago.[96]

Because of the CYO, the settlement houses, and other youth programs, the church was often able to retain the loyalty of the immigrant second generation, even as they Americanized them. Working with immigrant and black youth daily in inner-city neighborhoods, Irish American clergy invoked a broader Catholic vision that incorporated progressive social and economic ideas—as well as centuries-old values regarding gender and sexuality.

"THE GOOD PRIEST"

The church had opposed some early manifestations of the labor movement, and many clerics held conservative social views. By the 1880s, however, as the laity turned increasingly toward liberal social reform, most parish clergy supported Irish workers' organizing efforts.[97] In 1886, some clergy condemned the surging Knights of Labor movement as a secret organization, but James Cardinal Gibbons (1834–1921) concluded that "the objects of the Knights are praiseworthy and in no way opposed to the views of the Church. *The Catholic prelates will to a man declare in favor of the organization of Labor.* Organization is the basis of all progress—political, social, and religious."[98] Gibbons's support was not based on principle alone. If the church were to condemn the labor movement, he reasoned, workers might well abandon the church.

Catholic sanctions against secret organizations had some logic. Masonic groups had provided a base for much of the nativism of the mid-nineteenth century, and in the 1890s the Protestant Orange Order generated much of the power of the American Protective Association (APA), which campaigned against Irish Catholics. The APA claimed that Irish Americans' strikes were part of a popish plot to undermine the republic. Its pledge bound Protestant workers not to join unions or strike with Catholic workers, which disrupted organizing drives among miners and other groups.[99]

The Reverend Dr. Edward McGlynn (1837–1900) tested the church's limits on the "social question." A handsome, towering presence and a powerful speaker, McGlynn was deeply loved by his flock at St. Stephen's, a large blue-collar parish in New York's Hell's Kitchen. Like many Irish Catholics of his time, McGlynn supported the single-tax radical Henry George and the Land League. He was part of a group of liberal second-generation Irish American clergy, the New York Academia, that exerted a radical influence in a conservative diocese. McGlynn's democratic radicalism was bound to cause him trouble in a hierarchical church.[100] He was fond of emphasizing a phrase in the Lord's prayer: "Thy will be done on *earth . . .*"

THE GOOD PRIEST:
a cartoon rendering of the single-tax economist and mayoral candidate Henry George (right, 1839–1897) with the radical priest Edward McGlynn (left, 1837–1900), both favorites in late-nineteenth-century Irish communities, 1889.

McGlynn was critical of clerical celibacy, papal infallibility, and the divine inspiration of the Bible; he refused to establish a parochial school (feeling that public schools would better inculcate democratic values), and he supported woman suffrage; a church populated by the poor, he even observed, should take its lead from them. John Cardinal McCloskey (1810–85) tolerated McGlynn's gibes, but Michael Corrigan (1835–1902), McCloskey's successor as archbishop of New York, moved quickly against the radical priest. He forbade him to take part in United Labor Party activities or to speak in support of Henry George, who ran for mayor for New York in 1886; Corrigan called George a supporter of socialism, communism, and anarchism. He directed priests to read his pastoral letter on the "rights of private property" from every pulpit in the city and then had it printed and distributed widely.

Corrigan removed the beloved McGlynn from St. Stephen's and in 1887, with the Vatican's support, excommunicated him. McGlynn was unrepentant: "I am a Roman Catholic and I have not excommunicated myself. Nobody can change what I am."[101] He took an active role in the George campaign and the Anti-Poverty Society, which was organized in the wake of George's defeat. "You may go on forever with hospitals and orphan asylums and St. Vincent DePaul Societies," he wrote, "but with them you can't cure the trouble."[102]

Corrigan's actions sparked a huge protest. McGlynn, known as *Sogarth Aroon*, "the good (or precious) priest" in Gaelic, was a friend not only to the labor movement and the working poor, but also to African Americans and the new Italian immigrants.[103] Seventy-five thousand marched to Union Square to demand his reinstatement. McGlynn's portrait was plastered onto the walls of tenement flats along with those of Christ, the Virgin, and the saints. Priests declined positions replacing him; the parish janitor would not stoke the furnace; and the Sisters of Charity organized their orphans to stage skits in support of him. Enraged, the archbishop ordered the orphanage closed and the nuns disciplined.[104] "The servant girls were the worst," Corrigan wrote to his friend Bishop Bernard McQuaid of Rochester. When a replacement priest was finally located, "the cook would not prepare the dinner . . . Tonight all kind of violence was threatened."[105] Writing back to Cuba, the revolutionary José Martí reported, "Nothing happening today in the United States can compare in transcendence to the struggle developing between authorities of the Catholic Church and the Catholic people of New York."[106]

"Dr. McGlynn lost a parish and gained a continent," wrote the *Catholic Herald*. "He will regain the parish and retain the continent."[107] And indeed, the Vatican reinstated McGlynn in 1892. His story illustrates both the resolve of conservative clerics and the persistence of a progressive Irish American tradition with the church. The tension between these traditions divided many Irish American communities. Communist leader Elizabeth Gurley Flynn's immigrant mother and Irish American father refused to raise their children within the church, a rare decision even for radicals, while Margaret Sanger's embittered Socialist father covered all the bases by naming her brother Henry George McGlynn Higgins.[108]

Though George's movement was based heavily in New York's Irish and German American communities, he solicited the votes of "all citizens, rich or poor, white or black, native or foreign born."[109] "The intensely active supporters of Henry George for Mayor, when grouped together, present a spectacle of cosmopolitan harmony never before seen on American soil," *The Irish World* reported with pride. "They include German, Irish, French, Italian, Hebrew, Bohemian, and a number of other organizations representing distinctive nationalities . . . [and] almost every trade of wage-workers known to American industry."[110] Irish American women did much of the organizing for George, even though they could not vote.[111] By the time the dust had settled from the George campaign, however, the new immigrants were arriving in American cities, bringing the danger of new divisions between the Irish and non-Irish working poor.

THE CATHOLIC PLAN FOR A PATRIARCHAL WELFARE STATE

In the early twentieth century, "labor priests" championed workers' rights and advocated trade unions and social welfare reforms, basing themselves on Pope Leo XIII's 1891 encyclical *Rerum Novarum*, which supported workers' organizations while defending private property.[112] These activists also fought growing socialist influence.

By the 1910s, organizing campaigns were sweeping millions of immigrant workers into unions. In 1919, the largest strike wave in U.S. history climaxed with a series of general strikes and one out of every four American workers on a picket line. The Socialist Party's antiwar position won it many recruits among the most recent immigrants, and a series of local labor movements emerged throughout the country.

In this situation, the Catholic Church staked out its own position on the "social question." The 1919 "Bishops' Program of Social Reconstruction" reads like a blueprint for the coming welfare state: it called for workers' legal rights to organize, bargain collectively, and strike; a living wage; old-age pensions; public housing; social insurance; and the regulation of public utilities.[113]

What Socialist author Upton Sinclair called a "Catholic miracle" was not simply an application of papal pronouncements but also a natural outgrowth of activism among Irish and German laity and clergy in a variety of social reform movements. During the 1910s, it had finally reached the hierarchy. The program's author and the church's main spokesperson on social welfare was the Catholic University economist Monsignor John Ryan (1865–1945). First exposed to the injustices of both rural Ireland and the industrial United States in the pages of Patrick Ford's *Irish World*, Ryan's perspective, like those of so many other Irish Catholic radicals and progressives, was also shaped by his reading of Henry George's theories on land, taxes, and social inequality. In the 1920s, Ryan and his National Catholic Welfare Council developed an ambitious program that presaged Roosevelt's New Deal.[114]

The bishops' plan for a new welfare state had roots in the church's ancient hostility to materialism and especially in its view of natural law and the family as the sacred basis for society. This orientation complemented union demands for a "living" or "family wage," the notion that employers must provide earnings adequate to support a family without the paid labor of the wife and mother. Especially among Catholic immigrant workers, the ideal of a family wage fueled organizing campaigns and strikes. A powerfully gendered value, its profoundly conservative vision placed the mother at the center of family life and precluded any outside economic role for her. "The welfare of the whole family and that of society likewise," Ryan wrote, "renders it imperative that the wife and mother should not engage in any labor except that of the household."[115]

The same bishops' letter containing a "Program of Social Reconstruction" also fiercely condemned any artificial form of birth control. Both elements showed the hand of John Ryan.[116] It would be convenient but misleading to separate the two teachings. The same values that dictated a radical new approach to social welfare also dictated a reactionary position on family planning. Indeed, Ryan expressed his opposition to birth control in decidedly class terms: the problem was not too many children but rather, social and economic inequality.[117]

This position led the church to bitter confrontations with that quintessential Irish "rebel girl" Margaret Sanger (1879–1966). Sanger became the great symbol for the "new woman" of the 1920s, and her rebellion is justly celebrated, but its roots are often misunderstood. Her confrontations with the church over sexuality and birth control certainly put her at odds with the mainstream of the Irish American community. But Sanger's own background as one of eight children in an Irish working-class family explains her trajectory as well as the modernist impulses at large in the 1910s and 1920s. Her earliest influences and even her bitterness toward the church were deeply rooted in Irish American life. Her career choice as a public health nurse in New York's immigrant slums was characteristic of many second-generation Irish women, as was her rebellion.[118]

Sanger's father was a stonecutter and factory worker, a Knights of Labor activist, and an ardent anticlerical follower of Henry George, the atheist orator Robert Ingersoll, and Father Edward McGlynn. He was also, she wrote, "the spring from which I drank." His iconoclasm put an end to his stonecutting business and marginalized the family in the largely Catholic factory town of Corning, New York.[119] Sanger associated her family's poverty and alienation, and her mother's miserable life, with the

MRS. MARGARET SANGER (1879–1966):
the Irish American birth control advocate and women's rights activist, pictured
with one of her immigrant clients, Lower East Side, Manhattan, circa 1920.

power of the church. Despite some early Catholic schooling, Sanger was
not baptized until the age of thirteen and then only at her devout mother's
insistence. She considered herself an atheist from her teenage years and
joined first the Socialist Party and then the Industrial Workers of the
World (IWW), organizing immigrant women workers in mass strikes.
Her early ideas and actions in support of birth control and women's public health were framed in the context of these radical working-class movements. It was an attachment she clearly inherited from her father. Her
personal and often public explorations of sexuality mirrored Irish Catholic sexual repression; her emphasis on contraception reflected the poverty
and class discrimination she encountered first in Corning and later on the
Lower East Side and in Brooklyn.[120]

Church authorities employed their political connections to pursue Sanger and undermine her movement. Wherever it had political influence, the church lobbied elected politicians, prosecutors, and police to crack down on the movement. As a result, rallies in support of her were banned and dispersed, clinics were closed, and Sanger and other advocates were taken to court and imprisoned for their activities. The opposition from clergy and hierarchy was so bitter in part because Catholic working-class women of several ethnic backgrounds welcomed her movement, attended birth control clinics, and experimented with Sanger's instructions. Many had abortions. Though Catholic women sought the procedure proportionally less often than Protestants and Jews, early Depression studies in New York indicated that 29 percent to 35 percent of Catholic patients had had at least one abortion.[121]

In the 1920s, as Sanger's attacks on the church became increasingly shrill and her attachment to the eugenics movement more profound, the Irish Catholic community—embattled by anti-Catholicism—viewed her more and more as a traitor. Its venom derived not only from church doctrine or even from the issue's obvious implications for millions of women but also from the community's old impulse to close ranks and strike out against any threat. What is often seen as a "Catholic" response was more narrowly Irish Catholic in its values. And Sanger's own reaction reflected not only a wish to defend herself against recent Catholic attacks but also her older resentments against the church.

Margaret Sanger's rebellion was part of a more general opposition to the church and its influence that was deeply rooted in Irish tradition. "No Gods, No Masters," the masthead on her newspaper *Woman Rebel*, reflected the era's anarchism and "new woman" feminism but it also harkened back to the radical anticlericalism of the Fenian movement. Ironically, it was her childhood experience in a working-class Irish home that carried Sanger to the bohemian salons of Manhattan and to her birth control work in the immigrant slums.

John Ryan, as leader of the National Catholic Welfare Council, went on to become "Reverend New Deal," an important adviser to President Roosevelt and the industrial union movement, even as he worked behind the scenes to keep New Deal agencies from broaching the subject of birth control. He was also a vocal opponent of another Irish clerical leader, Father Charles E. Coughlin, a persistent and pervasive source of anti-Semitism and political reaction. Like Ryan's support for social democratic reforms, the church's support for the industrial union movement of the 1930s and 1940s had deep roots in older Irish American social movements.[122]

But the Irish Catholic support for industrial unions had clear boundaries. The Association of Catholic Trade Unionists, launched in 1937, provided a factional structure and strategy in the struggle against Socialist and Communist influence in the AFL and especially in the new CIO. At the same time, it elaborated Catholic social ideology, inspiring thousands of local and national labor leaders.[123]

FROM IMMIGRANT CATHOLICS
TO AMERICAN CATHOLICS

Irish-dominated Catholic organizations engaged new immigrant groups slowly: even as ethnic tensions continued within the church, Irish Americans were ambivalent about surrendering the church's distinct Irish identity. Only gradually did a shift in Irish American consciousness permit the emergence of a broader interethnic Catholic identity. "If the Irish wished to forge a new group identity out of a diverse array of ethnics and to defend their leadership of it," historian Timothy Meagher has argued, "they would have to emphasize what they had in common and not what distinguished them as Irishmen." This process advanced more quickly in smaller cities, like his Worcester, Massachusetts, where the small size of ethnic communities made it harder to sustain ethnically homogeneous groups.[124]

The Ancient Order of Hibernians (AOH), an Irish fraternal organization, was established as a defensive body in the face of Protestant bigotry in 1836, at a time when *Catholic* appeared to be synonymous with *Irish*. In the nativist 1840s and 1850s, the AOH provided guards for Catholic churches; in the 1860s and 1870s it provided meeting halls for the radical miners' group the Molly Maguires; and it provided leadership and protection for early St. Patrick's Day parades. But around 1900, the AOH, so closely identified with Irish Catholic defense, took on a more cosmopolitan tone and emerged as a major defender of immigration and immigrants in general.

Likewise the Knights of Columbus, established in 1882 for the defense of Irish Catholics, gradually opened themselves to other immigrant groups amid mass immigration. As political scientist Robert Putnam noted in his renowned *Bowling Alone*, the Knights of Columbus "bridge[d] cleavages among different ethnic communities while bonding along religious and gender lines."[125] In 1907, in the face of continuing anti-Catholicism, the order changed its ritual to reflect its multinational character, emphasizing Catholic heroes from various ethnic backgrounds. Thereupon its membership took off, rising from 42,000 in 1899 to 782,000 in 1922. As the Knights welcomed Catholics of various nationalities (though they tended to organize them into separate councils), they also embraced an intense American patriotism and an aggressive, interethnic American Catholic identity. In a sense, it organizationally expressed Americanist trends in the church.[126]

Established in 1911 by a group of retired military officers, the Guardians of Liberty emerged as a power in upstate New York state politics in 1914, reflecting a new round of anti-Catholicism nationally, especially in rural areas. The Populist Party leader Tom Watson directly attacked the Knights of Columbus as the linchpin of a giant Catholic conspiracy. The Guardians' main organ, *The Menace*, was only one of sixty anti-Catholic papers at the time; by April 1915, it reached a circulation of more than 1.5 million. In response, the Knights launched a new Commission on Religious Prejudices, which, during wartime, defended all Catholics in ostentatiously patriotic terms. The success of the campaign reflected the growing strength of Catholic organization and influence. By 1917, only three of the anti-Catholic papers were still in circulation.[127]

The anti-Catholicism of the early 1900s coincided with a strong surge of anti-immigrant racism and calls for immigration restriction. The Knights mobilized to defend not only the church but other Catholics and the immigrant tradition upon which the church was based and from which they themselves sprang. Knights leader Thomas H. Cummings argued for a new, multicultural conception of Americanism: "Like the crew who sailed with Columbus on the first voyage, we have men of various races and languages. But by drawing close the bonds of brotherhood, we make for the best type of American citizenship . . . For the best type of American is he who best exemplifies in his own life . . . a country of all races and creeds, with one great . . . creed of fair play and equal rights for all."[128] The Knights aimed at a new type of Catholic manhood, quite different from the one promoted by the Irish street gangs: a respectable form of manly self-improvement.

After World War I, with increasing centralization and the emergence of a standard parish school curriculum, children in Polish and other national parishes bore the mark of the Irish American hierarchy. From the 1920s on, as immigrant families gradually moved into more ethnically mixed neighborhoods, they sometimes found their children in Irish-dominated parish schools that conveyed an implicit Irishness. In this sense, Irish American nuns played a critical role in the acculturation of new immigrant children. "Every one of us Poles understands that in the Irish parochial schools our children are being systematically deprived of their Polish soul," a religious paper observed, and that finally the children would "yield to the process of Irishization."[129] The same paper drew a distinction between "Americanization" (which supported "the welfare of our new fatherland") and "Irishization" (which was "fertilizer for the degenerate national Irish organism").[130]

Given their own rather complicated history, it should not be surprising that the legacy Irish Catholics passed on to their coreligionists was one that mixed a defensive, parochial mentality with elements of nationalism, patriotism, and social justice. Frozen out of elite society, the Irish and, later, other Catholics used the church and its networks to create effective political organizations and to promote public activism. Catholic leaders—be they Knights or Americanist bishops—saw "Catholicism and

American democracy as dwelling in a complementary, almost symbiotic relationship." In the generation after World War I, they were eager to merge Catholicism, ethnicity, and Americanism and to assert themselves as "Catholic Americans."[131]

In 1923, the national president of the AOH urged its international convention to "wage war" on the resurgent Ku Klux Klan in the interests not of Catholics alone but also of Jews, Negroes, and all foreign-born. A series of physical confrontations with the Klan followed: the most spectacular occurred the following spring at South Bend, Indiana, where Notre Dame University undergraduates attacked and routed a large group of Klan marchers, leaving dozens injured.[132]

Such language and behavior did not necessarily portend a true equality between the Irish and other Catholics in a heterogeneous church. Beneath the rhetoric, it was clear that Irish Americans would be in charge of panethnic American Catholicism. They envisioned "melting down and remaking other Catholic ethnics in the image of the American Catholic ideal, the Irish American."[133] Nor would the expanded Catholicism open itself to mainstream American values and ideals: "Even though in theory Catholics upheld the values of Americanization and of pluralism, in practice they chose to justify separation by claiming superlative social programs were based on Catholic principles." Finally, the model for panethnic Catholicism was close at hand. "It is a special blessing of the church in this country that it has been founded along the lines of the Irish church," a Worcester, Massachusetts, priest argued in 1915, "and no matter how great the flood of immigrants may be in years to come, the tradition and custom has been established and it will continue along the lines of the dear church of Ireland."[134]

The Knights of Columbus took an Italian's name, but Irish Americans retained control. They allowed the establishment of a separate Ansonia Council for Italian Americans in Boston, but they kept a tight grip on the national organization. In New York City, Italians feared they could never achieve equality in such groups as long as the Irish controlled them, so they formed separate Italian associations, such as the Sons of Italy. In effect, the Irish were arbiters of the newer immigrants' "in-between" status. They integrated the newcomers into the broader Catholic community and were even prepared to fight for their rights, but they insisted on retaining the church's ethnic hierarchy.[135]

Even in the first generation, early Italian parishes might be served by Italian-speaking Irish priests, while Irish nuns taught many Italian parochial schoolchildren, and Irish laywomen taught Italian children in public schools. In the 1920s, Italians and other new immigrants who moved out of the older enclaves often found themselves in territorial parishes inhabited and staffed by Irish American laypeople and clergy. In larger Catholic high schools, it became increasingly difficult for non-Irish to maintain any sort of ethnic homogeneity. An Italian observer in Chicago feared that a generational conflict would emerge between Italian parents and their children, who would practice the religion "as the most fervent Irishman."[136]

By the 1920s, many New York Italian parishes were adding English sermons, confessions, and other services—simply to hold on to their Americanized second generation, who encountered the "American" world every day in city streets. Polish, Italian, and other immigrant youth entered remarkably diverse diocesan high schools, welfare organizations, and youth programs, led by Irish priests, nuns, and laity. As second- and third-generation Italians settled into American Catholic culture, they tended to conform to Irish norms, in religious terms at least, and Italian Americans more and more came to resemble the Irish.[137]

By the 1920s, second-generation Italians, Poles, and other Europeans, under Irish auspices, gradually gave up particular ethnic devotions and embraced "postethnic" devotions to the Sacred Heart, Saint Thérèse of Lisieux, Our Lady of Lourdes, and Saint Jude.[138] They began to think of themselves as part of a broader American Catholic community and culture.[139]

Father Dominic Cirigliano's story shows how this gradual integration occurred in the very heart of New York's Italian community. Born in Italy, Cirigliano was raised in the original Italian mission of Our Lady of Lo-

reto in Greenwich Village. Trained by Irish American Jesuits, Father Cirigliano took over the Nativity parish in 1927—it had previously been run
by a succession of Irish American pastors; it now underwent one of the
earliest shifts from Irish to Italian. Cirigliano took less interest in *feste*
and other Italian rituals and promoted "American" devotions. Confession,
sermons, and missions were conducted in English. Rather than running
a parish school with Italian-language instruction, Cirigliano conducted
catechism classes in the neighborhood public schools. He also established
branches of the citywide Boy Scouts and the Catholic Youth Organization, which provided badly needed recreational outlets for the parish
youth from various ethnicities and helped bring them into the Catholic
mainstream.[140]

At Harlem's Our Lady of Mount Carmel, New York's most famous *festa*
persisted, but by the 1930s it had lost some of its more colorful trappings.
Pilgrims on their knees in the streets were less common. The food stalls
remained, but hot dogs and watermelon were sold alongside Italian sausage and cakes. More was at work here than the Irish model and influence;
Italian American pastors were trying to maintain their hold on the second
generation, who showed much less interest in old-world Italian culture
than in the city's ethnically mixed popular culture. The Irish-dominated
hierarchy, in making assignments, preferred American-born to Italian-
born clergy, and no Italian joined the hierarchy until the 1950s. In the
process, a new "Italian American" ethnic culture was invented.[141]

Given Irish Americans' turbulent history with African Americans
and the church's checkered history on integration, race remained the great
barrier, both in the church and in the community. In the mid-1930s, the
pastor of a Philadelphia African American parish noted that "the various
National Catholic Immigrant groups—Polish, German, Irish, Italian,
etc.—are slowly merging and are losing their spirit of European parochialism." Why, he wondered, must African Americans still worship in segregated parishes?[142] The church's racial prejudice, too, became part of the
broader "American Catholic" identity that immigrants embraced.

The Irish Catholic version of civic identity differed, then, from that of the WASP mainstream. At its best, it stressed a broad American Catholic identity that nonetheless recognized the integrity and worth of distinct ethnic cultures, and the rights of ethnic minorities to maintain these cultures. In the 1950s, Jewish American writer Will Herberg argued that a panethnic Catholic identity was key to American postwar religious pluralism—Protestant, Catholic, and Jew. The locally minded first-generation immigrants, he argued, had developed as nationalities, while the second and third generations developed affinities based on religion. If these many nationalities did not produce a single "melting pot," then certainly three religiously based melting pots produced broad American identities out of the nation's ethnic groups.[143]

Herberg oversimplified. The complex process of identity formation varied significantly, even among Catholics, from one ethnic group to another; most Catholic ethnic groups sustained a degree of self-identity, and ethnic tensions persisted. But the notion that a broader Catholic identity emerged gradually in the interwar years rings true. Its appearance helps to explain the increasing number of marriages that crossed ethnic but not religious lines in the second and third generation.[144] The fact that anti-Catholicism remained an acceptable form of discrimination on the part of some American liberals as late as the 1950s enhanced the cohesion between otherwise distinct ethnic groups and also helps account for the postwar "Catholic ghetto" phenomenon.[145]

As religion did for second- and third-generation Jews, the church provided a vital vehicle by which Catholic immigrants could maintain a level of ethnic solidarity even during their gradual acculturation to a new identity as American Catholics. The church cultivated the vision of a patriotic, multiethnic Catholic minority. The Catholic Commission for American Citizenship, established in 1938 to promote this patriotic identity, produced its own readers, textbooks, youth magazines, and a popular comic book, *Treasure Chest*—all designed to convey the Catholic position in the American polity.[146]

This broad Catholic American identity helps explain what sociologists have described as the "muted ethnic identity" among many whites from European immigrant backgrounds.[147] Irish Americans did much to create it, in their roles as clergy and lay leaders. Thanks to their positions, the devotional character of American Catholicism incorporated many aspects of Irish American culture.[148]

THREE

THE WORKPLACE

For Chicago's remarkably diverse immigrant workers and their families, Easter Sunday 1918 held the promise of a better life. The meatpacking industry, dominated by one of the era's most powerful corporate oligopolies, had seemed impervious to union organizers. But over the past year, a new Stockyards Labor Council had swept through the crowded wooden tenements and greasy slaughterhouses in Packingtown, a slum made notorious by Upton Sinclair's muckraking 1906 novel *The Jungle*. It drew thousands of immigrant laborers as well as recent black migrants. The impoverished laborers, badly divided along ethnic and racial lines, had recently confronted the "Big Five" packers, winning an unlikely victory—substantial wage increases and the eight-hour day.

On this Easter afternoon, John Fitzpatrick (1871–1946), the architect of this new movement, rose to speak amid the church steeples and smokestacks of Packingtown. Born in County Westmeath, he arrived on Chicago's South Side and went to work in the stockyards at the age of twelve. Fitzpatrick soon immersed himself in the city's vibrant union movement. He married a schoolteacher and they settled into a modest Bridgeport home. In 1902, a group of reformers persuaded him to run for president of the Chicago Federation of Labor (CFL), a position he would hold until his death.

Tall and powerfully built, Fitzpatrick embodied the promise of a new, aggressive labor movement that would embrace all workers without regard to race, nationality, gender, or skill. He infused it with idealism and a sense of purpose. In a city famous for rampant corruption, he was a straight arrow. He gave up drinking at an early age and shunned labor meetings in saloons. An ardent Irish nationalist, he demonstrated a deep respect for other nationalities and a special affinity for the city's recent immigrants. A devout Catholic, he refused to countenance anti-Semitic or racist remarks in his presence. He was also a progressive. He worked with radicals like Anton Johannsen, an anarchist woodworker-intellectual, and with William Z. Foster and Jack Johnstone, who both would become leading figures in the Communist Party of the United States. He supported woman suffrage and facilitated the organization of Chicago's women workers.[1]

CREATING A NEW LABOR MOVEMENT:
John Fitzpatrick (1871–1946), president of the Chicago Federation of Labor, addresses a huge crowd of immigrant workers during the organizing campaign in the Chicago stockyards, 1918.

Looking out over the huge mixed crowd, with a large American flag billowing in the distance, Fitzpatrick congratulated the workers and their families on their hard-fought achievement. "It's a new day," he began, "and out in God's sunshine you men and you women, black and white, have not only an eight hour day but you are on an equality." The crowd roared.[2] In the ensuing months, on sunny days immigrant parents could be seen holding their children on a row of benches in front of the University of Chicago settlement. These came to be known as the "eight-hour-day benches," in honor of the victory that gave stockyard laborers a bit more time to spend with their children.

Little more than a year after Fitzpatrick's Easter speech, in the summer of 1919, Irish gangs from Bridgeport led attacks on black packinghouse workers and the black community. The Chicago race riot ushered in an era of racial contention and ended for more than a generation the prospects for the interracial labor movement Fitzpatrick had envisioned.[3]

Irish American workers often struck out at "outsiders" who appeared to threaten their jobs and communities. Entrenched in workplaces and unions by the late nineteenth century, they were positioned, as labor historian Bruce Nelson notes, to play a dual role—as guides to the lessons of race and class in the city and the workplace, and "as gatekeepers who were afforded the opportunity to harass and humiliate and to sharpen the lines between the hyphenated American and the greenhorn." As waves of migration transformed the working-class population, Irish American workers were strategically positioned to chart a course for the labor movement amid great racial and ethnic diversity.[4] Too often, they interpreted their interests narrowly, and their decisions marginalized other immigrants, unskilled workers, women, and people of color.

But their response to new immigrants was by no means exclusively hostile. People like Fitzpatrick—organizers and shop stewards, labor activists and local union officers, rank-and-file workers and middle-class sympathizers—reached out to them and, less often, to black or Mexican migrants, offering a different sort of Americanism from the one the newcomers found in government, corporate, and settlement house programs. Irish efforts to socialize and acculturate immigrant workers in workplaces, unions, and political organizations is a crucial part of the story of how newcomers negotiated the American city.[5]

Irish Americans achieved their dominant position in the labor movement just as the new immigrants flooded into American workplaces. Irish workers had closely identified with republicanism, land reform, and labor activism, as exemplified by the Knights of Labor, with its broad social aims and ethnically diverse membership, and participation in the 1886 "Great Upheaval" of strikes and organizing. Again in the World War I era, the promise of an interethnic, progressive labor movement emerged in the context of transnational social upheaval and revolution. By contrast, Irish Americans also led many of the craft-based "business unions" that accepted the capitalist order and narrowed their aims to improving their own members' wages and benefits. As business unionism emerged as a national movement in the early 1900s, German and Jewish immigrants both played critical roles, but the Irish tended to predominate.[6]

LACE CURTAIN AND SHANTY

For Irish Americans, upward mobility was slow at first, but by 1900 some had "risen." "The Irish hod carrier in the second generation has become a bricklayer," pioneering urban journalist Jacob Riis wrote, "if not the Alderman of his ward." They had created networks of outstanding secondary schools and, remarkably, were attending college in proportions as high as those of WASPS. Their overall occupational distribution was roughly comparable with that of native-born whites of all ethnic backgrounds. This mobility varied considerably by region; the Irish rose highest, it seemed, the farther west they traveled.[7]

The aspiring Irish could point to some striking examples of success. William Grace, a shipping magnate and philanthropist, became the first Irish Catholic mayor of New York in the 1880s. Patrick Collins—Famine emigrant, Fenian revolutionary, and labor organizer—became a wealthy businessman in the 1890s and the first Irish Catholic mayor of Boston in 1901. Most of the rising middle class, however, made more modest achievements. As of 1900, roughly 6 percent were classified as middle class, and another 10 to 15 percent as lower middle class; many among this latter group were saloonkeepers and other small-business people in working-class communities. Though the Irish were underrepresented among lawyers, bankers, and brokers, they were overrepresented among lower-level white-collar workers like clerks and teachers. As of 1880, only 6 of Chicago's 222 Board of Trade members were Irish Catholics, as were only 2 of that city's 42 bankers, and only 5 of its 161 doctors. The phrases "lace curtain Irish" and "steam heat Irish" came into use in the 1890s, to distinguish the upwardly mobile from the more recently arrived or persistently poor "shanty Irish," who labored alongside Slavic and Italian immigrants.[8]

While some "Famine Irish" rose to respectability, poor immigrants, or "greenhorns," continued to arrive in large numbers. Between 1871 and 1920, two million entered the United States, constantly reinvigorating older communities and cultural institutions. As late as 1930, nearly a million Irish-born people lived in the United States. They were highly concentrated in New York—almost half, in the 1920s; more than 57 percent of New York's Irish-born still lived in older Manhattan neighborhoods and another large number in Brooklyn.[9] These newer immigrants, who hailed from Ireland's impoverished, remote western regions, had great adjustments to make in the new environment. Upwardly mobile Irish saw the newcomers as threats to their hard-won respectability.[10]

Even many American-born Irish had failed to rise. In the late nineteenth century, a residual group from the first and second generations still worked in unskilled jobs and still lived in urban slums. "The result is a sediment," Riis wrote, with apparent distaste for the Irish poor, "the product of more than a generation in the city's slums." In the early 1900s, the Irish poor outnumbered those of any other white ethnic group in the United States. As late as 1915, the Irish death rate was the highest in New York City and twice as high as that for Ireland. Irish death rates—from industrial accidents, contagious disease, and alcohol-related illness—were generally much higher than those for other ethnic groups.[11] Even as some Irish moved up and out of the old immigrant enclaves, impoverished Irish immigrants continued to arrive, mixing with new immigrants from Italy, Russia, and eastern Europe and later with black and Mexican migrants. And so the Irish community, in addition to experiencing the usual generational divide between old-world parents and American children, was also divided along class lines.

Even for those Irish who had risen in status and wealth by 1900, a measure of insecurity and grievance persisted. Overviews of Irish American success place great emphasis on the upward mobility of the Irish middle class, especially in the West.[12] Frustrated ambitions and persistent discrimination facing the emerging Irish American elite help to explain their support for nationalist agitation, though much of the more radical activity continued to have a working-class base.[13] Kerby Miller's narrative of an Irish American middle class wracked by status anxiety has become the standard interpretation. Even "lace curtain" families remained "remarkably estranged from the dominant culture of their adopted country," he writes, wondering "whether full assimilation was possible or even desirable." Deeply devoted to a religious tradition despised by many Protestants, even the wealthier occasionally felt the sting of prejudice that "embittered the Irish middle class and kept old, inherited wounds fresh." Periodic bursts of nativism and anti-Catholicism and the persistent specter of poverty haunted the middle class, leaving some Irish Americans "crippled with self-doubt" and "morbidly sensitive to real or imagined snubs . . . to any perceived threat to their tenuous grasp on respectability."[14] "We are only half way up the ladder," an Irish Catholic teacher wrote in the 1920s.[15]

In fact, Irish American voluntary and nationalist organizations were often directed by businessmen, lawyers, judges, and doctors, while middle-class anxieties indeed shaped Irish American society and culture. For the Irish working poor (still the vast majority of the community well into the twentieth century), the threats were real enough. Their vulnerability helps to explain a strong defensive mentality in the streets and workplaces, in churches and political organizations, and even on the vaudeville stage. Irish Americans felt that their efforts to retain such status and resources justified such responses, but newer immigrants often saw them as aggressive and intolerant. Yet Irish workers also did more than any other group to lay the foundations of the American labor movement in its various incarnations.

THE LABOR REFORM TRADITION

The key to labor reform in the late nineteenth century was its relationship with Irish nationalist organizations. In New York, Chicago, Pittsburgh, the anthracite fields, and elsewhere, the two movements shared personnel and resources and often acted out of similar impulses. The Knights of Labor (by far the largest and most important of the late-nineteenth-century labor reform organizations) and the Land League (which aimed to give Ireland's peasant class control of the farms on which they worked but also agitated for social reform in the United States) were both elements of a broad reform movement heavily based on working-class Irish. Indeed, nineteenth-century Irish nationalism was based less on the emerging middle class than on industrial workers.

Strategically and organizationally, American unions owed a great deal to Irish social movements. The Molly Maguires, a secret miners' terrorist group, was directly linked to Irish secret societies like the Whiteboys, who terrorized landlords and their agents on behalf of poor farmers and agricultural laborers. In Chicago as well, this kind of violence was common in early labor protests among Irish immigrants.[16] The secrecy and rituals of the Knights of Labor were shaped by employers' hostility to the group and by American Masonic traditions, and despite the church's denunciation of all secret societies, the Knights' heavily Irish Catholic membership embraced the approach. The constituencies of the Land League and the secret Clan na Gael organizations often overlapped with Knights of Labor assemblies, but it was the Knights who carried these approaches to ethnically diverse workers.[17]

The most important strategy for the early labor unions was the boycott. Developed by Land League organizers in Ireland in the 1870s, the boycott was originally aimed at rural landowners, at their agents, and especially at fellow tenants who dared to take up land from which another had been evicted. What journalist James Redpath called the "terrible power of social excommunication" was outlined by Charles Stewart Parnell at a mass meeting in 1880. The tactic required the country folk to punish an internal enemy "by leaving him severely alone . . . isolating him from the rest of his fellow countrymen." There would be no man "so lost to shame," Parnell said, "as to dare the public opinion . . . and transgress your unwritten code of laws." Irish immigrants carried the tactic to American cities. An early and successful industrial use occurred during an 1881 Chicago streetcar strike. During the 1882 freight handlers' strike in New York and Jersey City, the Irish laborers resented the Italians brought in to take their jobs, but the full weight of community disapproval came down on a small number of Irishmen who went back to work—they were "left severely alone."[18]

Moving from Irish to German and Bohemian workers in New York's Central Labor Union (itself the product of an 1882 mass meeting in support of the Irish Land League), the tactic spread across the United States in the early twentieth century. Bringing solidarity and sanction to bear, communities used consumer boycotts to support labor actions against unfair employers during strikes and lockouts. They boycotted struck goods and took sympathetic action, such as refusing to handle any coal during a coal heavers' strike.[19] Eventually, workers from a wide range of ethnic backgrounds launched thousands of boycotts against manufacturers of hats, shoes, beer, bread, and other commodities.

In this context, the union label became a class weapon, and the union button a badge of honor. These were ways to draw the line, to decide who was with them and who against them. But this line could also be drawn on racial grounds, as in the use of the boycott against the products of Chinese immigrant labor.[20] Later, students and civil rights activists, Mexican and Filipino farmworkers, and consumer advocates employed the boycott, but its roots lay in rural Ireland.

PADDY'S JOB

In 1900, about two-thirds of the Irish American workforce still worked in manual labor. They dominated the labor movement partly because they were dispersed throughout the workforce but also because they rose out of the working class more slowly than other, older immigrant groups. Those Irish who did rise often found themselves not in professional and white-collar occupations but running saloons and other small businesses in working-class communities or laboring in the skilled trades as foremen and petty bosses, or as small contractors. Many who remained on the railroads, steel mills, coal pits, and other industrial environments were foremen of ethnically mixed gangs. So even these upwardly mobile Irish workers remained among and often at odds with eastern and southeastern European immigrants and black and Mexican migrants.

Where they endured in manual labor, Irish Americans carved out higher-wage, more or less unionized niches where they predominated. They were disproportionately concentrated in building construction (characterized by the highest rates of unionization and strike activity by 1900), coal mining (another arena of considerable industrial conflict), waterfront work, and the metal trades. Most Irish American craftsmen were steam fitters, plumbers, boilermakers, stonecutters, and masons. Their success in establishing these desirable niches and excluding others from them was striking.[21]

But at the turn of the century, about one in seven male Irish American workers and one in four Irish immigrants remained in poorly paid unskilled jobs, disproportionately in the ranks of casual laborers. As late as 1890, 65 percent of Irish-born males in Boston worked as unskilled laborers and only 5 percent held skilled positions. Large numbers worked on the docks or as teamsters. The newer Irish immigrants entered these unskilled positions, which brought them into direct contact with Slavic, Italian, and black laborers. Occupational achievement tended to be higher as one moved west; but on the East Coast and even some places in the Midwest, the Irish American community of 1900 was overwhelmingly working class.[22]

These hazardous jobs took a high toll on Irish American families. In

RATHER SENSITIVE

Boss. "What's the matter, Pat? You're not leavin'?"
Pat.   "Oi am that."
Boss. "Why, ain't the work and the wages all right?"
Pat.   "The wur-ruk is all roight, an' the wages is all roight, an'yer not so bad yersilf, but oi'll not wur-ruk on the same job wid a thing that looks as much loike a munkey as *that*!"

"RATHER SENSITIVE":
Harper's *conception of the lowly Irish laborer's prejudices against his competitors in the market for casual labor, 1891.*

New York in the 1880s, the Irish led all groups in job-related accidents. Walls of earth buried them while they were tunneling, heavy loads crushed them on the docks, and trains ran over them in the yards. Work fatalities and the late age of men at marriage meant that the Sisters of Charity and other religious orders spent a good deal of time caring for widows and abandoned women with many children.[23] Italians and other more recent immigrants shared the extreme dangers with the old-timers, but the Irish knew best how to do the work and how to avoid accidents. Experienced Irish laborers sometimes saved their Italian counterparts on worksites, but more often relations were contentious, and the Irish usually held the advantage.[24]

By 1900, Irish Americans could rely on their social networks and political patronage to secure employment in public transportation, streets and sanitation, and the police and fire departments, as well as in building and other parts of the private sector. The "Irish ethic" of intraethnic patronage could usually provide immigrants and their children with work. Their influence in AFL craft unions assured them control of apprenticeship and hiring and, thus, the training of a new generation of Irish American skilled workers. Irish building contractors and factory and worksite foremen often provided spots on the job for friends and relatives. By 1900, their extensive network of parish voluntary groups provided contacts even for newcomers. An Irish person did not "enter a City where you don't know anyone," an immigrant wrote home. "He can rely on his cousins to promote his interests in procuring work."[25]

Ironically, such networks could constitute what one political scientist has called a "blue-collar *cul de sac*" that concentrated Irish men particularly in stable but relatively low-wage manual positions (the great bulk of city jobs) rather than allowing them to rise into white-collar work. In a strange way, the strength of Irish economic and political networks may actually have retarded upward mobility.[26] Undoubtedly, however, such networks also excluded newcomers from many jobs.

In New York, immigration during the Land War and the agricultural crisis of the 1880s reinvigorated the various county societies. Along with the church, the county societies gave even Irish-speaking greenhorns from the island's rural west access to their English-speaking predecessors. In New York, greenhorns were quickly "connected"; in Chicago they soon had "clout." The societies facilitated employment in particular industries. Kerry men were found in large numbers among the paper handlers, people from Donegal in construction and tunnel work, and those from Clare on the lower West Side docks. Irish domestics provided leads for sisters and nieces on the best homes in which to become a maid or a cook. It went without saying that where Irish Americans were in a position to hire or at least to "put in a good word," as on the New York docks, others were at a disadvantage. Where a connected Irishman got the job, a newcomer

THE WEST SIDE DOCKS:
construction work on the new Chelsea Piers, West Side of Manhattan, 1909.

was often excluded. The county societies persisted through the early twentieth century not only because they sponsored popular dances and outings but also because they were excellent places to find work.[27]

Violent nineteenth-century conflicts involving Irish laborers were not simply carryovers from a truculent old-world culture: they were usually struggles for jobs and scarce resources, with one group trying to drive the other off the work site. The functioning of this market, carefully cultivated by the shippers, virtually guaranteed ethnic competition over jobs. Some of the worst violence occurred in the West Side Irish dock neighborhoods. Dock work was casual labor: thousands of would-be longshoremen thronged the waterfronts each morning for the "shape-up" where the unemployed lined up, hoping to be picked by the dock foreman for a day's work. The competition was fierce: New York Harbor in 1914 had about three longshoremen for every job. On the Chelsea waterfront, twenty-five hundred men might be hired on a typical day, but five thousand or more would shape up. If the policemen proved unable to drive off disappointed job seekers, foremen used clubs and water hoses.

As the composition of the waterfront workforce changed, confrontations between strikers and strikebreakers might cut across ethnic lines. In Chelsea, longshoremen needed to be close to their work for the morning shape-up, and in a volatile casual labor market, it helped to know someone: they relied on neighborhood word-of-mouth, the famed "Longshore Gazette," to locate and retain jobs. Whatever conflicts arose from cultural tensions, employers' habits of hiring outsiders at lower wages and breaking up labor organizations reinforced Irish hostility toward newcomers.[28]

Driving out competitors from other ethnic groups was a tactic the Irish later employed on docks and worksites in New Orleans and elsewhere. Many early-nineteenth-century dockworkers were slaves and free people of color, but in the wake of the Great Famine, Irish immigrants poured into the cities with few skills and desperate for work. They drove African Americans from one dock after another. Job competition between blacks and the Irish had become "a stark and dangerous reality" by the 1860s. The waterfront thereafter became an overwhelmingly Irish space, where dock jobs were considered "akin to a hereditary birthright."[29]

By the 1880s, an estimated 90 percent of New York dockworkers were Irish or Irish American. Foremen had to assign numbers to the many Pat Murphys and John Sullivans on a single dock in order to distinguish them from one another. When blacks resisted their exclusion, as they often did, Irish laborers attacked them with great ferocity. The "blind and un-reasonable hatred of the Negro" that one historian found among Irish American workers in Reconstruction-era New Orleans thrived in other late-nineteenth-century port cities as well. Such conflicts, together with Irish support for the Democratic Party and their reputation for resistance to abolition, fueled black resentment of them.[30]

The peculiar character of dock work, which required considerable strength and dexterity, could lead to close relationships. Laborers worked in pairs on heavy lifting that required careful coordination. The pairings seldom crossed ethnic and racial lines; early-twentieth-century work gangs were usually segregated by race and ethnicity.[31] An employer might induce Irish longshoremen to accept Polish or Jewish laborers, but the introduc-tion of Italians or African Americans often brought a stoppage. Where Italians and blacks made inroads, they were often confined to less skilled and lower-paid work.

At times, however, the logic of social class trumped that of race. In New Orleans, as it became clear that dock employers would go on indefinitely pitting heavily Irish white workers against blacks, the two groups de-vised a racial balance: they divided available jobs as well as union positions along racial lines in order to undercut any competition.[32] In New York Harbor, the American Longshoremen's Union (ALU), founded by follow-ers of Henry George, took as its motto "all men are brothers" and refused to make distinctions based on race, color, or creed. In 1898–99, the ALU organized somewhere between thirteen thousand and twenty thousand men, mostly Irish but also Italians and other nationalities. With so much surplus labor, however, it was difficult to keep the port organized. The ALU's successor, the Longshoremen's Union Protective Association, with strong roots among both Irish and Italians, led an unsuccessful strike in 1907. In its wake, the International Longshoremen's Association (ILA) gradually consolidated its strength in this and other ports. Dominated by the Irish, the ILA handled ethnic conflict by chartering ethnically based

"SHAPING UP":
workers waiting to be chosen for employment on
Manhattan's West Side docks, 1927.

locals and carefully integrating a few blacks and Italians into lower-level leadership positions in the national union.[33]

In the face of the massive early-twentieth-century immigration, the Irish reacted to Italians, eastern Europeans, and other interlopers as they had to African Americans. In 1887, the New York Knights of Labor were conducting a highly successful strike—when Italians arrived to break it. Bloody rioting erupted. In Boston, Irish-dominated unions barred both Italians and African Americans. When employers tried to introduce blacks or recent immigrants, riots often ensued. The tactic usually failed, but it helps to explain persistent tension between the Irish and later groups.[34]

As white ethnic groups were gradually integrated on the various waterfronts, Irish dockworkers passed their prejudices on to Italians, Poles, and others. Black longshoremen in New York reported that among the various ethnic groups on the docks, they faced the most hostility from the

Irish.[35] When sociologist E. Franklin Frazier interviewed New York's black longshoremen for a 1921 study, they reported that Italian longshoremen showed "less racial antipathy" than the Irish and were more likely to accept them on the docks. Their other observation was more ominous: the Italians seemed to be "assimilating the prejudices of the *white* men, in order apparently to insure their own standing."[36]

New York in 1900 was undergoing a building boom. Huge public works projects brought the prospect of unskilled construction jobs, tunneling for sewer systems and subways, digging foundations for large buildings, laying and repairing track. "The time was, when the heavy work of this country was done by men of Irish birth," the *Brooklyn Eagle* recalled as early as 1893. "That time has passed[.] Their places are taken on the railroads and in the cellars by Italians."[37] When a contractor arrived to take measurements for a subway tunnel between Lower Manhattan and Brooklyn in March 1900, word passed quickly through the city's ethnic communities. Hundreds of Irish, Italians, Swedes, African Americans, and other groups showed up, tools in hand, ready to claim fifty to seventy-five jobs. Police were called in to avoid a riot.[38]

As Italian laborers entered building and subway excavations, these confrontations frequently took place in an underworld of tunnels and trenches below respectable New York society. "Git out of me way, yez Guineas," Thomas Coney shouted, seeing Italians as he arrived at a Manhattan site with a wagonload of bricks. "Wait," shouted one of the Italians, "we getta da brick to the sidewalk first." Coney jumped from his cart and started to unload his bricks. A fight ensued: the Irish laborers supported Coney, and the Italians defended their own. "The combatants were soon fighting hand to hand all over the street." An Italian bit off a piece of an Irishman's nose as bricks, barrel staves, and other weapons filled the air.[39]

Ethnic fights on large public construction sites could easily develop into full-scale riots. In 1903, at the excavation for a hotel at the corner of Broadway and Twenty-ninth Street, laborers John Kennedy and Lorenzo Vito traded blows—and soon the whole crew of fifty Italian laborers faced off against seventy Irish rock drillers. Hearing the commotion, Irish truck

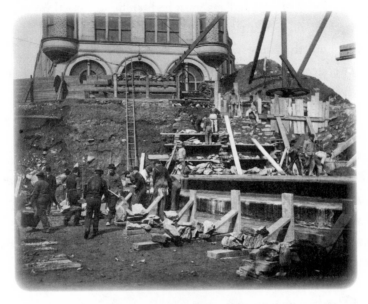

BELOW MANHATTAN'S STREETS:
laborers in the excavation for the Sixtieth Street subway station, 1901.

men started stoning the Italians from above. A policeman ended the fracas by arresting Vito, but when the prisoner was brought to the surface, a large crowd of Irishmen attacked him. At the excavation site for Grand Central Station, a string of Italian deaths had occurred under suspicious circumstances: several years later, while investigating, the city coroner uncovered a simmering dispute between Irish and Italian laborers. It had erupted when an Italian had misused a dynamite charge, killing an Irish laborer.[40]

In Brooklyn in 1903, the construction of a new telephone exchange employed Irish laborers. When Italian hod carriers arrived, the Irish immediately voted to strike (even though the newcomers were unionized in an Italian laborers' local). Their elected representative explained that it was "against their constitution and by-laws to work wit' Dagoes." When the contractor put several black laborers on to replace the Irish, the Italians went on strike. During an earlier such "racial" strike, a correspondent for the *Brooklyn Eagle* argued that the only solution to such conflicts was territorial. The Irish and Italians must be literally separated from one another, working on separate streets.[41]

Throughout the country, Irishmen bossed ethnically mixed construction crews, steel mill workers, and factory labor gangs. The topography of Pennsylvania's steel towns rather vividly reflected their power structures: immigrant laborers' families lived down in the "flats" on the riverbanks; the superintendents and the professional middle class lived atop the hills overlooking the towns; and Irish skilled workers and foremen lived in the middle, partway up the hill. Having entered the industry during a period of rapid expansion in the late nineteenth century, the lives of the Irish were very different from those of the recent unskilled immigrants. They achieved significant upward occupational mobility, moved into lower-level management positions, remained longer in the communities, and purchased homes.

In the early twentieth century, superintendents in Pennsylvania's mills and foremen at blast and open-hearth furnaces were usually Irish Catholics, supervising recent overwhelmingly Slavic immigrants.[42] Some immigrant laborers, of course, admired their bosses, taking them as role models for what a good American should be, but stories of brutal Irish foremen at blast furnaces, and in slaughterhouses, rolling mills, and freight-yards, were not unusual. Foremen at the Ford assembly plant in Highland Park, Michigan, had to learn at least one phrase in Polish, Italian, and other languages—"Hurry up!" Polish workers writing home often employed animal metaphors to describe their work and their treatment.[43] Bosses, whether Irish American or not, had lessons to teach immigrant workers, and one of them was who held power in the workplace.

BIDDY'S WORK

Like the Irish male laborers who filled America's docks and construction sites, Irish women entered nineteenth-century American society on its lowest rungs. Around 1900, over 73 percent of Irish-born women worked outside the home, unlike women in some other immigrant communities, who were restricted to the home for cultural reasons. In Boston and elsewhere, married Irish women were the most likely to work outside the home. And even many of those who remained at home supplemented family income by laundering or taking in borders, pursuits that brought them into contact with the native-born middle class and with other ethnic groups.[44]

The quintessential work for most Irish immigrant women was domestic service. To some degree, it was a carryover from Ireland: in the post-Famine years, with little else available to them, many Irish women had turned to service work. Wages, though low, were better than in many other available jobs. The work was considered ideally suited to young single women, and securing employment often involved traveling to the city, which held its own attractions. In 1911, domestics represented nearly half of the female Irish labor force, and it remained the most common female occupation until 1911.[45]

Irish women soon dominated household service in most American cities outside the South, and even in southern port cities, they often displaced black servants.[46] As late as 1900, at least 60 percent of Irish immigrant working women were domestic servants, and over 40 percent of the nation's 320,000 servants were Irish-born.[47] "There was nothing else we could do," Lillian Cavanaugh recalled of the employment opportunities when she arrived in New York at age fifteen.[48]

Even after the influx of new immigrants, Irish women still predominated, as many other immigrant cultures considered service in the home of another family unacceptable. Even if cultural barriers did not apply, however, there was still a stigma attached to service, and most young women preferred factory work.[49] Domestic service was difficult for many reasons. An 1890s Massachusetts survey set the servant's average work week at about 85 hours and her average weekly salary at $4.15. The day usually started by 6 a.m. and ended no earlier than 7 p.m. Many servants were then on call to answer the door or serve guests. In the early twentieth century, most domestics still worked seven long days each week, engaging in grueling tasks.[50]

Bridget or "Biddy" became the great symbol of the American servant class, the colorful Hibernian partner of "Paddy," stock subjects in jokes and cartoons. "They defile, they corrupt, they encourage one another to sin," a Presbyterian minister and employer of Irish household servants explained, "and if they have any scruple of conscience, by confession to the priest, he puts all right."[51] Biddy was "ignorant" and "stupid" yet also "defiant," "insolent," and "impertinent."[52] The humiliation caused by these prejudices left a lasting impression on the Irish. As late as the 1920s, experienced immigrants counseled young Bridgets to change their names. Adopting a WASP name bothered some of the young women. When Bridget Devlin's aunts, domestic servants in the Boston area, urged her to change her name to Bertha, she did so; but "I wish I never did have it changed," Bertha recalled many years later, "because I liked Bridget."[53]

Biddy served as a bridge between the working-class Irish and the respectable Protestant middle class. Domestic service provided the Irish a rare intimate glimpse of middle-class life, and such observations, as scholars of the Irish servant note, "certainly increased and refined, if they did not create, bourgeois aspirations both material and socio-cultural."[54] Irish maid Mary McGowan used domestic skills she had learned at her Irish national school, but she also picked up a good deal of social knowledge in the homes of her wealthy employers, who taught her to make hors d'oeuvres and to recognize good shoes by lending her some for Chicago's Irish dances. "Mom would refer to our front hall at home as a 'vestibule,'" Mary's daughter recalled, "a word I am sure she never heard of in Kilasser."[55]

Irish women who came from farms were likely rather removed from the domestic ideal embraced by middle-class American families. When they married, some tried to emulate the standards of cleanliness, organization, and punctuality they had observed in the elite American homes where they had worked.[56] Catherine Riordan, grandmother of the Irish American writer Peter Quinn, never spoke of her experiences in wealthy New York households, possibly because of some traumatic experience.

"Living in the homes of New York's elite introduced Catherine to an entirely different way of living, none of which was lost on her," Quinn observed. She educated her daughter in a Catholic women's college and showered her with the knowledge she had absorbed in her years as a maid, "how to dress, act, speak, furnish a home, set a table, hold a cup of tea. Catherine was determined that no one would ever mistake her daughter for a servant girl, or treat her as such."[57]

Yet the extent to which Irish domestics adopted the practices and values of the WASP middle class can easily be exaggerated. The homes to which Irish domestics traveled and where they sometimes lived were distinctly different from their own. The social distance between master and servant was often keenly felt, especially when it was reinforced, as it usually was, by religious and ethnic difference. Relations between servants and employers could be close and long lasting, but most Irish maids remained outsiders, "present but invisible in a very intimate setting."[58] They could rarely afford to emulate their employers in their own domestic spaces; the furnishings in Irish women's homes reflected their very different cultural and religious lives.

Late-nineteenth-century domestic service presented particular dangers for young Irish women. Far from being the warm, safe environment that many middle-class observers portrayed, domestic service was often a site for sexual exploitation. Stories of liaisons between master and servant led some to associate domestic work with prostitution. Middle-class reformers tended to attribute the problem to the women's character rather than to harassment and exploitation by wealthy employers. Domestic service, they thought, attracted women with low morals.[59] The church concerned itself not only with the young women's chastity but also with their religious lives: Catholic advice books circulated widely, admonishing the women to read only the Catholic Bible, insist on the right to attend Mass, and emulate the Blessed Virgin.[60]

In fact, prostitution was rare in Ireland. In Dublin, the incidence fell steeply, from low levels, during the nineteenth century, and it was extremely rare in rural areas due to state and church programs.[61] In American cities, the sexes had far more opportunity to interact than in Ireland, yet sexual promiscuity, illegitimacy, and prostitution increased only modestly. The earliest Irish immigrants showed up in large numbers among New York's prostitutes, undoubtedly due to the community's desperate poverty, but as the Irish settled in, prostitution became rarer and rarer. Between 1840 and 1870, most of New York's prostitutes were either young women from the rural northeastern United States or recent Irish arrivals in the metropolis. While native-born women populated the brothels, Irish women tended to find their customers on the streets or in the balconies of popular theaters, where the erotic character of some acts helped them to drum up business. By 1900, however, Irish and Irish American women rarely appeared in studies of prostitution; they had established a presence in many areas of the economy and had even begun moving into white-collar and professional positions.[62] Even the most ardent anti-Irish bigots tended to acknowledge the striking sexual discipline of Irish women.[63]

Working at low wages in sumptuous environments, subject to their employers' constant demands, often separated from their families and communities, domestics objected most to their mistresses' control of their time. "It's the very lowest on the scale," Mary Condon recalled of her work as a New York domestic. "Most of them . . . expected you to . . . sort of belong to them."[64] "If there was such a thing as fixed hours and some time certain to yourself, it might be different," an Irish mill worker explained, "but now I tell every girl I know, 'Whatever you do, don't go into service.'"[65] Where they continued in domestic service after 1900, Irish immigrants increasingly demanded greater control over their time, usually by "living out" in their own homes.[66]

Irish maids developed a reputation for feistiness and group solidarity. The experienced, assertive women among them provided role models for recent immigrants. "The cook is a very nice girl," the young maid Mary Cleary wrote home, ". . . a Murphy, Irish American . . . as smart a piece as

I ever saw. She makes the Boss think that she is just as good as him—she wouldn't take a word from the best of them, nor neither will I."[67] Marion Harland, the author of *Common Sense in the Household* (1872), noted that "the bad influence of fellow servants amounted to a de facto labor union," and indeed Irish servant women organized local Knights of Labor assemblies in St. Louis and elsewhere during the Great Upheaval in 1886.[68] Wealthy matron Caroline White blamed all of her servant problems on what she called "Irish fidelity" and declared herself "heartily sick of the Irish . . . sick of all the race." Her husband concluded that "the best excuse a suicide could leave behind was 'I kept Irish domestics.'"[69]

If Irish immigrant women often settled into unskilled work, they also valued education, perhaps because an earlier generation had been denied its advantages.[70] By the late nineteenth century, when many of the more recent immigrants were leaving Ireland, school textbooks focused on domestic skills—cooking, sewing, laundry, and needlework. Training that was intended to equip them better for agricultural life and work in Ireland, historian Janet Nolan observes, often instead encouraged young Irish women to try their hands at domestic work for better wages in U.S. cities. Having broadened their horizons a bit, "Ireland's classrooms unintentionally opened a window of opportunity for young women."[71] As a result of strong schooling, the Irish were among the most literate of turn-of-the-century immigrants—as of the 1890s, about 95 percent read and wrote English.[72]

Mary McGowan, a country girl from County Mayo, invested her own frustrated desires in her daughter's prospects. "Get a good education," she told her. "No one can ever take that away from you."[73] This peculiar turn of phrase conveyed not only the notion that education was an avenue of upward mobility, but also the fear that "they," presumably some amorphous WASP elite, were apt to take things away from the children of the poor.

BIDDY'S REVENGE

One effect of domestic service was rapid social mobility in the second generation of Irish women. In 1900, over 61 percent of Irish immigrant women worked as domestics or waitresses; but in the second generation the proportion had already fallen to only 16 percent. The American-born daughter of an Irish cook warned her peers against the occupation, lest they "always be prisoners and always looked down upon."[74]

The striking mobility of second-generation Irish women belies the old story of slow Irish mobility out of the working class. In the late nineteenth century, even most American-born Irish men were moving up, though often only into skilled manual work. But Irish American women, bearing deep resentment at past discrimination, and possessed of striking ambition, saved their wages as domestic servants and laborers and entered the professions, particularly teaching and nursing, in disproportionate numbers. In Chicago, only 16 percent of second-generation Irish men entered white-collar jobs, but for women the proportion was over 25 percent. Nationwide figures were comparable. Given the sorts of occupations they entered, they had even more influence on later migrants than did Irish men.[75]

With their room and board covered by their employers, even low-wage Irish domestics bankrolled their parishes, Irish nationalist groups, and their daughters, nieces, and younger sisters.[76] Irish families, whether because of an old-world tradition or a determination to help their daughters leave low-status domestic service, placed a heavy emphasis on young women's education. "It will always redound to the credit and glory of the Irish immigrants," Chicago's George Cardinal Mundelein noted, that "they always gave their daughters the chance of a better education. The father may only have been a laborer in the trenches, the mother without any education, but where the daughter showed signs of ability and a desire to study, they bore every sacrifice that she might have intellectual advantages."[77] In Boston and other cities, second-generation Irish girls showed up in high school far more often than boys (who often entered apprenticeship programs or clerk positions) and in unusually large numbers in teacher-training colleges and in nursing schools.[78]

School teaching became almost as important an occupation for the second generation as domestic service had been for the first. The work was steady, even in economic downturns. The expectation that teachers would be single facilitated the entry of late-marrying Irish women into the profession. By 1908, over 20 percent of New York and Boston public schoolteachers were the children of Irish immigrants. In Chicago, the proportion was more than one-third; in San Francisco and Worcester, Massachusetts, about one-half. By 1920, Cardinal Mundelein estimated that about 70 percent of Chicago's teachers were Catholic, most of them second-generation Irish.[79]

Yankee school boards worried that Irish women were "inundating" their systems and that Irish politicians were using teaching jobs for patronage. In an era of heightened anti-Catholicism, they feared that large proportions of Irish Catholic teachers would result in the "Catholicization of the public schools," and that immigrant children would be subject to "Hibernicization." In Boston, Protestant board members tried to restrict the number of Irish Catholics entering their normal schools by instituting new, more rigid curricula, tightening up exams, and setting quotas for Catholic high school graduates. Everything failed. The proportion of Irish among city schoolteachers continued to rise until the 1920s, when second-generation Jews gradually displaced aging Irish women from the profession.[80] If one includes nuns, a large proportion of first- and second-generation immigrant children were taught by Irish American women.

Their lessons could be rough. A teacher in the Bronx turned up a Polish boy's dirty collar in front of the entire class, instructing his sister to "see that he washes better." Even more subtle lessons left a mark on immigrant youth. "You go to the first grade," an Italian boy told a sociologist, "—Miss O'Rourke. Second grade—Miss Casey. Third grade—Miss

Chalmers. Fourth grade—Miss Mooney. When the Italian boy sees that none of his own people have the good jobs, why should he think he is as good as the Irish or Yankees?"[81]

There were also close and loving relationships between teacher and pupil. Rare glimpses appear in the very popular fictionalized accounts written by the Irish immigrant teacher Myra Kelly. Born in Dublin in 1875, Kelly grew up on the Lower East Side. She taught at PS 147 near the Bowery at the end of the nineteenth century and then as a supervisory teacher in the laboratory school at Columbia University in 1902–3. The teacher's role as an Americanizer of her immigrant pupils is the central theme in her *Little Citizens* (1904). Her Irish American heroine, Constance Bailey, struggles with authoritarian associate superintendent Timothy O'Shea, who has seen "his birthplace changed to a squalid tenement, and the happy hunting grounds of his youth grown ragged and foreign—swarming with strange faces and noisy with strange tongues." O'Shea bears a sullen grudge against the immigrant children in his school's Lower East Side classrooms. "I hope you remember that it is part of your duty to stamp out the dialect," he lectures Constance, but she observes, mindful of her own background, that his is "not an English voice, nor is O'Shea a distinctively English name." Constance Americanizes in a more nurturing way, and she shows sensitivity and an abiding love, if also a bit of condescension, toward her immigrant Jewish charges, who look up to her as a role model—an example of what it means to be an American. Student reminiscences about their Irish nuns often show a thorough mixture of fear and great love.[82]

Reformers' claims of collusion between politicians and teachers were not wrong. In many cities, Irish political influence helped young Irish American women enter the profession, as teaching was as subject to patronage operations as municipal employment. The connections are apparent in Tammany boss "Big Tim" Sullivan's recollection of his favorite teacher, Miss Murphy. When he missed school because his family could not afford shoes, she brought him directly to Tammany leader Brennan, who promptly fitted him with a new pair. (The experience left Sullivan

THE BOSS'S BENEFICENCE:
*Timothy "Big Tim" Sullivan's (1862–1913) annual distribution of shoes
to his needy constituents, the Bowery, Lower Manhattan, 1910.*

with a soft spot for shoeless people. On his mother's birthday each year, he distributed two thousand pairs to the denizens of the Lower East Side.) Tim had thus learned the importance of connections but also the vital role that a good teacher played in Irish New York.[83]

In some cases, city school administrators actually *preferred* Irish American women over WASPs when dealing with large immigrant populations. One superintendent told sociologist E. A. Ross that offered the choice, he would likely appoint the Irish woman because she would mean "less trouble with discipline, and hits it off better with parents in the neighborhood."[84]

Second-generation Irish women entered other professions and low-level white-collar jobs that brought them into contact with more recent immigrants. Many of them were nuns, but the attractions of the caring profession were felt outside the religious orders as well.[85] When Margaret Sanger and her sister entered nursing, the only profession other than teaching open to Irish women as late as the 1880s, they were following a well-worn path in the Irish community. By that point city hospitals and nursing programs were loaded with Irish women.[86]

Where they did not rise into the professions, Irish American women entered clerical and retail occupations. Again, parish and political networks were vital. A job at the Boston telephone exchange, for example, signified Americanness. By 1913, a majority of the city's telephone operators were high school graduates, most from Catholic girls' schools, at a time when that educational level was rare. In fact, the large number of young Irish American women completing high school increased the social distance between them and later immigrants. A training school run by the former chief operator at Boston's main exchange served as the conduit. Jobs were advertised only by word of mouth, with Catholic school officials or priests making the recommendations. Inadvertently, the exchange hired a few Jewish girls, but otherwise operators were nearly all "American," which usually meant second- and third-generation Irish, whom other immigrant girls viewed as the American standard.[87]

Garment manufacturing and other factory work shifted from Irish to more recent immigrant women; few Irish Americans were left in the clothing factories by 1914. Increasingly, to speak of factory workers was to speak of foreigners. Carving out such ethnic niches was not only a way of reserving the better jobs for Irish American women, but also an observation of the racial boundaries between them and later immigrants.[88]

Their relatively high educational levels, their experience in running community institutions, their commitment to public service, and their demeanor as strong role models all placed Irish women in a relatively good position compared to their sister female immigrants. Some have speculated that the high rates of psychological problems, alcoholism, and other pathologies among Irish men are actually related to the dominance of women in Irish American families.[89] One need not accept that dubious correlation to conclude that this was a society in which women occupied a particularly important position and that through their roles in family, church, school, trade union, hospital, and city street, they shaped the process by which Irish and other immigrants became American. The Irish American family conveyed not only cultural and political traditions, but also a sense of class distinctions, from one generation to another. Biddy had endured years of poverty, hard work, and the condescension of respectable WASP society; but she wreaked a vengeance of sorts through the vital role the next generation of Irish women played in shaping American urban society.

THE IRISH COMMUNITY ON STRIKE

The slights and hardships experienced by Irish laborers and servants enhanced their enclaves' defensive, communal nature, which became more desperate during strikes. Having faced bitter hostility themselves a generation earlier, and now confronted with a new wave of migrants, the Irish turned their neighborhood networks against the newcomers. Strong Irish labor solidarity, and the fact that newcomers were often first introduced as strikebreakers, made hostility and conflict all but inevitable.

In Chicago's Bridgeport and Back of the Yards, large crowds of women and children engaged in rioting during the 1877 railroad strikes, the 1886 strikes in the stockyards and neighboring plants, and the great Pullman boycott of 1894. Trains passing through the neighborhoods during the Pullman conflict presented attractive targets.[90] The strong community sanction against strikebreaking seen in crowd actions, which one historian has termed "collective bargaining by riot," and the central role of women and children, underscore the mutually reinforcing character of class and ethnic identity in Irish American communities over time.[91] In an era when formal labor organization was still weak, such riots were transitional forms of protest behavior between spontaneous eruptions and disciplined union strikes. Stable unions arrived in big-city neighborhoods by the 1880s, whereupon workers relied increasingly on negotiation and mediation, but as long as the threat of easily importing unskilled immigrant and black migrant strikebreakers was present, riots remained critical.[92] The developing class identity could spread beyond the Irish community and link with other ethnic groups, but it could also accentuate racial and ethnic antagonisms.

The key union in turn-of-the-century Chicago was the powerful teamsters' organization. Its leadership and the majority of its members were Irish, but the union also included substantial numbers of blacks, Poles, and others. The teamsters touched off "street strikes" when they came out in sympathy with other trades and attacked strikebreakers' vehicles. In 1905, when the teamsters stopped the city's wagons in sympathy with a group of women's garment workers, employers finally confronted the union in a huge conflict that left 21 people dead and 416 injured.[93]

The few black union teamsters, 5 to 10 percent of the total, supported the strike. Only an estimated 800 of the 5,800 strikebreakers were black, while the others were a mixture of immigrant and native-born laborers. But the teamsters targeted the more visible African American strikebreakers, and the conflict left a bitter legacy of Irish hatred against the "scab race." Particularly among the thoroughly unionized Irish, strong class sentiments reinforced white racism.[94]

These class attitudes soon spread to the newer immigrants. The settlement house pioneer Graham Taylor was surprised to find his neighbors, largely Polish and Italian unskilled nonunion families, attacking the scab wagons. Women and even small children chased the wagons and hurled objects from tenement windows and playgrounds, shouting epithets in English and Polish. "It was then we learned," recalled Taylor, ". . . that on occasion the class-conscious spirit emerges from the whole working class, expressing the personal claim to the job as inviolate."[95]

When class solidarity reinforced racial prejudice, it lent Irish American racism a ferocious quality. During a 1904 strike in Chicago's packinghouses, a "nigger scab" was lynched in effigy—even though most of the interlopers were again white. White effigies were also lynched, though they targeted particular individuals rather than a whole race. Thus, "Flynn, the traitor sausage maker" was hung in effigy in the heart of the old Irish neighborhood, while Bessie Undreshek returned home to the Slavic

STREET STRIKE:
the cart of a strikebreaker overturned on Chicago's near South Side, 1902.

RITUAL LYNCHING:
a strikebreaker hanged in effigy in an ethnic neighborhood
on the South Side of Chicago, 1904.

neighborhood closer to the yards after a day's strikebreaking to find a lynched image bearing her name.[96]

Irish Americans conveyed such attitudes about race and class at work, at home, and in the neighborhood. The public school was another venue. Chicago's unionized teachers were represented in the city's labor federation, which lent them important support and linked them to unions throughout the city. Strikes by schoolchildren were fairly common, as "skilled pupils' unions" patterned their behavior and values on those of their unionized teachers and parents.[97] Neighborhood gangs could also be enlisted, formally or informally, in labor conflicts. During a 1911 garbage strike led by the Irish but which included thousands of Italian and African Americans, gangs kept a careful watch for strikebreakers and overturned cans and bins, leaving mountains of stinking refuse in city streets. Recalling his boyhood in a South Philadelphia slum in the 1890s, Communist leader William Z. Foster condemned his Irish Catholic gang for its racism and

SCHOOL STRIKE:

*an ethnically mixed group of boys on strike in front
of their school, West Side, Chicago, 1902.*

anti-Semitism but remembered fondly the Bull Dogs' "real proletarian spirit" during a streetcar strike in 1895, when they wrecked every car that came through their territory, even those with armed police escorts.[98]

The history of New York's dockworkers showed both the possibilities and the limits of ethnic solidarity. Irish unionists reached out to black and Italian newcomers as early as 1887, but employers continued to introduce new groups in the midst of strikes. In 1887, Italian strikebreakers helped demolish an effective Irish-based Knights of Labor organization, and by the late 1890s they had mostly displaced the Irish from docks in Brooklyn and parts of Manhattan. The dockside Irish neighborhoods of Chelsea and the West Village remained among the last Irish preserves. Here strikebreakers, often under police guard, were attacked not just by strikers but by women and children as well. Fleeing a large crowd during a 1907 strike, one strikebreaker was met with a fusillade from the surrounding tenements—"from every window peered an angry woman who hurled all kinds of missiles." When the strike was finally abandoned and a group of discharged black and Italian strikebreakers tried to reach an elevated station on Christopher Street, a crowd set upon them with hooks, clubs, and stones. When mounted police arrived, the crowd attacked them, and the full day of rioting ended with scores of people injured.[99]

A leader in the International Longshoremen's Association Chelsea branch claimed that memories of black strikebreakers in the neighborhood had created the "greatest possible racial antagonism" and that the union had accepted African American members largely to solve this problem.[100] The leader of a black longshoremen's local in Brooklyn agreed. "We are in the union today," he said, "because the white man had to take us in for his own protection. Outside the Organization, the Negro could scab on the white man. Inside he can't. In return for this we get a share of the work, the protection of the union contract and organization support."[101]

The significance of Irish American networks for successful strikes was exemplified by Boston's telephone operators. In their organizing, the young women could call upon not only the Irish-controlled Boston Central Labor Union, with its membership of more than a hundred thousand, but also the city and state Irish American political elite. "It was not only that the Irish were now 'American,'" historian Sarah Deutsch has observed, "but that America (at least Boston), in some sense, was now Irish." Following a successful 1913 strike, the Irish American operators emerged as mainstays of Boston's Women's Trade Union League, leading campaigns among scrubwomen and among candy and garment factory workers. During a telephone strike in 1919, a year when the police themselves went on strike, policemen openly fraternized with the young women pickets, bringing them lunches and lending them their raincoats when the skies opened. When the federal government threatened to replace the phone strikers with soldiers, one hundred war veterans in uniform—the strikers' brothers and boyfriends—joined them with flags flying. MIT undergraduates and other strikebreakers arrived at the main telephone exchange, but the soldiers and strikers attacked them, questioning the young men's masculinity. The telephone company held out for only five days.[102]

In contrast, during a 1923 telephone strike, the courts granted the company sweeping injunctions and jailed and fined the pickets. Police protected strikebreakers far more effectively than in 1919, clubbing and arresting the operators. The reason for the change was straightforward: with the help of the federal government, the city had broken the 1919 police strike. The authorities discharged the mostly Irish Catholic strikers and recruited a whole new police force to take the strikers' positions. Many hailed from outside the Irish American community and had little or no connection to the labor movement. Beyond the reach of community and labor networks, they were far more willing to take action against the young Irish American women.[103]

THE REBELS

Twentieth-century Irish American labor activism embraced two traditions: mainstream business unionism (represented by the AFL and the Railroad brotherhoods) and a radical labor tradition (with roots in the Knights and Henry George's ideas). To all appearances, Irish American workers maintained their distance from organized labor radicalism, due to their success within the AFL, their close association with the Democratic Party, the opposition of the Catholic Church to most radicalism, and hostilities between them and other ethnic groups with strong Socialist influence. But all the major radical movements of this era—the Socialist Labor Party (SLP), the Socialist Party (SP), the Industrial Workers of the World (IWW), and the Communist Party (CPUSA)—counted Irish Americans among their leaders: Joseph McConnell, James Larkin, James Connolly, Elizabeth Gurley Flynn, William Z. Foster, the Dunne Brothers, James Cannon, and "Mother" Mary Jones. Flynn explicitly connected her Irish background to her conversion to socialism.[104] During the high tide of Irish nationalism, from the 1880s to the 1920s, labor radicalism had more relevance for typical Irish Americans than it would if we confine that radicalism to adherence to Marxism.

Irish women's labor activism had roots in the labor reformism and upheavals of the 1880s. Elizabeth Rodgers, master workman [*sic*] of Chicago District Assembly 24 and the Knights' most prominent female leader, was born in County Galway and arrived in the United States at the age of six. By the height of the Knights' power in 1886, she had delivered twelve children, nine of whom survived. Rodgers organized and led Chicago's Working Woman's Union in the 1870s and presided over the Eighth Ward Irish National Land League, and she served as a delegate to the Illinois Trades Assembly for many years. Labor historian David Montgomery concludes that until the 1909 general strike led by Jewish women in the New York garment industry, "virtually all the prominent activists in either the Knights of Labor or the AFL were Irish Americans."[105]

Within and beyond the Irish Catholic community, many Irish women were assertive enough to transgress standard sexual roles and behavior (even if they are seldom seen in that light). They also played a strong role in the nationalist, suffrage, and revolutionary movements in Ireland and then in American society.[106] And while many of these activists fused their progressive views of working-class organization and politics with fairly traditional Catholic attitudes about marriage and family, a tradition of "rebel girls" like Elizabeth Gurley Flynn and Margaret Sanger consciously broke with the church and embraced not only radical politics but a revolutionary lifestyle.

Before and during World War I, Leonora O'Reilly (1870–1927) embodied all these influences. Born in Brooklyn, her printer father and dressmaker mother were freethinkers and humanists. She left the church at an early age for a political life with immigrant Jewish Socialists, middle-class progressives, and women workers from a variety of backgrounds. Even so, a close friend described her as "Irish to her very finger tips with a passionate Irish temperament."[107]

An early member of the Knights of Labor, O'Reilly's father died when she was only three. Her mother held the impoverished family together by taking in boarders and sewing at home. She imbued Nora with a strong sense of social justice and took her to labor meetings and lectures

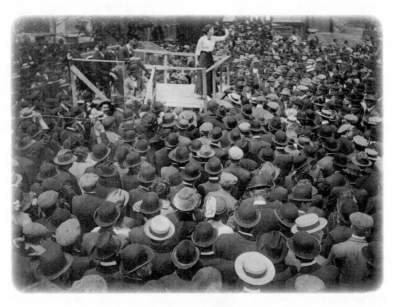

A REBEL GIRL:
Elizabeth Gurley Flynn (1890–1964), Socialist orator,
IWW organizer, and later a Communist Party leader, addressing
a large crowd of immigrant workers in Patterson, New Jersey, 1913.

at Cooper Union. The girl's other major influence was "the good priest" Father Edward McGlynn, who modeled for her a commitment to social and political radicalism. Education was her passion. She took courses at the Pratt Institute, moved with her mother to the Henry Street Settlement in Lower Manhattan, and later taught working-class girls at a trade school.[108]

Nora O'Reilly went to work in a shirt factory at age eleven. In the wake of Henry George's mayoral campaign and the Great Upheaval strikes in 1886, she joined the Knights and never looked back. Joining George's Social Reform Club in the 1890s, she became the first woman organizer for the United Garment Workers Union and emerged as a spellbinding soapboxer. In 1903, after joining the Socialist Party, she helped launch the Women's Trade Union League (WTUL). Along with the reformer Helen Marot, she brought New York's WTUL out of the tearoom and into the streets and factories. She organized immigrant women in the garment industry, and during the giant strike of 1909, which helped to establish the International Ladies' Garment Workers' Union, she became close friends with Rose Schneiderman, Pauline Newman, and other Jewish activists.

At the same time, O'Reilly recruited some of the league's most enduring and valuable middle-class activists, though she sometimes clashed with the middle-class reformers, finding some in this "overdose of allies" condescending. Despite the tensions it caused, the class collaboration represented the WTUL's great promise.[109] (The same class tensions plagued the Chicago WTUL. In 1908, when its leaders decided to move their headquarters from Hull House to the offices of the Chicago Federation of Labor, one settlement worker objected, preferring to "convene amid attractive furnishings instead of facing walls covered with union labels and tobacco juice." Still, moving its headquarters brought the WTUL into the city's progressive labor movement.)[110]

O'Reilly left the WTUL in 1915 and became active in suffrage work. By combining union and suffrage organizing, she and the Jewish immigrant women with whom she worked closely provided a crucial link between working-class immigrant and middle-class native-born women progressives.

O'Reilly's social justice activism recognized no national or racial boundaries: she saw a common struggle among diverse peoples. An active supporter of the NAACP and an ardent internationalist, she worked with advocates of Indian independence and attended the 1915 Hague Women's Conference on international peace along with Jane Addams. There she met peace and justice activists from around the world, as well as Irish independence and suffrage campaigners. Tiring of the Socialist Party's factionalism, O'Reilly moved, after Easter 1916, toward radical Irish nationalism. From 1918 through the early 1920s, she threw herself into the radical wing of that movement, helping to establish the Irish Progressive League. [111]

Nora O'Reilly was one of a generation of Irish American women progressives who expanded their movements' horizons by creating alliances with middle-class women and with working women from other ethnic communities. Others included "Mother" Mary Jones; Chicago needle trades worker and labor reformer Agnes Nestor; Margaret Haley, founder of the Chicago Federation of Teachers and a leading figure in the Chicago Federation of Labor; Mary Kenney O'Sullivan, a bookbinder and the AFL's first full-time woman organizer; Kate Kennedy, a Famine child immigrant who worked first as a needle trades worker and then as a school principal and teachers' union leader in San Francisco; and Margaret Mahoney, a physician and a public school teacher who became the first president of the San Francisco Federation of Teachers. [112]

The generation also included thousands of local activists like Julia O'Connor and the dozens of Boston telephone operators who organized the first women's local in the International Brotherhood of Electrical Workers; and Hannah O'Day, a rank-and-file organizer in Chicago's stockyards. Early-twentieth-century Chicago was a hotbed of women's unionism, often led by Irish Americans: Mary McDermott of the scrubwomen's union, Josephine Casey of the Elevated Road Clerks, Margaret Duffy of the Telephone and Switchboard Operators, and Elizabeth Maloney of the waitresses' union. [113]

Several characteristics stand out among these women. Although Mother Jones was born in Ireland, most were children of immigrants. Like their male counterparts, they were products of the American city more than the Irish countryside. Compared to other immigrant groups, they were unusually well educated in English. Often influenced by their parents' participation in the Knights of Labor, they inherited a commitment to the labor movement and cherished ideals of social justice learned from Henry George. But as they took an active role in the public sphere and in social reform movements, they charted their own course, cultivating links with middle-class reformers and with new immigrants. Their community's strong networks, and their physical and social proximity to other impoverished immigrants, gave Irish women ample opportunity and encouragement to enter public service as teachers or nurses or to participate in union or reform organizations.

Devoted to Catholic social teachings, most radical Irish men and women encountered tensions between their social and religious commitments, and some went on to reject the church and its teachings altogether. Others promiscuously mixed Catholicism, nationalism, and socialism, recognizing the church's grip on Irish workers and that a fusion of religion and nationalism lay at the heart of Irish working-class radicalism. James Connolly (1863–1916) lived and organized in New York from 1903 to 1910, maintaining close links with the Socialist Party and the IWW. He helped launch a small Irish Socialist Federation and a left-wing paper, *The Harp*. The federation's statement of purpose, which he wrote, pledged to educate Irish American workers to socialist principles and "to prepare them to cooperate with the workers of all other races, colors, and nationalities in the emancipation of labor."[114] He occupied a position on the far left, advocating the organization of radical industrial unions and revolutionary action (rather than reformism): his dream was always to link the Irish national struggle with the international workers' movement. Yet he continued to embrace Catholicism and remained at the very heart of the Irish community.

In 1910, Connolly returned to Ireland to lead the radical wing of the nationalist movement. He turned to armed struggle in the 1916 Easter Rising, an insurrection that set the stage for the Irish revolution and national independence. Following the rebellion, he was executed by British troops and became a martyred saint. The fact that he was a revolutionary Socialist seemed to bother no one—so long as he was also a Catholic.[115]

Jim Larkin (1876–1947) organized the Irish Transport and General Workers' Union, Ireland's premier labor organization, and led the 1913 Dublin General Strike. On the eve of World War I, he arrived in the United States, dividing his time between Chicago, New York, and various prisons. He led a series of wartime strikes on the docks and in the munitions industry, activities for which he was eventually jailed. He helped to launch the American Communist movement and to establish connections between the Communist International and the Irish labor movement. Throughout it all, he unnerved Communists and Catholics alike by publicly insisting on his adherence to the church. "I condemn certain political activities of the Irish bishops," Larkin declared in 1923, "but I am and will remain a Roman Catholic."[116] Larkin and Connolly were determined to remain Catholics even as they overturned the existing social and political order; they embodied a revolutionary tradition rooted in Irish soil, then transported to American cities.

For other Irish American radicals, like Elizabeth Gurley Flynn (1890–1964), socialism appeared to be a kind of replacement for Catholicism. During the McCarthy era, when she was serving time at the Women's House of Detention, an Irish officer observed, "I guess Socialism has always been your religion." "And, in a certain sense," she agreed, "this is true. I found the Socialist movement at a very young and impressionable age. To me it was the creed of the brotherhood of man or 'to do on earth as it is in Heaven,' and I was an intense believer in Socialism during my whole life."[117] Flynn, a vocal internationalist and champion of immigrant, minority, and especially working women's rights, never lost her father's ardent nationalism.[118]

Other radicals like William Z. Foster (1881–1961) reacted strongly against

Catholicism and their Irish identity. Raised by a devout mother and a Fenian father, a local brawler of some repute, Foster was originally intended for the priesthood. In his adolescence, he read voraciously in natural science, history, and rationalism; rejected his mother's Catholicism as well as his father's nationalism; and soon developed an active intolerance for all religion. "I have never failed to marvel at how intelligent people can believe . . . in the idea of a human-like Deity, who rules over the immense universe," Foster wrote. The only way modern people could accept such ideas was on blind faith. "The days of heaven and hell are past for men and women who actually think about such matters."[119] Like Flynn, Foster had a special rapport with immigrant workers from diverse backgrounds, but he identified only as an internationalist and seldom spoke of his own family background. Yet Catholicism's grasp seems to have reached even Foster: a family member recalled that on his deathbed in a Moscow hospital, he called for and received the last rites.[120]

BUSINESS UNIONISTS

Business unionism and AFL craft unionism generally embraced only skilled workers: it focused narrowly on issues of wages and working conditions and was far more conservative in its influence. Exclusionary by definition, it could easily turn to nativism, racism, and the prohibition of women and minorities in the workplace and the union. The Irish community often equated labor's cause narrowly with its own—which lent it internal strength by mobilizing the whole community behind strikes, but also accentuated craft unionism's exclusivity. Irish American leaders led the campaign against Chinese immigration in California and supported the immigration restrictions and literacy tests embraced by the AFL and many Socialist Party activists.[121] John Roach, the AFL's head organizer in New York, refused to print leaflets or union constitutions in foreign languages because, he said, "foreigners should be forced to learn English."[122] When economist David Saposs investigated union attitudes toward immigrants in the 1910s, he found one Irish American union leader after another who insisted they were unorganizable—often in the face of considerable evidence to the contrary.[123]

When the new immigrants did organize and launch huge strikes in the 1910s, often under the auspices of the radical IWW, Irish policemen confronted them. Irish American business unionists denounced immigrant radicals as volatile and dangerous. The 1919 Lawrence textile strike welded together a dozen different immigrant groups; recalling it, Italian radical Anthony Capraro concluded that it was the Irish—priests, policemen, and AFL leaders—who had represented the main enemies of the strike.[124]

Irish Americans had a firm grip on the AFL's top leadership positions. By 1910, nearly half the AFL's 110 national unions had Irish American presidents—even though the Irish represented only 10 percent of the nation's native-born and only 3 percent of its immigrants. Even in AFL unions where they were small minorities, they often dominated the leadership.[125] While we have no reliable study of the intermediate and lower levels of union activism, many city and state federations, union locals, and shop floor organizations appear to have had Irish leaders. In Boston in the 1920s, for example, nearly 90 percent of the city's 347 elected union officials were Irish Americans.[126] The typical Irish American labor leader of the early twentieth century was the child of immigrants who had grown up in an industrial city or town, steeped in urban society.

The Irish-controlled building trades unions became famous for their corruption and duplicity. Again the force of neighborhood solidarity was often turned against any outsiders. Martin B. "Skinny" Madden (1855–1928), president, treasurer, and "business agent for life" of Chicago's Steamfitters' Helpers' Union, maintained his control of the city's labor federation and the building trades council through a network of sluggers. Racketeers used their control of apprenticeship programs to keep African Americans and recent immigrants out of the most prized jobs. They exploited their connections with political machines and their relationships with Irish contractors to secure favorable treatment. In the worst cases, they sold "strike insurance" to employers, undermining their own members' ability to protect wage rates and work rules.

But the bricklayers, ironworkers, and workers in other trades were an employer's worst nightmare. Organized through powerful building trades councils, they used the sympathetic strike liberally to enforce elaborate work rules and ensure a tightly closed shop on all construction sites. Their "walking delegates" were happy to settle any dispute—for the right price. When asked what an employer needed to do to end a strike, Sam Parks, president of New York's United Board of Building Trades, allegedly responded, "I'm it, you pay me . . . You can go back to work when you pay Sam Parks $2,000." The income from such extortionate practices could be enormous. Government prosecutors claimed that "Umbrella Mike" Boyle (1879–1958), a business agent for Chicago's electricians, was worth $500,000 when he went to trial. For well-connected Irish Americans and labor bosses, the system worked well. For workers frozen out of quality jobs, it represented corruption.[127] These business unions came closest to what the IWW called "jobs trusts."

The collaboration of such crooked unionists and bosses did not preclude industrial conflict and often encouraged violence. The building trades, coal mining, and railroads—industries with large numbers of Irish American leaders and rank and file—all posted unusually high levels of strike activity.[128] During the depression of 1921–22, when builders' organizations became strong enough to take on the unions, such practices resulted in open warfare and increased the prospects for labor sluggers, most of them drawn from Irish neighborhoods. Conventional wisdom holds that these purveyors of urban violence were open to the highest bidder, but a division of labor developed between neighborhood-based sluggers (who maintained connections with and worked exclusively for the unions) and "professionals" from organized crime or labor spy outfits (who specialized in breaking up picket lines, guarding strikebreakers, intimidating union members, and assassinating leaders). The unions maintained their own pool of talent, and professionals often found themselves outmuscled by

CHICAGO LABOR BOSSES:
Martin B. "Skinny" Madden (right, 1855–1928), "Business Manager for Life"
of the Steamfitters' Helpers, and "Umbrella Mike" Boyle (left, 1879–1958),
business manager of the Electrician's Union, 1909.

some of the neighborhood boys. The open shop conflict of the early 1920s was the bloodiest in Chicago, where a building employers' group put up $3 million, imported twenty-one thousand strikebreakers, and employed a private police force of seven hundred men to protect them.[129]

Mainstream Irish AFL leaders who eschewed corruption and embraced broader reform goals were likely to have a Catholic vision that was in opposition to the major radical groups, albeit sometimes linked to the cause of Irish nationalism. The turning point for Catholic social thought was Pope Leo XIII's 1891 encyclical, *Rerum Novarum*. Leo recognized that if the church was to retain its working-class base, it must take a position on the social question, so he advocated trade unionism, cooperatives, and basic protective labor legislation. But he adamantly condemned socialism. Later encyclicals reinforced these teachings. U.S. clergy and hierarchy varied in their opinions, depending often on their proximity to their working-class flocks and labor organizations. Some priests clearly supported strikes and even more radical organizations and protests, while others fulminated against any union or strike.[130]

In the everyday realm, the new emphasis on the social question was embodied in the careers of "labor priests" like Father Peter Yorke of San Francisco, who combined labor, Irish nationalist, and radical activism. Most clergy, however, fell in line behind the pope, welcoming conservative unionism and denouncing socialism. William Cardinal O'Connell of Boston concluded simply, "There is not and cannot be a Catholic Socialist," while New York archbishop John Farley called socialism "the heresy of the hour."[131] The 1912 national convention of the Ancient Order of Hibernians condemned socialism as both "un-American" and "un-Christian." The Anti-Boycott Association, a conservative business group, reprinted an address by Archbishop James Cardinal Gibbons of Baltimore, a leading "liberal," that eloquently defended private property against the Socialist threat. Bishops urged their priests to preach on the issue and establish parish study groups to promote the Catholic perspective on issues concerning social class. An extensive array of Catholic papers and periodicals carried the anti-Socialist message in a range of languages.[132] In socialism, the church perceived a threat to both its theology and its influence.

Within the AFL, Irish activists played a major role in launching and sustaining resistance to radical influences. In Boston, the campaign was led by Peter Collins of the Central Labor Union. Father Peter Dietz's Militia of Christ for Social Justice, a secret faction established in 1910 to coordinate anti-Socialist activities within the unions, had close ties to the German Catholic Central Verein, but at least six of its seven directors and five of its six officers were Irish Americans. Though it boasted only seven hundred members and lasted only a few years, the militia remained an ongoing conservative influence at the highest levels of the AFL precisely because it provided what David Montgomery called "an ideological antidote for socialism" that appealed to many workers. But Catholic activists also advocated the labor movement as a defense of the sacred family against corporate greed. Their position remained closest to the hearts of those steeped in Catholic values, but patriarchal pleas for the sanctity of the working-class family appealed to millions of workers beyond the church's reach.[133]

Catholic attacks did not prevent rank-and-file immigrant workers from supporting the Socialists. In the 1910 municipal elections, Socialist Party candidates carried the thoroughly Polish Catholic wards in Milwaukee and attracted Catholic working-class votes in Chicago's immigrant wards. Within the International Association of Machinists, a major battleground between right and left, Socialist lodges in the Northeast and parts of the Midwest were largely Catholic, while conservative lodges in the South were largely Protestant.[134]

Continuing immigration brought new radical influences from Ireland but could also accentuate the parochial perspective. By the 1920s, many Irish immigrants had participated in both the Irish republican and the Irish labor movements and tended to see class and national solidarities as linked. An immigrant laborer in a New Jersey saloon put the equation simply: "My father was Irish, my mother was Irish, and so am I Irish. I am a union man and proud of it . . . I was in a union ten years before I came to this country and twelve years in this country . . . I never scabbed in my life . . . I'd always stick by the union and by the Irish."[135]

AMERICANIZATION THROUGH UNIONIZATION

While these two Irish American labor traditions were often at odds, it would be a mistake to exaggerate the distance between them. In order to succeed, craft unions had to control the flow of skilled labor into the various trades, but during the early twentieth century, in many industries, the division of labor and mass-production processes rendered this approach futile. Especially in heavy industry and manufacturing, employers relied ever more on unskilled immigrant labor, often assiduously dividing their workers by accentuating racial and ethnic animosity. If not because of an inclusive ethic and tolerance, then through sheer necessity, union organizers broadened their vision. Irish American labor progressives—in the

WTUL, in labor unions, and in many state and municipal federations—
worked to integrate the new immigrants and black migrants into the
movement. These challenges, as well as the nineteenth-century traditions
of labor reform and radical nationalism, help explain how a group of progressive unionists emerged at the very heart of the AFL—and how they
conveyed these values to later immigrants.

In the spring of 1900 in Chicago, Hannah O'Day led a group of young
Irish American women, friends from her South Side parish, to protest a
succession of piece-rate cuts at the canning factory where they worked.
O'Day tied a red kerchief to her umbrella and marched her co-workers
through the giant Union Stock Yards, garnering support as they went. The
packers brought in Slavic women as scabs and blacklisted the Irish women,
thereby breaking the strike. Thereafter the Irish women organized the
Maud Gonne Club, a name that fused Irish nationalism, class-conscious
unionism, and early feminism. Maud Gonne (1866–1953), a spirited Socialist feminist actress who had been active in the Land League, founded In-
ghinidhe na h'Éireann, the original Irish women's nationalist organization.[136]

O'Day's unsuccessful strike helped to spark an organizing drive by the
Amalgamated Meat Cutters and Butcher Workmen of North America.
Two years later, when the campaign reached its zenith, the composition
of the female labor force in the stockyards was changing. Hundreds of
Polish and Bohemian and a smaller number of African American women
had joined the Irish in the canning rooms, and the Maud Gonne Club
became the nucleus for the Amalgamated's Women's Local 187.[137]

Visiting a meeting of the local in 1903, Mary McDowell of the University of Chicago Settlement House witnessed a fascinating exchange
between two members. A black woman rose to accuse a Polish woman of
insulting her, and the Irish American chairwoman asked the two to come
forward.

Now, what did yez call each other?

She called me a nigger.

She called me a Pollack [*sic*] first.

Both of yez oughta be ashamed of yourselves. You're both to blame. But don't you know that this question in our ritual don't mean that kind of griev-e-ances, but griev-e-ances of the whole bunch of us? Now shake hands and don't bring any more of your personal grievances here.[138]

The exchange demonstrates the promise of interethnic and interracial labor organizing: the experiences and grievances that the women shared were more important than the racial and ethnic differences that separated them. All their efforts to improve their own lives and those of their families depended upon their ability to stick together. In the workplace and the union hall, Irish American workers helped immigrants and migrants of color come to understand their new lives.

As early as 1900, as unskilled workers poured into American industry, some mainstream Irish American AFL leaders called for the integration of new immigrants and racial minorities into the existing unions. As African American and later Mexican migrants moved into industrial centers, the same dynamic was at work. Even when a union's official position discriminated against immigrants and demanded restriction, the situation on the ground often required union activists to reach out to the unskilled newcomers. Chicago's Union Stock Yards was a good place to see the process at work. As late as May 1902, the union's journal still reprinted nativist articles. That fall, however, J. A. O'Brien reported that the immigrant shop stewards, newly integrated by himself and other local activists, were "the very best union men we have got."[139]

A 1905 *Bureau of Labor Bulletin* quoted Irish American stockyards workers: "However much it may go against the grain, we must admit that common interest and brotherhood must include the Polack and the Sheeny."[140] Michael Donnelly, a Kansas City sheep butcher who led the stockyards campaign, put the matter more eloquently: "Experience has taught us that this latter class in their unorganized condition are a menace." The man who wiped the blood from the slaughterhouse floor was "entitled to the same consideration I am. I cannot forget that he is a human being, and that he has a family. It should be our purpose to make the injury of the common laborers the concern of the skilled workman . . . It is our duty to educate them in the labor movement."[141]

In coal mines and factories too, the Irish activists conveyed to newcomers, in distinctly working-class tones, what it meant to be an American, emphasizing basic civil liberties, particularly free speech, and encouraging immigrant workers to speak up for themselves. These ideas were not abstract: union organizing in steel and coal company towns depended directly upon the freedom to exercise such rights, so immigrant workers often learned of their value in the midst of organizing drives and strikes. Organizers frequently infused their material demands with the rhetoric of democracy and patriotism, particularly during World War I. They spoke of an "American standard of living," by which they meant higher wages, shorter hours, and safe working conditions. In the past, that phrase had been employed to exclude Chinese workers; now it served to integrate new immigrants and impart the movement's basic message. Immigrants responded because the unions appealed to their deepest value: the preservation of their families and communities. Finally, organizers stressed cultural pluralism and class solidarity as an antidote to ethnic antagonism.[142]

For many immigrants, the union represented what U.S. commissioner of labor Ethelbert Stewart called "the first, and for a time the only, point at which [the immigrant] touches any influence outside of his clan." "The labor union has been the only institution," settlement house reformer Mary McDowell observed, "that has brought the immigrant in touch with English-speaking men for a common purpose and in preparation for self-government."[143]

An immigrant worker was far more likely to be introduced to the American political and economic system by informal conversations at work, by discussion and debate at union meetings, and by union publications written in his or her own language than by formal government or employer attempts at Americanization. The de facto Americanizers might be knowledgeable workers either from his or her own community or from others, but many of them were Irish Americans.

In Chicago's slaughterhouses and meatpacking plants, Irish Americans represented only 25 percent of the labor force in 1904, but they held 57 percent of local union offices and led what economist John R. Commons called "a strike of Americanized Irish, Germans, and Bohemians in behalf of Slovaks, Poles, Lithuanians, and negroes."[144] The process of unionization generally spread from the long-unionized skilled Irish and German "knife men" to Slavic and black unskilled laborers. As in politics, effective labor organization rested on local parish networks. When Patrick Coakley, a hog butcher, arrived at his local's first meeting, he found that nine of the twelve charter members were Bridgeport neighbors of his, most of them had been his classmates at the local parish elementary school.[145]

A Lithuanian male laborer told a reporter that the union's successes had given him more time to learn to read and to enjoy life "like an American." He served the labor movement as an interpreter, bringing the union gospel to his fellows in their own tongue.[146] In the nation's remarkably diverse workplaces, the unions combined nationalities in a common cause—and created a generation of workers with their own notions of what it meant to be an American.

The danger of ethnic conflict, however, was always present in these movements, and massive black migration from the South brought the further threat of racial violence. Promising strikes were often wrecked when native-born workers failed to support immigrant workers, as in the 1919 steel strike, or when racial conflict erupted between ethnic whites and African Americans, as in the Chicago stockyards.[147] Some Irish American steelworkers held back from joining a "Hunky" union, populated largely by Slavic immigrants, while their sons might be actively attacking black workers. But other Irish American labor activists were busy integrating black and immigrant workers into new unions and, in the process, building a new labor movement.

Irish Americans acted as gatekeepers for job sites and labor unions; they defined what the term *labor* meant in the diverse industrial city; as foremen and foreladies, they disciplined recent immigrant and migrant workers and enforced the regimen of the industrial workplace; as older, more experienced workers, they taught newer workers to subvert that regimen; as local activists, they organized newcomers into unions and political movements; and in the process they conveyed a distinctly working-class notion of "American."

FOUR

THE STAGE

I n January 1907, at Manhattan's Hammerstein's Victoria Theater, hundreds of Irish American men in the audience heckled the actors onstage and pelted them with eggs, potatoes, and rotten vegetables. The same thing happened a few days later at Brooklyn's Orpheum. Twenty-two men were arrested in one melee alone, though an Irish American judge later dismissed all charges. Organized by the United Irish Societies, representing more than ninety organizations, the protests were aimed at a vaudeville skit called *The Irish Servant Girls*. The Russell Brothers, once one of the most popular acts on the vaudeville circuit, had been performing the act without incident for many years. Dressed in drag, the actors depicted dim-witted Irish maids. In response to earlier objections from the Irish American community, the brothers had changed the name of the act and cut some of the more offensive lines, but when they brought their new version of the routine back to New York in 1907, the complaints turned into riots. The protests forced the Russells out of New York and eventually out of vaudeville entirely.[1] *The Irish Servant Girls* reflected vaudeville's preoccupation with ethnic stereotypes, while the protests were part of a broader movement against ethnic caricature.

The new popular culture that reflected urban themes and a sense of realism would reach full flower during the Great Depression, but it originated in the ethnically diverse turn-of-the-century city. Themes of social class difference emerged on stage and screen, in musical comedies, in vaudeville routines, in realist novels, in Tin Pan Alley song lyrics, and in the newspaper observations of Finley Peter Dunne's philosopher-saloonkeeper "Mr. Dooley." Vaudeville—variety shows encompassing music, comedy, and dance acts—became synonymous with the new urban culture. This culture was the product of interactions among Irish and other city dwellers from various backgrounds, as they tried to interpret that urban diversity to themselves, to the immigrant peoples around them, and to the mainstream public.

From the music hall to the vaudeville stage, and from the comics and humor columns of newspapers to realist novels, Irish Americans portrayed class and gender tensions within their own communities and with other racial and ethnic groups. Their cultural expressions ranged from low humor to high literature, but all reflected life in the streets of America's great cities.

BLACKFACE IRISH

Due in part to their English-language skills, their earlier arrival in the United States, their predominance, and the persistence of their musical and comic traditions, Irish Americans did much to construct the identities of more recent immigrants through popular literature and theater. Irish American performance was a distinctly urban art form, appealing above all to the inhabitants of ethnically diverse neighborhoods. The stage Irish became arbiters and interpreters of American ethnic cultures. As long as they lacked their own popular English-language interpreters, Chinese Americans, African Americans, and others found their lives introduced and explained, in print and on stage, by the Irish.[2]

The Irish immigrants' own social footing was rather tenuous: by the time they reached the United States, they had been the main focus of ethnic humor on the English stage for centuries. Irish comic figures appeared in Shakespeare's plays, and they remained a central feature of

British theater from the seventeenth century through the Victorian era. The "stage Irishman" stereotype transferred easily to nineteenth-century America, and traces of the tradition continued into the twentieth.[3]

Irish American performance was not simply an adaptation of Irish forms but rather the product of interaction with other ethnic cultures. Up to the Civil War, Irish and African Americans, living and working in close physical and social proximity in Lower Manhattan's Five Points neighborhood, mixed their distinctive performance styles in dance halls. Irish music fused with African beats, and contests pitted Irish champions against "Master Juba," an expert in intricate African dance steps. "Each group incorporated favorite steps from their competitors' dance idiom into their own," notes Tyler Anbinder, historian of the Five Points. "It was from this interaction between African Americans dancing the shuffle and the Irish dancing the jig that 'tap dancing' developed."[4]

But as Irish became involved in racial assaults on blacks, a distancing occurred. During the course of this shift in relations, Irish performers on the minstrel stage donned blackface, interpreting the black character for a generation of audiences. This performance allowed Irish Americans to separate their own collective persona from that of African Americans and, in the process, earn a more secure place in the racial hierarchy.[5]

The Irish did not invent blackface minstrelsy. The first truly popular American cultural form, it dated back to the early republic and was employed in a number of ways. But it appeared on the Irish stage at midcentury, as Irish support for abolitionism was waning.[6] And for the rest of the century, Irish immigrants dominated the form, in hundreds of national touring companies and thousands of local performances. Profoundly racist, minstrelsy was the sort of ethnic composite that characterized Irish American performance. After the Civil War, as the country became increasingly diverse, Irish Americans in minstrel shows took on the personae of absurd black characters in story, song, and dance, but also absurd Polish, Italian, German, and Irish characters in polka, opera, folk song, and other performances.[7]

Blackface minstrelsy was central to the formation of white suprema-cist values—generally and among the despised Irish Catholic minority in particular.[8] In the course of establishing their own white identity, Irish performers employed blackface to distance themselves from Afri-can Americans, thereby playing a crucial role in the formation and repro-duction of racist values. They took on other ethnic roles as well, and actors from other ethnic backgrounds took on comic Irish personae. In the process, stage performers, with the Irish prominent in their number, interpreted a complex social world to audiences from a variety of back-grounds.

Through blackface minstrelsy, Irish Americans introduced recent im-migrants to American understandings of race, on the vaudeville stage and even through church fund-raisers and settlement house programs. They transmitted the racist cultural form throughout immigrant communities. Minstrelsy's continuing popularity well into the twentieth century indi-cates its potent value as a cultural form that allowed artists to transgress the color line even as they enacted racist values.[9]

The stock characters in nineteenth-century ethnic music hall and the-ater were Paddy, the drunken and stupid stage Irishman, and his partner Biddy, the lovable but dense Irish maid; they probably reached the height of their popularity during the later Irish immigration of the 1880s. Like Black Sambo and Mose in minstrelsy, Paddy and Biddy were comic char-acters that thrived amid extreme racism and discrimination. Even when the Irish themselves laughed at them, they deeply resented such stereo-types. [10]

John Boyle O'Reilly (1844–90), Irish America's most important public intellectual of the late nineteenth century, found a particularly effective means to denounce blackface minstrelsy. A poet, a writer, and editor of the mass-circulation *Boston Pilot*, O'Reilly compared the ridiculous and demeaning Sambo character to the stage Irishman. Toward the end of his life, O'Reilly grew ever sharper in his denunciations of white racism and his demands for African American equality. Yet the Irish American as-sociation with minstrelsy continued.[11]

THE "AMERICAN DICKENS"

Straddling the musical variety shows of the 1860s and 1870s and the emerging vaudeville explosion at the turn of the century was the musician, performer, and playwright Edward Harrigan (1844–1911), who became known as the "American Dickens." Harrigan's enormously popular plays portrayed ethnic life on the Lower East Side. Born in that classic crucible of immigrant life and steeped in Irish American culture, Harrigan witnessed the city's ethnic transformation firsthand. He and his collaborators, his father-in-law David Braham (the son of an Orthodox Jew) and Tony Hart (1855–91) (a second-generation Irish American), shared extensive minstrel experience. Having graduated from songs, sketches, and dialogues, their full-fledged musicals captured the imagination of New Yorkers who saw their city changing about them. Twenty-three of his plays ran for more than one hundred performances, while hundreds of thousands of copies of his songs circulated on sheet music throughout the United States. Harrigan's main themes were social class and the relations between the Irish and other ethnic groups.

However one interprets the plays, Harrigan's goal was clear enough. "Though I use types and never individuals," he wrote, "I try to be as realistic as possible." His characters were exaggerated but easily recognizable: assorted immigrant politicians, petty merchants, washerwomen, laborers, and cops. His setting, carefully designed with an eye to detail, was invariably Five Points or another New York slum. The performers wore costumes that he purchased directly from individuals on the streets of New York, and they spoke familiar slang and dialect.[12] The middle-class nationalist John Finerty's complaint that Harrigan and Hart produced "drama from the slums" was not far off the mark. "Mr. Harrigan realizes in his scenes what he realizes in his persons," the critic William Dean Howells wrote at the time. "He cannot give it all . . . and he has preferred to give its Irish American phases in their rich and amusing variety, and some of its African and Teutonic phases."[13]

Harrigan brought his own well-developed sense of racial hierarchy to his creations and held the Irish up as a sort of model.[14] But he also genuinely appreciated the city's diverse peoples. His lyrics captured *both* the casual ethnic prejudice *and* the unmistakable fascination with urban diversity that characterized much of Irish American culture.

> *It's Ireland and Italy, Jerusalem and Germany,*
> *Oh, Chinamen and nagers, and a paradise for rats,*
> *All jumbled up together in the snow and rainy weather,*
> *They represent the tenants of McNally's row of flats.*[15]

Relations among these groups were often antagonistic. The *Boston Herald* called Harrigan's plays a "war of the races in cosmopolitan New York," especially in the case of the Chinese.[16] In Harrigan's 1881 musical *The Mulligans' Silver Wedding,* Honora Dublin, an Irish washerwoman, carries a special grudge for Hog Eye, the Chinese laundryman whose business is undermining her own. Hog Eye is "the heathen's heathen." Honora expresses her frustration in a long diatribe, describing him in both feminine and animal terms: "You're not half a man. You're a nagur . . . You're a monkey, you have a tail growing out of your head . . . Why don't you have whiskers on your face like a man, you baboon you . . . walking around in your petticoats and calling yourself a man. Bah."[17]

Yet Harrigan's play also alluded to the presence of Chinese-Irish couples, a common theme in late-nineteenth-century song lyrics and musical variety performance but a sensitive issue nonetheless.[18] This composition hit the New York stage before audiences made up of Irish Americans who resented the encroachment of the Chinese. The laundry became a frequent site of ethnic tension and the source for racism among Irish women, as in the popular song "Since the Chinese Ruint the Thrade":

> *It makes me wild, whin I'm on the street,*
> *To see those haythen signs:*
> *Ah Sung, Ah Sing, Sam Lee, Ah Wing,*

An' the ilegant spread on ther lines.
If iver I get me hands on Ah Sing,
I'll make him Ah Sing indade—
On me clothesline I'll pin the leather skin
Of the haythen that ruint the thrade.[19]

Harrigan's lyrics resonated among Irish Americans because they re-flected very real attitudes toward the Chinese as a result of the changes in New York's labor market. In the late 1870s, when anti-Chinese agitation began to gather steam in New York, Irish women and Chinese men were competing for laundry work. "They have already two hundred laundries in New York," *The Irish World* reported in 1879. "Six months ago they had not

"AMERICAN DICKENS":
Edward Harrigan (left, 1844–1911); an unidentified African American
youth (center); and Harrigan's partner, Tony Hart (1855–1891),
in their Mulligan Guard outfits, 1879.

twenty." "Their passage to San Francisco costs less than a steerage passage from Liverpool to New York. And crowded up in China there are some 400,000,000 of them, and they can live on ten cents a day." As often with working-class racism against the Chinese, the immigrants' debased status represented the direct threat, but the solution to such competition also involved the taming of the corporations that were thought to drive the immigration.[20]

What separated Harrigan's plays from earlier minstrelsy and later musical theater, which also included extensive ethnic performance, was their portrayals of interactions among ethnic groups. In *The Mulligan Guard Ball*, interethnic marriage was a central theme. Dan Mulligan and wife Cordelia are at odds with their neighbors the Lochmullers in part because they fear that their son Tommy will marry Katrina Lochmuller. While the Lochmullers are just as concerned about the prospect, mother Bridget hails not from Germany but from the Mulligans' own County Cork—she has married a German. Meanwhile, another of Dan Mulligan's antagonists, Sim Primrose, leader of the competing African American Skidmore Guard, runs a barbershop where characters from the various communities gather. Sim complains loudly that the Irish washerwoman charges too much to launder his towels and threatens to shift his business to the neighborhood's Chinese laundryman. Class tensions and anxieties abound. The main characters are not workers but small-business people looking for ways to rise—an accurate reflection of Irish America's struggling lower middle class. The play's denouement comes when the competing black and Irish guard units schedule their fancy balls on the same day at the same hall, but on different floors. The black couples dance with such enthusiasm that the floor collapses, and they literally fall to the level of the Irish.[21]

These comic scenes differed significantly from those in minstrelsy, where stereotypical characters like Mose or Pat appeared on stage only briefly to sing, dance, or deliver stock gag lines. They seldom interacted, and the show had no story line. Harrigan's narratives allowed him to invest his

African American, Irish, and other characters with depth and agency and to bring them into sustained conversation with one another.

VAUDEVILLE: AMERICANIZATION ON THE STAGE

With their urban tenement setting, their concern with ethnic difference and race relations, their often crude characterizations of racial and ethnic groups, and their great popularity among settled immigrants and their children, the Harrigan-Hart musicals represented a kind of overture to George M. Cohan's vaudeville.[22] Around 1900, vaudeville theater stood at the very center of popular culture in the increasingly diverse American city. Through its songs, dances, and jokes, vaudeville integrated immigrant city life in a way that set the stage for modern show business.[23]

Characterized by cheap variety acts that ran continually through the day and evening, vaudeville was designed as family entertainment with a little something for everyone. Like minstrelsy before it, it spoke to the displaced rural migrant coping with daily life in the big city and trying to make sense of the people around him or her. No group had been more deeply immersed in this experience and its expression on stage than the Irish. For them, blackface performance had been a ritual of Americanization, and with the emergence of vaudeville in the late nineteenth century, they remained center stage.[24] But now the performers, their audiences, and the urban life they sought to re-create were far more diverse.

Vaudeville theaters of various sizes and quality sprouted in big-city neighborhoods; and when their performers toured smaller towns around the country, they brought aspects of urban life and culture before a much larger national audience and set the stage for the mass culture of the interwar years.[25]

The vaudeville audience was far more diverse than that of the music hall—large numbers of women and children often attended. According to a 1911 study, New York audiences were drawn from a wide social spectrum.

Nearly two-thirds came from the working class. (The comparable figure for the "legitimate theater" was only 2 percent.) But the vaudeville audience also included vagrants and "gamins," and more than one-third came from clerical occupations. The overwhelming majority of the audience comprised working adults, and more than a third were female.[26]

Because of the language factor, vaudeville attracted more settled immigrants and their children, but skits often employed a mixture of English, Yiddish, and other languages, and physical comedy ensured laughs even from audiences that faced a language barrier. After small, cheap "nickelodeon" arcades were added to many neighborhood houses, even recent immigrants were drawn into the vaudeville orbit, as the new silent films required little command of English.[27] Increasingly, mass leisure was an experience that older immigrant groups like the Irish shared with more recent arrivals.

Vaudeville offered a common ground among the city's working-class ethnic groups, but it also presented a challenge to the native-born middle class. While immigrants encountered a popular culture rooted in their own ethnic worlds, the middle class found their more refined culture of restraint confronted by brash immigrant comedians, singers, and dancers.[28]

Long after 1900, a strong Celtic presence characterized the vaudeville stage, its audiences, and its entrepreneurs, but it was vaudeville's *diversity* that marked it as the quintessential urban entertainment.[29] Irish performers could appeal to mixed audiences by taking the personae of other ethnic groups and peppering their performances with good doses of self-deprecation—a characteristic of Irish humor. Even vaudeville that focused on Irish American themes resonated across ethnic lines, as immigrants tried to grasp the striking social differences in the urban world around them. City life furnished the main source for the material. The characters were stereotypes, but they were based on people of different races, classes, sexes, and ethnicities encountered in city streets.[30]

As they morphed from minstrels to vaudeville performers, the Irish developed a distinctive urban sensibility. The onetime minstrel performers portrayed a variety of ethnic groups—blacks, Italians, Germans, Jews, and

"ST. PATRICK'S DAY IS A BAD DAY FOR COONS":
the sheet music for a racist vaudeville number composed by Irving Jones, 1891.

Chinese—who likewise took on an Irish persona. In the 1870s, late minstrelsy competed with the racialized musical variety shows by adding comic German, Jewish, and Chinese to supplement their stock Irish and black caricatures, but they often still performed these other ethnic groups in blackface.

As vaudeville blossomed, artists from a bewildering array of backgrounds performed "Dutch" (German), Jewish, Irish, black, and Italian acts. This tendency to ethnically cross-dress owed a great deal to minstrelsy. Like its forerunner, vaudeville was a distinctly American art form due precisely to its preoccupation with ethnic and racial difference. This humor could be intentionally crude and even insulting to the targeted group, but its popularity among immigrants themselves demonstrates what the cultural historian Joyce Flynn calls a "cautious cosmopolitanism." The stereotypes served to categorize the multitude of others inhabiting the city. They might console the Irish and other older groups about their higher place in the evolving ethnic hierarchy, while they helped immigrants and especially their children grasp the diversity that characterized their neighborhoods and their daily lives.[31]

While late-nineteenth-century songs and musicals had often reflected tensions between the Irish and the Chinese, turn-of-the-century vaudeville songs and skits tended to focus on racist comparisons between Chinese and African Americans. Kelly and Catlin's routine *The Coon and the Chink* featured the comedy team in blackface and "yellowface," portraying derogatory stereotypes. Drawing on decades-old tropes often employed by Irish American minstrels, such routines were and remained popular.[32] Irish American impersonators of the Chinese had performed on stage in yellowface at least since the 1870s, and Chinese impersonations of the Irish had arrived by the early 1900s. In 1906, Lee Tung Foo toured the East Coast singing his own songs, including "My Irish Molly" in a brogue, while Yip Lee's Chinese version of the Irish ballad "Mother Machree" was well received as comic theater, if not as serious music. Chinese vaudevillians also performed in blackface and took on other personae, but their Irish and Scottish stock characters were particularly popular. Likewise, African American performers often displayed an uncanny ability to mimic the Irish brogue.[33] Again, it was the transgression of ethnic lines—the spectacle of a Chinese performer singing in Irish dialect, sometimes in Irish dress—that attracted audiences.

Numerous immigrant communities sustained their own foreign-language theaters that performed very different social functions from vaudeville. The Yiddish and Italian theaters especially offered ways to preserve valued aspects of old-world culture. By celebrating shared values, these ethnic theaters provided a sense of community and helped maintain group solidarity in the chaos of daily life in extremely diverse cities. Ethnic caricatures in mainstream venues served a very different function, interpreting the mysterious foreign-born to middle-class audiences—and to the foreign-born themselves.[34]

Around 1900, vaudeville was filled with stage "Dagos," "Hebrews," and others. One trade publication referred to a "Hebrew Craze," even as immigrant Jews were pouring into the Lower East Side, eliciting widespread xenophobia among the native-born.[35] Irish comics, singers, and dancers, by doing just such interpreting, undoubtedly perpetuated and exploited negative racial stereotypes.[36]

Some commentators have interpreted ethnic caricatures negatively as a sign of xenophobia or positively as a kind of boundary marking on the part of native middle-class audiences, but the character of the performances likely had more to do with the immigrant audience, and the skits reflected far more than an attack on one or another immigrant group. In many vaudeville houses, both the audience and the performers were ethnically mixed—a variety upon which comedic performance thrived. "The show dramatized the spectrum of humanity in the city," urban historian Gunther Barth wrote, "and the diversity of urban life through its subject matter and variety."[37]

Although the ethnic stock characters were stereotypes, they often bore a resemblance to people whom immigrants and their children were apt to encounter on the streets of the Lower East Side, Chicago's Near West Side, and other immigrant neighborhoods. A critic noted "how quick patrons of vaudeville are to recognize an act that comes near to the truth."[38] These stylized depictions reduced each ethnic group to a distinct set of characteristics, either favorable or unfavorable, with just enough reality to make the scenes familiar, if not entirely plausible.[39] Performers often integrated issues of local interest into the shows—political scandals, strikes, or international events. This perceived authenticity, as much as any slapstick humor, gave the acts their enormous popularity.

While racially segregated seating and admission were common in many cities, audiences comprised a wide range of immigrant groups, and it was in these darkened theaters that many immigrants formed impressions of their new urban world. The great Jewish American writers of the mid-twentieth century, literary critic Alfred Kazin wrote, were shaped not in the universities or in journalism but in vaudeville theaters, music halls, and burlesque houses, "where the pent-up eagerness of the penniless immigrant youngsters met the raw urban scene on its own terms."[40] Greenhorn caricatures were particularly popular, perhaps because they allowed the more experienced immigrants and the Americanized second generation to distinguish themselves from these symbols of their old-world past and to feel themselves sophisticated American city dwellers.[41]

By the early 1900s, Irish performers continued to exercise an important influence, but they increasingly shared the stage with Jews and African Americans. Transgressing ethnic boundaries appealed most to ethnically mixed vaudeville audiences. Interracial romance remained a theme in vaudeville, and mixed-race performers, usually of Irish and Chinese origin, found a place on the popular stage.

One of the most popular acts around 1900 was the Jewish comedy team of Weber and Fields, who appeared in blackface impersonating African Americans, Germans, and Irish. The Irish minstrel pair of McIntyre and Heath was a major influence on them; in 1889, Joe Weber and Lew Fields had joined a company specializing in Irish two-acts. But the team's material was not nostalgic. Rather, they sang of work, wages, and urban conflict. Such comics sailed through depictions of ethnic groups at the lightning speed characteristic of vaudeville's quick-change pace. "Here we are, a colored pair," Weber and Fields announced in heavy Yiddish accents and minstrel outfits. Then they quickly changed their ethnic makeup and costumes to fit the next stereotype—green satin breeches, black velvet coats, green bow ties, and green derbies to signal the Irish—but changed not a word of their jokes. The audience loved seeing the Jewish comics singing "Achushla Gall Machree" and other Irish songs in their Yiddish accents (with words they likely never understood).[42] Audiences likewise considered an Irish comic impersonating a Jewish or Chinese immigrant in heavy brogue hilarious.

"In the hands, disproportionately, of Irish and then of Jewish entertainers, this ethno-cultural expression served a melting-pot function," political scientist Michael Rogin writes. Faced with nativist resistance and depictions of them as racially suspect others, immigrants in pursuit of American identity crossed and recrossed the racial line.[43] Blackface performance spread to church fund-raisers and settlement house programs throughout immigrant communities.[44] Minstrelsy and ethnic vaudeville skits resonated with immigrants creating identities in a confusing new setting. When ethnic skits did not signal outright hostility toward one group or another, they offered immigrant audiences a way to work toward some understanding of one another.

DOWN WITH THE STAGE IRISHMAN

In the late 1880s and early 1890s, a time of surging anti-Catholicism, negative Irish caricatures were rife. But as the Irish gradually rose in the early 1900s, the crudest of the ethnic stereotypes declined in the legitimate theater and even became less acceptable in vaudeville.[45] A more complex character like Mike Haggerty, for example, now wore *both* the laborer's hobnailed boots and a respectable frock coat, reflecting the Irish American audiences' anxieties about social climbing and the tensions between their middle and working classes. This fading of caricatures recurred in the music, theater, literature, and song not only of Irish Americans but also of Jews and other immigrant peoples.[46] One explanation is a quest for respectability on the part of old Pat and Biddy or their offspring, who by the early 1900s had generated considerable social capital and political influence.

The theater protests of which the Russell Brothers riots were a part highlighted a special concern with the status of Irish American women. In 1906, the largely WASP student body at Chicago's Hyde Park High School were planning to perform *Mrs. Mulcahy* as their upcoming school play. They plastered their neighborhood with flyers advertising it, illustrated with stereotypical cartoon features. The city's Catholic weekly, the *New World,* reprinted the flyer and asked, "Are you contented that your mothers, daughters and sisters, the ornament and glory of their sex, should be misinterpreted in this gross, sensual, bestial manner?"[47] Boston audiences received Irish dialect comedians with stony silence. Elsewhere viewers showered offensive actors with eggs and vegetables.[48]

In Chicago and Philadelphia, the Ancient Order of Hibernians launched protests and boycotts against stage Irishmen, and by 1904 the AOH was also calling for an end to Irish comic stereotypes in cartoons and newspaper features. New York's United Irish Societies collected reports of performances "that brought the Celtic people into plain contempt."[49] Reporting on a comedian, a Boston manager wrote to the home office in 1903: "Look out and have him cut his comedy Irishman if your town is strongly A.O.H."[50] The protests had some effect. Comic Irish characters, which had been a staple in the 1890s, diminished considerably.

In 1910–11, the AOH and the nationalist Clan na Gael launched a boycott of the Dublin Abbey Theatre ensemble's performances of John M. Synge's *Playboy of the Western World*, arguing that its portrayal of an idealized Irish peasant society reflected badly on Ireland and Irish women in particular. Riots broke out at performances in Philadelphia and New York, where Irish policemen at first refused to intervene.[51] Film caricatures were also protested. Proposed 1927 legislation would have empowered the New York commissioner of licenses to revoke the license of any theater showing a film that "maligns, ridicules or gives offense to any racial or religious group." Though the bill's proponents were largely Irish Catholics, representatives of the city's Jewish community also supported it. "We believe in liberty," a speaker for the United Irish Societies declared at a public hearing, "but we are opposed to license which openly insults any race or creed. This is a free country. Let us make it free from prejudice."[52]

While watching Harrigan's plays and in musical variety shows, Irish Americans had roared at some of the cruder caricatures; now many of them had stopped laughing. Why? Social class, social mobility, and audience composition certainly are part of the explanation. Subdued Irish comic caricatures persisted in vaudeville, where audiences were more mixed in class and ethnic terms. Audiences at legitimate theater and musical plays, however, were relatively more respectable by 1900, and the Irish

Americans among them were often particularly sensitive. In this sense, the reaction was an instance of what literary historian Charles Fanning has called "the seismic shocks to the Irish-American community brought on by the emergence of a middle class."[53]

Historian Kerby Miller has found that the late-nineteenth-century Irish American bourgeoisie was "morbidly sensitive to real or imagined threats to their tenuous grasp on respectability." The resurgence of anti-Catholicism in the 1890s undoubtedly heightened such anxieties.[54] This search for respectability helps to explain why some of the most brilliant Irish American writers, like Eugene O'Neill, F. Scott Fitzgerald, and John O'Hara, pursued acceptance from upper-class WASPS and were isolated from and even despised by the Irish American middle class, whom they satirized.[55]

But there was another source for such protests: a newly militant, more muscular Irish nationalism. The riots at the Russell Brothers' performances were driven by a broad nationalist mobilization that agitated against ethnic stock characters like the dumb Irish maid. The Russell riots and other such protests were organized by the Gaelic League, Clan na Gael, and the AOH, whose working-class male membership constituted the physical-force wing of the nationalist movement. Now they also brought their belligerent masculinity to the fore in the theater riots.[56] This militant nationalist culture would reach its zenith in the early 1920s as a mass movement embracing thousands of working-class Irish Americans. Performances caricaturing the Irish touched a nerve in the broader Irish American community, not just its middle class. Irish caricatures in the 1910s were relatively more benign than some other ethnic caricatures, but to the chagrin of the community, they persisted on stage and reappeared in early film. In Ireland and in their new cities, Irish Americans were still close enough to their despised origins to resent any slight.[57]

"Some day," a vaudeville manager wrote the home office in 1903, "the Hebrews are going to make as big a kick as the Irish did against this kind of burlesque of their nationality."[58] And indeed similar sensitivity soon spread to other ethnic communities, who voiced their objections. Negative

African American stereotypes were particularly persistent; but in the early 1900s, agitation by the black community forced vaudeville management to limit the number and roughness of "coon" acts.[59]

When Jews later launched their protests, they distinguished, as Irish protesters had, between ethnic humor per se and offensive caricatures. They also modeled their boycotts and agitation on those of the Irish. Dr. Emil Hirsch, a founder of the Anti-Defamation League in Chicago in 1913, highlighted the difference in the depictions of Irish and Jews. "A stage Irishman is funny and not offensive because he is a good humored caricature," Hirsch reasoned. "We wouldn't mind being laughed at in that way." But many Jewish stage characters were more sinister.[60] Hirsch, who considered himself an "Irishman by adoption" and was a frequent guest at Chicago's Irish Fellowship Club, noted an affinity between the Irishman and the Jew. Irish priests and community leaders generally supported efforts to discourage negative ethnic and racial stereotypes.[61] Irish comic caricatures, which had been a staple at the turn of the century, declined in the early 1900s, while "Hebrew" and other caricatures persisted. By the early 1920s, when a second generation was maturing in more recent immigrant communities, vaudeville performers themselves expressed reservations about ethnic acts and hesitated to employ ethnic dress and stock ethnic caricatures.[62]

Irish Americans used vaudeville to stress their patriotism and loyalty to their new home, a tendency that reached its zenith in the career of Broadway giant George M. Cohan (1878–1942). The consummate vaudeville star, from an Irish American show business family, he embodied the ostentatious patriotism of the second generation in songs like "You're a Grand Old Flag," "Over There," and "Yankee Doodle Boy." But while his plays and songs traded on nostalgia for Irish American roots, Cohan also represented the community's rising bourgeoisie. In 1919, Actors Equity launched a strike, but by that time Cohan was a major producer and owned interests in a range of theaters, so he established his own patriotic Actors' Fidelity League and worked to break the movement. While Irish

American patriotism dated back to the Civil War, Cohan's lyrics and his very image on stage helped to make the Irish, as Senator Daniel Patrick Moynihan observed, "almost a symbol of American nationalism."[63] "I like the way you Irish wear your patriotism on your sleeve," a fictional President Roosevelt says to the Cohan character in the 1942 film *Yankee Doodle Dandy*.[64]

As vaudeville matured, became a big business, and morphed into the classic Broadway musicals, Irish Americans continued to shape the performances. The bill of fare at the premier theater, the Palace at Forty-Seventh Street and Broadway, was set by booking manager Pat Casey, who emerged as an arbiter of metropolitan tastes.[65] Entrepreneurs who had developed social and financial capital in politics or gambling now invested it in live theater, the center of New York's emerging multiethnic culture. "Big Tim" Sullivan, boss of Lower Manhattan, whose political outings, parades, and festivals always had a flair for the theatrical, mixed politics with vaudeville. His Sullivan-Considine Circuit comprised forty small theaters that brought vaudeville acts to cities and towns throughout the West. By the late 1920s, as movies displaced musical theater, Irish American theater owners transformed their houses into movie theaters, and a whole generation of performers, such as Jimmy Cagney and George M. Cohan, transitioned into radio and film.[66] This new mass culture became the world of second-generation immigrant youth.

THE IRISH AND THE JEWS

Tin Pan Alley songs, which enjoyed huge popularity from 1900 to the late 1920s, were often based on traditional Irish melodies and themes, invoking nostalgia for an idealized Ireland that city dwellers pined for—even if it never existed. To the extent that the Irish *were* moving up, it was precisely this distance from their roots that produced such nostalgia in the second and third generations. The Irish remained as both creators and subjects of Tin Pan Alley lyrics in sheet music, recordings, and live performances, but they were often in dialogue with people of other races and ethnicities. In "The Kellys," a young immigrant from Cork encounters both the ubiquitous Irish and their diverse neighbors:

> *I went to the directory me uncle for to find*
> *But I found so many Kellys that I nearly lost me mind.*
> *So I went to ask directions from a friendly German Jew*
> *But he says please excuse me but me name is Kelly too.*
>
> *Dan Kelly runs the railroads, John Kelly runs the seas*
> *Kate Kelly runs the suffragettes and she looks right good to me.*
> *Well I went and asked directions from a naturalized Chinese*
> *But he says please excuse me but me name it is Kell Lee.*[67]

Filled with a good deal of self-congratulation and nostalgia for the "old sod," lyrics were less the products of the immigrants themselves than of their children, probing their place in American society in relation to other ethnic groups. Stock Irish characters, who in vaudeville skits had frequently been depicted as drunks or buffoons, were less common in Tin Pan Alley songs, partly because of Irish social mobility. Some songs reflected close relations between the Irish and other ethnic groups.

Tin Pan Alley lyrics depicted Irish men and women roaming the world and encountering a wide range of others. In "I've Got Rings on My Fingers" (1909), a shipwrecked Jim O'Shea washes up on an isolated island, where the natives immediately embrace him as their king. Intermarriage was a common theme in lyrics—Irish men married or courted Indian, Hawaiian, or Arab women.[68] Audiences laughed at the thought of the Irish man in exotic locations, so central was he to images of the working class and the American city.

By far the most common pairing, however, in such comic romantic songs was the Irish-Jewish match, as in "My Yiddisha Colleen" (1911) and "It's Tough When Izzy Rosenstein Loves Genevieve Malone" (1910). The humor, which tended to be at the expense of the Jews more than the Irish, displayed a clear affinity between the two groups. "If at times the results sounded more *klezmer* than Hibernian," music scholar William Williams notes, "no one seemed to mind."[69] Irish Catholics and Jews, two of the nation's most successful ethnic groups, shared a history of oppression in the old world, conspicuous urban settlement and persistence in the new. Between them, they dominated the entertainment industry.[70] The 1912 William Jerome (Flannery) and Jean Schwartz song "If It Wasn't for the Irish and the Jews" conveys these affinities:

> *Talk about a combination,*
> *Hear my words and make a note,*
> *On St. Patrick's Day Rosinsky,*
> *Pins a shamrock on his coat.*
> *There's a sympathetic feeling,*
> *Between the Blooms and McAdoos,*
> *Why Tammany would surely fall,*
> *There'd really be no hall at all,*
> *If it wasn't for the Irish and the Jews.*[71]

Interethnic love and marriage was a common theme in vaudeville and then in film, at least as early as the 1912 silent *Becky Gets a Husband,* but it became particularly popular with the second generation. In the early 1920s, the movie, play, and novel *Abie's Irish Rose* captured the public's imagination. It sympathetically told the story of love between Abraham Levy, a second-generation Jewish immigrant, and Rosemary Murphy, a second-generation Irish American woman. Rose's father, Patrick, a contractor from County Kerry, objects to the proposed marriage on the basis of stereotypes. Patrick is full of ethnic humor and stories about youthful Jewish-Irish fights in the streets of New York. Father Whalen, who represents ethnic and racial tolerance, confronts Patrick on his anti-Semitism. The play was wildly successful, despite some hostile reviews, running for more than 2,300 performances on Broadway, a record that persisted for

LOVE BETWEEN THE IRISH AND THE JEWS:
a scene from the Broadway version of Abie's Irish Rose, *showing
where the young lovers' families intervene, 1922.*

fourteen years. It also set records in Erie, Pennsylvania, and South Bend, Indiana, home of Notre Dame University. By the summer of 1926, some five million people had seen it. The play spawned film adaptations, in 1928 and 1946, a weekly radio show during World War II, and two revivals on Broadway.[72]

With its roots in vaudeville ethnic humor, *Abie's Irish Rose* embodied the second and third immigrant generations' anxieties and aspirations. Irish-Jewish relationships were also featured in scores of ragtime songs, in many other stage productions, and in twenty-one other films between 1921 and 1930, including *Kosher Kitty Kelly* (1926) and *Clancy's Kosher Wedding* (1927). Irving Berlin, who broke into show business singing in saloons on the Lower East Side, had an early hit with "Abie Sings an Irish Song" (1913), whose lyrics tell the story of a Jewish merchant who increases sales among his Irish neighbors by singing Irish songs from his storefront. Quintessentially nostalgic Irish songs like the Tin Pan Alley "'Twas Only an Irishman's Dream" (1918) were actually creations of Jewish-Irish teams. Comic and romantic pairings were a staple on the vaudeville stage, and sports fans followed the antics of Jewish and Irish roommates on the New York Giants and the Chicago White Sox.[73] By the 1920s, rabbis and other representatives of the Jewish community often spoke at St. Patrick's Day celebrations. Clearly, stories of Irish-Jewish couplings resonated widely and had meaning for audiences. What was going on here?

One distinct possibility was that the Irish-Jewish pairing was so unlikely, given cultural differences and frequent conflicts in politics and on the streets, that it was inherently comical. Though they shared city neighborhoods and the vaudeville stage, the Irish and Jews were far more likely to be enemies than friends.[74] Some of the humor may well have been comparable to Weber and Fields singing "Mother Machree" in their Yiddish accents. But the popularity of the songs, plays, and films and their often subtle treatments of these relationships indicate some affinity between the two groups, if not in real life, then in the imaginations of readers and viewers.

Such films and plays were particularly popular with second-generation ethnic audiences in New York and Chicago. As they constructed their new identities, older stock ethnic characters helped them distance themselves from their parents' generation and work out their attitudes toward their counterparts in other communities. Vaudeville's ethnic cross-dressing reappeared as young Jewish and Irish Catholic characters assumed one another's ethnic backgrounds in unsuccessful efforts to reassure their families. Such performances foregrounded the available Irish American woman as a vehicle for both comedy and assimilation. "If the melting pot existed," Riv-Ellen Prell concludes, "it was in the cultural imagination of the 1920s."[75]

The films displayed a preoccupation with social class. Most of the Irish as well as the Jewish families portrayed were at least middle class; others were clearly wealthy. Some projected a prosperous future for the second generation but also anxiety over leaving behind one's lower-class roots.[76]

Ethnic communities felt considerable anxiety over the issue of intermarriage, the ultimate test of interethnic relations. Discussions of inter-marriage gauged the attitudes of groups toward one another. As in the fictional interethnic relationship in *Abie's Irish Rose*, tension continued in mixed marriages: Would the Irish and new immigrants mix and if so, on what basis? What identities would the children of such "mixed marriages" carry?[77] In *Abie's Irish Rose*, Rose and Abie symbolically sidestep the loom-ing conflict by marrying before neither a priest nor a rabbi but a Method-ist minister.

Many Irish-Jewish plays and films seemed genuinely concerned with using interethnic love affairs to depict an affinity between the two com-munities. At their best, they registered a cultural reaction against the in-tolerance so widespread in the 1920s. In the film version of *Abie's Irish Rose* (1928), a young Abie pledges allegiance to the flag alongside black and Asian youths. Given the strength of ethnic and religious prejudice, it would be a mistake to read too much into these images, but the great popularity of these plays and films indicates that many second-generation immi-grants longed for the sort of tolerance they showed.[78]

Underlying all these performances was a striking social reality: there were far more young, single Irish American women in American cities than women from other ethnic communities. They were viewed as more eligible than most for intermarriage, especially with men from immigrant groups that had far fewer women. Memories of earlier marriages between Irish women and African and Chinese American men likely enhanced their reputation as eligible partners—and fears among some whites of racial amalgamation. Irish-Chinese marriages were still fairly common around 1900; the couples often lived either in Chinatown or in Irish Cath-olic neighborhoods.[79]

Irish women who married outside the community were most likely to choose German or British-born (possibly ethnic Irish) immigrants, but their marriage partners came from a broad spectrum of races and nationalities. They were far more likely than women from any other eth-nic group and twice as likely as Irish men to marry non-Irish. Inter-marriage, even in small numbers, was highly visible. By the 1920s, in the large Irish American third generation, rates of outmarriage were relatively high, anticipating later patterns of intra-Catholic, interethnic marriages uniting Irish Americans with new immigrants.[80] Relations at this most intimate level meant the creation of interethnic families—still a rare phenomenon.

URBAN MATINEE IDOLS

The persistence of Irish American cultural influence through the interwar years had a lot to do with film. American popular culture was a potent force for acculturation in the American-born generation, and film was a vital constituent of a new urban mass culture. Movie audiences in darkened city theaters comprised a wide variety of ethnic, class, and regional groups, transcending politics and language. Indeed, during the 1920s and 1930s, immigrant workers and their children made up the overwhelming majority of movie audiences.[81]

Film served to acculturate immigrant children, who were defining their identities in a rather complex world. As a Chicago sociology student observed of the city's Mexican community, "The Mexican children attend the American schools and learn English. They also attend the movies and get acquainted with American culture as it is portrayed on the screen . . . Mexican children are rapidly becoming Americanized and already living in a very different world from that in which their parents live."[82]

The growing Irish self-confidence expressed in Tin Pan Alley lyrics came across clearly in film. As the Irish had learned America's racial folkways through black minstrelsy, so the new immigrants discovered their identities through Hollywood movies, which celebrated the American melting pot while excluding African Americans.[83]

In film's silent era, Irish Americans were directors, producers, actors, actresses, and managers. Early short films integrated varieties of the stage Irishman, as in the *Happy Hooligan* shorts (1901–3); later, in wartime, immigrant audiences watched the heroic accomplishments of model immigrants in *How Molly Malone Made Good* (1915) and *Son of Erin* (1916). In the late 1920s, popular comic characters like the Keystone Kops, Laurel and Hardy, and Our Gang were the creations of Irish American writers and directors.[84] When the motion picture industry moved to Hollywood, most of the large studios were established by first- or second-generation Russian and East European Jews. Dozens of Irish American actors and actresses continued to populate the screen, providing powerful and tantalizing role models for immigrant youth: the selfless Irish parish priest, the smart-aleck tough guy, the Irish American glamour girl. Catholic priests

THE IRRESISTIBLE GANGSTER:
James Cagney (right, 1899–1986), on the verge of stardom, in the Broadway production of Penny Arcade, *1930.*

were portrayed by Pat O'Brien in *Angels with Dirty Faces* (1938) and later by Bing Crosby in *Going My Way* (1944) and *The Bells of St. Mary's* (1945). Their parishes were ethnically mixed, but the Hollywood priests themselves were all Irish, very handsome and appealing. The effect was to reinforce tendencies toward an Irish-inflected American Catholic identity.[85]

No Irish American film actor had a more dramatic impact than Jimmy Cagney (1899–1986). Born on the Lower East Side, the son of an Irish American bartender and amateur boxer, Cagney made his way into vaudeville. During the Depression, he emerged as the quintessential urban tough guy in films like the enormously popular *The Public Enemy* (1931), *Smart Money* (1931), *Taxi!* (1932), and *Angels with Dirty Faces* (1938) and as a tough, crusading federal agent in *"G" Men* (1935). All these films showcased Cagney's masculinity and pugnacity.[86] When immigrant youth took to the streets in New York or Chicago, they likely had Cagney's image before them.[87]

The greatest Irish impact on Hollywood films, however, was the campaign for public purity. As early as 1907, Catholic efforts resulted in the first censorship law in Chicago. They then pressed for federal decency legislation. In 1930, Hollywood moguls, with an eye on the huge first- and second-generation immigrant audiences, developed their own Hollywood Production Code, or Hays Code, seeking the church's seal of approval for Hollywood's product. Written by a Jesuit priest and sold to the industry by a fervent Catholic journalist, the Code was less an industry prescription than what one film historian has called "a statement of Catholic moral philosophy."[88]

Initially the Code was voluntary, so sex and violence remained on the screen during the early Depression. Cagney's sexual magnetism and graphic brutality in *Public Enemy* mark it as a pre-Code film. But in 1934, the church established the Legion of Decency, with its own elaborate code: it gave every film a rating and published it widely every week. Once a year at Mass, Catholics were required to formally pledge to support the system, and many parents used it to monitor their children's cinema viewing. Eleven million Catholics more or less adhered to the Legion's Code at its height, so the industry quickly fell into line with a more rigid Code and an enforcement system, overseen by yet another Irish Catholic. In line with conservative Irish sensibilities, the enforcement body showed far more concern with sex than with violence. By 1938 the new Code system was reviewing about 98 percent of all films viewed in American theaters.

Studios also submitted films and sometimes even preproduction scripts directly to the Legion of Decency.[89] Hollywood's choice of personnel not only indicated the church's influence on popular culture, it clearly signaled the critical position of Irish Catholics as arbiters of decency.

The Irish American contribution to film, then, could be urbane and even provocative: Irish American actors and directors helped to interpret the urban world for an ethnically diverse audience. But Irish Catholic insistence on censoring what they deemed immoral sexual content reflects the "morbid obsession" with respectability that was an important element in Irish Americans' cultural legacy.

URBAN REALISTS

The Irish mark on American popular culture was a product of literacy as much as timing and inclination. Irish Americans were an unusually literate segment of the immigrant working-class population.[90] Having absorbed a modicum of education, immigrant youth were now perched between their parents' struggles and their own uneasy reach for respectability and recognition. Second- and third-generation Irish American authors interpreted the urban experience—to their own generation, to middle-class society, and eventually to the newcomers' second generation. They offered realism, and in the process, they told the stories not only of their own people but of many others as well.

George Washington ("Chuck") Connors (1852–1913), a child of Irish immigrants and the quintessential urban guide, told such stories. Raised on Mott Street, he spent much of his youth terrorizing Chinese immigrants, yet he developed long-lasting relationships with his neighbors, even learning a bit of Cantonese. Connors worked as a newsboy, small-time boxer, bouncer, and sailor, then settled into a Bowery saloon and found his calling as the "Bowery Philosopher." Well connected with both Tammany and the Chinese tongs, he spent much of his time telling stories of the Lower East Side in German, Yiddish, Chinese, Cockney, and Irish dialects. He became a living symbol of the "low life" in the slums of

Manhattan and of the connections between these slums and respectable society.

In the 1890s, a time of massive immigration and imperialist expansion, middle-class Americans yearned to know more about cosmopolitan experiences. In those years, Connors made a living as the "Mayor of Chinatown," providing tours of the neighborhood and interpreting Chinese life for upscale visitors, including royalty. With a foot in each world, Connors fed a developing taste for the "exotic." He soon took his act on the stage, first as a hoofer in the Bowery but soon in a loosely autobiographical show, *From Bowery to Broadway*, at George Hammerstein's theater on Broadway. Every year his Chuck Connors Association held a ball in Tammany Hall with Chinese and American orchestras, a wild mixture of uptown celebrities, politicians, and Lower East Side denizens. All proceeds went to Chuck Connors; the event became a prototype for numerous such balls held in Lower Manhattan at the turn of the century. In 1904, Connors collected his lurid anecdotal sketches into an autobiography, *Bowery Life*, edited by Richard J. Fox, publisher of the *Police Gazette*. By the time he died in 1913, Connors and his association had been taken over by Frank Salvatore, an Italian immigrant operator who styled himself the Young Chuck Connors.[91]

Like Edward Harrigan, Connors was almost a parody of himself, but both men were significant for the formation of racial knowledge in New York. Harrigan and O'Connor lived at a time of close contact and occasional intermarriage between Chinese and Irish. By 1900, the Irish were, as Asian American John Tchen notes, "in a unique position to build up their own image in mainstream society while creating new 'heathens' to displace their longstanding negative image," but they also interpreted newer immigrants, to the broader society and to one another.[92]

If Connors brought the respectable middle class to New York's Chinatown, Finley Peter Dunne (1867–1936) brought daily life in an Irish American working-class neighborhood in Chicago to millions of Americans through his philosopher-saloonkeeper Mr. Dooley, perhaps the most memorable Irish character in turn-of-the-century American culture.

In those years, the Irish (along with the Germans) dominated that great institution of immigrant working-class culture and Mr. Dooley's bailiwick: the city saloon. Given the saloon's central functions as cafeteria, bank, meeting room, library, and social center, the bartender occupied a particularly important role in urban industrial life. Early-twentieth-century Chicago's streets had more saloons than groceries, meat markets, and dry goods stores combined.[93] As in Ireland, married women in Boston, Chicago, and elsewhere ran the unlicensed "kitchen bar" trade, informal workingmen's drinking establishments aimed at supplementing the family economy. In Ireland, such establishments were called *shebeens*, a Gaelic word that caught on in the United States, South Africa, and elsewhere.[94]

While more recent immigrants developed their own distinct ethnic saloons, Irish bartenders and saloonkeepers served ethnically mixed clientele, as the proportion of Irish saloonkeepers to saloons and the location of their establishments indicate. Trade unions, fraternal organizations, and political organizations of all stripes met regularly in saloons. Young couples and their families celebrated weddings in the back rooms. Where workers lacked adequate clean eating space, as they often did, saloons served as cafeterias, offering cheap or free lunches for the price of a drink. To the extent that one can speak of an early-twentieth-century saloon culture, it had a strong Celtic influence.[95] It is hardly surprising that the saloon emerged as an important venue in Irish American realist writing.

Dunne's genius, like Harrigan's, lay in his evocation not simply of Irish American life but of relations between the Irish and other ethnic groups, as well as the tensions inherent in the group's gradual social ascent and acculturation. As with Harrigan, Dunne's aim was urban realism. Dunne told a friend he wanted the world "to see itself through a picture of the simple life of the Irish immigrant in Chicago."[96] Cities were filled with the monuments to the rich and powerful, Mr. Dooley observed, "but there's none but th' widdy f'r to break her hear-rt above th' poor soul that died afther his hands had tur-rned to leather fr'm handlin' a pick."[97] Dunne's columns convey a remarkable sense of place and a preoocupation with classic urban settings. His column celebrated Bridgeport's "sacred sites," like the regular Democratic ward organization clubhouse and Schaller's Pump. The *Chicago Post* called Dunne "the Boswell of the Sixth Ward." For their part, later urban realists like novelist Theodore Dreiser recognized in Dooley the roots of a "genuine American realism."[98]

Dunne clearly based his philosopher-saloonkeeper on real personalities in Chicago's ethnic communities. A product of an upwardly mobile working-class household, Dunne knew the city well. His immigrant father had started out as a carpenter but acquired a bit of wealth through real estate investments and a bit of political capital through his activities on behalf of the Democratic Party. Raised on the city's West Side, Dunne received a good education through high school and went to work for newspapers, quickly rising to first a reporter's and then an editor's position. He joined a bohemian circle of writers and journalists, the Whitechapel Club. While writing for a conservative Republican paper, he created Mr. Dooley as a medium for his own liberal beliefs. Despite early middle-class protests against yet another Irish dialect character, Mr. Dooley became wildly popular. Dunne's national and international fame came with his departure for New York and the appearance of his satires of American jingoism in the 1898 Spanish-American War.[99]

Dunne is remembered most for his political commentary, but his most touching columns involved the widening class divide within the Irish American community. As some of their countrymen and their children moved up in the world and decorated their parlors with the ubiquitous piano, working-class Irish gazed with a mixture of envy and contempt from lower rungs on the social ladder. Mr. Dooley's monologues exposed both the pretensions and the class tensions within the Irish community and in the increasingly diverse urban world. Not coincidentally, bourgeois Irish nationalists denounced his use of a heavy brogue, what one called "the devil of dialectism," and his emphasis on the lives and foibles of the Irish poor. For his part, Dunne often lampooned the new Irish American middle class.[100]

From his vantage point behind the bar of his saloon on Chicago's Archer Avenue, Dooley surveyed and interpreted the political, social, and cultural world of Irish America. Dunne's satires of Irish pride and vanity often worked in the interests of greater tolerance. Assessing the gradual ethnic transformation of Bridgeport's Tenth Precinct in the 1890s, Dooley noted that its "ancient Hellenic" heroes from Mayo and Tipperary, the Hannigans and the Caseys, had moved up and out, making way at the "sacred sites" for "Polish Jews an' Swedes an' Germans an' Hollanders." A "Polacker" had even taken over the patronage job controlling the great symbol of Bridgeport, the "red bridge" over the South branch of the Chicago River.[101]

Dunne's themes—the halting Irish lurch toward respectability, their class tensions, and their deep ambivalence over their rise—also emerged clearly in the transformation of Irish caricature from the 1890s to the 1920s in that quintessential American mass culture product, the cartoon. In the 1870s and 1880s, the frankly racist editorial cartoons of Thomas Nast and Frederick Opper depicted the Irish as grotesque simian characters, at a time when many middle-class Anglo-Protestants considered the Irish far beyond the pale of respectable society.[102] Around 1900, while continuing to look ridiculous, Irish characters softened a bit, though cartoon strips like *Happy Hooligan* and *The Yellow Kid* still contained negative stereotypes that signaled the working-class Irish, like drunkenness and a propensity for crime, along with odd-shaped heads and bodies, fractured pronunciation, and urban slang.[103] As Irish American cartoonists began to draw their community, they integrated the deep ambivalence at its heart.

George McManus's *Bringing Up Father*, introduced in Joseph Pulitzer's *New York World* in 1913, brilliantly captured immigrants' ambivalence toward their own backgrounds and their quest for acceptance. The satirical comic strip portrayed the striving Irish American middle class critically and, increasingly, looked back with nostalgia at the community's working-class roots.

In McManus's strip, Maggie and Jiggs unexpectedly come into some money. The prodding and pretentious Maggie craves acceptance by the Van Snoots, who represent Manhattan's old-money aristocracy. But Jiggs prefers the company of his working-class mates and is at constant risk of

FROM THE SHANTY TO LACE CURTAIN:
Jiggs plots to invite his old buddy Dinty Moore to one of Maggie's soirees. From George McManus's wildly popular comic strip, "Bringing Up Father," 1921.

slipping back into his more authentically Irish habits and attitudes. Both characters have the physical features of their comic predecessors as "a convenient marker of Irish otherness," but they are clearly more sympathetic and less ridiculous. Their daughter Nora, "an idealized, thoroughly Americanized fashionable Gibson Girl," represents the promise of assimilation in the second generation, but it is Jiggs who is the star of the comic strip. Predictably, the least sympathetic character is Nora's insufferable British husband, Lord Worthnotten. Jiggs spends much of his time and energy trying to flee the pretentious upper middle class, where he is a permanent outsider, for the warmth and sincerity of his card games and pub life.[104]

McManus (1884–1954), the educated child of Irish immigrants, was clearly reflecting his own anxieties in *Bringing Up Father*. He based the strip on a play he had seen at his own father's St. Louis vaudeville theater a decade before. *The Rising Generation* was one of scores of popular plays that took as their central theme the dangers and frustrations of upward mobility. Like Irish American writers of the same era, McManus hoped his characters would "begin to take on real life . . . that the constant readers would see something of themselves reflected in them."[105] Readers probably viewed the strip from the perspective of a self-deprecating or anxious middle class. But what drew second-generation blue-collar readers was what cultural historian Kerry Soper has called the "leveling pleasures" and Jiggs's "unapologetic working-class physicality."[106] Like Harrigan before him and James T. Farrell after, McManus stimulated his readers' consideration of their own situation through his comic portrayal of a real social experience. It was an image that they saw every day in the newspapers and came to embrace. The strip remained extremely popular for more than forty years.

Some Irish American writers directly confronted ethnic prejudice within their community. James W. Sullivan, journalist and labor organizer, lampooned the anti-Semitism among New York's Irish middle class in a story called "Threw Himself Away" (1895). Members of an Irish American reading society bemoan the marriage of one of their number to a "common Jew Sheeny," ignoring a member's observation that "for a long time we Irish were ostracized." A club officer soon discovers that it is the young Jewish seamstress who had thrown herself away on their profligate friend.[107] Sullivan's work, not only a parable regarding tolerance but also a cautionary tale about social striving, was representative of a new group of writers who abandoned romance and sentiment to probe the realities of city life and the seamier side of Irish American culture.[108]

In this respect, they prefigured the stark urban realism of Irish America's greatest twentieth-century novelist, James T. Farrell (1904–79), author of the epic *Studs Lonigan* trilogy (1932–35). The premier chronicler of Irish American urban culture, Farrell was also a major interpreter of social class, youth culture, and racial and ethnic relations and cast his unblinking gaze on the community's repressed, intolerant, and parochial side.

Farrell was born to poverty in a Chicago tenement. His parents—a second-generation Irish American teamster and his wife—realized they could not provide the upbringing they desired for him and so sent him to live with his "steam heat" grandparents in Washington Park. This move up the social ladder undoubtedly attuned him to the status anxiety of the middle-class Irish, who were often only one step from poverty.

In the 1910s and 1920s, thousands of black migrants arrived in Chicago, accentuating this anxiety. Farrell's Washington Park neighborhood became a great venue for racial division, the site of frequent clashes as it changed from largely Irish to African American. Between 1920 and 1930, the neighborhood's black population grew from 15 to 92 percent.[109] Having only recently fled the poverty of their old enclaves, most Irish had been in Washington Park for less than a generation when this transition started. "When he bought his building," Studs's father, Patrick, recalls, "Wabash Avenue had been a nice, decent, respectable street for a self-respecting man to live with his family. But now, well, niggers and kikes were getting in."[110]

Much of *Studs Lonigan* unfolds in a succession of South Side Chicago neighborhoods, against the backdrop of the Irish American oscillation between security and terror, their strivings for respectability, and their fear of "invasion" by African Americans and more recent European immigrants. The racial anxieties of Irish American culture emerge dramatically. The Lonigan family hopes that Father Gilhooley's construction of a new church and school will anchor their parish and keep theirs a "white man's neighborhood." As John McGreevy has shown, this defensive parochial conception of urban space later shaped opposition to neighborhood racial integration by Catholics from a variety of ethnic backgrounds.[111]

The trilogy's characters and settings are rooted firmly in particular locations and in actual events. Father Gilhooley and St. Patrick's stand in for Father Michael Gilmartin of St. Anselm's parish. The new church was completed in late 1925 in the midst of racial transformation, and by the late 1920s St. Anselm's was one of the largest African American parishes in Chicago.[112] Yet as journalist William Shannon notes, Farrell's intimate portrait of his own turf stands in for all Irish Americans in an increasingly diverse city: "The boys around 58th Street on Chicago's South Side could just as well have been living on Manhattan's West Side or in South Boston."[113]

Farrell's character Old Man O'Brien conveys this siege mentality—his whole world seems under stress from waves of colored people: "Baseball's the only game we got left. The Jews killed the other games . . . I say kikes ain't square. There never was a white Jew, or a Jew that wasn't yellow . . . And now I'll be damned if they ain't coming in spoiling our neighborhood. It used to be a good Irish neighborhood, but pretty soon a man will be afraid to wear a shamrock on St. Patrick's Day."[114] As African Americans and others arrive on the scene, O'Brien's world is closing in on him, and the prospects for the next generation seemed dim: "My kid here wanted to wrestle in that tournament over at Carter Playground last winter, and I'da let him, but he'd have to wrestle with niggers . . . You got to keep these smokes in their place."[115]

Each ethnic group required its own special treatment. O'Brien berated a black laborer for working too slowly as he loaded coal: "You got to put pepper on the tails of these eight balls." A Jewish customer, angry because the delivery was late, required an operator's charm: "You got to soft soap some of these Abie Kabbibles."[116]

The appearance of blacks at Washington Park, the beachfront, and other recreation venues most irritates Studs and his young mates: "I came around the boathouse last Sunday, and it stunk with niggers . . . They ruin the park . . . That's why I say we ought to get the boys together some night and clean every nigger out of the park."[117] Farrell had grown up surrounded by such racial antagonisms. He later admitted to belonging to a gang called the Merry Clouters, which engaged in attacks on blacks. A friend, Clarence "Clackey" Metz, undoubtedly the model for Clackey Merton in

Farrell's short story "The Fastest Runner on Sixty-first Street" (1950), was actually stabbed to death in a confrontation with black youth.[118]

Eventually, the Lonigan family's only recourse seems to be flight, the occasion for a deep sense of loss reminiscent of the exile from Ireland but now with racial undertones. "Bill, I'd rather let the money I made on this building go to hell and not be moving," his father tells Studs. "This neighborhood was kind of like home. We sort of felt about it the same way I feel about Ireland, where I was born." Yet there was no question of remaining with their African American neighbors. "Hell, there is scarcely a white man left in the neighborhood . . . Goddamn those niggers!"[119]

Farrell's narratives were not the unmediated reflection of his life in a changing South Side; nor were his characters intended only to represent Irish Americans. His strong sense of racial and ethnic urban place, his emphasis on the relations between social groups, his preoccupation with social pathologies, and his rather dark image of life in the socially diverse city were all shaped by his intellectual encounters at the University of Chicago. The university's urban sociologists were riding high with their ecological approach to urban society, a special interest in ethnic succession in city neighborhoods, and their use of an American "race relations cycle" to explain urban history in terms of conflict and accommodation among ethnic groups.[120] Intellectually unleashed as he moved from Washington Park to Hyde Park, the brilliant young Farrell absorbed their ideas and turned violently against his own background, even as he was drawn to understanding and interpreting it. Above all, Farrell sought a realistic depiction of the Irish in relation to other urban peoples around them. Once he left Hyde Park for New York City, his style was also influenced by his conversations with an earlier urban realist, Jewish American socialist writer Abraham Cahn.[121]

Another influence was socialism, which led Farrell first to the Communist Party and then to Trotskyism. In *Studs Lonigan*, John Connolly, the Irish American soapboxer, denounces racism as a phony racket and urges working-class organization and struggle. The fact that the argument comes not from a Jewish or black Communist speaker but from one of his own particularly infuriates Studs.[122] Rare in the Irish American community, socialism was a commitment Farrell shared briefly with youthful black and immigrant writers in the 1930s.[123]

It is difficult to overstate the significance of vaudeville and other forms of urban popular culture in shaping the perspectives of recent migrants to the city, and the Irish American impact is striking. As historian Timothy Meagher concludes, Irish Americans were not simply consuming American popular culture, "they were making it."[124] Their song lyrics, prose, and theater performance focused on the relations among the various groups crowded into urban neighborhoods and helped to create a new, multiethnic city culture. When immigrants from various backgrounds embraced new styles, behavior, and values, they were not those of some distant WASP mainstream, but rather those of a newly emerging hybrid ethnic working-class culture. The Irish provided both a rather strict moral compass for what appeared on the nation's movie screens and also the model for the urban movie gangster and for the Hollywood glamour girl, who became the idols of immigrant youth. At its best, as in Farrell's unrelenting portrayal of his own community and culture, Irish culture could offer a trenchant, transcendent view of American society. Even at its worst, it shaped much of what it meant, in the interwar era, to be an American.

FIVE

THE MACHINE

On September 15, 1913, seventy-five thousand people lined New York's old Bowery for the funeral of "Big Tim" Sullivan, boss of the Lower East Side. It was one of the longest funeral processions in the city's history. The diverse crowd was filled, according to the *New York Sun,* with "statesmen and prize fighters, judges, actors, men of affairs, police officials, women splendidly gowned and scrub women." Tammany Hall's power elite were all in attendance, but so too were Jewish, Italian, and Irish petty criminals, political operatives, and schemers.[1] "Side by side with the man of wealth, who came down to the Bowery in his limousine," the *Times* reported, "came the hobo or 'down and out' in rags; behind the Irishman walked the Jew, the Italian, the German, the Frenchman, the Chinese . . . It was, in fact, a procession of all nations."[2] Twenty thousand people visited the coffin as it lay in state at Sullivan's clubhouse on the Bowery. It was then carried through the streets to Old St. Patrick's Cathedral. Italian families crowded tenement windows and fire escapes to get a glimpse of the boss's procession as it passed.

From his origins in a squalid tenement on Baxter Street in Five Points, Timothy D. Sullivan (1862–1913) went to work at the age of seven as a newsboy and bootblack. Elected at the age of twenty-three to represent New York's most famous slum in the state legislature, he went on to dominate Tammany politics on the Lower East Side during its dramatic

DEATH OF A BOSS:
*throngs of mourners line the streets of the Bowery for the
funeral of Timothy "Big Tim" Sullivan, 1913.*

transformation from an Irish to a largely Jewish and Italian slum. An imposing figure at six feet tall and two hundred pounds, he was good with his fists and good at organizing voters.

Sullivan was a bundle of contradictions, but his system worked. He identified with his Irish working-class roots but organized a small army of Jewish and Italian lieutenants to turn out the votes. A saloonkeeper early in his career, Sullivan never drank alcohol. He built a fortune and an extensive network of contacts in the theater world (where he ran a chain of music hall and vaudeville houses) and in the underworld (where he was deeply involved with gambling operations). Sullivan thrived on the diversity of his home turf—he often showed up for events in the Jewish community wearing a yarmulke. He showed a marked sympathy for the underdog, persuading restaurant and music hall proprietors to employ only union waiters and musicians. Twice elected to Congress, he grew bored in Washington and pined for the Bowery. Late in his life, working behind the scenes in Albany, he vigorously supported woman suffrage and played a crucial role in shepherding gun control and social legislation, including New York's rigorous factory inspection act, through the legislature.[3] "The ethnic coalition that Sullivan put together, and its curious amalgam of party regularity, social-welfare reform, and organized vice," journalist William Shannon observed, "typified the Irish political machines that began to emerge in the 1890s and flourished in the first forty years of the twentieth century."[4]

No symbol is more central to Irish American mythology than the big-city political boss. Machines emerged in New York as early as the 1830s, and in the antebellum period Boss William Tweed (1823–78) perfected a city-wide organization based heavily on the immigrant Irish; its rampant corruption led to attacks by reformers. The Irish turned some of their earliest networks, based in volunteer fire units and street gangs (and often it was difficult to distinguish between the two), into political assets. "As Tammany Hall looked for new recruits to their political organization," journalist Terry Golway writes, "they beat a path to the fire house."[5] As political machines reemerged nationwide in the 1890s, the continuing Irish grip on them was striking, given the dramatic transformation in city populations between the 1880s and the 1920s. In the peak immigration period, 1901–10, the new immigrants accounted for half the population growth in many of the nation's largest cities—where the Irish had already established some measure of influence.[6] What a contemporary journalist termed "the dominion of our Hibernian oligarchy" grew even as their proportion in city populations dwindled. By 1890, machines dominated half of the nation's twenty largest cities, and the Irish were in control of most of them.[7] In the next half century the machine was transformed as Irish politicians strove to maintain their power and influence in a vastly more diverse and complex metropolis.

Irish politicians' power relied not exclusively on their own community but also on their relations with others. In 1910, "Big Tim" Sullivan's district

HOME OF THE MACHINE:
*Tammany Hall on Fourteenth Street West, the seat of all political power
for generations and the headquarters of the Irish machine, 1914.*

on the Lower East Side was 85 percent Jewish and Italian and only 5 percent Irish. But from 1908 to 1933, every Lower East Side Tammany candidate for the board of aldermen, the state assembly, and the state senate was Irish. In 1919, the Irish controlled twenty-six of the city's thirty-five Tammany district leadership positions. And as late as 1932, on the eve of the machine's decline, three-quarters of the Tammany leaders in the district were still Irish, only one-fifth Jewish.[8]

In other cities, where the Irish made up a smaller proportion of the population, the regular Democratic organization was forced to assimilate the newcomers more readily than Tammany. But even in Chicago in 1890, when the Irish constituted only 17 percent of the city's population, they held twenty-three (more than a third) of the council seats and fourteen of eighteen positions on the Democratic Party central committee. As late as 1926, they controlled two-thirds of the city's vital ward committeemen positions.[9] The phenomenon extended beyond the large cities to mining and industrial towns. "After all, it was his party," an Italian miner recalled, "the priest, the precinct captain—they all gravitated around the church . . . the Irish retained the leadership for themselves."[10] Why were the Irish so successful in dominating city politics? And how was it, during the Great Depression, that they fell from power?

IRISH BOSSES AND NEW IMMIGRANTS

Many professional reformers thought they understood the Irish machine well enough: its power lay in an innate, if flawed, political sensibility among the Irish, combined with the ignorance of the migrant voter. An 1896 *Atlantic Monthly* article concluded that the hard-nosed Irish approach to politics derived from their Celtic blood. The Irish lacked "the stolidity, the balance, the judgment, the moral staying power of the Anglo-Saxon," but the Irishman "imbibes with avidity the theory of equality, and with true Celtic ardor pushes it to excess."[11] The "taproot" of the machine's prowess, wrote the early sociologist E. A. Ross, "is the simple-minded foreigner or negro, and without them no lasting vicious political control has shown itself in any of our cities . . . Until they get their eyes open and see how they are being used, the foreigners constitute an asset of the established political machine, neutralizing the anti-machine ballots of an equal number of indignant intelligent American voters."[12]

Others saw the machine as reproducing, in city streets, the personal, reciprocal relations of village life. The face-to-face style of many Irish machine bosses was indeed a key to their success.[13] But the urban boss's relationship with his immigrant constituents was critical. As Jane Addams noted in the most famous contemporary discussion of the system, recent immigrants derived a wide range of services from the machine. They supported it not only due to bribery but also because the boss convinced them that he was a good man, of "simple kindness."[14] Thus the machine was a reflection less of the Irish village than of the city neighborhood. It was shaped by the interaction between two distinct generations of immigrants contending with the vagaries of city life.

Cultural factors—especially a talent for politics ingrained in the national psyche as a result of experiences in Ireland—surely played some role in achieving Irish political influence. Likewise, territorially the network of Irish parishes resembled the city's political districts. But many of the newer immigrants had also conducted struggles against imperial authorities. What singled out the Irish was that, having created a mass movement against British penal laws, they had developed extensive skills in negotiating complex British political and legal procedures. Their confrontation with British domination also produced in them a highly instrumental view of politics. The object, as historian Chris McNickle concluded, "was to secure power by all conceivable means, hold onto it and exploit it."[15]

Their literacy in English (the result of changes in the Irish school system and the suppression of Gaelic) gave Irish politicians a vital advantage over most other groups. By 1900, an estimated 96 percent of Irish Americans were literate in English. This knowledge and language facility allowed them to serve as brokers for more recent immigrants, an edge they employed to maximize their influence.[16]

To impoverished immigrants trying to understand how the system worked, practical economic considerations loomed important. Where they voted, many immigrants had little choice but to respond to Irish power. Saloon, pushcart, and store licenses, as well as patronage jobs, were at stake. In the early 1900s, recent immigrants were largely excluded from such jobs, but the modest integration of a few into the machine through patronage employment provided the illusion of opportunity. "If ya needed a job," a New York Italian voter recalled, "ya went over and saw some Irishman."[17]

Any explanation for Irish dominance must embrace this broad range of factors, especially the physical and social location of the Irish in relation to the newcomers. The key to Irish American influence in the twentieth century lies not in the concentrated ethnic homogeneity of their communities but rather in their presence throughout the city and in their strategies for dealing with newcomers. Unlike other older immigrants, the Irish remained scattered around the inner city. In Chicago, they concentrated in large numbers on the West and South Sides, yet in 1890 they were the city's most dispersed ethnic group. Smaller concentrations lived in wards from Lake Michigan to the city limits and from Evanston in the north to the South Chicago steel mill district. In 1890, on the eve of the new immigration, New York's Irish were concentrated heavily in Midtown and Lower Manhattan, but substantial numbers were present in every single ward in Manhattan and Brooklyn.[18]

Neither the earlier arrival of the Irish, then, nor their greater facility in English wholly explains their political influence, though both were important. It was vital that they set down firm roots in American cities and stayed there, developing elaborately networked social, political, and cultural institutions. The newcomers who arrived in ever larger numbers from the 1890s on found the Irish firmly entrenched.

Political machines helped integrate newer immigrants into urban society, but unions, the Catholic Church, and voluntary organizations were also critical in strengthening political influence. "It was by working in tandem, consciously or otherwise," historian Evelyn Sterne concludes, "that these institutions provided an education and a venue for new Americans in the late nineteenth and early twentieth centuries."[19] Political integration relied on networking, which greatly favored the Irish, who had cultivated networks through family and community ties. The Catholic Church, the Democratic Party, the police and fire departments, the unions, the social athletic clubs and street gangs, and other vital bonding institutions all recruited from the same Irish American communities, which facilitated political organization and mobilization.

Cultivating these bonds took time, often more than a generation. In precisely these years, the newer immigrants' ties to their old-world cultures were strong and their immersion in the new culture rather weak. While they busied themselves creating the sort of ethnic community institutions that the Irish had created a generation earlier, the second-generation Irish consolidated their power and created bridges to new immigrant communities.

For this reason, those with the strongest loyalties to the machine were *not* Irish immigrants but rather their children. They achieved success through a political institution based not on old-country loyalties but on a new urban culture.[20] Tammany's political clubs succeeded, urban historian Richard Wade observes, because they were rooted in the clubhouse, the saloon, the vaudeville theater, and the street: "The boss system was simply the political expression of inner city life." This culture produced unusually high Democratic voter turnout and ensured party loyalty in Irish urban enclaves.[21]

THE OLD MACHINES

Irish American political power has often been misconstrued, due to our fascination with the all-powerful boss, exemplified by Chicago's Richard J. Daley. Yet even in the Tammany machine, which had a strong chief at the top, local bosses exercised considerable influence in their districts. In cities where political power translated into patronage jobs, business licenses, and legal flexibility, a great deal was at stake in gaining and maintaining such power. In the early 1900s, machines' political power was built from the street corner up and resided at the neighborhood or ward level.

Irish political bosses used many strategies, and their careers followed many trajectories, but many of the most successful were saloonkeeper-politicians. The saloon occupied a peculiarly important position in neighborhood political life, often serving as a clubhouse, a space where the local boss met with ward heelers and constituents alike, where deals were brokered and slates hammered out. The fact that the saloon was also a central component of working-class culture, crossing all lines of ethnicity, facilitated its functions as a political center—even as it excluded women and racial minorities.[22]

Local power in Chicago rested with two distinct types of Irish politicians: the "neighborhooders" and the "levee and lodginghousers." Neighborhooders were men of the streets, like Johnny Powers and Edward Cullerton, who commanded respect in part through personal prowess, personal friendship, and ward-servicing methods that became a model for future machine politicians.[23]

In New York, Tammany's neighborhooders included George Washington Plunkitt (1842–1924) and Charles Francis Murphy (1858–1924). In his early career, Murphy engaged his constituents literally in the street, standing for hours on end beneath a streetlamp in front of his East Side saloon. Anyone who needed him could find him there. As he rose in the machine, he migrated from the street corner to a sumptuous room upstairs in Delmonico's famous restaurant, but his door remained open to politicians and common citizens alike. Many ward bosses were undoubtedly corrupt, but as settlement house reformer Jane Addams observed, they also provided a personal connection of sorts to distant public institutions. Neighborhooders like Tim Sullivan of the Lower East Side maintained extremely close relations with their constituents, whatever their ethnic backgrounds, and could often be seen on the street.[24]

Community-focused machine politics offered exciting spectacles and free public entertainments in crowded immigrant communities. "The neighborhood political club was always the center of all activity," New York governor Al Smith recalled of his boyhood community in Manhattan's old Fourth Ward. The George Washington, Thanksgiving, and St. Patrick's Day parades, immortalized in Edward Harrigan's song "The Mulligan Guards," were not only political events aiming to galvanize the community's political attention; they were also entertainments that engaged the whole community, including its recent arrivals. Tom Foley, "Big Tim" Sullivan, and other Tammany politicians organized outings that brought families out of the slums and to the seaside and amusement parks. Tammany seems to have copied such activities from the remarkable reform movement organized in 1886 around Henry George, the hall's most serious radical challenger.[25]

On the other hand, the "levee and lodginghouser" bosses built their political fortunes on the connections between criminal activities and legitimate city politics. In Chicago, the "Lords of the Levee" delivered votes

ST. PATRICK'S DAY ON FIFTH AVENUE:
having started out as an embattled religious ritual, the parade became a
symbol of Irish power and influence in New York and other cities, 1904.

to the mayor and in return he turned a blind eye toward their lucrative gambling and prostitution activities.[26] This kind of environment favored a rough-and-ready brand of masculinity. Colorful politicians like Michael "Hinky Dink" Kenna (1848–1946) and "Bathhouse" John Coughlin (1860–1938) built their political careers on close relations with the mayors. In New York, Tammany's Richard Croker (1843–1922), who led the machine in the 1890s, had graduated to politics through prizefighting and leadership of the Fourth Avenue Tunnel Gang. He had been accused of murdering a political rival but was acquitted when he explained that he never carried a gun and always used his fists to settle any scores.[27] "You had to have a fist like a ham in those days," Chicago's Jimmy "Hot Stove" Quinn explained.[28]

Irish politicians drew on a common class and religious background and, occasionally, on racism to galvanize first Irish Americans and later their new immigrant constituents. New York's mayor Abram Hewitt (1822–1903) was the last WASP Swallowtail within the Democratic Party. Starting out as a reformer with a strong appeal to working-class Catholics and immigrants, in the late 1880s Hewitt came out against the Saturday half-day holiday, against the Knights of Labor, and for Sunday blue laws. He questioned the patriotism of Irish nationalists and the morality of immigrants generally, and he refused to fly the Irish flag on St. Patrick's Day. All of this allowed Tammany to mark the Swallowtails as antilabor, anti-immigrant, elitist bigots. Attitudes like Hewitt's, on the crest of the great wave of immigration, allowed Irish American politicians to position themselves as defenders of the foreign-born, to seize firm control of Tammany, and to dominate New York politics for more than a generation.[29]

Nowhere did Irish resentment fuel machine politics more than in Boston. Here a pinched local economy and a haughty Brahmin ruling class enhanced Irish insecurity and defensiveness. Journalist William Shannon describes a new generation of Irish politicians who "came roaring out of slums and tenement houses propelled by a hard, aggressive urge to strike out at the world, to choke down all inner feelings of inadequacy. Politics was the obvious open road . . . They expressed an insurgency—born of pride, resentment, and ambition . . . no longer the eager pathetic hope for tangible tokens of acceptance." Now the Irish insisted they were not equal to but better than the Yankees who had despised them and relegated them to the city's worst jobs. The Brahmin's day was done.[30]

Boston's most successful boss, James Michael Curley (1874–1958), the son of an Irish scrubwoman, built his machine on just such resentments. He held up Harvard, the great symbol of Brahmin power and prestige, as a target for the Irish, and never tired of flogging the establishment in his efforts to weld together an effective Irish American political organization. His constituents rewarded him with two terms in Congress, four as mayor of Boston, and one as governor of Massachusetts. His political demise came only in the late 1940s, by which time he had been indicted twice for felonies.[31]

Political divisions often accentuated ethnic animosities, and political boundaries provided a tangible basis for racial hostility; the political contest the Irish loved so well could take on explicit racial overtones. In Chicago, a shift toward the politics of nativism and an increasing Republican reliance on the black vote facilitated Irish American political aims:

Democratic politicians told the newcomers, with an element of truth, that the Republicans were a party of ethnic intolerance and privilege. Across the Wentworth Avenue deadline, Chicago's strongest Republican organization in the Black Belt faced off against its strongest Democratic machine in Irish Bridgeport. Close elections often brought conflict during the 1910s and 1920s. In this era, Mayor "Big Bill" Thompson's Republican machine represented for the Irish not only a black threat but also anti-Catholicism.[32]

Originally sensitive to immigrant voters, during Prohibition Thompson emerged as the great symbol of both African American prospects and a wide-open, gangster-ridden Chicago. Born to an influential middle-class family, he was athletic and had been a cowboy out West. Possessed of a flair for the dramatic and comic, he frequently campaigned in a ten-gallon hat on horseback. To shore up support among the native-born and cultivate relations with the burgeoning black community, he increasingly manipulated nativist and anti-Catholic sentiments. In 1920, the Democratic candidate for governor visited various ethnic neighborhoods, campaigning less against the GOP's gubernatorial candidate than against Thompson, for threatening the city and state with "criminal Negro domination." In the wake of the 1919 race riot and a series of exposés on crime and prostitution in the Black Belt, the message resonated.[33]

Aspiring Irish American politicians could achieve a measure of influence through alliances, and federations of local bosses stretched across each city. In New York in the 1860s, WASP Boss William M. Tweed had built Tammany Hall into the nation's most notorious and powerful machine; "Honest John" Kelly's rise to the position of Tammany's Grand Sachem in 1871 ended the worst of the corruption and initiated an Irish ascendancy that lasted for generations. In 1880, William Grace, a rare Irish Catholic millionaire, was elected mayor and was reelected in 1884. In Chicago, Irish-born politicians represented nearly half of the city council as early as 1874; and in 1893, John Patrick Hopkins became the city's first Irish Catholic mayor.[34] Yet in neither of these increasingly diverse cities was political power settled in the hands of one all-powerful boss. Usually, Irish

Americans' positions as brokers between mayors and the various ward-based machines enhanced their political influence.

When recent immigrants naturalized, it was most often under the supervision of Irish Democratic Party politicians, whom the *Chicago Tribune* called the "governing race." Because voting depended on citizenship, early Irish machine bosses were great supporters of Americanization, often working through ethnic middlemen in the various communities of their wards or districts. "Big Tim" Sullivan, whose organization controlled the Lower Manhattan wards that were packed with recent immigrants, "took them as fast as they came [and] flung them into his melting pot . . . He naturalized them, registered them, and voted them for Tammany Hall."[35]

"IN A TAMMANY HALL NATURALIZATION BUREAU":
the urban machine as Americanizer, 1893.

The system in Chicago in the 1890s had a wide scope and wisely integrated a proportion of the more recent immigrants into the process. The Democrats opened a naturalization bureau in party headquarters and each month secured a list of new immigrants. Party stalwart John O'Brien then broke the list down into ethnic groups, sent a letter to each immigrant inviting him to naturalize at the expense of the party, and copied the relevant list to city workers representing the various groups. Each immigrant patronage worker took charge of his or her respective group. The immigrants met their ethnic sponsors in O'Brien's office and were escorted before Democratic Party judges, where they were naturalized in large batches. "In this way," the *Tribune* reported, "the Democratic foreign vote is being swelled at the rate of about two thousand per month." The Republicans' feeble naturalization efforts were "left to a few zealous Swedes in the Twenty-third Ward."[36]

Such efforts were hobbled by greater enforcement of existing naturalization and voting laws, the effect being to greatly slow down naturalization and reduce immigrant voting. Ironically, such laws may actually have facilitated the naturalization of well-connected, English-speaking Irish immigrants, while inhibiting that of most other groups.

As the proportion of new immigrant voters grew and they began to show signs of political independence, however, Tammany and some other machines became less enamored of the naturalization and mobilization of recent immigrants, turning instead to targeted populations, above all the Irish, upon whom they could depend. Low naturalization rates among the newer immigrants worked to the bosses' advantage, as the newcomers appeared to constitute a threat to Irish control. In most cities, only a fraction of immigrants voted between the 1890s and the mid-1920s. Partly because of high geographic mobility, Italians and Poles naturalized and voted in low numbers. More than one-third of the later immigrants returned home between 1908 and 1923; for southern Italians, Poles, and some other eastern Europeans, the proportion was more like one-half. Those who remained in American cities naturalized only very slowly.[37] In an Italian district on Chicago's Near West Side, about half of those present in 1900 were gone only two years later. By 1924, two-thirds of the city's Italians and Poles remained nonnaturalized, even though most nonnaturalized immigrants had been in the city for more than twenty years. Low Italian naturalization sustained Irish power in Boston's North End long after most Irish had left the community.[38]

The effect was to dramatically reduce immigrant voting. In 1911, at the height of the Italian immigration and more than a generation after they had begun arriving in large numbers, only fifteen thousand of New York's half-million Italians voted.[39] In the area around the Chicago Commons Settlement House, while the ward's population had increased from 940 to 1,911 with heavy Italian immigration, its number of voters had fallen substantially. In some years, unregistered immigrants outnumbered registered voters two to one.[40] But nearly all the Famine-era Irish had settled in permanently and naturalized quickly. They and their offspring proceeded to vote in disproportionate numbers and to provide a reliable base for early twentieth-century machines. Newer immigrants and their children began voting in large numbers only in the late 1920s, when a series of ethnic issues, including Prohibition, the drive for immigration restriction, and anti-immigrant sentiment more generally, galvanized Al Smith's campaign and ignited immigrant political ambitions.

As later immigrants entered Irish-dominated wards, the first instinct of voters, politicians, and patronage workers was often to fight it out with the newcomers. The result was election-day violence. In the South Chicago steel mill district, where the voting population was rather evenly divided between Irish, Germans, and Poles, a major riot broke out during an 1893 Democratic primary. In an effort to assuage the various constituencies, the ward organization had slated one Pole, one German, and one Irishman as candidates and secured a promise of separate polling places located in the various enclaves. Instead, the Democratic central committee established only one polling place immediately adjacent to an Irish saloon. Chaos ensued. Hundreds of Poles marched in a body to occupy choice spots in line. Shortly before the polls opened, large groups of Irish and Germans arrived. Fierce fighting erupted, with police reinforcements called from surrounding districts. Possibly because of police collusion, a largely Polish crowd was turned away when the polls closed, and the Irish candidate prevailed.[41]

Machines also turned to ballot stuffing and other electoral shenanigans, simply counting out the opposition. For days after the closely contested 1886 mayoral race, which pitted an Irish- and German-based working-class insurgency against Tammany Hall, New York City residents observed hundreds of uncounted Henry George ballots floating in the Hudson River.[42] As Irish ward bosses retreated in changing neighborhoods, they sometimes managed to redraw ward boundaries, consolidating large Italian, Polish, or black populations into one ward rather than fighting them for control of several. This had happened in Greenwich Village and on the near West Side of Chicago by the early 1930s. Irish ward committeemen split up their bailiwicks to undermine Italian, Polish, or Jewish rivals.[43]

But the impact of gerrymandering and outright vote fraud can be easily exaggerated. In the face of huge immigrant waves, such desperate measures were never a viable long-term strategy for retaining power. Demographics alone argued for a more sophisticated approach. A survey of Chicago ward committeemen in the early 1930s showed that half the Democratic committeemen were still Irish American. One well-educated Irishman was repeatedly elected committeeman in an overwhelmingly Polish ward because he kept an open house and spent all his time serving his constituents. His job seemed to consist of sitting on his front steps, listening to his Polish neighbors' concerns, and trying to address them. He was good at it. Clearly, some neighborhood-level party functionaries held their positions not through subterfuge but because their neighbors continued to trust them.[44]

OPENING THE MACHINE

Since after 1900 Irish Americans were always a minority, ambitious Irish politicians could maintain power only by systematically building interethnic coalitions. This strategy was more pronounced in Chicago, which had a smaller Irish population than New York and an incoming torrent of immigrants. As populations changed in their wards or assembly districts, smart bosses integrated ambitious young immigrants to help them connect with their constituencies and to provide the impression that they were prepared to share the spoils. "Bathtub" John Coughlin and Michael "Hinky Dink" Kenna, the very incarnations of the corrupt Irish ward boss, carefully recruited talented young men from the various ethnic groups—and continued their reigns, as did Tim Sullivan on the Lower East Side.[45]

This strategy could produce conflict, however, when immigrant politicians decided to make their move. So it did in 1912, when Tom Foley, the strongest boss in Lower Manhattan, refused to advance his trusted lieutenant Michael A. Rofrano as Tammany Hall's congressional candidate over an old Irish warhorse. So Rofrano launched his own ward organization, allied with anti-Tammany reformers, and competed with Foley for votes. The resulting political war lasted two years, punctuated by eleven stabbings and at least four murders. Foley's ultimate control rested not on violence, however, but on jobs; Rofrano had little that was tangible to offer ward workers—the critical players responsible for turning out the votes. Within a couple of years, most of the Italians returned to the Foley organization. The lesson was not lost on other would-be challengers. The ethnic composition of the district continued to evolve, but Foley retained his hold.[46]

John ("de Pow") Powers, immortalized in Jane Addams's famous 1898 essay "Why the Ward Boss Rules," reigned as alderman in Chicago's Nineteenth Ward for sixteen consecutive terms, from 1888 to 1927. Originally an Irish stronghold, by 1919 the Nineteenth was about 80 percent Italian. Powers, chair of the City Council Finance Committee and the Cook County Democratic Committee, was a towering figure in Chicago politics, but he recognized the importance of negotiation in his ethnically diverse ward. He sought to incorporate his main Democratic rival, Anthony D'Andrea, a defrocked priest, convicted counterfeiter, and labor boss, but D'Andrea challenged Powers in the 1921 Democratic primary.

The resulting carnage demonstrated not only a deep resentment of Irish control but also how much was at stake in such a conquest. The violence, largely between Italians supporting the respective candidates, featured several bombings and a total of thirteen shootings, including the eventual assassination of D'Andrea.[47] Powers remained in office.

At the same time, smart bosses became increasingly sensitive to the interests of their diverse constituencies. The relationship between New York's Irish politicians and the burgeoning Jewish community represents a case in point. Many Italians seemed indifferent to electoral politics, but Jews showed a strong interest and a dangerous propensity for independence and reform, so they drew the attention of the Irish bosses. In 1886, many Jewish workers had supported the radical reformer Henry George. In 1894 and 1901, the Democrats lost the mayor's office to reformers, in part as a result of Jewish votes. By 1920, Jews made up almost 30 percent of the city's population. Tammany's early advances to the Jewish community were largely symbolic. In 1902, when Irish and German factory workers pelted Rabbi Jacob Joseph's funeral cortege with stones and bolts, a Tammany leader instructed his minions to break every window in the factory. In the 1890s, Irish American machine politicians in Chicago, New York, and Boston all publicly denounced anti-Semitic attacks occurring in Russia and eastern Europe.[48] If they were not drawn together by mutual affection, discrimination pushed the Irish and Jews closer. When Al Smith ran in the 1914 gubernatorial election, the opposition warned, "If a Catholic is elected, perhaps a Jew next."[49]

Manhattan borough president John F. Ahearn (1853–1920), who also built his career on the Lower East Side, was what one Tammany stalwart called a "cosmopolitan," since he adapted easily to an ethnically mixed constituency. Ahearn ate corned beef and kosher meat "with equal nonchalance," George Washington Plunkitt explained, "and it's all the same to him whether he takes his hat off in the church or pulls it down over his ears in the synagogue."[50] When Ahearn died, a Jewish operative reported, "women wept, peddlers turned over their pushcarts, black crepe was draped over their fire escapes, stores closed, and thousands followed the funeral cortege. Prayers were heard at more than one synagogue for this devout Catholic."[51]

Charles Francis Murphy's Tammany Hall administration (1902–24) represented an advance over such symbolic gestures, moving the machine into its "maturity."[52] Born in the ethnically diverse Gas House district along the East River, Murphy left school after the ninth grade to work at a variety of jobs, including streetcar driver. He was a devout Catholic, a puritan who seldom drank or gambled—in his spare time he read church history and *The Lives of the Saints*. Yet he built his early career out of a saloon and social athletic club in his old neighborhood. He soon became a true urban statesman and succeeded the flamboyantly corrupt Richard Croker as Tammany boss. Murphy was ideal to lead the machine into a new era—his genius lay in building a coalition that responded to the city's changing technical and demographic complexity. He had an agile mind and maintained a decorum unusual in the great Tammany Wigwam. His

SILENT CHARLIE:
Tammany's consummate boss, Charles Francis Murphy, at the funeral of "Big Tim" Sullivan in the Bowery, Lower East Side, Manhattan, 1909.

tendency to avoid interviews and the public spotlight earned him the sobriquet "Silent Charlie."[53]

As boss, Murphy recognized the need for technical experts in health, education, and finance. Along with other second-generation Irish politicians, he seemed to relish fighting anti-Semitism. It reminded them of their own persecutions. He abhorred the machine's moral taint and set out to win the support of Jewish voters, and the emerging middle class in other ethnic communities, by cleaning up the worst of the corruption and addressing issues that concerned them.[54]

Murphy was perfectly capable of playing hardball politics. In the World War I era, when Socialists were winning increasing support from immigrant workers, especially on the Lower East Side, Irish bosses first turned to intimidation and fraud. Murphy sent wrecking crews to break up radical meetings; Tammany operatives used the police to harass speakers, banned the Socialists from halls, and fired their supporters from city jobs. But between 1910 and 1917, even in the Irish strongholds of Hell's Kitchen and the Lower West Side, the Socialist vote tripled to about 10 percent.[55] As it continued to rise, especially among Jews, Irish politicians turned toward social reform. They were motivated in part by political expediency, of course, but also by a need to fulfill demands from the Irish-dominated city labor movement. The popular juxtaposition of corrupt Irish machine politicians, on the one hand, and native-born, elite progressive reformers, on the other, is somewhat misleading. Many machine politicians pursued social and economic, if not political, reform goals.

The American-born and Dublin-educated Judge Edward F. Dunne (1853–1937) led the quintessential blue-collar progressive alliance that drew support and expertise from the teachers' union, the Chicago Federation of Labor, and the city's strong middle-class reform movements. As mayor of Chicago (1905–7), Dunne fashioned an unusually broad coalition by supporting school reform and municipal ownership of public transportation, objectives that particularly appealed to the city's Democratic rank and file. He appointed Jane Addams to the school board and Clarence Darrow, a radical lawyer with close ties to the labor movement, as corporation counsel. Dunne went on to a distinguished career as governor (1913–17), but in Chicago the collapse of his coalition ushered in a period of Republican rule and corruption.[56]

In New York, Tammany Hall was originally resistant to union demands because of a commitment to low taxes, but it increasingly courted the unions and endorsed many of their demands, including state child and women's labor laws; factory inspection; regulation of public utilities, insurance, and banking; and workmen's compensation during the first two decades of the twentieth century. Political pragmatism undoubtedly played a role in the conversion of Boss Murphy and other bosses to social reform, but their own backgrounds also inclined them to sympathize with the immigrant poor. Ed Flynn, another New York City boss-reformer, observed that Murphy's social conscience developed as he governed. He "adjusted his thinking to a real belief that government might, through an expansion of its functions, serve the people in new and helpful ways."[57]

Murphy placed honest candidates on the Tammany slate, including two avid reformers, Robert F. Wagner and Alfred E. Smith. Smith (1873–1944) was strictly an organization man, but far more socially conscious than most: in the upsurge of the 1880s, his parents had read Henry George's *Leader,* though they voted for Tammany.[58] He sprang from an ethnically mixed family and neighborhood, New York's old Fourth Ward, where Germans, Poles, Italians, Swedes, African Americans, and Spaniards mixed with Irish and Chinese. As Tammany leader, Smith was a new sort of machine politician, opening the process to the city's Jews and favoring social reform. Although he identified as an Irish Catholic, Smith represented what a *New York Times* columnist called "the great composite"—a broad identity of diverse ethnic groups. He liked to remind listeners that he had grown up literally under the Brooklyn Bridge, with Yiddish, Greek, Italian, and other immigrant languages ringing in his ears. As he rose through the ranks of New York politics, from the assembly to the statehouse and, in 1928, to presidential candidacy, he surrounded himself with Jewish advisers.[59]

Smith was both a symbol and a vehicle for a new, inclusive American

UP FROM THE STREETS:
New York governor Alfred E. Smith (1873–1944)
campaigning in Manhattan, circa 1928.

ethnic identity, based heavily on Catholics but maintaining close relations
with and relying on Jews, and speaking the language of reform at a moment when working-class voters were desperate for change. Particularly
for second-generation immigrants, Smith symbolized all that was exciting
about the city. He made an instant connection with young people from
immigrant families and could sing Broadway and vaudeville lyrics by
heart. The entertainer Eddie Cantor remembered Smith as a "ward-heeler
and do-gooder . . . a young, good-looking guy . . . he was our hero."[60]

Tammany had both its constituency's class and its ethnic interests in
mind. In 1911, the Triangle Shirtwaist Factory fire killed 141 young Jewish

and Italian women; in its wake, Smith and Wagner, now both state legislators, wrote rigorous new factory safety legislation. As early as 1907, Smith sponsored an unsuccessful bill to make Columbus Day a state holiday. In 1912, he and Wagner introduced a bill that banned discrimination on the basis of religion, an appeal to both Jews and Catholics: it passed unanimously.[61] Settlement house and labor activists like Lillian Wald and Rose Schneiderman informed Smith about the details of current social issues; his inclination to address them stemmed from his own slum childhood. As governor of New York (1918–20, 1922–28), Smith opposed the Red Scare and church-supported censorship efforts, and his state appointments were notably enlightened. By the late 1920s, Tammany was opening positions in the city's legal department and on the judicial bench to Jewish supporters.[62] And New York State's reforms echoed in cities across the country. Plenty of corruption remained in the old Irish machines, but many of them integrated new ethnic groups in the 1920s and pursued a range of social reforms.

CELTIC SUFFRAGISTS

When Irish American women took up the cause of woman suffrage, the church and many Irish American men, harboring traditional attitudes about women's proper role, opposed them. In the early 1900s, Irish American suffragists fought an ongoing struggle within nationalist organizations that failed to support women's rights. Most machine politicians followed this line. Meanwhile, nativists opposed them precisely because, as historian Barbara Solomon notes, they "thought 'Patrick' was bad enough and did not want to add 'Bridget' to their problems."[63]

Many Irish Catholics claimed that the woman suffrage movement was anti-Irish and anti-Catholic. The claims had some cause: nineteenth-century suffrage literature had depicted Irish politicians and voters as a major obstacle and featured Irish jokes and caricatures. Well into the twentieth century, middle-class suffrage campaigners contrasted their own marginalization with the political rights of ignorant working-class men.

For these reasons and also because of the church's strong opposition, most Irish women at the turn of the century opposed woman suffrage.[64]

From that point on, however, Irish American women increasingly represented the suffrage movement's main link to ethnic working-class communities. Mr. Dooley's Bridgeport neighbor Molly Donahue was a fictional "new woman"—convent-educated, bicycle-riding, pants-wearing, pursuing the vote—the kind of woman the *New World*, Chicago's Catholic paper, inveighed against regularly. But Molly had real-life counterparts.[65]

Chicago's Agnes Nestor, a glove maker; Mary Kenney O'Sullivan, a bookbinder and AFL organizer; Leonora O'Reilly, a garment worker; Margaret Foley, a hat trimmer; and others helped to make what women's historian Nancy Schrom Dye has called the "industrial branch of the women's suffrage movement." In Chicago, waitress union activist Elizabeth Maloney organized the Self-Supporting Women's Equal Suffrage Association, while O'Reilly helped to build bootmaker Emma Steghagen's Wage Earners' Suffrage League into a major organization. Kenney O'Sullivan raised the suffrage issue continually at national AFL conventions, which endorsed her resolutions in 1904 and again in 1906, while Agnes Nestor led the lobbying in the Illinois legislature.[66]

Class tensions permeated the suffrage movement. In Boston particularly, it was tinged with Brahmin anti-Semitism and anti-Catholicism, and the problems of working-class women remained opaque to many middle-class reformers. Margaret Hinchey (1870–1944), a veteran of nationalist and labor activism both in Ireland and in the United States, said of her participation in a New York Woman Suffrage Party conference, "I feel as if I have butted in where I was not wanted, not a word of labor spoken at this convention so far."[67]

Organizers like Hinchey brought the issue of suffrage directly to laboring men at union meetings, in workplaces, and in the streets. In 1915, during a referendum campaign, Hinchey led a small brigade from the Woman Suffrage Party down to the West Side docks and into the subway excavations to talk to Irish and other immigrant laborers about votes for women. Under a green banner, the group was warmly received when they distrib-

CELTIC SUFFRAGIST:
*Margaret Hinchey (1870–1944), Irish-born labor activist and
suffragist, speaking to a street meeting, circa 1913.*

uted flyers in German, Yiddish, Italian, and one in English with a large
shamrock on top. Hinchey displayed her Irish union card and asked,
"Brothers, are ye going to give us the vote in November?" "Sure, we are,"
came the reply.[68]

Maggie Foley, a tall, beautiful native of Boston's Dorchester and Roxbury neighborhoods, also provided contacts between middle-class feminists and working-class organizations. As historian Sarah Deutsch notes,
Foley "transgressed barriers more when entering the elite parlors of the
suffrage leaders than when she spoke from street corners." Serving as a
bridge between the WTUL and suffrage groups, on the one hand, and
black churches, Jewish temples, and Catholic parishes, on the other, Foley
spoke before immigrant factory workers but also before the Women's
City Club and the Boston Yacht Club.[69]

Frequent conflicts across class lines within the suffrage and women's
movements usually involved second-generation Irish American women.

When activists crossed barriers of class and ethnicity, they often found that mainstream suffrage reformers blocked their efforts to create a broad interethnic, transclass movement. Foley offered herself as a conduit to ethnic workers. "The surest and best way to reach the alien is through the churches," she wrote to a suffrage leader. "Most of the aliens are Catholics and if I could interview the priests . . . you would get the largest attendance and best attention. Of course, this would have to be done by a Catholic to get the best results." She had little luck.[70]

The Boston movement thrived when it went out on the streets, but during World War I, when suffrage organizations shifted to a more legally oriented approach, Foley found herself sidelined. Marginalized and unemployed, she turned back to her own community, receiving help through the Democratic machine. "Margaret Foley's story," Deutsch concludes, "epitomized the possibilities and limits organized elite women's patronage held for working-class women in the decade surrounding women's suffrage."[71]

Many middle-class reformers like Jane Addams and Florence Kelley became involved in labor activity. With help from a largely Irish American group of suffragists working through WTUL, they increasingly won the support of working-class voters for woman suffrage. Once the opinion of their constituents began to turn, Irish bosses generally followed. And machine politicians gradually took a more pragmatic view and bent to women's demands for the vote.[72]

Too often viewed from the perspective of native-born middle-class feminists, Irish American women are often portrayed as backward. From the vantage point of the new immigrant communities, however, these women were assertive and engaged. They helped create political opportunities for other immigrant working-class women.

THE LIMITS OF PATRONAGE

Irish American machines tended to reserve patronage jobs for their own, withholding access to employment and influence over city services from newer migrants. There was a lot of patronage to distribute. Between 1900 and 1930, public sector employment skyrocketed in many of the Irish American strongholds, as an expansion of government jobs and huge public works projects put the building trades to work, fueling patronage machines. In New York, the number of city employees jumped from 54,386 to 148,421. Of these, nearly 52 percent were Irish. In an 1897 sketch titled "A Polacker on the Red Bridge," Finley Peter Dunne's Mr. Dooley worries about the appointment of a Pole to "the notoriously un-strenuous job of bridge-tender" at a point of entry to an Irish neighborhood. The bridge, which connected Bridgeport to Chicago and the rest of the world, was a metaphor for patronage and Irish political prowess. Dooley lamented that the Irish American commissioner of public works had chosen "to re-pose that sacred thrust in th'hands iv a man that no wan' . . . can swear at an' be answered dacintly." Dooley allowed, however, that "th' foreign iliminits have to get recognition nowadays. They're too strong to be left out."[73]

Actually, those "ilimints" often *were* left out. *Dziennik Chicagoski* reminded its readers that squabbles among the other ethnic groups allowed the Irish, "the most notorious tricksters in the entire country," to promote their own narrow interests.[74] In New York and elsewhere, the machines doled out only minor shares to their most serious ethnic challengers. If Tammany served as an employment agency for working-class New Yorkers, historian Chris McNickle concludes, "then bosses conceived of that class as largely Irish Catholic."[75] In 1900, first- and second-generation Irish controlled more than one-third of all municipal employment in New York, Chicago, Boston, San Francisco, Albany, and Jersey City. By 1930, when New York City's foreign-born Irish population had fallen to 15 percent, somewhere between one-fourth and one-third of all first-, second-, and third-generation Irish worked in the public sector—the fire and police departments, the publicly owned subways and buses, the waterworks and port facilities, and the public schools.[76]

As newer immigrants crowded into cities, changing wards and assembly districts, Irish politicians faced a dilemma. Newly franchised voters had to be rewarded lest their grievances against the machine multiply and they become ripe for reform movements and other parties. And some Irish ward bosses did reach out to their new constituents, but most tended to concentrate on what sociologists would call "bonding social capital" over "bridging social capital." That is, their efforts went more into consolidating their relationships with the Irish through patronage jobs and other benefits rather than into sharing such spoils equally in order to establish relations with the newer groups. They doled out enough food and favors to other immigrant constituents to keep their hopes alive, but they retained most of the jobs for the Irish.[77]

By refusing to share patronage across ethnic lines, machines sowed the seeds of their own demise. By the early 1930s, a range of ethnic groups were complaining loudly about being frozen out of these jobs. Why didn't the bosses make the smart move by integrating them enough to undercut such claims?

Particularly in Depression conditions, ethnic groups competed over jobs and other spoils of municipal government. In New York City, Albany, and Jersey City, per capita municipal spending rose by a remarkable 111.8 percent from 1902 to 1932, in large part, presumably, to provide patronage jobs. To integrate new immigrant groups into the patronage pool and still maintain the core Irish constituency's overrepresentation would have meant a much higher increase in the size of the city payroll.[78]

But to reapportion existing jobs—reducing the Irish share of patronage positions—would have undermined the machines' base of stalwart supporters. It would have meant sacrificing bonding social capital in favor of bridging social capital. Irish Americans had generated much bonding social capital in mass nationalist politics, in parish organizations, and as a defense mechanism and a route to upward mobility. Given the timing of their migration, their location in the U.S. social structure, their persistence in inner-city neighborhoods, and their efforts on behalf of other ethnic groups, they had also been able to generate considerable bridging capital. But the two could not always be effectively yoked. Under such constraints, "minimalist" politics—dispensing social services as well as food, loans, and licenses—made sense, but widely distributing city jobs apparently did

THE PATRONAGE TREE BEARS FRUIT: MACHINES REWARD THE IRISH, 1900–1930

MACHINE CITIES	LOCAL GOVERNMENT EMPLOYMENT, 1900			LOCAL GOVERNMENT EMPLOYMENT, 1930			PERCENTAGE OF IRISH WORKFORCE EMPLOYED BY LOCAL GOVERNMENT	
	IRISH	ALL	PERCENTAGE IRISH	IRISH	ALL	PERCENTAGE IRISH	1900	1930
New York	19,926	54,386	36.6	76,734	148,421	51.7	5.8	23.6
Jersey City	1,293	3,052	42.4	4,254	7,297	58.3	5.1	20.8
Albany	530	1,764	30.0	1,128	2,735	41.0	4.6	14.8

Source: Steven P. Erie, *Rainbow's End: Irish-Americans and the Dilemmas of Urban Machine Politics, 1840–1945* (Berkeley: University of California Press, 1988), 88.

not—even if systematically favoring Irish Americans threatened to antagonize the new immigrants.[79]

In New York and elsewhere, the machines' failure to resolve this dilemma ultimately encouraged anti-Irish insurgencies. Italian resentment surfaced early, linked to more general grievances. They had felt the sting of Irish prelates' distaste for their religious practices and discrimination by Irish foremen and straw bosses on the docks and in other workplaces. Italians also held Irish Americans responsible for the 1891 lynching of eleven Sicilians following the murder of New Orleans police chief, David Hennessy. (Significantly, Hennessy, an assimilated Irish American, represented New Orleans's broader white Anglo-Saxon population.) As the editor of *L'Italia* observed of the lynchings, "It is only during elections for public office that these ill-bred knaves accept the Italian as an equal, so that he may vote for the rotten Irish, who when arrived in power, insult our co-nationals or vilely massacre them as in New Orleans."[80]

Tight Irish control of patronage jobs and candidate slating created room for Republicans and third parties. As in New York and other big cities, many of Chicago's Jews and Italians remained Republicans as late as 1926.[81] When second-generation ethnic politicians finally rose to positions of power within the Democratic Party, it was often in concert with Irish American advisers and handlers. Boss Charles Murphy finally began to integrate Tammany in the early 1920s, including small numbers of Jews, Poles, Italians, and others at the district level. At the city level, change proceeded more slowly. Where Democratic machines gradually integrated second-generation ethnics as top leaders, Irish bosses often remained as close as possible to the levers of power. In the 1920s, Caroline Ware observed, New York's Italians "took on the techniques, assumptions, and the manner of the Tammany Irish." When Carmine DeSapio became leader of Tammany Hall in 1949, it did open up more patronage positions for Italians and others, but he was surrounded by Irish American aides whose influence persisted.[82] Growing Italian American influence was realized through the organization of social athletic clubs with close ties to political organizations and, often, organized crime—a model that owed a great deal to Irish strategies a generation earlier.[83]

THE RISE OF THE INTERETHNIC MACHINE

Though Irish power survived in some places until recent years, its decline began earlier than historians assume. The decisive moment for many machines came during the Depression, when naturalized new immigrants and their American children achieved a greater level of organization and challenged the old Irish bosses. The results depended upon the new generation's strength and on Irish flexibility. James Michael Curley, who dominated Boston politics during the 1920s, fell to a new ethnic coalition and recovered his influence only after he had successfully wooed the city's more recent immigrants. In New York, Italians and Jews represented nearly half of the city's population in the 1920s, while the Irish had fallen to less than one-fifth. Finally, Fiorello La Guardia harnessed Italian and Jewish resentment and disgust with Mayor Jimmy Walker's extravagantly corrupt regime to broader class issues raised by the Depression. Then in the 1930s, Mayor La Guardia forged an alliance with the rising American Labor Party movement. Tammany's influence receded.

Chicago's first citywide machine was created in 1931, but not by the Irish. Bohemian boss Anton Cermak crafted a coalition around ethnic issues like Prohibition and immigration restriction. After Cermak's assassination in 1933, however, the Irish gained considerable influence over slates and patronage, producing a succession of Irish bosses and the last of the great political machines. In all three cities, the new organizations tended to be cleaner and more politically progressive, but they learned and adapted strategies from an earlier generation of Irish politicians.[84]

When the nation's most powerful Irish American machine finally fell, it was due to a remarkable confluence of events. Charles Francis Murphy's death in 1924 was followed by a resurgence of weak leadership and corruption, including gambling and prostitution, which weaker and less talented leaders tolerated. Tammany's new mayor, Jimmy Walker, observed of Murphy's demise, "The brains of Tammany Hall are buried in Calvary Cemetery."[85] The Great Depression hit New York, with its huge patronage rolls, particularly hard, resulting in wage and budget cuts. Jewish professionals, only recently integrated into the city payrolls as teachers and social workers, particularly resented the large layoffs. When a rigorous corruption investigation implicated Tammany's flamboyant Walker and forced him from office in 1932, reformers saw an opening.[86]

Even then, Tammany's Irish might have held on if it were not for a great mobilization of newer immigrant voters between 1928 and 1936. By 1930, three million first- and second-generation Italians and Jews made up 40 percent of New York City's population. Al Smith's 1928 presidential campaign drew an unprecedented number of newly registered Italian, Jewish, and other ethnic voters to the polls, while Roosevelt's 1932 campaign planted them firmly in an emerging "New Deal Coalition." The number of New York's voters increased by 40 percent between 1924 and 1928 and by another 26 percent between 1932 and 1936.[87] Reformers, not Tammany, harvested most of these new voters. Turnouts were comparable in other big cities and were even higher in Chicago, where many new ethnic voters and those who had been voting Republican turned to the Democrats. The issues of Prohibition and immigration restriction were both vital to these immigrant voters, but so were the longtime neglect and discrimination that they now aimed to change.

Smith's defeat amid widespread anti-Catholic agitation, including within the Democratic Party, demonstrated that most of those outside New York viewed him as just another Irish Catholic boss. Kansas editor William Allen White found that "the whole Puritan civilization which has built a sturdy, orderly nation is threatened by Smith." His nomination, wrote Methodist bishop Edwin Mouzon, "signalized the uprise of the unassimilated elements in our great cities against the ideals of our American fathers."[88] Thus, the election at once cultivated a panethnic Catholic identity and rekindled the sort of defensive impulse that had been characteristic of Irish Americans since the mid-nineteenth century.[89] Nationally, these newly mobilized voters turned toward the New Deal Democratic Party, but the New Yorkers among them had had enough of Tammany Hall. In New York's 1933 municipal election, the new ethnic voters were presented with a very attractive alternative to the Irish machine that had marginalized them for so long.

More than any other political figure of the era, Fiorello La Guardia embodied the overdue immigrant upsurge and symbolized aspirations for an honest, effective, multiethnic urban politics. Born to an Italian Jewish mother and a nonpracticing Italian Catholic father, and married to a Protestant German American, La Guardia was "a balanced ticket all by himself."[90] He was a recovered-alcoholic teetotaler but opposed Prohibition. He ran on an ethnically diverse Republican fusion slate but embraced a progressive political position very foreign to the old GOP. Tammany's Democrats smoothed La Guardia's way by splitting along factional lines. Projecting an idealism and energy sorely lacking in aging Tammany politicians, he swept through New York's crowded ethnic neighborhoods, campaigned in half a dozen languages, and galvanized a tough new reform organization that rivaled the old Irish machine in turning out the new voters. "His is the keenest political mind that has been operating in many a day," Tammany mayor Jimmy Walker observed, "but he's a great showman too. His rivals talk English, good, bad, or indifferent. But Fiorello is the cosmopolite of this most cosmopolitan city. In the ghetto he talks Yiddish . . . In Little Italy he talks Italian . . . When he talks of the Germans, he can do so in their own language."[91]

Part of LaGuardia's genius lay precisely in the fact that he was *not* a typical reformer. He well understood deep ethnic tensions and was not above exploiting them to optimize his position. When the smoke cleared in the 1933 election, La Guardia had garnered 40 percent of the popular vote and Tammany was clearly on borrowed time. Although he drew ethnic voters and some of the native-born middle class, all of them tired of Tammany, his greatest support came from the long-suffering Italians, who gave him more than 80 percent of their vote. He repeated his success in 1937 and again in 1941, running with the support of the American Labor

THE ONE-MAN BALANCED TICKET:

Fiorello La Guardia (1882–1947) on the campaign trail in Manhattan, circa 1933.

Party and effectively freezing Tammany out for twelve years running. "For all practical purposes Tammany Hall was finished," historian Jay Dolan concluded, "and along with it, the Irish ascendancy in New York City politics."[92]

The reform-oriented machine actively naturalized and registered the recent immigrants, turning out their vote in large numbers in areas where Tammany had sought to avoid their participation. Election violence was common. Italians and Hispanics in Harlem embraced the new Labor Party, supporting first La Guardia for mayor and then Vito Marcantonio for Congress. The remaining Irish continued to support Tammany and resented La Guardia as "anti-Irish."[93] In a striking metaphor for the shift in power, Tammany's mortgage on its famous Wigwam was sold to the progressive, Jewish-led International Ladies' Garment Workers' Union.[94]

By rigorously enforcing civil service laws, La Guardia integrated more Italians and Jews into city jobs, nudging out Irish patronage workers. The proportion of Irish department heads fell from 40 percent to 5 percent.[95] Using the heavily Jewish and Italian needle trades unions and a variety of ethnic organizations to mobilize New Deal voters, he convinced Roosevelt to place much of the city's federal works employment under his control. The Irish remained entrenched in the police and fire departments, but the reforms and the cooperation of the federal government deprived Tammany of thousands of jobs, the cement that had held the machine together for so long.

La Guardia's ascent and the hiring of other ethnic groups for city jobs during a period of unemployment bred resentment among the Irish. Their divergent positions on the Spanish Civil War, in which the Catholic Church opposed and most Jews supported the new republic, undoubtedly aggravated tensions between Irish and Jewish Americans, but the main flashpoints had to do with practical matters, above all jobs.

Particularly in teaching, social work, and other positions requiring college education, second-generation Jews excelled. In 1900, only 11 percent of New York's teachers were Jewish; by 1930, the number was 44 percent. As Jewish women entered teaching, they displaced the Irish, and the older instructors resented their intrusion into what had been largely their domain. As Jewish teachers unionized during the 1930s, they confronted entrenched Irish American administrators and even anti-Semitism among some older Irish and German teachers. The left-wing character of many teachers and union activists, and the upsurge of radicalism, more generally raised fears of communism among Irish Catholics and eventually split New York teachers into rival unions.[96]

The anti-Semitic demagogue Father Charles E. Coughlin (1891–1979) thrived on the resulting anxiety, and the persistent defensiveness common to Irish American communities resurfaced with great force. "We see all around us the people of other races forging ahead," *The Irish World* observed.[97] Coughlin had started out denouncing the Klan, castigating the rich, and supporting FDR's New Deal, but his Christian Front fulminations turned increasingly paranoid and reactionary. He tapped into deep insecurities in the Irish American working and lower middle class. They had enjoyed strong local unions in the AFL and political capital in Democratic machines like Tammany Hall. Steeped in the parochial culture of their parishes and local voluntary associations, they faced a bewildering wall of change in the 1930s—CIO industrial unionism, a modest upsurge of political radicalism in Labor Party and Communist activities, and the entry of the new immigrants' second generation into politics.

Many resented the ethnic transformation of city neighborhoods as second-generation Jews and Italians moved in, to be followed after World War II by a massive influx of Puerto Rican and African American migrants. The Irish remained anchored to their old moorings—family, parish, and neighborhood, Tammany machine politics, and the conservative AFL unions. Feeling their way of life threatened on all sides, some responded to a leader, particularly a priest, like Father Coughlin.[98] In desperate economic conditions, many Irish Americans turned to their own: to the church for charity, to the Democratic Party for patronage or access to city relief; to the craft unions with their seniority systems and apprenticeships for the few jobs still around.

Anti-Semitism fed on status insecurities, particularly in Boston, where the Irish had never achieved the level of acceptance they had in other cities and Brahmin anti-Catholicism persisted. In 1936, devastated by the Depression, Irish South Boston and Charlestown turned in votes of over 11 percent for Coughlin's right-wing Union Party candidates. Throughout the 1930s and early 1940s, Irish attacks on Jewish youth and even on synagogues proliferated in Boston and New York.[99] While Boston's William Cardinal O'Connell condemned Coughlin, the New York diocese remained largely silent, even in the face of Jewish calls for the church to speak out. Coughlin attracted Germans and others, particularly among older skilled blue-collar workers, but his was essentially an Irish

Catholic organization. With working-class and lower-middle-class members as well as lawyers, priests, and college-educated leaders, Coughlin's constituency was a cross-section of New York's Irish community.[100]

During World War II, May Quinn, a right-wing teacher activist in New York's public schools, drew attacks from Jewish Americans and liberal groups and considerable support from the Catholic Church and the Irish American community.[101] During the McCarthy era, Irish Catholic clerics and union activists organized and led attacks on left-wing unions and other groups with large Jewish constituencies. A new conservative icon emerged: the Irish FBI agent.[102] Yet the concept of a pervasive "Irish-Coughlinite" worldview oversimplifies the situation. Once again, the community was divided. Many Irish Catholics strongly opposed the Christian Front and Father Coughlin, notably through unions and publications like *Commonweal* and the *Catholic Worker*, but the burst of anti-Semitism strained Jewish-Irish relations.[103]

La Guardia's reform of the civil service, as well as the Democratic Party's ambitions to serve more ethnic groups, had lessened Irish power. But ironically, as Irish American political influence wavered at the city level, it surged at the national level. Irish-controlled Democratic county organizations that were friendly to Roosevelt—in the Bronx and Brooklyn, Albany, Jersey City, and elsewhere—received much federal patronage. Here Irish candidates continued to win elections, and New Dealers like Edward Flynn of the Bronx and FDR's postmaster general James Farley held posts high in the national party hierarchy. More Irish Catholics were elected to Congress than ever, and Roosevelt appointed more Irish Catholics to his cabinet than any of his predecessors and many more Catholics, mainly Irish, to the federal bench than the three previous presidents combined.[104]

During the Depression, Chicago's emerging Democratic machine faced the same fiscal and political crises as New York's but with very different results. Chicago's heavy industrial and manufacturing base had collapsed, throwing huge numbers of white ethnic workers out of jobs. Conditions in the large African American community were much worse. But unemployment and ethnic political mobilization only consolidated the Chicago machine, though its ethnic composition changed significantly.[105]

Long the most powerful group in the city's Democratic Party, the Irish had established regional machines throughout Chicago and forged alliances with a succession of mayors, but they had never consolidated these bases to achieve the kind of power that New York's Irish had realized by the 1890s. Where they had influence in 1900, the Chicago Irish slated their own candidates and kept most of the spoils for themselves. This practice retarded integration of the new immigrant groups into the slowly evolving machine. It took a gruff, talented Czech politician to build the citywide multiethnic machine for which Chicago became famous, albeit with the vital support of a faction of Irish bosses.

Born in Bohemia, Anton Cermak (1873–1933) grew up in the mining town of Braidwood, Illinois, but lived most of his life in the heart of Chicago's Czech community. Confrontations between the entrenched Irish and the more recent Slavic youth were common, but Cermak emerged as a leader, as much through his quick wit as through his strength and toughness. He was also particularly attuned to immigrant sensibilities. These characteristics served him well in his project of creating an interethnic machine. Before World War I, Cermak had emerged as the key figure in the United Societies for Local Self-Government, which sought to simplify the laborious system under which ethnic fraternal groups applied for liquor licenses. In 1918, the United Societies took up a desperate fight against Prohibition, mobilizing groups that had hitherto shown little interest in politics: the issue encouraged various ethnic groups to conclude that they had much in common with one another. Working as a lieutenant for Democratic boss George Brennan, Cermak hit upon the brilliant stroke of holding a series of referenda on Prohibition. These demonstrated massive opposition across wards made up of a wide array of ethnic groups.[106]

In the 1927 mayoral election, the Republican "Big Bill" Thompson sought to regain the office he had held in 1915–23. Thompson, a shrewd politician, had incorporated a range of social groups into his Republican machine, but he relied heavily on the large and well-organized African American electorate, which in previous elections had turned out for him in huge pluralities. "The Black Belt of Chicago," Carl Sandburg wrote, "is probably the strongest effective unit of political power, good or bad, in America."[107]

His Democratic opponent was a rare Irish reformer, William Dever. The Irish-dominated Democratic machine staked its prospects on an explicitly racial appeal to whites; in the wake of the city's 1919 riot and subsequent racial violence, that appeal struck a responsive chord. Dever would win, Cook County party chair George Brennan announced publicly, because the people of Chicago would never "turn the city over to be ruled by the Black Belt." Chicago, he concluded in another speech, "is a white man's town." Racist posters appeared throughout the city, and sound trucks rolled through neighborhoods blaring the song "Bye, Bye, Blackbird." The basic issue in the election, South Side Irish boss Michael Igoe declared, was "Shall the white people continue to rule Chicago?" The *Chicago Herald Examiner* called the campaign "the largest torrent of appeals to race and religious prejudice ever known in Chicago's history."[108] Thompson garnered 93 percent of the black vote by emphasizing the Democrats' hostility to blacks. He held on to a substantial number of Italians and Jews as well as older Protestant immigrants, winning handily.[109]

The lesson was not lost on Cermak, who made his move when the heavy-handed party chair Brennan died in 1928. He broke with the racism of the 1927 election and welded together not only the Jewish and Slavic constituencies, united by a common hostility to the Irish, but also some Irish dissidents. Rather than try to defeat the Irish in open confrontation, he accentuated Irish factionalism and then incorporated a powerful minority led by West Side boss Pat Nash (1863–1943). Cermak established a new countywide organization; unlike Tammany, it integrated a vast array of ethnic groups from the executive down to the precinct level. Cermak doled out patronage on the basis of election performance more than ethnicity, and the overwhelmingly Irish candidates of Brennan's reign were replaced by slates representing the city's largest ethnic groups.[110]

As in other big cities, Al Smith's 1928 campaign galvanized Chicago's newer ethnic groups, but much of the impetus was local. Cermak, who actually ran ahead of Smith on the ticket, stressed issues of concern to ethnic groups, like Prohibition, immigration restriction, and blue laws. In the process, he assembled a coalition of often-warring groups by focusing on goals they shared.[111]

By late 1930, Cermak had built Chicago's first effective interethnic machine. Like Jimmy Walker's corrupt Tammany administration in New York, the flamboyantly corrupt Thompson had managed to make Chicago look ungovernable; and just as general disgust with Walker opened the way for La Guardia, Thompson inadvertently paved the way for Cermak by fighting the 1931 campaign on a platform of 100 percent Americanism. He called Cermak "Pushcart Tony" and derided his and other Slavic names on his ticket. The strategy was political suicide: many of Chicago's huge population of first- and second-generation immigrants were now naturalized and registered to vote. Poles, Czechs, and others took Thompson at his word, seeing the election as a contest between "the Slavic and the Anglo Saxon," and turned out in huge numbers for Cermak. *Dziennik Chicagoski* told its readers that in voting for Cermak, they were voting "for their own interests, for the due recognition of Poles."[112]

The results of the 1931 Chicago mayoral election were striking. Poles, Czechs, and Lithuanians registered large pluralities for Cermak, who won even the few ethnic groups that had gone for Thompson in 1927. Depression conditions and the hope for a "New Deal" certainly cemented the newer ethnic groups into Chicago's new coalition. In the 1932 national election, Poles, Italians, Lithuanians, Czechs, and Yugoslavs voted on average 76 percent Democratic, up from 40 percent in 1924. Jews voted 73 percent Democratic, up from only 19 percent.[113] But it was the 1928 election that had first turned ethnic voters toward the Democrats and laid the foundation for an interethnic Democratic machine. As in New York, the electoral shift was less a turn away from the GOP than a massive mobilization of new voters; thereafter any new machine would have to be an ethnic coalition, not a creature of the Irish bosses.

Cermak lost only two of the city's major ethnic groups—African Americans and Italians. As mayor, he integrated Italian ward committeemen, placed Italians on the 1932 ticket, and renounced the Irish bosses' tradition of racism.[114] He made overtures to Irish Americans by allying closely with Pat Nash, one of the few Irish politicians considered friendly to blacks. Cermak cultivated connections in the black community, but once elected, he fired black Republican patronage workers and clamped down on South Side gambling and policy operations. "The entire city is closed up like a drum," the *Defender* observed. "The lid went on five minutes after it was certain Mayor Thompson had lost."[115]

Cermak was open to a new relationship with the black community, but only if its political allegiances changed. Over the next three decades, the more ambitious black politicians constructed a strong Democratic machine in the ghetto, and Black Belt policy bosses wasted little time. Within a year the major operators were in Democratic ranks, and the rackets were open again. By 1936, Chicago's African American community was part of a durable Democratic coalition that would persist into the twenty-first century.[116]

But the Irish were never far from the levers of power. If Cermak was the architect of the new machine, Pat Nash was its engineer. Nash had spent decades organizing for the party but was alienated from the mainline Irish politicians. Cermak turned to him to chair the new county organization. When Cermak was assassinated in 1933, Nash remained behind the scenes but controlled city politics for a generation. The Democratic-controlled city council elected Nash's nominee, Ed Kelly, to the mayor's position. An efficient administrator with an engineering background, Kelly would hold office through World War II. Working closely with Nash, Kelly demonstrated the new machine's prowess with a 630,000-vote victory (83 percent Democratic) and a truly massive turnout (89 percent of registered voters) in the 1935 municipal election and in FDR's victory in federal elections the following year. The key to this achievement was the naturalization and mobilization of thousands of immigrant voters, but Kelly also publicly supported racially integrated housing and schools in a successful effort to draw more blacks to the Democratic Party.[117]

This performance assured the Kelly-Nash machine tight control over federal public works jobs. In the wake of their 1936 election feat, they reaped an unprecedented windfall of patronage positions: in 1936, Chicago had sixty thousand city jobs and an estimated sixty-eight thousand WPA jobs under the control of the Cook County Democratic Party. Political appointees were assessed at 2 percent of their salaries to finance party campaigns and were expected to get out the vote and encourage people to attend rallies and other political events. Precinct-level operatives carefully facilitated applications for federal assistance and then returned to recipients to collect their votes. The machine continued to favor Irish Americans in certain areas. The city's police and fire departments, for example, remained firmly under their control. But in the interests of party strength, Kelly and Nash carefully integrated all the major groups into the party machinery and other city jobs. They particularly targeted southern and eastern Europeans, who were still smarting over the Irish seizure of power.[118]

The Chicago machine flourished. For the next half century, strong Irish-dominated South and West Side political organizations retained control over the mayor's position and much of the county board and city council. But they did so by paying careful attention to the ethnic groups that Cermak and Nash had so skillfully woven together during the 1920s.

The Irish came late to effective citywide political power in Chicago, and they did so only by ethnically balancing the machine. The model proved extremely durable, however, and Chicago's Irish politicians retained considerable control long after New York's had lost theirs.[119] New York's New Deal coalition began to unravel after World War II, but Chicago's Irish-led multiethnic machine persisted until the late 1970s, some would say down to the recent past. Irish mayors occupied Chicago's city hall for eighty-two of the eighty-eight years between 1933 and 2011. (In 1983, Chicago elected Harold Washington as its first black mayor, the result not only of massive minority voter mobilization but also of factionalism among the ruling Irish.) As late as 1970, Irish American politicians, representing a tiny proportion of the city's population, held more than one-third of its key ward committee positions. Chicago's diversity may have actually made Irish politicians more skillful.[120]

Irish American politicians used the machine to maximize their group's influence, often at the expense of other immigrants, but they had little choice but to integrate newcomers at some level if they were to maintain their power. The process had very different effects from one city to another. The massive mobilization of ethnic voters for Smith in 1928 and then for FDR in the early 1930s provided a broad base for machines that succeeded in making the interethnic turn, as in Chicago. The more intransigent organizations, like Tammany, receded and were replaced in the 1930s by new multiethnic political coalitions.

Machine politicians could display ethnic group and party loyalty, a remarkable degree of political efficiency, and even an ethic of public service. But the Irish American orientation to urban politics was largely instrumental: to gain power and influence for the few, and to provide jobs and services for a larger, loyal group. This approach frequently involved corruption, bribery, and undemocratic procedures, but Irish American machine politicians provided basic services to immigrants, and over time, self-interest forced them to assimilate newer groups into their organizations. In this sense, the machine was a flawed system for power sharing among ethnic groups but a vital mechanism for integrating them through naturalization, legal representation, and employment.[121] Later ethnic groups easily grasped and adopted the model.

The problem, of course, was that so long as the Irish machine retained its grasp on party organizations, slating, and patronage jobs, it was also a way to exclude non-Irish ethnic and racial groups and to enrich the Irish American middle class. It integrated some ethnic groups more readily than others; African American and recent Latino communities were marginalized for decades and suffered as a result.

The Irish American political machine embodied contradictory tendencies, but it stood at the center of the American city's emerging multiethnic political culture. As late as the 1960s the Irish remained disproportionately engaged in electoral politics.[122] But where Irish American political influence remained potent, it did so only through extensive integration of the newer groups: first Jews, Italians, and eastern Europeans, and later African Americans and Hispanics. Because of the long Irish dominance of city politics, many felt its loss all the more keenly. "New York used to be an Irish city," wrote Daniel Patrick Moynihan in the early 1960s, "or so it seemed. There were sixty or seventy years when the Irish were everywhere. They *felt* it was their town. It is no longer and they know it."[123]

SIX

THE NATION

O n March 5, 1916, New York Supreme Court judge Daniel Cohalan stepped to the podium at the Irish Race Convention. More than two thousand nationalist leaders had descended on New York from Nome to Tampa—"all that is best in the Irish race," according to Cohalan. The purpose of the event was to demonstrate the distinctive history and culture of the Irish people, so as to display the respectable character of the Irish American community. Amid merciless attacks on the British Empire, Cohalan and other speakers memorialized the contributions of the Irish race to American and world civilization.[1]

Four years later, on August 2, 1920, the black nationalist leader Marcus Garvey took the podium at the international convention of his Universal Negro Improvement Association in Harlem. For six years, the group had been recruiting among African Americans, advocating black pride and solidarity among the African diaspora communities and urging African Americans to go "back to Africa." Now, however, Garvey had another movement in mind. He read from a telegram he had sent to Éamon de Valera, the first president of the new Irish republic, invoking the historic struggle of the Irish people against British imperialism and urging support for their efforts. "We believe Ireland should be free," Garvey wrote, "even as Africa shall be free for the Negroes of the world."[2] When he sent greetings to the new republic on behalf of African peoples throughout the world, *The New York Times* observed, the twenty thousand delegates "roared their approval."[3]

BLACK MOSES:
Marcus Garvey (1887–1940), pioneer black nationalist, orator, and admirer of the Irish fight for freedom, 1924.

The social distance between these gatherings of Irish and African American nationalists was less than we might assume today. Domestic and international events between 1916 and 1920 seemed to offer the possibility of solidarity among subject peoples.[4] Small nations throughout the world were contemplating the decline of the old empires and the rise of new republics. The timing of the Irish Race Convention, in March 1916, was particularly propitious: the Easter Rising was already being planned in Dublin, war sentiment was rising in the United States, the Russian Revolution was on the horizon, and the greatest upsurge in American labor history was gathering steam.

The migration experience; the burning memory of the Famine; the integration of later immigrants from Ireland into social, political, and religious organizations; the ongoing depredations of British colonialism; the persistence of nativism and anti-Catholicism in the new world—all these factors had nurtured a diasporic nationalism in late-nineteenth-century Irish American enclaves. Their bitter exile after the Civil War had produced what historian Thomas N. Brown has called a "nursery of nationality." Irish nationalism thrived in the era of expansive class conflict, deeply rooted in Irish American working-class communities and closely associated with the era's sweeping labor reform movement. The Irish colonial legacy, Anglo-Saxon triumphalism, and continuing discrimination inclined many Irish Catholics to resist the imperialism that ushered in the new century.[5]

But by 1900, Irish nationalism in the United States had largely dissipated. Writing in 1896, newspaper editor Patrick Ford (1837–1913), who had raised huge sums for the movement from immigrant laborers, gave up on the prospect of finding American support: "I judged it would not be wise to approach any of our 'Irish Irishmen' in the United States . . . These men, as a class, must not be expected to do anything that will not repay themselves, and with interest."[6]

At the turn of the century, the American-born second and third generations outnumbered the Irish-born by three to one. Immersed in making a living, in building their own institutions, and in navigating rough-and-tumble urban politics, most Irish Americans viewed old-country affairs at a considerable distance. The Ancient Order of Hibernians' membership declined. Even in hardscrabble mining and factory towns like Butte, Montana, and Lowell, Massachusetts, the new "lace curtain" generation was detaching itself from the Irish struggle. A hard core of revolutionary nationalists continued to operate through Cohalan's secretive Clan na Gael, but they did not get much of a hearing from the great mass of Irish Americans.[7]

But during and after World War I, Irish American nationalism underwent a huge resurgence. Heralded by Cohalan and Garvey, it had roots in the romantic nationalism surrounding the Easter Rising of 1916 but also in social eruptions around the world. The new Irish nationalism thrived amid domestic labor mobilization, diasporic nationalism in other ethnic communities, and transnational revolutionary and anticolonial movements. International and local events not only reenergized Irish American nationalists, they brought them into contact with other racial and ethnic groups who were experiencing these events in their own terms.

During World War I and the postwar reaction, many Irish Americans embraced *both* a radical commitment to the emerging Irish nation *and* an intense American patriotism. Their nineteenth-century trials had enhanced their attachment to crowded American cities and undoubtedly strengthened their determination to be accepted as good Americans. When the Grand Army of the Republic, a Civil War veterans' organization, launched a program at the turn of the century to provide flags to each school, Irish Catholic schools snapped them up in large numbers. A similar program later established by the Ancient Order of Hibernians aimed to give every parochial schoolroom its own flag.[8] During World War I, many Irish Americans volunteered and distinguished themselves in combat, but this same period saw the peak of revolutionary Irish nationalism and a major American labor offensive often led by Irish American progressives.

Irish Americans' ambivalence toward recent migrants recurred in the movements of the war years and the 1920s, and Irish American youth were prominent in the most violent racial conflicts. But at the same time, labor activists invented a new movement that crossed lines of race, nationality, and skill. Irish belligerence in workplaces or on streets was paralleled by struggles for greater social tolerance and for the rights of workers, women, and minorities. In the midst of the "tribal twenties," a wave of reaction defeated Irish radicalism on both sides of the Atlantic. Most Irish Americans finally settled into mainstream American life as loyal devotees of the Catholic Church and an increasingly conservative American republic.

DIASPORIC NATIONALISM AND IRISH ANTI-IMPERIALISM

During the Great Upheaval of 1886, Irish American nationalism fused with the labor reform movements. The transnational Land League and Clan na Gael overlapped with the Knights of Labor and other unions in envisioning both an independent Ireland and a more socially just United States. In the Irish west, the Land War of the 1870s and 1880s spawned both sectarian conflict and rural radicalism; late-nineteenth-century Irish immigrants from those regions tended not only to reinvigorate the nationalist movement in the United States but also to push it toward a broader social and political vision.[9]

As a constitutive element of their identity, nationalism could separate Irish Americans from other racial and ethnic groups, certainly from the Anglophile elite and most Protestant Irish. Some could not be bothered about "the niggers in the Pacific," as Tammany stalwart George Washington Plunkitt termed Emilio Aguinaldo's Philippine resistance fighters. Plunkitt's constituents were busy earning a living and defending their West Side turf. "It is not more than two months since ye learned whether they were islands or canned goods," Finley Peter Dunne's Mr. Dooley observed of the Philippines.[10]

But a broader, more tolerant tradition of Irish nationalism stretched back to Ireland's own Great Emancipator, Daniel O'Connell, and beyond. "Ireland and Irishmen should be foremost in seeking to effect the emancipation of [all] mankind," O'Connell admonished his countrymen, precisely because "the Irish people . . . had themselves suffered centuries of persecution."[11] Irish struggles against British imperialism and the perennial struggle for independence made international politics and sympathy for colonial peoples central to the lives of many second- and third-generation

Irish Americans, particularly in the era of high imperialism from the 1890s through the 1910s. "My father saw the whole picture clearly back in 1898," Elizabeth Gurley Flynn recalled. "When one understood British imperialism it was an open window to all imperialism."[12]

Although some Irish Americans enthusiastically supported imperial ventures, and the respectable Irish American middle class was mostly reticent, many working-class Irish Americans rejected a world order that sustained and condoned old empires.[13] Their nationalism denounced social injustice and imperial violence and expressed solidarity with the experience of colonial peoples in India, Egypt, Afghanistan, South Africa, and China. When Irish nationalists in the United States established a "skirmishing fund" to buy arms, ammunition, and dynamite, they justified it in terms of the British Army's cruelty in the far reaches of the empire; in turn, when Irish American operatives bombed Westminster, the Tower of London, and the Houses of Parliament on "Dynamite Saturday" in 1885, their actions resonated among colonial peoples around the world.[14]

The Irish were most loyal to U.S. policy when their own cause could be squared with it. The plight of "little Cuba" generally elicited great sympathy and, thus, support for what many Irish Americans saw as an anticolonial war with Spain. Some nationalists wondered why there was so much concern for "Cuba Libre" and so little for a Free Ireland; others were torn between Catholic Spain and Catholic Cuba. Most, however, had little trouble choosing sides. They embraced Teddy Roosevelt's notion of the American army as a sort of crucible mixing together the various white ethnic groups (not Asian or African Americans) to produce a new and stronger American race, and they trumpeted the Irish American role in the war. Recruitment centers were thronged; Irish American regiments sprouted up in San Francisco, Boston, New York, and Chicago; and huge crowds, often mobilized by the AOH and Clan na Gael, saw the troops off with parades and Irish and American patriotic music. New York archbishop Michael Corrigan displayed Irish American patriotism most dramatically by draping an enormous American flag between the soaring steeples of St. Patrick's Cathedral.[15]

Irish American enthusiasm for the liberation of Cuba from "Iberian Orangemen" did not extend to fighting Filipino guerrillas. They detected, in justifications for American colonialism, the same sneering arrogance aimed at Filipinos that had also been aimed at them. "We who have been the destroyers of oppression," New York congressman William Bourke Cockran told an Irish American audience, "are asked now to become its defenders."[16] Some Catholic hierarchy supported the project, but "the vast body of organized Irish-America trenchantly opposed American imperial expansion in 1898–1901," historian David Doyle concludes, "with unanimity not to be found on social issues." When some conservative hierarchy founded the American Federation of Catholic Societies in order to provide support for the war in the Philippines, most Irish-American groups refused to join, and the Irish Catholic press denounced the organization, which soon faded.[17] British calls for an Anglo-American alliance in support of their colonial struggles induced Irish and German patriotic organizations to organize and lobby jointly, a cooperation that would re-emerge in opposition to World War I and, later, the Versailles Treaty.

In the 1900 election, Cockran, Patrick Ford, John Devoy, and other prominent nationalists broke with the Republican Party over President McKinley's imperialist policies and supported William Jennings Bryan. When Father McKinnon, the chaplain for a California regiment sent to Cuba, supported American expansionism and pronounced the Filipinos incapable of understanding the meaning of freedom, some in the audience heckled him for parroting "the English argument." Others asked simply, "Why shouldn't they be free?"[18] In a phrase pregnant with bitter meaning for his readers, Patrick Ford referred to General Adna Chaffee, in charge of suppressing Aguinaldo's rebels, as "the Cromwell of the Philippines." Like African American troops, Irish American soldiers sometimes sympathized with the insurgents they were fighting, whom they referred to as "smoked Irish." Their letters questioning American policy circulated in hometown papers.[19]

Devotion to the Cuban cause and sympathy with the Philippine resistance were products of Irish Americans' continuing struggle against the

Anglo-Saxonist ideology that had relegated them for so long to an inferior status in the pantheon of American races. On the eve of war with Spain, the American Protective Association had mobilized five million Protestants, largely in cities, around the claim that Catholics were disloyal and could not be trusted.[20] Cuba in particular was a chance to prove their loyalty in a great struggle in support of an oppressed colonial people.

After 1900, the Irish were increasingly accepted in theory as "honorary" Anglo-Saxons or Nordics, but in daily life the old prejudices persisted through the 1920s. In 1911, a renowned eugenicist determined that the Irish were genetically given to alcoholism, mental abnormalities, and tuberculosis. Even their noted clannishness and political chicanery could be attributed to their defective genes.[21] Irish Americans remained stranded, in Matthew Guterl's memorable phrase, "between whiteness and Anglo-Saxondom."[22] So long as such prejudice and Irish American nationalism remained, Matthew Jacobson notes, "any and all attempts at the complete and total assimilation, 'Americanization,' and whitening of the Irish race were doomed to failure."[23]

Here was a fate that the Irish, despite their growing political influence, shared with newer immigrants and all colonial peoples. Some sought to rally them all against the Anglo-Saxon threat. James Jeffrey Roche, editor of *The Boston Pilot*, asked, "Shall we add 10,000,000 Malays . . . and set out to 'civilize' them by means of lynching and Ku Kluxism for the benefit of a new brood of Carpetbaggers? Or is it about time to put a halt to the mad career of Anglo-Saxonizing the world?"[24] Patrick Ford called on every non–Anglo Saxon element in the population to unite to "block the Anglo-Saxon game. We will not be Anglicized!"[25] It was this racist ideology that Roche assailed in his satirical poem "The White Wolf's Cry":

> We are the Chosen People—Look at the hue of our skins!
> We are the heirs of the ages, masters of every race,
> Proving our right and title by the bullet's saving grace . . .
> We are the Chosen People—whatever we do is right—

> Feared as men fear the leper, whose skin like our own is
>   white![26]

As obvious as the relationship appears in retrospect, Roche was one of the few writers of his day to explicitly connect anti-imperialism with anti-racism, and he published the work of a young black intellectual, W. E. B. DuBois, who did the same.[27]

At its best, the Irish struggle against Anglo-Saxonism asserted the rights of all peoples to self-determination and projected an American society where racial and ethnic difference was perceived not as a problem but as a great strength. "The American is neither Anglo-Saxon nor Celt, nor German, nor French, nor anything else individually," *The Boston Pilot* asserted. It was not in racial purity that the nation's strength resided, but rather in its diversity.[28]

Even their opposition to imperialism, however, often reflected Irish Americans' ambiguous history and status in American society. Some based their opposition on their experiences as a colonized people, others on American racial conventions and a desire to distance themselves from all people of color. During the Boer War, Irish Americans embraced the Boer cause, filling halls for large rallies throughout the United States. Here was another small nation trying to throw off the yoke of British imperialism. Recruiters did a brisk business sending Irishmen to fight the British in Africa, and the Boer colors showed up on houses, apartment buildings, and whiskey bottles in Chicago's South Side, Midtown Manhattan, and Brooklyn. What went without saying in all this celebration of the Boers' fight for freedom was that it projected a new African republic based on white supremacy.[29]

John Finerty (1846–1908), Chicago's leading Irish nationalist, saw no contradiction between his adamant condemnation of Anglo-Saxonism and his crudely racist role as an army officer in the annihilation of Native Americans in the West. Indeed, some Irish American anticolonialism, like that of the WASP elite, was actually based on racism. Writing in *The*

Catholic Citizen, Henry Desmond explained that Catholics should oppose annexation of the Philippines because it would mean "that our American democracy is to stand the trial of working itself out among inferior people." The watchword, Desmond concluded, should be "No new negro problem! No Malay annexation policy! No coolie citizens!"[30] If America's imperial adventures provided the Irish another opportunity to teach recent immigrants a lesson about race, the message was clearly mixed.

PATRICK FORD AND IRISH CONSERVATISM

In many ways, the journalist Patrick Ford (1837–1913) embodied the ambiguous character of Irish nationalism in the era of imperialism. Born in Galway and emigrating to Boston in 1845, Ford apprenticed at age fifteen to the abolitionist printer William Lloyd Garrison on *The Liberator*. The sight of a captured fugitive slave being led in shackles through Boston's streets on his way back to slavery in the South deeply moved him. Parallels between the situations of the black slave and the colonized Irish leaped to Ford's mind and remained there for a lifetime. He fought at Fredericksburg and during Reconstruction edited a radical Republican newspaper in Charleston. He founded *The Irish World* in New York in 1870, and the newspaper achieved a circulation of 125,000 by the turn of the century, making it by far the most important Irish American newspaper. Renamed *The Irish World and Industrial Liberator*, by the early 1880s the *World* had become what historian Eric Foner has called "the voice of the politically conscious Irish American working class," but labor radicals from other ethnic backgrounds read it too. Between the 1850s and the 1880s, Ford supported the causes of abolitionism, American and Irish republicanism, the labor reformism of the Knights of Labor, and the radical single-tax land reform of Henry George. Like many labor reformers of his generation, he held to a primitive labor theory of value. His belief that "Nothing is a man's own property, except it be the result of his labor," led him to strongly support the Irish Land League.[31]

Despite its middle-class leadership, the strongest support for the Land

League lay not in the cosmopolitan centers of New York and Boston but rather in the slums of Chicago and Pittsburgh, the mine and mill towns of the Pennsylvania anthracite region, and the hard-rock mining towns of the Far West: Leadville, Colorado; Butte, Montana; and Virginia City, Nevada. Here, according to Foner, the movement represented a "symbiotic relationship between class-conscious unionism and Irish national consciousness." At times it also represented a broadening of Irish American politics, as English, Welsh, Hungarian, and other miners also took part.[32]

The land issue seized the imagination of nineteenth-century organized labor. "The No Rent Battle of Ireland," read a giant banner at a New York City labor meeting, "is the battle of workingmen the world over." In New York's labor demonstrations, radical German workers held aloft a green banner emblazoned with a harp. It was this movement that produced New York's ethnically mixed Central Labor Union, which took as one of its principles that the nation's land was "the common property of the people."[33]

Above all, Patrick Ford was an ardent Irish nationalist. The early 1880s convergence of the Irish Land League and the radical labor movement was fertile soil for his gospel of independent labor politics and land reform. His newspaper provided a link among transnational radicals in the United States, England, and Ireland. Conservative middle-class nationalists like Chicago's John Finerty and New York's John Devoy denounced people like Ford who wanted "to use Ireland as a means of working out a social revolution in other countries," and they characterized Ford's agitation as "humanitarian cant."[34] But such "lace curtain" nationalists, Ford contended, "do not relish this land question with its logical deductions applicable to America as well as Ireland."[35]

In the late 1880s, however, Ford and other radical nationalists themselves took a more conservative path. *The Irish World* underwent a severe economic crisis, and Republican Party financial support offered a way out. As a devout Catholic and an increasingly important member of the Irish American establishment, Ford came to see Father Edward McGlynn's defiance of the church hierarchy as a threat to the institution and Henry

THE AGING RADICAL:
Patrick Ford (1837–1913), newspaper editor, Irish nationalist,
advocate of the black freedmen and colonial peoples, circa 1913.

George's single tax movement as a threat to the status of the rising Irish American political and economic elite. All of this undermined his enthusiasm for working-class radicalism, and he broke with both men shortly after the 1886 election in New York. He muted his support for land nationalization and strikes and later dabbled in notions of anti-Semitic conspiracies.

Ford's conservative turn reflected the craving, on the part of the new Irish American middle class, for respectability. Hitherto for most laboring Irish, respectability had been unimaginable; now for their "lace curtain" compatriots, it became an obsession.[36] More settled Irish like Ford developed a skepticism toward more recent immigrants, who seemed to be challenging the Irish at every turn—in their hard-won control of urban territory, jobs, political influence, and even church leadership. Defensiveness shaded into intolerance, not only for the new immigrants but for all forms of radicalism. By the early twentieth century, Ford and those around him were denouncing militant trade unionism as well as socialism.[37]

Still, long after he fell into hock to the Republican Party, broke with George and McGlynn, and lost his radical edge, Ford remained an Irish nationalist. In his defense of the Irish, he continued to employ the metaphor of the black slave. He embraced the causes of Native Americans, the Cuban and Filipino insurgents, and other colonized peoples. *The Irish World* staunchly opposed U.S. imperialism and, after Ford's death, American entry into the First World War. Ford's only break with the Republicans came in 1900, when he supported William Jennings Bryan for his opposition to imperialism and the formal acquisition of colonies. Though he eschewed the "physical force" approach (which held Ireland could gain its freedom from the British only through armed struggle), Ford remained committed to the Irish cause. His concept of a strong and proud Irish race reinforced his intolerance of the more recent immigrants; yet his abhorrence of Anglo-Saxonism fueled his opposition to immigration restriction.[38]

Ford's ambivalence reflected the ambivalent outlook of the Irish American middle class. As they rose in respectability, many feared social radicalism and became intolerant; but they also remained committed to the advancement of working people through organization and action. Even as they resented the encroachment of newer immigrant groups, many of them opposed immigration restriction and sympathized with the world's oppressed, owing to their own nation's plight, militant Anglo-Saxonism, and anti-Catholicism. This ambivalence shaped Irish American nationalism in the age of revolution and war.

CREATING THE IRISH RACE

On both sides of the Atlantic, the issue of "moral force" parliamentarism and "physical force" revolutionism divided the Irish nationalist movement philosophically and strategically, as did social and economic issues.

In Ireland, the nationalist movement was deeply divided over tactics and aims throughout the late nineteenth and early twentieth century.

Charles Stewart Parnell's Irish Parliamentary Party (IPP), which had led the campaign for Home Rule and land reform in the 1880s, represented the political dimension of the nationalist movement, but it splintered badly and declined in the 1890s.[39] In 1901, John Redmond emerged as leader of a reunified IPP, which concentrated almost entirely on achieving Home Rule. Since 1798, a "physical force" Fenian wing of the movement had advocated armed struggle against the British. But until World War I this agitation attracted only a small core of revolutionaries. Neither of these movements paid much attention to the larger question of the social character of the new Irish society once independence was achieved. By contrast, Michael Davitt's radical Land League had aimed to achieve not only independence but a social and economic transformation of the island nation. In 1916, in the wake of the brutal suppression of the Easter Rising, the plight of impoverished farmers, landless peasants, and increasingly militant urban workers produced a new, socially radical nationalist movement in Ireland. [40]

In the United States, the new middle class, increasingly suspicious of the activists below them on the social ladder, protective of their hard-won gains, and resentful of the new immigrants, devised a nationalist movement in its own image, one that struggled against a resurgent Anglo-Saxonism but also opposed labor unions, strikes, and women's rights.[41] The American movement reached a high point with the staging of the Irish Race Convention in March 1916 in New York City.[42] The convention was the brainchild of an unlikely team. Daniel Florence Cohalan (1865–1946) personified the growing Irish American middle class. The college-educated son of immigrants, he had risen to the status of New York Supreme Court justice in 1911. Well connected in both Tammany and the national Democratic Party, he was a leading figure in Clan na Gael, the secret revolutionary group that did most of the nationalist organizing in the United States in the late nineteenth and early twentieth century. As journalist Terry Golway notes, Cohalan, like other Clan na Gael notables, "walked a tightrope between respectable and revolutionary politics." His main goal was to achieve independence for Ireland and, at the same time, respectability and acceptance for Irish Americans.[43]

John Devoy (1842–1928) was a revered Irish Fenian exile. Sentenced in 1866 for organizing among Irish soldiers in the British Army, he was released in a general amnesty in 1871 and made his way to New York. A pragmatist, Devoy was a key figure in the "New Departure" of 1879, which aimed to unify the movement's transnational "moral" parliamentary and physical force wings. In 1900, following a period of bitter factionalism, Devoy reunited the Clan na Gael under new leadership: more radical in tactics and proletarian in membership, it nonetheless focused entirely on the struggle's political dimension. In 1903, Devoy had become editor of the just-established *Gaelic American*.[44]

Between them, Cohalan and Devoy guided the secret Clan na Gael and hatched the plan for the Irish Race Convention. They represented two distinct generations of the movement, but they were in agreement in their views. The Race Convention launched a broad new organization, the Friends of Irish Freedom (FOIF)—more plebeian and youthful in its base, open to women, less subject to church influence.[45]

In April, one month after the Race Convention, the Easter Rising occurred. Resources for the rising had originated in New York; Cohalan, Devoy, and other Clan na Gael leaders had been in close contact with the rebels. In the short run, the rising seemed to have been a tragic blunder: it elicited little sympathy on either side of the Atlantic. But once the British executed its leaders, Irish nationalism became, for the first time since the 1880s, a mass movement. Revulsion over the executions, and despair at the apparent emptiness of Home Rule hopes, moved Irish Americans en masse into the movement's physical force wing. Rallies and demonstrations erupted not only in New York, Philadelphia, and Chicago but also in smaller cities and towns. The British ambassador Sir Cecil Spring-Rice concluded, "Our cause for the present among the Irish here is a lost one."[46]

The reborn nationalist movement caught fire: the new FOIF built a membership of more than 225,000 by 1920. With the U.S. declaration of war in April 1917, however, Cohalan and his allies faced a dilemma: they sought to win Irish freedom while maintaining loyalty to the American state, which was now allied with Britain. The Irish Progressive League opposed the war, but most FOIF leaders fell in line behind the war effort, and refused to recognize the new Irish Republic when it was proclaimed in 1919. The American Association for the Recognition of the Irish Republic, a rival group launched the following year by the Irish revolutionary Éamon de Valera, soon claimed a membership of 700,000 and contributions of $10 million in Irish Republican bonds.[47]

Within the AFL, Chicago Federation of Labor president John Fitzpatrick and other labor activists pushed unsuccessfully for a boycott of all British goods, while in the broader Irish American community, boycott organizers had more success, linking their 1921 boycott calls with those of Gandhi and other Indian nationalists against Lancashire cotton. The new radical groups thrived in big-city neighborhoods and small manufacturing and mining towns throughout the United States.[48] At a time when the increasingly successful third generation might have been inclined to distance itself from Ireland, British policies cemented Irish American ties to Ireland, and many Irish Americans continued to see themselves as a race apart.

Before World War I, just at the point when lawyer-anthroplogist Madison Grant and other racists and eugenicists were finally welcoming them into the ranks of genetic respectability, Irish Americans were busy imagining themselves as a distinct race. The notion was not new; in nineteenth-century Ireland, it had served as an important antidote to British racism. The earliest Irish Race Convention, a small affair, had been held in Chicago in 1881, and in September 1896 an Irish Race Convention in Dublin had drawn two thousand delegates from the rest of Ireland as well as the United States, Canada, South Africa, and Australia. In the wartime context, however, support for the Irish revolution and opposition to the war and the Anglo-American alliance had rendered Irish Americans once again suspect and somewhat subversive.[49] After the war, the resurgence of Irish nationalism actually fed notions of the Irish as a separate race, quite distinct from and, in some formulations superior to, that of the Anglo-Saxon. "Both U.S. and Irish nationalisms," Matthew Jacobson concludes, "generated a racial crosscurrent that placed a high premium indeed upon the differences between the white races, the Anglo-Saxon and the Celt."[50]

As the Irish literary scholar Luke Gibbons has observed, the argument for a native Irish civilization, advanced and independent of the other classical civilizations, "provided a cue for race to enter the proceedings on the nationalist side, [employing] the image of an embattled people surviving intact and maintaining unity in the face of two thousand years of upheaval, invasion and oppression."[51] During World War I, the notion of an Irish race provided a basis for mobilizing Irish Americans in support of the emerging republic and, sometimes, for bringing them into solidarity with Indians, African Americans, and other oppressed groups. This notion of a distinct Irish race informed the first meeting of the Irish Dail in 1919, when it addressed the "Free Nations of the World." And in asserting the integrity of the Irish race, Irish American nationalists embraced the new cultural pluralism advanced by Randolph Bourne, Jane Addams, and other American intellectuals and reformers as an alternative to the melting pot and the war's shrill ultra-nationalism.[52]

At the same time, as "small nations" sought self-determination, diasporic nationalism also ran through the Polish, Czech, Indian, African, and other American ethnic communities. This commonality, and the fact that some Irish activists were genuine internationalists, opened the possibility for greater understanding among the groups. The more radical Irish merged with an ethnically and racially mixed anti-imperialist movement based in New York, drawing the attention of U.S. Military Intelligence in the process. The progressive labor lawyer Frank Walsh, an official representative of the new Irish Republic and nationalist leader Dudley Field Malone, son of a Tammany stalwart, both served as officers of the Friends of Indian Freedom and spoke often before racially mixed audiences on behalf of Indian independence. The Indian cause also drew the support of John Fitzpatrick and other progressive Irish Americans.[53]

Black, Indian, and other contemporary nationalist movements recognized the significance of the Irish independence struggle in their own campaigns. Often considered a nineteenth-century phenomenon, Irish American nationalism peaked during and immediately after World War I, a time when diasporic nationalist movements seized the imagination of workers throughout the industrial United States. Polish and other eastern European immigrants mobilized in support of their national aspirations, and African Americans embraced Marcus Garvey's vision of a pan-African society. This diasporic ethnic nationalism could be a barrier among workers of diverse groups, but it could also create sympathetic bonds among them.[54]

In the context of world war, revolution, and labor mobilization, and in the wake of the brutal suppression of the Easter Rising, some Irish American activists saw this new movement as part of a broad mobilization of working people. They could link Irish prospects for national liberation with the issues of industrial and social reform. Or they could root their own movement firmly in the settled, defensive Irish American community, develop strategies based on the two-party system, and accept leadership from the "steam heat" elite. This latter, more respectable form of nationalism came to predominate, but that should not obscure efforts to link the Irish cause to movements embracing millions of new immigrants and black migrants.

The socially radical faction of the nationalist movement picked up steam in both the old world and the new. In Ireland, the revolutionary Sinn Fein movement, which aimed at securing independence through open conflict with the British, erected an elaborate network of clubs, displacing remnants of Redmond's Home Rule movement. When nationalists staged the first Irish general election of 1918 in anticipation of declaring an independent republic, Sinn Fein won 70 percent of the vote. The Irish Transport and General Workers' Union grew from twelve thousand members in the summer of 1917 to more than a hundred thousand in late 1919, becoming the linchpin of an urban workers' movement. Between 1919 and 1920, "soviets" were established in the course of factory occupations, while in the rural parts of the West, land seizures by agricultural workers led to widespread conflict.[55] During these years, revolutions and strikes broke out throughout Europe, while the United States experienced the greatest strike wave in its history, and support for the Socialist Party, especially its left wing, grew substantially among immigrant workers.

WAR AND REVOLUTION AS AN OPENING

In the short run, the war crisis seemed to highlight the subversive potential of Irish Americans. Many Irish Catholics at first resisted American involvement in World War I on the grounds of Irish nationalism and hostility to the British. German and Irish fraternal and nationalist organizations had been cooperating since 1890s, and the Ancient Order of Hibernians and the National German-American Alliance had created a coalition as early as 1907 to oppose U.S. intervention and a possible Anglo-American alliance. A pattern of Irish-German resistance to close ties with Britain had emerged by 1914. In the early stages of the war, numerous demonstrations and rallies opposed the prospect of American intervention and denounced any moves in Ireland to support it. Irish American newspapers tended to be pro-German, and the church's official position of peace and neutrality tended to accommodate Irish nationalist sympathies.[56]

By the war's end, Secretary of State Robert Lansing was worried about President Wilson's rhetoric favoring self-determination for "small nations," because it raised the expectations of a whole host of subject peoples throughout Europe and beyond—the Irish, the Indians, the Egyptians. "The phrase is simply loaded with dynamite," Lansing observed. "It will raise hopes that can never be realized."[57]

Irish American progressives used patriotic discourse and Wilson's own rhetoric in support of the interracial industrial union movement, independent labor politics, and radical Irish nationalism. In Chicago, this movement coalesced around John Fitzpatrick and the Chicago Federation of Labor. In New York, the Irish Progressive League (IPL), formed in

October 1917, worked to harness the more radical nationalists to a politically inclusive progressive movement that included the Socialist Party. The IPL, which endorsed not only Irish independence but also social and economic transformation on both sides of the Atlantic, was much smaller than the Chicago Federation, but it had the support of some American clergy and the services of Irish exiles and veterans of James Connolly's old Irish Socialist Federation, including Connolly's daughter Nora, Liam Mellows (a central figure in the Easter Rising), and others. It also attracted a cadre of experienced American organizers, including the poet and actor Peter Golden and the indomitable Leonora O'Reilly.[58]

The IPL's first public meeting, on May 4, 1917, drew seven thousand activists from around the country; they endorsed Morris Hillquit, who was then running for mayor of New York City on a strong antiwar platform. "That the league would support a Jewish socialist over two Irish Catholics for mayor of one of the world's most Irish cities," historian Bruce Nelson concludes, "speaks volumes about the forces that were coalescing on the left wing of the nationalist movement."[59] Even more strikingly, a wide range of Irish publications, including the Catholic *Freeman's Journal*, endorsed Hillquit, support that undoubtedly helped him increase the Socialist vote from 32,000 to 145,000 over a period of two years.[60]

Hillquit beat the Republican candidate and finished close behind the patrician incumbent reform mayor John Purroy Mitchel. The grandson of a much-beloved Irish nationalist and a darling of middle-class reformers, Mitchel had defeated the Tammany candidate in the 1913 mayoral election. Many Irish Americans rejected him in 1917, underscoring the growing social gulf between "lace curtain" and "shanty" Irish. He enraged public schoolteachers, by demanding that they work longer hours for less pay; immigrants, by wrapping himself in the flag and questioning their patriotism; ethnic Catholics, by confronting the church over its connivance with Tammany Hall; and Irish nationalists, by clamping down on their street protests against the war.[61] In the 1917 election, the Democratic candidate crushed Mitchel, and Tammany, which some reformers had assumed was finished, recovered and dominated city politics through the 1920s.

The FOIF convention held in June 1917 vividly displayed nationalist divisions over the war. The Clan na Gael's Judge Cohalan and the old nationalist John Devoy urged the members to support the war in the interests of winning Irish independence. But Liam Mellows, the exiled Irish revolutionary, and other activists insisted on opposing the war and calling for a social and political transformation of Ireland. Their clash was the latest installment of the tension between socially radical activists and the middle-class element who sought only national independence.[62]

In the longer run, their great ambition for acceptance and respectability pushed most Irish Americans toward patriotism and support for the war effort. The church hierarchy strongly endorsed it once the United States entered, and most Catholics followed this lead. Still, a breach opened in the community over the meaning of the conflict: while many nationalists opposed providing any assistance for the British, and others saw the war mainly as a chance to push for Irish independence, most clergy and hierarchy and many rank-and-file Catholics came to support the war effort with great fervor.

In a joint statement, cardinals Gibbons, Farley, and William O'Connell urged American Catholics to "fight like heroes and pray like saints." The hierarchy established the National Catholic War Council to coordinate support, while the Knights of Columbus opened field canteens and launched a huge Liberty Bond drive.[63] Irish Americans poured into the armed forces, sensing once again an opportunity to prove themselves good Catholics and good Americans. Of nearly four thousand conscientious objectors in the nation, less than 1 percent were Catholic. The number of Catholic chaplains quickly shot up after American entry, from 28 to over 1,500 ministering to about one million Catholics among the U.S. troops.[64] Once again, the Irish were striving to be "more American than the Americans."

Some priests resisted the call to war, like those at the Carmelite Monastery in Lower Manhattan: the full weight of the church fell upon them.

Cardinal Farley demanded that parish priests stop distributing Sinn Fein material at Mass and that the Irish Christian Brothers return their portraits of Woodrow Wilson to their normal positions in classrooms. (The brothers had turned the president's face to the wall when he rejected the pleas of nationalists to support the Irish cause.) He instructed Father Peter Magennis, who had been elected president of the Friends of Irish Freedom, to either desist from attending protest rallies or leave the diocese.[65]

When Irish Americans organized against U.S. involvement in the war, the federal government went after them. The 1917 Espionage Act, passed with the Irish movement's radical wing much in mind, made it illegal not only to send money to the revolutionary movement in Ireland but also to organize any meeting for this purpose. The government sanctioned the American Protective Association's efforts to root out "Bolsheviks" and antiwar traitors in Irish communities. Mass-circulation papers like *The Gaelic American* and *The Irish World*, which had assumed a progressive antiwar line, were suppressed. The government lumped Sinn Fein in with the IWW and the Bolsheviks as a major threat to American security. Government spies kept Irish radicals under constant surveillance and infiltrated nationalist meetings; police broke up Irish freedom rallies. Irish immigrants who failed to register for the draft as British subjects were arrested and imprisoned (though later freed). Federal authorities indicted the IPL's Jeremiah O'Leary for obstructing the draft with his street corner speeches and banned O'Leary's popular satirical magazine *Bull* from the mails.[66] At the same time, the division between the radical and moderate wings weakened the movement, a split that foreshadowed the division in Ireland between nationalists who accepted partition and those demanding a unified "workers' republic." After the war, Irish activists would be among the major targets of the Red Scare.

In the realm of popular culture, the war became a crucible in which the nation's ethnic groups met one another and were transformed into Americans. New York's Seventy-seventh "Melting Pot" Regiment became the great symbol of this wartime integration: "Men who had recently been subjected to the pogroms of Russia, gunmen and gangsters . . . Italians,

Chinamen, the Jews and the Irish, a heterogeneous mass, truly representative both of the varied human flotsam and the sturdy American manhood which comprise the civil population of New York City."[67] The government conceived of its ethnically mixed training camps as "gigantic 'universities' for educating Americans of every region, race, and creed in the fundamentals of an American national identity," historian David Kennedy wrote. "In this sense the war itself provided a striking site for 'Americanization.'" "The military tent where they all sleep side by side," Teddy Roosevelt wrote, "will rank next to the public school among the great agents of democratization."[68]

Films like *The Lost Battalion* (1919) and *The Fighting 69th* (1940), with James Cagney as a war hero and Pat O'Brien as Father Duffy, developed the theme of Americanization through combat. In the 1922 play *Abie's Irish Rose*, the quintessential interethnic love story of the 1920s, Rosemary Murphy begins her romance with Corporal Abraham Levy when she dresses his wounds in a French field hospital. The immigrant priest Father Whalen silences Patrick Murphy's intolerance with stories from the battlefield: "I saw those Negroes fight in France . . . and they covered themselves in glory . . . yet we still place them in the same old category . . . What would you say . . . if I told you that on the battlefield I, as a chaplain, administered the Last Rites to Catholics, Jews and Gentile Protestants? . . . One night in a shell hole I came across a chaplain who was a rabbi at home and who had just given the Last Rites to a Catholic boy." Abie's best war buddy, killed in combat, was Patsy Dunne. "He saved my life on the field," Abie tells Rosemary. ". . . Do you think we ever thought about his being an Irishman and I a Jew? It ought to be that way at home."[69]

In reality, the war sometimes cast Irish Americans in unaccustomed roles. The Knights of Columbus developed a good reputation among black soldiers for integrating their field dispensaries, while those of the YMCA remained segregated. An army investigator reported, "There was absolutely no discrimination practiced by this organization."[70] Cultural historian Richard Slotkin writes that officers now often saw the Irish, once the most despised of the immigrant groups, as the "most Americanized . . . still differentiated by their 'racial' propensity for whiskey and brawling, but generally up to the Strenuous Life standard." Veterans from various ethnic backgrounds recalled that ethnic soldiers "saw the Irish as the model minority for Jews, Italians, and Chinese to emulate."[71]

Despite the historic tensions between Irish and African Americans, New York City's "Fighting Sixty-ninth" developed good relations with New York's black soldiers. Drawn heavily from Irish county societies and athletic clubs, the Sixty-ninth traced its roots back to General Thomas Meagher's Civil War Irish Brigade. Despite the everyday anti-Semitism on the streets of New York City, relations between Irish Americans and

"GO TO THE FRONT WITH YOUR FRIENDS":
a World War I recruitment poster for the Fighting Sixty-ninth infantry unit, drawn largely from the Irish county and social athletic clubs of Manhattan, 1917.

the estimated seventy Jewish soldiers in the Sixty-ninth were good. Though largely Irish, then, the Sixty-ninth was ethnically diverse, including some Germans, ethnically mixed men, and the famous "Sergeant Abey Blaustein of the Irish."[72] Father Francis Duffy, who came from the more intellectual and liberal wing of the church in New York and represented the spiritual heart of the Fighting Sixty-ninth, took pride in the tolerance such mixture symbolized.[73]

Mixing these city soldiers with southern whites at Camp Mills in Spartanburg, South Carolina, proved volatile. Hometown papers reminded the Alabama troops that during the Civil War, at Fredericksburg, the Fourth Alabama and Manhattan's Sixty-ninth had almost annihilated each other. Relations deteriorated further with the arrival of the Fifteenth New York National Guard. Better trained than the Sixty-ninth, with a band of musicians drawn from Chicago's South Side and Harlem's Cotton Club, the Fifteenth personified the new urban black culture thriving in the wake of the great migration. With their syncopated march rhythms and fancy stepping, the black unit delighted the white New Yorkers, who welcomed them with great enthusiasm. When the African American soldiers came in contact with the Alabama unit, however, fights erupted all over the place. The Sixty-ninth became as famous for fighting in camp as on the battlefield. When regimental authorities confiscated the black unit's ammunition, the Sixty-ninth soldiers supplied it, and they traded taunts with the Alabamans. When they assaulted the Sixty-ninth's encampment, the New Yorkers repulsed the Alabamans at bayonet point, killing one of their soldiers.[74]

By all accounts, the Fighting Sixty-ninth served with great bravery. They sustained heavy casualties in the fields of France, but their patriotism coexisted with a deep strain of Irish nationalism. When army brass sent a large consignment of British Army tunics to supply the poorly equipped Irish, a near riot ensued. Soldiers discovered British Army buttons on the uniforms and threatened to burn the whole consignment. General Pershing was forced to send an officer up with a large box of American eagle buttons, which were switched for the British buttons. "The changes were made," he recalled, "and the regiment turned out looking both smart and serene."[75]

CREATING A NEW LABOR MOVEMENT

Under Irish American leadership, progressive traditions thrived in the AFL mainstream, especially in early-twentieth-century Chicago. For a moment, the diverse American working-class population seemed as if it might become part of a transnational social movement. In the 1880s and 1890s, the Chicago Federation of Labor (CFL) had been dominated by powerful and corrupt men like Martin B. "Skinny" Madden, boss of the Chicago Building Trades Council. Aligned with Democratic bosses, CFL leaders put their energies into lining their own pockets. Comparable Irish American labor bosses operated in New York and Brooklyn. At the other end of the spectrum, remnants of Chicago's Haymarket-era labor radicalism remained, particularly in immigrant communities, although they had been isolated since the defeats of the 1880s. John Fitzpatrick (1871–1946) offered honest leadership and an opening for aggressive organizing and progressive labor politics.[76]

In this struggle, two distinct elements in the Irish American community competed for the soul of the labor movement. The gangsters saw the CFL as a closed world of job trusts, which they could use to freeze out the newcomers who threatened their operations. For progressives like Fitzpatrick, the CFL was a chance to spread the solidarity and protection of unions to every corner of the city and beyond. During the conflict, labor sluggers beat reformers, and delegates often went to CFL meetings armed. When the reformers moved decisively against the racketeers at the federation's 1906 election, fistfights broke out, and 120 policemen were stationed inside and outside the hall.[77]

Fitzpatrick, who became president of the CFL in 1902, forged the federation into an invigorating amalgam of industrial unionism, independent labor politics, and progressive internationalism. He and his largely Irish American colleagues created a genuinely interethnic and to some extent interracial movement. CFL organizers penetrated the city's various ethnic communities with a new language of "Americanism" that stressed ethnic and racial tolerance while demanding industrial as well as political democracy.

A militant unionist, Fitzpatrick led a remarkable burst of organizing. On Saturday afternoons, he held open office hours to help immigrant workers trying to organize. In 1910, he worked with Sam Levin and Sidney Hillman to launch the new Amalgamated Clothing Workers of America, an ethnically diverse industrial union led by Jewish immigrant radicals. He did so even though it caused trouble with the old United Garment Workers craft union and the AFL leadership. When the Amalgamated struck the major garment manufacturers, Fitzpatrick coordinated relief efforts.[78] By the 1910s, he and his colleagues had built the CFL into the strongest and most progressive urban labor federation in the United States, with 350 local unions representing over 350,000 workers.[79]

Fitzpatrick acquired an outstanding reputation for his support of black workers. He investigated allegations of racial discrimination and advised black trainmen on their independent organizing, appointed black organizers, served on the federal government's Negro Workers' Advisory Committee, and sought the sanction of black religious leaders.[80] During the 1910s, unions or loose federations of unions launched organizing drives in steel, coal and metal mining, textiles, and garment manufacturing to integrate the new unskilled immigrants and migrants. Fitzpatrick put the radical William Z. Foster in charge of an organizing drive in the slums around Chicago's stockyards; in 1917, the massive and remarkably successful drive brought black and white, native and immigrant, skilled and unskilled—in more than forty distinct ethnic groups—together into one powerful movement, the Stockyards Labor Council.[81] The achievement marked a rare (and temporary) breach of the color line.

With the stockyards organized, Fitzpatrick and Foster moved on to the open-shop bastion of steel by forming the National Committee for Organizing Iron and Steel Workers. Sweeping into the steel towns of South Chicago, the Calumet region of Indiana, the "steel valley" around Pittsburgh, and other mill towns throughout the nation, their organizers built the largest strike movement in the nation's history, bringing three hundred thousand largely unskilled immigrant workers out on strike in late 1918 and holding many of them out for almost a year. The great steel strike of 1919 was crushed by an employers' offensive and the Red Scare of 1919–22, but Fitzpatrick and Foster had demonstrated a crucial lesson: that given proper support, unskilled immigrant workers could be organized.[82]

At the national level, Fitzpatrick emerged as a leading opponent of Samuel Gompers's conservative brand of business unionism; he demanded the integration of African Americans and more recent unskilled immigrant workers. Radicals like Foster hoped Fitzpatrick would wrest control of the AFL from Samuel Gompers and lead a progressive national movement to new heights. Fitzpatrick helped found the Labor Party movement in the United States and in 1919 ran for mayor on the Cook County Labor Party ticket. He balanced the top of his ticket with Polish and Scandinavian candidates, while black, Italian, and other immigrant men and women ran for alderman in various wards. The Labor Party established machine-style clubs in ethnic neighborhoods including the Black Belt, winning considerable support for Irish independence at mass meetings in ethnic neighborhoods and projecting a "Chicago for the workers." Though the party garnered only 8 percent of the total vote, its slate ran particularly well in some of the South Side immigrant wards. Fitzpatrick launched a spirited weekly, *New Majority*, which covered the CFL's industrial and political exploits but also revolutionary events internationally.[83]

Chicago progressives saw no contradiction between the various ethnic nationalisms and militant trade unionism. Thus, the demand for Irish or Polish freedom often shared platforms with demands for labor rights and support for the Russian and Mexican revolutions. The CFL supported the cause of Indian independence and the formation of workers' republics in Ireland and Russia. Its unfulfilled plans called for a League of Oppressed Nationalities, including Lithuanians, Koreans, Chinese, Liberians, and Filipinos as well as Poles and Irish.[84] When the Irish revolutionary James Larkin set up shop in the United States (see chapter 3), he headed first to Chicago, where he could expect a ready welcome and material support. When he was arrested in the midst of the 1919 Red Scare, Fitzpatrick launched a defense committee and coordinated the involvement of Norman Thomas of the Socialist Party and Roger Baldwin, who was in the process of organizing the American Civil Liberties Union.

Fitzpatrick was important both as a symbol and as a leader because he embraced Irish nationalism, class-conscious labor militancy, and anti-racism at a particularly important moment. His "Irishness," far from constituting a barrier separating him from other ethnic and racial communities, encouraged his goal of building a genuinely inclusive movement. Fitzpatrick perceived logical connections between the movement for Irish liberation and those of other oppressed peoples around the world; between the workers' movements of Ireland, Britain, and Russia; and between the discrimination facing African Americans and that which had faced the Irish. His embrace of the Irish republican cause was of a piece with efforts to organize immigrant and black meatpacking and steelworkers into one cohesive industrial and political movement that could transform the United States into a more democratic society. Fitzpatrick was an effective Irish nationalist because he was an effective and class-conscious labor organizer, and his nationalist ideals fueled his labor activism.

The contrast between conservative, exclusive business unionism and a new progressive multiethnic movement was not peculiar to Chicago. The hard-rock mining town of Butte, Montana, was a particularly graphic case. Nowhere did the conservative brand of Irish American unionism have a tighter grip than here, where the giant Butte Miners' Union (BMU), dominated by immigrants from west Cork, "stood guard over the best paid work in America." The copper mine's owner, Marcus Daly, an ardent immigrant nationalist, hired workers through the Ancient Order of Hibernians, often posted job notices in Gaelic, and worked closely with the BMU. As a result, in its thirty-six-year life, the BMU never engaged in a strike.[85]

Everything changed after 1900, when Daly died. The Anaconda Corporation introduced new, more rigorous work rules, and over the next two decades immigrant miners from every corner of the globe—Finland, Italy, Serbia, Montenegro, Ethiopia—poured into Butte. Among them were young immigrants from an Ireland that had been transformed between 1900 and 1917 by industrialization, class conflict, and nationalist agitation. These new immigrants rejected the BMU, the AOH, and the Irish labor aristocracy. During the 1910s, the radical Metal Mine Workers' Union embraced all ethnic groups, and the Irish immigrants formed the Pearse-Connolly Irish Independence Club. Between 1914 and 1921, they joined with the other immigrant workers in four major strikes.[86]

In Butte and elsewhere, the two generations of Irish immigrants "viewed one another from across a deep and widening cultural divide."[87] After World War I, Irish American progressives founded Connolly Clubs, named for the socialist leader of the Easter Rising, in working-class communities.[88] But church authorities, abhorring the rising tide of immigrant radicalism, launched a major campaign in Boston to link Irish nationalism and Irish American identity with anti-Bolshevism. Their efforts led to a major riot in Roxbury on May Day 1919 that pitted patriotic Irish American crowds against a large group of immigrant radicals. The riot left two dead and dozens injured.[89]

Manhattan's West Side had been an Irish stronghold: in the mid-nineteenth century Irish dockers had driven blacks off the piers, then fought ferocious battles against Italians and others. But now radical nationalism expanded the Irish American perspective even here, providing a momentary link to other groups. In August 1920, Irish longshoremen in New York launched the "Great Patriotic Strike," perhaps "the first purely political strike of workmen in the history of the United States." They and other unionists across the country demanded the release of Sinn Fein leader and Cork lord mayor Terence MacSwiney, who was being held in a London prison for his revolutionary activities. Italian longshoremen and British coal handlers joined them. The Irish Progressive League set up a speakers' bureau, and Leonora O'Reilly's impassioned speeches spurred newly enfranchised Irish American women, and other immigrant women, to spread the strike to warehousemen near the docks, then to Brooklyn, Hoboken, Boston, Philadelphia, New Orleans, and other ports.[90]

When employers brought in hundreds of black strikebreakers, women pickets marched with signs proclaiming, "The Emancipation of the Irish is the Emancipation of All Mankind" and "Ireland for the Irish. Africa for the Africans." Black dockers walked off the ships and fell in with what labor historian Bruce Nelson termed "a remarkably diverse line of march." A group of Irish dockworkers, along with attorney Dudley Field Malone and other nationalist leaders, went up to Harlem to negotiate an arrangement with the Universal Negro Improvement Association, offering support for its Black Star Line and promising to allow blacks to work on Chelsea's "Irish piers" indefinitely. Seeing a chance to strike a blow against British colonialism, Marcus Garvey sent a representative down to the Chelsea docks to appeal to black longshoremen to support the strike. Following the strike's collapse, most Irish dockers reverted to "older and more familiar patterns of localism" but Pier 60, the most "Irish" on Manhattan's waterfront, continued to accept black dockworkers from that point on. "Thus, for a moment," Bruce Nelson concludes, "two parallel nationalisms had converged to create genuine bonds of sympathy and a tangible redistribution of resources among workingmen who had long regarded each other with suspicion and even hatred."[91]

RENAISSANCES AND NATIONALISMS, GREEN AND BLACK

Contacts between black and Irish nationalists during the 1920 strike were not a coincidence. For some time, radical black nationalists had been drawn to the Irish movement. Marcus Garvey saluted Éamon de Valera and hailed the declaration of a new Irish Republic at the Universal Negro Improvement Association international conference on the eve of the New York dock strike of 1920. Black radicals Claude McKay and Cyril Briggs (who called the Irish independence struggle "the greatest Epic of Modern History") maintained contacts with Irish radicals, a development monitored by government spies.[92] Briggs modeled his African Blood Brotherhood on the Irish Republican Brotherhood (IRB), while Garvey named

Harlem's Liberty Hall after the Dublin headquarters of Connolly's Irish Transport and General Workers' Union, home of the working-class wing of the Irish revolutionary movement that launched the Easter Rising.[93] The West Indian working-class intellectual Hubert Harrison, a Socialist and nationalist and the era's most sophisticated African American radical, spoke and wrote often of the Irish struggle. He repeatedly held up the Irish American movement as a model for his community's struggles in the Caribbean, in Africa, and in the United States and as a way for African Americans to establish their "political manhood."[94] "With its race conventions and its sponsorship of IRB revolution," historian Matthew Guterl observes, "Irish American nationalism had become the standard by which all other subversive nationalisms were to be judged."[95]

The Harlem Renaissance, the black cultural awakening in the 1920s, had some of its roots in an earlier Irish Renaissance. In 1893 in Dublin, Douglas Hyde founded the Gaelic League to encourage a Celtic cultural revival rooted in Irish folk traditions and the Gaelic language. Hyde urged Irish artists and intellectuals to "de-Anglicize" Ireland through the recovery of the nation's own language and culture. They then consciously enlisted this newly invented "Gaelic" culture in the revolutionary cause. Arthur Griffith's Sinn Fein movement (founded in 1905) drew its inspiration largely from that renaissance and from a group of poets—Patrick Pearse, Thomas MacDonagh, and Joseph Plunkett—who would all later be executed for their parts in the Easter Rising. Employing local Irish dialects, folk themes, and realist rural Irish settings, William Butler Yeats, John Synge, and other playwrights associated with Dublin's Abbey Theatre created plays that reflected the lives of common Irish people and served the nationalist cause. Sean O'Casey later employed similar principles in his own plays based on life in Dublin's slums.[96]

The Irish Renaissance influenced many African American artists and intellectuals. Claude McKay, Countee Cullen, and other black American poets and writers admired and corresponded with their Irish counterparts. A new "Negro Theater" took as its model Dublin's Abbey Theatre.[97] The black critic Alain Locke, speaking of what he termed "race welding," compared Harlem with "other centers of folk expression and race determination" and concluded that "Harlem has the same role to play for the New Negro as Dublin has had for the New Ireland."[98] The Harlem Renaissance, linked to the insurgent African American radicalism of the 1920s and drawing on the higher living standards and psychic energy generated in the course of the great migration, was a cultural explosion inspired in part by a similar movement born halfway around the world.

The two movements, based on a persistent if elusive affinity between black and Irish Americans, shared a nationalist impulse and many aesthetic characteristics: appeals to a forgotten and noble past, themes based on the experience of common people, and language based on their dialects. "Nationalism usually conquers in the name of a putative folk culture," political theorist Ernest Gellner has written. "Its symbolism is drawn from the healthy, pristine, vigorous life of the peasants . . . If the nationalism prospers it eliminates the alien high culture, . . . it revives, or invents, a local high . . . culture of its own, though admittedly one that will have some links with the earlier local folk styles and dialects."[99] In both cases, oppressed people, in the process of struggling against their colonial enemy, invented a new culture stressing the virtues of the common folk and a vital sense of national pride. Both embraced elements of primitivism in their efforts to locate an authentic nationalist past and a racial essence. In both cases too, a rising, better-educated middle class, for whom the nationalist struggle was more a cultural than a political concern, rejected this primitivism.[100]

Precisely because of the severe political and cultural reaction of the 1920s, a broad range of ethnic and racial groups might have come together in opposition to Anglo-Saxon racism. This is clearly what W. E. B. DuBois had in mind when he denounced "a renewal of the Anglo-Saxon cult [and] worship of the Nordic totem" and urged a "great alliance between disadvantaged groups like the Irish and the Jews and the working Classes everywhere . . . to keep down privilege as represented in New England and Old England."[101]

Given the deep Irish American ambivalence toward blacks, however,

"New Negroes" remained wary, "celebrating [Irish Americans'] every success in the struggle for freedom and castigating them for their repeated
and continued violence against 'the Negro' in America."[102] "I shall at all
times defend the right of Ireland to absolute independence," W. E. B.
DuBois wrote a friend in 1921, "[but] there can be no doubt of the hostility of a large proportion of Irish Americans toward Negroes." Cyril Briggs,
who had welcomed the Irish revolution as much as anyone and remained
committed to cooperation between African American and white radicals,
nevertheless included the Irish "within the charmed circle of the dominant race."[103] Indeed, it was the grip of white racism in Irish American
communities that explained the widespread participation of the community's youth in race riots in Chicago and other cities in these same years.

CONFRONTING THE KLAN

In the early 1920s, immigrants, Catholics, Jews, and others emerged as targets of the organized intolerance of Prohibition advocates, the Ku Klux
Klan, and nativists pushing for immigration restriction. In the face of
these threats, Irish American politicians and church leaders positioned
themselves as guardians of the immigrant, and thereby created new ethnic
coalitions built on inclusive notions of civic identity. As Michael Funchion
notes, "There was a degree of Catholic solidarity that could become for-
midable in periods of anti-Catholic nativism."[104]

The 1920s were such a period, as Prohibition presented a cultural as well
as an economic and political affront to Irish Americans, as did the resurgence of Ku Klux Klan activity. At the national level, a battle raged for the
heart and soul of the Democratic Party. On one side stood a developing
coalition of Irish American machine-based politicians and patrician reformers denouncing the Klan; on the other, the party's "Solid South" and
other elements opposing any anti-Klan plank in the party's platform. The
battle also raged at the local level. In communities with large, diverse
populations, the Klan targeted black migrants, Jews, immigrants, Catholics, and labor activists, raising the possibility of a rare alliance among

these groups. In New York City, the Klan was notably unsuccessful, although it had two hundred thousand members in the state and enough activity in the city's suburbs for it to be perceived as a threat to immigrant people and the church.[105]

In Chicago, the situation was more ominous: here "Klan and anti-Klan met head on." The besieged Anglo-Saxon minority poured into the Klan, which often used Masonic halls for its meetings and rituals. In January 1922, Klan organizers claimed that Chicago had the largest membership of any city in the United States. Anti-Klan activists estimated the city membership at about fifty thousand in late 1922, while Klan sources claimed a much higher figure, about 10 percent of the adult white native-born Protestant population. At least twenty klaverns operated inside the city, while others sprouted in its surrounding suburbs. The Klan was also organizing in the city's schools. It was strongest in neighborhoods where native-born Protestant populations were immediately adjacent to large black communities and were also facing an influx of Jews and Irish Catholics. In an overwhelmingly blue-collar city, the Klan was populated disproportionately by businessmen, salespeople, foremen, and professionals.[106]

Attorney Clarence Darrow and former mayor and governor Edward F. Dunne organized some of Chicago's earliest opposition to the Klan, but the most successful group was the American Unity League, established in June 1922. Dismissed by the Klan as "an Irish Roman Catholic clique," the league included Protestants and Jews, and an African American cleric served as it honorary chairperson. Its popular newspaper, *Tolerance*, sold at newsstands and bus stops throughout the city, published the names, addresses, and occupations of thousands of Klansmen. The entire list was then published as a pamphlet, "Is Your Neighbor a Kluxer?"—"the only major attempt in the nation to publicize the names of rank and file Klansmen on a systematic basis." With a circulation high of 150,000, *Tolerance* did a great deal to break up the Chicago Klan, as did demonstrations, bombings, and ritual lynchings of Klansmen.[107]

Alderman Robert Mulcahy, keeping a close eye on the increasingly diverse electorate, convened a special investigating committee to root out

Klan members on the city payroll. The committee, which Mulcahy chaired, consisted of African, Norwegian, Polish, and Jewish American alder-men.[108] The numerous Klan organizations functioned in the more homo-geneous outlying city neighborhoods, where Chicago's small native-born Anglo Saxon population lived, much divided from the sea of immigrants and black and Mexican migrants with whom they shared the city. This division surfaced in the 1923 municipal elections, when Republicans, appealing to Klan-oriented voters, circulated anti-Catholic brochures to undermine the Democratic candidate, William Dever. The strategy back-fired. Thousands of Catholic voters mobilized, and some African Ameri-cans voted against the GOP for the first time in their lives. Dever and anti-Klan aldermen swept the election throughout the city. Given Chi-cago's large population of Catholic immigrants, blacks, and Jews, the Klan never had much chance of achieving real power there. Mulcahy's com-mittee was significant mainly as a form of multiethnic political theater. And what Mulcahy staged in Chicago was repeated in performances by Irish American politicians in Washington, D.C., and in other American cities.[109]

Though remnants of the Chicago Klan remained, it was largely dead by the end of 1924, a point at which the national organization was still rising. But white racism in Chicago did not end. The 1927 mayoral cam-paign (as we saw in chapter 5) was notable for its expressions of white supremacism, particularly from the Irish-influenced Democratic Party. "What the Klan episode proved," urban historian Kenneth Jackson con-cludes, "was the futility of efforts to treat immigrants, Catholics, and Jews like nonwhites."[110]

DEFENDING THE IMMIGRANT

During the 1920s, a movement for immigration restriction emerged, aimed largely at immigrants from southern and eastern Europe. Peaking in tandem with—and related to—the Klan's rise, it contributed to a siege mentality among Irish Catholics. The Catholic Church's position on immigration had previously been somewhat divided: prominent Catholic social activists had promoted restriction in the interest of raising wages.

But as the rationale for such legislation turned more toward racial categorization, Catholic opinion hardened. As early as 1907 the Ancient Order of Hibernians had joined with the National German-American Alliance to oppose all immigration restriction. According to historian John Higham, in the resistance to restrictive legislation, "The Irish leaders who dominated the Catholic Church and in some sections bossed the Democratic Party championed the interests of their southern and eastern European followers."[111] A 1921 immigration law restricted other ethnic Catholics but did little to damage Irish immigration, which continued in large volume in the early 1920s. Then in 1924, the Johnson-Reed National Origins Act proposed to drastically curtail immigration from eastern and southeastern Europe—and to reduce the allowable quota from Ireland. At that point, Irish Americans reacted harshly.[112] As historian Gary Gerstle notes, the legislation not only racialized and politicized immigration but also "increase[ed] the rewards for assimilation and penalties for cultural difference for those immigrants already here."[113]

Some Catholics continued to support the principle of immigration restriction, but most objected to the prejudice against ethnic and religious groups upon which the new legislation seemed to be based. "Looking into the philosophy . . . that has guided or is guiding much of our present immigration policy," Bishop Edmund F. Gibbons of Albany wrote, "one cannot but see that it is unconsciously or consciously a prejudice against the Catholic immigrant."[114] Persistent anti-Catholicism, a burden the Irish felt keenly; the symbolic importance of continuing immigration to Irish American identity; and the self-interest of the Catholic Church and the Democratic Party—all dictated opposition to the act.

While a wide range of groups opposed the restrictive 1924 Immigration Act, the Jews and the Irish were the key groups in the opposition.[115] With dozens of representatives in Congress, control of the Catholic Church, and strong political organizations in most large cities, Irish Americans were well equipped to fight restriction at both the ideological and legislative levels. In congressional debates over the 1924 legislation, Irish American politicians and the Catholic Church made their influence felt.[116] The Knights of Columbus led the public fight, while Irish Catholic and Jewish politicians rallied opposition within Congress. "This is not the America I belong to," Congressman John O'Connor of New York said, referring to the bill. "That is not the America I want to be a part of." After the restrictive legislation was passed, the American Irish Historical Society, the Friends of Irish Freedom, Clan na Gael, AOH, and other organizations formed the Joint Committee on the Immigration Act of 1924 with the goal of repealing it. Tellingly, however, the solidarity among opponents of the bill did not extend to people of color. Some of the most vociferous opponents of the restriction on European immigration acquiesced in or even supported restrictions on the Japanese.[117]

Despite the conservatism of the church and the various Irish American groups, in insisting on the rights of immigrants and workers, they projected a civic identity based on tolerance and social solidarity.[118] In the process, they helped forge an inclusive Catholic ethnic identity and laid the groundwork for the ethnic-based Democratic coalitions of the late twenties and early thirties. By opposing Prohibition, immigration restriction, and the Klan, Irish politicians could position themselves as representatives of an aggrieved multiethnic community, while their increasing support for social reforms appealed to a class-conscious urban constituency.[119]

In response to postwar nativism, racism, and immigration restriction, the Knights of Columbus promoted a distinctive "Catholic Americanism." "The proudest boast of all time is ours to make," the group's oath read: "I am an American Catholic citizen."[120] It emphasized the pluralism of American society. In 1921, the Knights established a Historical Commission specifically to present an alternative to the triumphal Anglo-Saxonism and anti-immigrant and anti-Catholic sentiments they found in much mainstream historical writing. The result was a fascinating series of books on the "racial contributions" of various ethnic groups, including African Americans—authored by W. E. B. DuBois—Germans, and Jews.

The inspiration for the series was Edward F. McSweeney (1864–1928). A self-educated Boston trade unionist who left school for work at the age of eleven, McSweeney had a deep, lifelong love for U.S. history. Though he had shown an anti-immigrant bias earlier in his life, his tenure as assistant commissioner of immigration at Ellis Island from 1893 to 1902 convinced him to resist immigration restriction and to defend the role of immigrants in the development of the United States. McSweeney wrote an introduction to the book series that challenged the Klan's exclusivist vision of American history. The Knights' Historical Commission established a series of prizes for books and for graduate students doing research on topics that enhanced ethnic and racial tolerance. It abandoned its work only when the Knights decided to confront the Klan more directly through lawsuits and lobbying in state legislatures.[121]

Al Smith's bitter defeat in the 1928 presidential election signaled the limits of Irish Catholic acceptance, and during the Great Depression, mass unemployment served to remind millions of Irish that they remained in the broad working-class community. As Father Coughlin's popularity showed, economic insecurity could breed intolerance and reaction, but the Depression also had the effect of undercutting the worst of the prejudice against Irish Americans. "If Papists were really taking over the nation's institutions," historian Michael Kazin writes, "why were so many out there on the breadlines with other Christians?" Kazin overstates the case when he claims that "in the 1930s, no public figure of any influence still accused Catholics of being un-American." A genteel liberal anti-Catholicism remained among some of America's most influential intellectuals even after World War II. Where they surfaced occasionally, such attitudes sustained a sullen defensiveness among some Irish Catholics.[122]

Irish American politics was often a strange combination, then, of the parochial and the global, the progressive and the conservative. The concerns of one particularly talented Irish American congressman, William Bourke Cockran (1854–1923), who represented a Midtown Manhattan district, suggest the sinews of key components of the perspective. Born in County Sligo, Cockran was educated in Ireland and France before emigrating to the United States at the age of seventeen. He studied and practiced law in New York City, supported Tammany Hall, and was elected to Congress as a Democrat in 1887. He broke briefly with the Democrats over the silver issue in 1896, but opposed McKinley's imperialist adventures and soon returned to the fold. Cockran certainly considered himself a reformer: he was quite capable of criticizing the party yet remained a Democratic stalwart. Cockran's three great passions were free and open immigration, opposition to British and American imperialism, and the welfare of the Catholic Church. A brilliant orator, Cockran spoke often in support of Irish independence and in opposition to the U.S. occupation of the Philippines. He was a strong advocate of trade unions and woman suffrage but an adamant opponent of socialism.[123]

In the age of imperialism and the racist thinking that sustained it, many Irish Americans identified with oppressed colonial peoples, recognized in their struggles a reflection of their own, and opposed colonial expansion. But many more embraced both American patriotism and imperialism—to establish their status as good Americans and perhaps also as part of a process of distancing themselves from people of color, at home and abroad.

After the First World War, most Irish turned away from the idealism of the revolutionary nationalist movement as well as the progressive labor movement. All Americans were subject to the coercive nationalism of the war years, but few groups were as vulnerable as the Irish due to their active opposition to the war, their hostility to the British, and their pursuit of Irish independence in the midst of the war. Were the Irish truly "one hundred percent" Americans, or were they "hyphenated" Americans? During and after the war, the government cracked down both on the radical republican movement and on the leftist organizations to which it was allied. Neither the Versailles nor the Anglo-Irish treaty delivered the unified, independent Ireland of the nationalist dream. More depressing, in the wake of an exhausting revolutionary struggle to remove the British from the island, the revolutionaries turned on one another in a sustained civil war. A small minority of hard-core nationalists in the United States fell into either the pro-treaty or anti-treaty republican camp, but most Irish Americans became disaffected by the struggles in Ireland, whether from disgust, disappointment, or simply exhaustion.

The Red Scare of the early 1920s was part of a more general conservative turn in American society—regarding the status and culture of immigrant people, race and social class relations, and politics. At this time the parochial quality of Irish American culture reemerged, visible in the race riots of 1919. It reemerged also in the form of Father Coughlin's anti-Semitic and reactionary populism when the Depression once again threatened the tenuous Irish grip on success. Still, even in the reactionary 1920s, some Irish Americans reached out to the new immigrants and people of color through groups like the Knights of Columbus. When Prohibition, immigration restriction, and ultrapatriotism all targeted immigrant communities, many Irish Americans rightly perceived that this included them. Where they could envision solidarity, a progressive, internationalist form of Irish Americanism endured.

EPILOGUE

William and Paul O'Dwyer were two of eleven children born to Patrick and Bridget O'Dwyer in a small impoverished village in County Mayo. William (1890–1964) followed in many ways a classic Irish immigrant route. He came to the United States in 1910, landed in an Irish-run boardinghouse on New York's Upper West Side, and began making connections, working first as a laborer and then as a policeman while studying law at Fordham University in the evenings. He built a successful practice and worked his way through the Tammany ranks, serving first as a judge and then as district attorney in Brooklyn. After losing to Fiorello La Guardia in the 1941 mayoral election, he volunteered for war service, emerging as a brigadier general in 1945, and was shortly afterward elected mayor. He was reelected following a successful first term, but allegations of organized crime connections dogged him until he resigned in 1950.[1]

Paul O'Dwyer (1907–1998) followed his brother to New York, where political and union connections helped him get work on the West Side docks. He, too, attended Fordham's law school at night. An ambitious and ardent Catholic and a nationalist, Paul O'Dwyer was in many respects typical of twentieth-century Irish immigrants. But his instincts led him in a different direction. Deeply offended by the anti-Semitism he saw around him, he forged close ties with Jewish classmates, provided legal and logistical support to the Zionists in the 1948 Israeli war for independence, and pleaded the case for Israeli sovereignty before the United Nations. O'Dwyer joined Oscar Bernstein's law firm and worked his way up to partner, yet he never forgot his ethnic or class background. He supported both the radical republican movement in Ireland and the civil rights movement in the United States, often drawing parallels between them. "The Black and Tan used to drive through the town shooting things up," he recalled of the Irish revolutionary war against the British. "It was not that different from Mississippi." It was a comparison that Catholic civil rights campaigners in Northern Ireland commonly made at the time. Running for U.S. Senate in 1968, O'Dwyer once arrived at a television studio to find a strike going on. He refused to cross the picket line. "These are my people," he told the interviewer. At a time when most labor and many Democratic Party leaders supported the war in Vietnam, O'Dwyer joined young protesters in opposing it, as did an emerging Catholic left. He represented minority and working-class clients in labor and civil rights cases, often for free. "The one issue," O'Dwyer explained, "is fair play."[2]

Between them, the stories of the O'Dwyer brothers represent vital elements in the history of urbanized Irish Americans: an ambitious, assimilationist, and more conservative path; and a pluralist, progressive path based on idealism. While the former may have been more common, the two tendencies remained in tension in Irish American communities. The resulting ambivalence in values and behavior goes a long way toward explaining their relations with other ethnic and racial groups.

At the core of Irish influence in the American city was what sociologists have come to call social capital. "The theory of social capital is, at heart, most straightforward," sociologist John Field writes. "Its central thesis can be summed up in two words: relationships matter."[3] Those who would understand how certain groups exercise power and influence, French theorist Pierre Bourdieu writes, would do well to consider not just their material wealth but also their social and cultural resources, or "capital," generated through elaborate relationships over time. These various forms of capital are, in fact, linked. "The existence of a network of connections," Bourdieu writes, "is not a natural given, or even a social given . . . It is the product of an endless effort."[4]

Bourdieu had social elites in mind, but his concept can also explain the remarkable influence of working-class and "lace curtain" Irish Americans in cities between the 1880s and the 1940s. Irish Americans built and maintained relations with other ethnic and racial groups in the face of massive migration of other peoples to American cities. They proved to be masters at transforming everyday relations in extended families, neighborhoods, and workplaces into institutions that afforded them economic, social, cultural, and political power.[5] In the process, they shaped a world that later immigrants and migrants inhabited in their own transitions to American urban life. The short-term effect of this massive immigration was not to diminish but rather to enhance Irish influence.

Everything we know about nineteenth-century Irish American communities indicates that they were sustained by these dense networks, a distinct approach to religion, and a strong national identity forged in the struggle for national independence and in opposition to aggressive and pervasive nativist and religious prejudice. Such networks derived from informal neighborhood and parish connections, street gangs, political clubs, and saloons. They were then built into enduring institutions, notably the Catholic diocese and its allied organizations; the urban Democratic machine; and the city labor movement. In each case, Irish influence started locally and then expanded to the metropolitan level. Nativist hostility toward the Irish on ethnic, religious, and even racial grounds only enhanced their solidarity as they used a range of strategies to defend themselves and to maximize their influence.

The strong parishes, unions, and city political organizations that they developed, often in the face of considerable discrimination, constituted bonding social capital, which underlay their communities' strong defensive mentality. Its shared values and its sense of reciprocal social, economic, and political functions—what one historian has called the "Irish ethic" of intraethnic patronage—provided the framework for Irish American survival and advancement.[6] The rewards of such organization and bonding were not lost on later groups. The Irish "were treated worse than ever were the Jews at any time in the history of the country," the *American Monthly Jewish Review* observed in 1911. "But the Irish . . . organized into various leagues, and these instead of trying to crush one another out, joined hands for the common issue."[7] That was why the Irish ran city hall, the police department, and the schools, a Polish cop tells a troublesome Polish American youth in Nelson Algren's *Never Come Morning* (1942). The city's Poles should "do like the Irish."[8] It took well over a generation, but by the time new immigrants began pouring into American cities, the Irish had managed to create a great deal of such bonding capital.[9]

Of course, these networks could exclude and deny as well as integrate and empower.[10] Irish bonding could be employed to monopolize hierarchical positions in the church, to defend neighborhood turf and jobs, and to retain control over ballot slots and patronage positions. In the midst of massive immigration around 1900, Irish Americans used these networks and the social capital they had painstakingly created to dominate many aspects of urban life. The often-closed quality of these networks explains why the Irish so often came into conflict with other racial and ethnic groups, and how, in response, these groups developed their own networks and institutions, sometimes modeled on those of the Irish, to compete for power and resources. In the course of this conflict, Irish Americans helped to reproduce and convey racism and other forms of prejudice to more recent arrivals.

Something like the deadlines dividing neighborhoods can be discerned in Irish-dominated unions. Too often they functioned as "job trusts," blocking access of workers from other ethnic backgrounds to apprenticeship programs and job sites. Despite the fact that their own members often derived from immigrant backgrounds, early unions supported immigration restriction, in part to prevent unskilled immigrant labor from flooding the labor market, but also out of deeply held prejudices. In the Catholic Church, the Irish sought to maintain their power structure

and relegate more recent immigrant Catholics to the parish basement—
metaphorically and in fact. Irish vaudeville comedians, Tin Pan Alley
lyricists, and popular writers transmitted racial and ethnic knowledge to
native-born Americans, to the settled Irish, to the recent immigrants, and
especially to their children. Artists stigmatized and marginalized new
groups through crude ethnic humor and songs, but their efforts signal not
only hostility but also curiosity.

What makes the Irish experience crucial to understanding that of other
groups is that they also proved adept at developing bridging social capital. The attitude of Irish Americans toward more recent European immigrants and migrant peoples of color was never uniformly hostile. Thus
a tension between civic and racial nationalism lay at the heart of the Irish
American community.[11]

The Irish disseminated racism and ethnic prejudice against and among
the newcomers, but they also often helped them adapt to their new city
homes through their religious institutions and political and labor organizations, if only to retain their grip on power and influence. In some cases,
they would also reach out to more recent arrivals, following ideals of tolerance, inclusiveness, and human rights and worth that were derived from
Irish religious and political culture as well as from their own experiences
with discrimination and exclusion. John Fitzpatrick and Leonora O'Reilly
lived at the very center of the Irish American community, but they built
their social movements by reaching out to African Americans and recent
immigrants, personifying an Irish Americanism that was not only progressive but also cosmopolitan in its perspective and inclusive in its aims.

The social teachings of the Catholic Church, and the dark memories of
poverty and violence stretching from the west of Ireland to Lower Manhattan and Chicago's South Side, provided fertile ground for such progressive political activism long after many Irish Americans had become
respectable and some had even begun to turn toward political conservatism. "As a young person, impressionable, I almost forgot who I was, as
the Irish often do here," Paul O'Dwyer once commented on the roots of

his own commitments. "Because you are white you think you will be treated equally." The fact that this still was not always the case pressed him to consider the plight of people of color.[12]

Liberal Irish priests tried to accommodate black and Italian Catholics; the Knights of Columbus and the Ancient Order of Hibernians were first established to fight discrimination against the Irish but later adapted to oppose immigration restriction, the Klan, and intolerance against all immigrants. Community loyalty could spark violent reactions against outsiders in strikes, but broader notions of solidarity steeped in Irish nationalism and Catholic social values could also motivate activists like John Fitzpatrick, who spent his energies trying to create a progressive, interracial labor movement. In such situations, Irish Americans employed their considerable social capital to create bonds with more recent immigrant groups.[13] In the process, they passed on progressive political and social values and helped mobilize immigrants and migrants against social, economic, and political inequality. One ignores these more salutary effects, and focuses exclusively on tendencies toward exclusion, at the risk of fundamentally misunderstanding not only Irish Americans but also the groups with whom they shared the American city.

Irish American women played a decisive role in establishing and maintaining such "social bridges," due in part to the demographics of the Irish immigrant community and the resources they carried with them. Irish women's strong sense of social responsibility was born in Ireland and nurtured in the Catholic enclaves of the urban United States. They married other immigrants more often than did their counterparts in other ethnic communities, and they carried Irish values into these ethnically mixed families. They cared for immigrant youth in Catholic orphanages and settlement houses. As teachers and teaching nuns in public and parochial schools, they taught new immigrant, black migrant, and later Mexican migrant children and served them as nurses and nursing sisters. As early suffragists and union organizers, they provided contacts with middle-class reformers and drew working-class people into social and reform movements.

As working-class Catholics in a WASP-dominated society and as women in the patriarchal Irish American community, they were outsiders in a variety of ways. Unlike earlier generations, however, twentieth-century Irish immigrants assumed "white" status in a society where that opened many doors. Irish women's place in the nation's complex racial hierarchy was far more secure than that of the new immigrants they encountered on the streets and in the workplaces.[14]

The answer to the old question of what it means to be an American has never been static. Generations of immigrants have helped to transform the ideal. But the gradual evolution of a broader racial identity was crucial to the acculturation of immigrant peoples. If the second generation in the more recent immigrant communities was becoming American by the mid-twentieth century, sociologist Philip Kasinitz writes, "it was also expanding what it meant to be 'American.'" The incorporation of immigrants' children created a more inclusive society that was panethnic rather than mainstream Anglo-Saxon in its character.[15]

The effects of Irish strategies—those that restricted and excluded later migrants as well as those that sought to integrate them—were etched in millions of individual contacts between Irish Americans and others. It is difficult to conjure up any net effect, but in building and employing these social bridges, Irish Americans played a vital role in the creation of the multiethnic American city.

Since the Great Depression, Irish American influence has dissipated. "Irishness" has become more diffuse. By the 1960s, ethnicity was a matter of choice as much as of heritage, as sociologist Nathan Glazer and the late senator Daniel Patrick Moynihan maintained, but certainly most Irish Americans, including many from ethnically mixed backgrounds, clung to the identification.[16] Today's Irish American culture is very different from what we have described here. As they moved up in the social structure and out to the suburbs, as they intermarried more extensively, first with other Catholics and then with other racial and religious groups, Irish Americans certainly blended in. By 1980, they had surpassed most other groups in terms of occupational status, income, and educational levels.[17]

As Irish Americans rose in wealth and status, some abandoned the traditional urban liberalism of their parents and turned toward the conservatism of a new elite. Yet the continuing influence of the Irish, particularly in city environments, is unmistakable. They show up often in the leadership of the Catholic Church, the Democratic Party, and the labor movement, but they maintain influence only if they are able to work effectively with other ethnic groups. A new wave of immigrants primarily from Asia and Latin America has once again transformed the American city. The social networks of the twenty-first-century city are extremely diverse—not unlike those that emerged in the early twentieth. They form the basis of a new version of the multiethnic American city that Irish Americans have done so much to shape.

ACKNOWLEDGMENTS

Much of the inspiration for this book came from Jenny Barrett and our relationship over the past four decades. She helped me to appreciate the lasting influence of the Irish in some very unlikely settings. She discussed the research and writing with me at great length, read various versions of the manuscript, made numerous helpful suggestions, and facilitated the work through her own sacrifices. I thank her for all this and above all for her love and support.

I learned a great deal from my son Xian (Sean), whose own interests in race and ethnicity and his experiences as a teacher in the Chicago public schools and as a member of the labor movement have been important sources of ideas and encouragement. He constantly reminded me that the point of this exercise was not simply to describe American society but to change it. I thank Xian too for his love, support, and hospitality on research trips, for his commitment to building a more just city and society, and for having the wisdom to return to my family's old West Side neighborhood, where parts of this story are set.

I would especially like to thank an old friend and colleague, David Roediger. The book evolved in conversations with him about race and ethnicity and the peculiar role that the Irish played in this realm of American life. It took shape in a joint project regarding their role in teaching more recent immigrants about race and in helping to create a broader "white" ethnic identity. Parts of our coauthored essay, "Making New Immigrants

'Inbetween': Irish Hosts and White Panethnicity," which was published in *Not Just Black and White: Historical and Contemporary Perspectives on Immigration, Race, and Ethnicity in the United States*, edited by Nancy Foner and George Frederickson (New York: Russell Sage Foundation Press, 2004), appear at points in the present work, and I am grateful to David and to the Russell Sage Foundation for permission to use them here. Likewise, I thank David and the *Journal of American Ethnic History* for permission to reprint portions of our article "The Irish and the 'Americanization' of the 'New Immigrants' in the Streets and in the Churches of the Urban United States, 1900–1930," which appeared in the Summer 2005 issue of volume 24 of that journal.

Portions of the book dealing with immigrant youth culture and "The Irish and the Jews" first appeared in the Polish journal *Przeglad Polonijny*. Thank you to Dorota Praszalowicz, Adam Walaszek, and other Polish colleagues for their interest in my work.

My wonderful graduate students have served as research assistants or have contributed ideas and encouragement. Many thanks to Will Cooley, Mike Rosenow, Tom Mackaman, Martin Smith, Nicki Ranganath, Jason Kozlowski, Anthony Sigismondi, Dave Hageman, Steve Hageman, Melissa Rhode, Adam Hodges, Janine Giordano Drake, Dennis McNulty, David Bates, Kwame Holmes, Ian Hartman, Emily Pope Obeda, and Bryan Nicholson. Thanks especially to Bryan for his help on securing the book's images. The staffs of the New York Public Library, the Chicago History Museum, the Boston Archdiocese, and the Rare Books Room at the University of Illinois Library in Urbana, provided the images and permissions for their use. The Library of Congress was particularly important in this regard.

The late Rudolph Vecoli, Kerby Miller, David Montgomery, Tim Meagher, Gillian Stevens, Tricia Kelleher, and Donna Gabaccia made helpful suggestions. Kevin Kenny, Kathy Oberdeck, Diane Koenker, David Roediger, Antoinette Burton, and Alison Kibler read and commented on parts of the manuscript. I am particularly grateful to Kevin for an insightful reading of a very early draft and to Mark Leff, who read two different drafts and provided his usually astute comments. I presented various parts of the work at the History and Irish Studies Colloquia at Boston College; the Newberry Library Labor History Seminar; the American Conference for Irish Studies at Notre Dame University; the National University of Ireland, Galway; two different conferences at Jageillonian University, Cracow; a special conference on race and class at Roosevelt University in Chicago; and to the University of Illinois History Workshop, Working-Class History, and Migration Studies groups in Urbana. I benefited from all of these discussions, and I thank innumerable colleagues, students, and friends not named here for their suggestions.

I received research support and time off from teaching as a result of grants from the Research Board, the Center for Advanced Study, and the Center on Democracy in a Multiracial Society at the University of Illinois at Urbana-Champaign, an institution that has provided a consistently invigorating and supportive work environment over three decades. When you receive a semester off from teaching, the students are still there, so I also thank all of my colleagues for taking up the slack and encouraging me along the way.

Glenda Gilmore encouraged me to send the manuscript to Penguin Press. Laura Stickney oversaw the project there from beginning to very near the end, at which point Mally Anderson and Scott Moyers took over. Janet Biehl did a wonderful job copyediting it for Penguin. Julie Greene and Fred Hoxie provided some early advice regarding publishing.

The Barrett family—Pat, Jack and Bonnie, Mike and Teri, and in particular Tom Barrett and Janine Goldstein—have provided the requisite measures of skepticism and enthusiasm for the project and loving support for the author. My late father inspired my fascination with the multiethnic city and intrigued me with his stories of its diverse peoples. We argued constantly—and very productively—over many of the questions raised here. I am sorry that he is no longer with us to see the effects of my work.

This book is dedicated to the two most important women in my life. They share more in common than one might guess. Jenny Barrett and her experiences growing up in the city as the child of hardworking immigrants and our lives together inspired the book. My late mother lived much of this story, and her own life represents its brightest dimensions. She raised five children in the inner city, conveying all the right lessons and teaching us early on and every day of our lives that "it takes all kinds."

Jim Barrett, Chicago

NOTES

INTRODUCTION

1. Harry Golden, "Preface," in Hutchins Hapgood, *The Spirit of the Ghetto: Studies of the Jewish Quarter of New York* (1902; reprinted, Cambridge, Mass.: Belknap Press of Harvard University Press, 1967), ix. See also Moses Rischin, *The Promised City: New York's Jews, 1870–1914* (New York: Harper & Row, 1962), 263; Jacob Riis, *How the Other Half Lives: Studies Among the Tenements of New York* (New York: C. Scribner's Sons, 1890), 22.

2. Kevin Kenny, *The American Irish: A History* (New York: Longman, 2000), 131–41; Thomas N. Brown, *Irish-American Nationalism, 1870–1890* (Philadelphia: Lippincott, 1966), 18; Roger Daniels, *Coming to America: A History of Immigration and Ethnicity in American Life* (New York: HarperCollins, 1990), 121–45; John Paul Bocock, "The Irish Conquest," *Forum*, April 1894, 187.

3. Emily Greene Balch, *Our Slavic Fellow Citizens* (New York: Charities Publication Committee, 1910), 412.

4. Nathan Glazer and Daniel Patrick Moynihan, *Beyond the Melting Pot: Irish, Jews, and Puerto Ricans in New York City* (Cambridge, Mass.: MIT Press, 1970), 217; Timothy Meagher, ed., *From Paddy to Studs: Irish American Communities in the Turn of the Century Era, 1880–1920* (Westport, Conn.: Greenwood Press, 1986), 3–5; Tom Hayden, *Irish on the Outside: In Search of the Soul of Irish America* (London: Verso, 2001), 55–63, 78–80; Thomas M. Henderson, *Tammany Hall and the New Immigrants: The Progressive Years* (New York: Ayer, 1976), 73–75.

5. Rudolph J. Vecoli, "An Inter-Ethnic Perspective on American Immigration History," *Mid-America* 75 (April–July 1993), 234; Werner Sollors, ed., *The Invention of Ethnicity* (New York: Oxford University Press, 1989), xiv. See also Kathleen Neils Conzen and David A. Gerber, "The Invention of Ethnicity: A Perspective from the U.S.A.," *Journal of American Ethnic History* 12, no. 1 (Fall 1992): 3–41.

6. Henry Louis Gates, Jr., *Loose Canons: Notes on the Culture Wars* (New York: Oxford University Press, 1992), xvi.

7. James R. Barrett, "Americanization from the Bottom Up: Immigration and the Remaking of the Working Class in the United States, 1880–1930," *Journal of American History* 79 (December 1992): 996–1020. On the role of the Irish in the acculturation of the "new immigrants" of the early twentieth century, see James R. Barrett and David R. Roediger, "The Irish and the 'Americanization' of the 'New Immigrants' in the Streets and in the Churches

of the Urban United States, 1900–1930," *Journal of American Ethnic History* 24 (Summer 2005): 3–33; David R. Roediger and James R. Barrett, "Making New Immigrants 'Inbetween': Irish Hosts and White Panethnicity, 1890–1930," in Nancy Foner and George M. Fredrickson, eds., *Not Just Black and White: Historical and Contemporary Perspectives on Immigration, Race, and Ethnicity in the United States* (New York: Russell Sage Foundation, 2004), 167–96.

8. James S. Donnelly, "The Construction of the Memory of the Famine in Ireland and the Irish Diaspora, 1850–1900," *Éire-Ireland* 31, nos. 1–2 (Spring–Summer 1996), 26–61; Kerby A. Miller, *Emigrants and Exiles: Ireland and the Irish Exodus to North America* (New York: Oxford University Press, 1985), 551; Kerby A. Miller, " 'Revenge for Sibbereen': Irish Emigration and the Meaning of the Great Famine," and Mick Mulcrone, "The Famine and Collective Memory: The Role of the Irish-American Press in the Early Twentieth Century," both in Arthur Gibben, ed., *The Great Famine and the Irish Diaspora in America* (Amherst: University of Massachusetts Press, 1999), 180–95, 219–38; J. J. Lee, "Introduction: Interpreting Irish America," in J. J. Lee and Marion R. Casey, eds., *Making the Irish American: History and Heritage of the Irish in the United States* (New York: New York University Press, 2006), 18–23.

9. The Irish had an unusually low rate of return migration compared to virtually all other American ethnic groups, as low as 6 to 10 percent in the late nineteenth century. See David Fitzpatrick, *Irish Emigration, 1801–1921* (Dublin: Economic and Social History Society of Ireland, 1984), 6–7.

10. On persistent nativism against Irish Catholics throughout the mid-nineteenth century, see Peter Schrag, *Not Fit for Our Society: Nativism and Immigration* (Berkeley: University of California Press, 2010), 24–29; Dale T. Knobel, *Paddy and the Republic: Ethnicity and Nationality in Antebellum America* (Middletown, Conn.: Wesleyan University Press, 1986); Kenny, *American Irish*, 80–82, 116–18; Ray Allen Billington, *The Protestant Crusade, 1800–1860: A Study of the Origins of American Nativism* (New York: Macmillan, 1938), 53–165; David H. Bennett, *The American Far Right from Nativism to the Militia Movement* (Chapel Hill: University of North Carolina Press, 1988), 35–47; Sean Wilentz, *Chants Democratic: New York City and the Rise of the American Working Class, 1788–1850* (New York: Oxford University Press, 2004), 315–25; Iver Bernstein, *The New York City Draft Riots: Their Significance for American Society and Politics in the Age of the Civil War* (New York: Oxford University Press, 1990), 38–39; David T. Gleeson, *The Irish in the South, 1815–1877* (Chapel Hill: University of North Carolina Press, 2000), 112–19.

11. *Chicago Tribune*, February 26, 1855, quoted in Lawrence J. McCaffrey, Ellen Skerrett, Michael F. Funchion, and Charles Fanning, *The Irish in Chicago* (Urbana: University of Illinois Press, 1987), 26; see also Donald L. Miller, *City of the Century: The Epic of Chicago and the Making of America* (New York: Simon & Schuster, 1996), 136, 442; Benjamin Alexander, "Temperance, Slavery, and Nativism: Chicago and the Origins of the Know-Nothing Party, 1850–1856," B.A. honors thesis, University of Illinois at Urbana-Champaign, 2001.

12. Knobel, *Paddy and the Republic*, 90, 68–103; Matthew Frye Jacobson, *Whiteness of a Different Color: European Immigrants and the Alchemy of Race* (Cambridge, Mass.: Harvard University Press, 1998), 46–49; and Thomas F. Gossett, *Race: The History of an Idea in America* (Dallas: Southern Methodist University Press, 1963), 95–97, 109–10, 288–89. See also David R. Roediger, *The Wages of Whiteness: Race and the Making of the American Working Class* (London: Verso, 1991), 133–34.

13. Alexander Keyssar, *The Right to Vote: The Contested History of Democracy in the United States*, rev. ed. (New York: Basic Books, 2009), 81.

14. Roediger, *Wages of Whiteness*, 144–50; Jacobson, *Whiteness of a Different Color*, 48–49; Richard Williams, *Hierarchical Structures and Social Value: The Creation of Black and Irish Identities in the United States* (New York: Cambridge University Press, 1990); David M. Emmons, *Beyond the American Pale: The Irish in the West, 1845–1910* (Norman: University of Oklahoma Press, 2010), 119–21, 138–72.

15. William H. Williams, *" 'Twas Only an Irishman's Dream": The Image of Ireland and the Irish in American Popular Song Lyrics, 1800–1920* (Urbana: University of Illinois Press, 1996), 1.

16. Abraham Bisno, *Abraham Bisno, Union Pioneer* (Madison: University of Wisconsin Press, 1967), 55; Caroline F. Ware, *Greenwich Village, 1920–1930: A Comment on American Civilization in the Post-War Years* (Boston: Houghton Mifflin, 1935), 129; Williams, *" 'Twas Only an Irishman's Dream,' "* 175; and Howard Ralph Weisz, *Irish-American and Italian-American Educational Views and Activities, 1870–1900: A Comparison* (New York: Arno Press, 1976), 375. See also Michael Novak, *The Rise of the Unmeltable Ethnics* (New York: Macmillan, 1972), 55.

17. Kevin Kenny, "Diaspora and Comparison: The Global Irish as a Case Study," *Journal of American History* 90 (June 2003): 134–62; and Lawrence McCaffrey, *The Irish Diaspora in America* (Bloomington: Indiana University Press, 1976), 108.

18. On the importance of ethnic nationalism in eastern European working-class communities in the 1910s, see Victor R. Greene, *For God and Country: The Rise of Polish and Lithuanian Consciousness in America, 1860–1910* (Madison: State Historical Society of Wisconsin, 1975), 172–79; and David Montgomery, "Nationalism, Patriotism, and Class Consciousness among Immigrant Workers in the United States in the Epoch of World War I," in Dirk Hoerder, ed., *"Struggle a Hard Battle": Essays on Working Class Immigrants* (DeKalb: Northern Illinois University Press, 1986), 327–51. On the mass character of Irish American nationalism in this era, see Kenny, *American Irish*, 193–96; Kevin Kenny, "American Irish Nationalism," in Lee and Casey, *Making the Irish American*, 294–96; and David Brundage, " 'In Time of Peace, Prepare for War': Key Themes in the Social Thought of New York's Irish Nationalists, 1890–1916," in Ronald H. Bayor and Timothy J. Meagher, eds., *The New York Irish* (Baltimore, Md.: Johns Hopkins University Press, 1996), 357–73.

19. L. A. O'Donnell, *Irish Voice and Organized Labor: A Biographical Study* (Westport, Conn.: Greenwood Press, 1997); Helen C. Camp, *Iron in Her Soul: Elizabeth Gurley Flynn and the American Left* (Pullman: Washington State University Press, 1995); James R. Barrett, *William Z. Foster and the Tragedy of American Radicalism* (Urbana: University of Illinois Press, 1999); Elliott J. Gorn, *Mother Jones: The Most Dangerous Woman in America* (New York: Hill & Wang, 2001); and David Montgomery, "The Irish and the American Labor Movement," in David Noel Doyle and Owen Dudley Edwards, eds., *America and Ireland, 1776–1976: The American Identity and the Irish Connection* (Westport, Conn.: Greenwood Press, 1980), 205–6.

20. Kenny, *Irish in America*, 165–71, 204–9; Robert D. Cross, *The Emergence of Liberal Catholicism in America* (Cambridge, Mass.: Harvard University Press, 1958); Jay P. Dolan, *The American Catholic Experience: A History from Colonial Times to the Present* (Notre Dame, Ind.: University of Notre Dame Press, 1992), 294–346.

21. Ellen Chesler, *Woman of Valor: Margaret Sanger and the Birth Control Movement in America* (New York: Simon & Schuster, 1992).

22. Ronald H. Bayor and Timothy J. Meagher, "Conclusion," in Bayor and Meagher, *New York Irish*, 533.

23. On the fusion of Irish national and religious identity in Ireland and the United States, see Matthew Frye Jacobson, *Special Sorrows: The Diasporic Imagination of Irish, Polish, and Jewish Immigrants* (Berkeley: University of California Press, 2002), 66–68; and R. F. Foster, *Modern Ireland, 1600–1972* (New York: Penguin, 1988), 340. On Catholicism as the central component of hegemonic bourgeois culture in Ireland, see Kerby A. Miller, "Class, Culture, and the Immigrant Group Identity in the United States: The Case of Irish American Ethnicity," in Virginia Yans-McLaughlin, ed., *Immigration Reconsidered: History, Sociology, and Politics* (New York: Oxford University Press, 1990), 100–106.

24. Elizabeth Gurley Flynn, *The Rebel Girl: An Autobiography: My First Life (1906–1926)* (New York: International Publishers, 1955), 21, quote at 23; William Z. Foster, *From Bryan to Stalin* (New York: International Publishers, 1937), 11; Jacobson, *Whiteness of a Different Color*, 50; Kenneth Moss, "St. Patrick's Day Celebrations and the Formation of Irish-American Identity, 1845–1875," *Journal of Social History* 29, no. 1 (1995): 125–48.

25. Roediger, *Wages of Whiteness*, 133–34, 137–38; Gilbert Osofsky, "Abolitionists, Irish Immigrants, and the Dilemmas of Romantic Nationalism," *American Historical Review* 80 (October 1975): 889–98; Theodore Allen, *The Invention of the White Race* (London: Verso, 1994), 1:178; Catherine Mary Egan, *"I did imagine . . . we had ceased to be white-washed negroes": Racial Formation of Irish Identity in Nineteenth Century Ireland and America*, Ph.D. diss., Boston College, 2001; Lauren Onkey, *Blackness and the Transatlantic Irish Identity* (New York: Routledge, 2010); Colm Kerrigan, "Irish Temperance and U.S. Slavery: Father Matthew and the Abolitionists," *History Workshop* 31 (1991): 105–19; Angela F. Murphy, "Daniel O'Connell and the 'American Eagle': Slavery, Diplomacy, Nativism, and the Collapse of American's First Irish Nationalist Movement," *Journal of American Ethnic History* 26 (Winter 2007): 3–26; John T. McGreevy, *Catholicism and American Freedom: A History* (New York: W.W. Norton, 2004): 50–53, 56; Frederick Douglass to William Lloyd Garrison, September 16, 1845, in Philip S. Foner, ed., *Life and Writings of Frederick Douglass* (New York: International Publishers, 1950–55), 1:120; John F. Quinn, "'Safe in Old Ireland': Frederick Douglass's Tour, 1845–1846," *Historian* 64 (Spring–Summer 2002): 535–50; and Bruce Nelson, "'Come Out of Such a Land, You Irishmen': Daniel O'Connell, American Slavery, and the Making of the Irish Race," *Éire-Ireland* 42 (Spring–Summer 2007): 58–81.

26. Bertha Devlin, interview by Dana Gumb, September 19, 1985. See also Bertha Devlin, interview by Guggenheim Productions, February 22, 1987, quotes at 25, 22; Josephine Keenan Materia, interview by Janet Levine, June 22, 1994; Lillian Cavanaugh, interview, Oral History Collections, Ellis Island Immigration Museum. On Irish beliefs regarding a black devil, see also David R. Roediger, *Working Toward Whiteness: How America's Immigrants Became White: The Strange Journey from Ellis Island to the Suburbs* (New York: Basic Books, 2005), 137–38.

27. Meagher, "Irish Americans and Race," in Timothy Meagher, *The Columbia Guide to Irish American History* (New York: Columbia University Press, 2005), 220.

28. Roediger, *Working Toward Whiteness*, 111. On persistent prejudice toward the "travelers" and their subculture over the years, see Jane Helleiner, *Irish Travellers: Racism and the Politics of Culture* (Toronto: University of Toronto Press, 2000); Brian Lavery, "Old Prejudice Lives on in a Multiracial Ireland," *New York Times*, November 18, 2001, A12; and "Nomadic Group in Ireland Yearning for Recognition," *Chicago Tribune*, July 2, 2006, 18.

29. George Potter, *To the Golden Door: The Story of the Irish in Ireland and America* (Boston:

Little, Brown, 1960), 372; Frederick Douglass, *Life and Times of Frederick Douglass*, 2:249, quoted in Jay Rubin, "Black Nativism: The European Immigrant in Negro Thought, 1830–1860," *Phylon* 39, no. 3 (1978): 198. See also Luke Gibbons, "Beyond the Pale: Race, Ethnicity, and Irish Culture," in Andrew Higgins Wyndham, ed., *Re-Imagining Ireland* (Charlottesville: University of Virginia Press, 2006), 52–57.

30. John Higham, *Strangers in the Land: Patterns of American Nativism, 1860–1925* (New York: Atheneum, 1963), 234–63; John F. McClymer, "The Americanization Movement and the Education of the Foreign Born Adult, 1914–1925," in Bernard J. Weiss, ed., *American Education and the European Immigrant, 1840–1940* (Urbana: University of Illinois Press, 1982), 96–116; John F. McClymer, *War and Welfare: Social Engineering in America, 1890–1925* (Westport, Conn.: Greenwood Press, 1980), 105–52; Rivka Shpak Lissak, *Pluralism and Progressives: Hull House and the New Immigrants, 1890–1919* (Chicago: University of Chicago Press, 1989), 3–4, 74–81; and Edward G. Hartman, *The Movement to Americanize the Immigrant* (New York: Columbia University Press, 1948).

31. Quoted in "Americanism, Not Hyphenism," *Outlook*, October 20, 1915, 390. Roosevelt's version of civic nationalism made room for a diverse group of European ethnics as long as they submitted to a thorough Americanization. It excluded African and Asian Americans on the grounds that they were racially unfit. See Gary Gerstle, *American Crucible: Race and Nation in the Twentieth Century* (Princeton, N.J.: Princeton University Press, 2001), 14–80. On "coercive Americanization," see Desmond King, *Making Americans: Immigration, Race, and the Origins of the Diverse Democracy* (Cambridge, Mass.: Harvard University Press, 2000); and Gary Gerstle, "Liberty, Coercion, and the Making of Americans," *Journal of American History* 84 (September 1997): 524–58.

32. Barrett, "Americanization from the Bottom Up"; Gerstle, "Liberty, Coercion, and the Making of Americans," 527; Philip Gleason, "American Identity and Americanization," in Stephan Thernstrom, ed., *Harvard Encyclopedia of American Ethnic Groups* (Cambridge, Mass.: Belknap Press of Harvard University, 1980), 39–41. For a useful discussion of the changing and contested meaning of the term in more recent scholarship, see Russell A. Kazal, "Revisiting Assimilation: The Rise, Fall, and Reappraisal of a Concept in American Ethnic History," *American Historical Review* 100 (April 1995): 437–71.

33. New York and Chicago had the first and third largest Irish populations at the turn of the century. Philadelphia was ranked second, Boston fourth.

CHAPTER 1: THE STREET

1. Langston Hughes, *The Big Sea* (New York: Hill & Wang, 1963), 33; St. Clair Drake and Horace R. Cayton, *Black Metropolis: A Study of Negro Life in a Northern City* (New York: Harcourt, Brace, & Co., 1945).

2. "Whites Slug Man to Death on West Side," *Chicago Defender*, March 16, 1929, 1; Frederic M. Thrasher, *The Gang: A Study of 1313 Gangs in Chicago* (Chicago: University of Chicago Press, 1927), 139, quote at 278–79.

3. Chicago Commission on Race Relations, *The Negro in Chicago: A Study of Race Relations and a Race Riot* (Chicago: University of Chicago Press, 1922), 15.

4. Robert Ernst, *Immigrant Life in New York City, 1825–1863* (New York: King's Crown Press, 1949); Edwin G. Burrows and Mike Wallace, *Gotham: A History of New York to 1898* (New York: Oxford University Press, 1999); and Ronald H. Bayor and Timothy J. Meagher, eds., *The New York Irish* (Baltimore, Md.: Johns Hopkins University Press, 1996).

5. Bessie Louise Pierce, *A History of Chicago*, vol. 1: *The Beginning of a City, 1673–1848* (New York: Alfred A. Knopf, 1937), 49, 179–80; and Donald L. Miller, *City of the Century: The Epic of Chicago and the Making of America* (New York: Simon & Schuster, 1996), 441–42.

6. Ernst, *Immigrant Life in New York*, 551; and Michael F. Funchion, "Irish Chicago: Church, Homeland, Politics, and Class, 1870 to 1900," in Melvin G. Holli and Peter d'Alory Jones, eds., *Ethnic Chicago: A Multicultural Portrait*, 4th ed. (Grand Rapids, Mich.: Eerdmans, 1995), 58. On Boston, see Oscar Handlin, *Boston's Immigrants: A Study in Acculturation* (Cambridge, Mass.: Harvard University Press, 1941); on Philadelphia, see Dennis Clark, *The Irish in Philadelphia: Ten Generations of Urban Experience* (Philadelphia: Temple University Press, 1973); and on New Orleans and other southern ports, see Earl F. Niehaus, *The Irish in New Orleans, 1800–1860* (Baton Rouge: Louisiana State University Press, 1965), and David T. Gleeson, *The Irish in the South, 1815–1877* (Chapel Hill: University of North Carolina Press, 2001).

7. Reginald Byron, *Irish America* (Oxford: Clarendon Press, 1999), 68.

8. I recognize the significance of Protestant Irish emigration from Ulster, elsewhere in Ireland, and from Canada. See Donald H. Akenson, *The Irish Diaspora: A Primer* (Streetsville, Ont.: Institute of Irish Studies, Queen's University, 1993), 219. I am confining my discussion to immigrants and their children in large American cities since the late nineteenth century, a moment when and a place where Catholics predominated. An estimated 80 percent of post-Famine immigrants were Catholic, and this figure was undoubtedly higher in cities. See Kevin Kenny, *The American Irish: A History* (New York: Longman, 2000), 137. On a Catholic bias in Irish American immigration historiography, see Donald Harman Akenson, "The Historiography of the Irish in the United States of America," in Patrick O'Sullivan, ed., *The Irish in the New Communities: History, Heritage, Identity* (Leicester, U.K.: Leicester University Press, 1992), 2:99–127; and Donald Akenson, *Being Had: Historians, Evidence, and the Irish in North America* (Toronto: Meany, 1985).

9. Patrick Blessing, "Irish," in Stephan Thernstrom, ed., *Harvard Encyclopedia of American Ethnic Groups* (Cambridge, Mass.: Belknap Press of Harvard University, 1980), 530. On the Irish Americans as urban people, see David Doyle, "The Irish as Urban Pioneers in the United States, 1850–1870," *Journal of American Ethnic History* 10 (Fall 1990–Winter 1991): 36–53; and for their tendency to thrive in the early-twentieth-century city, see Peter Quinn, *Looking for Jimmy: A Search for Irish America* (Woodstock, N.Y.: Overlook Press, 2007), 19–42, quote at 51. See also Edward O'Donnell, "How the Irish Became Urban," *Journal of Urban History* 25, no. 2 (1999): 271–86; and Lawrence J. McCaffrey, "Diaspora Comparisons and Irish-American Uniqueness," in Charles Fanning, ed., *New Perspectives on the Irish Diaspora* (Carbondale: Southern Illinois University Press, 2000), 18.

10. Stanley Lieberson, *Ethnic Patterns in American Cities* (New York: Free Press of Glencoe, 1963); Edward R. Kantowicz, "Polish Chicago: Survival through Solidarity," in Holli and d'Alory Jones, *Ethnic Chicago*, 176; Lawrence J. McCaffrey, Ellen Skerrett, Michael F. Funchion, and Charles Fanning, *The Irish in Chicago* (Urbana: University of Illinois Press, 1987), map and table, 160–61; Robert Hunter, *Tenement Conditions in Chicago; Report by the Investigating Committee* (Chicago: City Homes Association, 1901); Deirdre Mageean, "Making Sense and Providing Structure," in Christiane Harzig et al., eds., *Peasant Maids, City Women: From the European Countryside to Urban America* (Ithaca, N.Y.: Cornell University Press, 1987), 239; Eileen M. McMahon, *What Parish Are You From? A Chicago Irish Community and Race Relations* (Lexington: University of Kentucky Press, 1995), parish map, vii.

11. Thomas M. Henderson, *Tammany Hall and the New Immigrants: The Progressive Years* (New York, 1976), 73–77; John Paul Bocock, "The Irish Conquest," *Forum*, April 1894, 186; Bayor and Meagher, *New York Irish*, table A.6, 558–559, maps, 565–73. The number of Irish in New York's Italian and Jewish neighborhoods was often quite small by the time of the 1920 census, though they continued to exert considerable influence. See John R. Logan, "The Ethnic Neighborhood, 1920–1970," Working Paper no. 113, Russell Sage Foundation, 1997. Thanks to Nancy Foner for this data.

12. Kerby A. Miller, *Emigrants and Exiles: Ireland and the Irish Exodus to North America* (New York: Oxford University Press, 1985), 522.

13. Hasia Diner and Beryl Benderly, *Her Works Praise Her: A History of Jewish Women in America from Colonial Times to the Present* (New York: Basic Books, 2003), 306; and David Montgomery, "The Irish Influence in the American Labor Movement," Cushwa Center Hibernian Lecture, Notre Dame, Ind., 1984, 10, 12.

14. Quinn, *Looking for Jimmy*, 33, 31, 41. See also David Nasaw, *Children of the City: At Work and Play* (New York: Oxford University Press, 1985), 33–34.

15. Claude M. Lightfoot, "From Chicago's Ghetto to World Politics: The Life and Struggles of Claude M. Lightfoot," mimeo, Chicago, n.d. On "Irish confetti," see Irving L. Allen, *The City in Slang: New York Life and Popular Speech* (New York: Oxford University Press, 1993), 46–47.

16. *Chicago Daily News*, August 2, 1919, quoted in John Landesco, *Illinois Crime Survey*, Part III: *Organized Crime in Chicago* (Chicago: University of Chicago, 1929), 171. See also Chicago Commission on Race Relations, *Negro in Chicago*, 11–17; Myron Davis, "Canaryville," research paper, University of Chicago, 1927, 20–21; and Chicago Historical Society, "Documents: History of Bridgeport," Document 1a. For other instances of "deadlines" between ethnic and racial groups in Chicago, see Thrasher, *Gang*, 175, 194, 197–98, 212.

17. Neal Samors and Michael Williams, *The Old Chicago Neighborhood: Remembering Life in the 1940s* (Chicago: Chicago's Neighborhoods, 2003), 49, 52, 110.

18. On Byrnes, see Timothy J. Gilfoyle, *A Pickpocket's Tale: The Underworld of Nineteenth Century New York* (New York: W.W. Norton, 2006), 249–54. On the New York origins of the term, see David R. Roediger, *Working Toward Whiteness: How America's Immigrants Became White: The Strange Journey from Ellis Island to the Suburbs* (New York: Basic Books, 2005), 167n22, 298; and Luc Sante, *Low Life: Lures and Snares of Old New York* (New York: Farrar, Straus & Giroux, 1991), 247.

19. Victor Hicken, *Illinois in the Civil War*, 2nd ed. (Urbana: University of Illinois Press, 1991), 357.

20. William Z. Foster, *Pages from a Worker's Life* (New York: International Publishers, 1939), 15–18, quote at 18.

21. On the Irish in Greenwich Village, see Charles W. McFarland, *Inside Greenwich Village: A New York City Neighborhood, 1898–1918* (Amherst, Mass.: University of Massachusetts Press, 2001), 36–48; on African Americans there, 11; Donald Tricarico, "Influence of the Irish on Italian Communal Adaptation in Greenwich Village," in Francis X. Femminella, ed., *Italians and Irish in America: Proceedings of the Sixteenth Annual Conference of the American Italian Historical Association* (Staten Island, N.Y.: American Italian Historical Association, 1985), 53; Caroline F. Ware, *Greenwich Village, 1920–1930: A Comment on American Civilization in the Post-War Years* (Boston: Houghton Mifflin, 1935), 12; and on their move north in the city, "The Black North," *New York Times*, November 17, 1901, 10. On the per-

sistent conflicts from the mid-nineteenth through the early twentieth century, see Iver Bernstein, *The New York City Draft Riots: Their Significance in American Society and Politics in the Age of the Civil War* (New York: Oxford University Press, 1990), 5, 22–23, 119–23; "About Things Theatrical," *Amsterdam News*, December 9, 1925, 6; Gilbert Osofsky, *Harlem: The Making of a Ghetto* (New York: Harper Torchbooks, 1968), 81; "Fierce Race Riot in Upper New York," *New York Times*, December 26, 1901, 1; "Battle of Washington Arch," March 11, 1904, 3; and "Race Riot Rages in Harlem Streets," August 5, 1907, 1. Similar disturbances occurred in Boston. See Dennis P. Ryan, *Beyond the Ballot Box: A Social History of the Boston Irish, 1845–1917* (Rutherford, N.J.: Fairleigh Dickinson University Press, 1983), 132.

22. Jeff Kisseloff, *You Must Remember This: An Oral History of Manhattan from the 1890s to World War II* (San Diego, Calif.: Harcourt, Brace, Jovanovich, 1989), quotes at 190; Stave, *From the Old Country*, 180–81.

23. Kisseloff, *You Must Remember This*, 268. On the Irish American reputation for racist, ethnically intolerant, and anti-Semitic language, see ibid., 189, 577; Bruce M. Stave and John F. Sutherland, with Aldo Salerno, *From the Old Country: An Oral History of European Migration to America* (New York: Twayne, 1994), 180–81; Harry Golden, *The Right Time: An Autobiography* (New York: Putnam, 1969), 49.

24. Alvin F. Harlow, *Old Bowery Days* (New York: D. Appleton & Co., 1931), 185; "Five Points House of Industry Slated for Destruction," *New York Times*, August 3, 1913, SM6. See also "The Poor of New York," *New York Times*, January 15, 1866, 8.

25. Graham Hodges, " 'Desirable Companions and Lovers': Irish and African Americans in the Sixth Ward, 1830–1870," in Bayor and Meagher, *New York Irish*, 107–24; Tyler Anbinder, *Five Points: The 19th-Century New York City Neighborhood That Invented Tap Dance, Stole Elections, and Became the World's Most Notorious Slum* (New York: Simon & Schuster, 2001), 197–99, 263.

26. Rev. Thomas McLaughlin, "In Darkest Chinatown," *Donahue's Magazine*, November 1897, quoted in Anbinder, *Five Points*, 378–79.

27. Mary Kingsbury Simkhovitch, *Neighborhood: My Story of Greenwich House* (New York: W.W. Norton, 1938), 143; Thrasher, *Gang*, 29–32; Nasaw, *Children of the City*, 33, 36; Pauline Goldmark, *Boyhood and Lawlessness: West Side Studies* (New York: Survey Associates, 1914), 39–48. (Thanks to David Montgomery for suggesting this last source.) On the informal, territorial quality of Irish American gangs in Chicago's Canaryville, see "The Neighborhood," (1922), especially 9, 18, 19–20, Ernest Watson Burgess Papers, Addenda, Box 38, Folder 1, Special Collections, Regenstein Library, University of Chicago. Although the word *turf* stretches back to Old English and German, its early meanings related rather narrowly to a piece of earth. The notion of turf as territory first appeared in the United States in the wake of the Great Famine in relation to criminal activity, a usage likely descended from Irish immigrants who also used the term to describe the peat they cut and used for fuel. The first use of the term in relation to street gangs did not come until the postwar period in relation to gangs in Brooklyn and the Bronx, areas with large Irish American populations. See *Oxford English Dictionary*, online ed., www.oed.com/view/Entry/207586.

28. McFarland, *Inside Greenwich Village*, 156–65, 167, quote at 156.

29. Ware, *Greenwich Village* 130.

30. Henry Roth, *Mercy of a Rude Stream*, vol. 1: *A Star Shines Over Mount Morris Park* (New

York: St. Martin's Press, 1994). See also Roth's collection of stories and essays, *Shifting Landscape: A Composite, 1925–1987* (Philadelphia: Jewish Publication Society, 1987); and Steven Kellman's biography of Roth, *Redemption: The Life of Henry Roth* (New York: Norton, 2005).

31. Thrasher, *Gang*, 212.

32. Ware, *Greenwich Village*, 52, 131; Virginia Yans-McLaughlin, *Family and Community: Italian Immigrants in Buffalo, 1880–1930* (Urbana: University of Illinois Press, 1982), 112–13; William Foote Whyte, *Street Corner Society: The Social Structure of an Italian Slum* (Chicago: University of Chicago Press, 1943), 195; Stave and Sutherland with Salerno, *From the Old Country*, 89, 106, 187; Michael La Sorte, *La Merica: Images of Italian Greenhorn Experience* (Philadelphia: Temple University Press, 1985), 139, 148–52; Ronald H. Bayor, *Neighbors in Conflict: The Irish, Germans, Jews, and Italians of New York City, 1929–1941* (Baltimore, Md.: Johns Hopkins University Press, 1978), 30–86; and Rudolf Glanz, *Jew and Irish: Historic Group Relations and Immigration* (New York: Waldon Press, 1966), 98.

33. A. J. Paulsen, "A Sociological Study of the Gimlet Gang" (1931?), 48–53, quotes at 48, 50, 51, Burgess Papers, Box 181, Folder 7.

34. Ibid., 53; *New York Times*, February 15, 1903, 33.

35. William F. Whyte, "Race Conflicts in the North End of Boston," *New England Quarterly* 12 (December 1939), 623–42.

36. "The Wickedest District in the World," *Chicago Tribune*, February 6, 1910, H7; Thrasher, *Gang*, 137; Herbert Asbury, *The Gangs of Chicago: An Informal History of the Chicago Underworld* (1940; DeKalb: Northern Illinois University Press, 1986), 211–22; Frank De Liberto, interview by Italians in Chicago Project, April 17, 1980, photocopied interview transcripts, 2, 22, Special Collections, University of Illinois at Urbana-Champaign. On comparable "sport" among Irish American youth in late-nineteenth-century New York, see James F. Richardson, *The New York Police: Colonial Times to 1901* (New York: Oxford University Press, 1980), 166–68.

37. Emanuel Steen, interview by Paul Sigrist, March 22, 1991, Oral History Transcripts, Ellis Island Immigration Museum, 27.

38. Ray Rivlin, *Shalom Ireland: A Social History of Jews in Modern Ireland* (Dublin: Gill & Macmillan, 2003), 29–34; Dermot Keogh, *Jews in Twentieth-Century Ireland: Refugees, Anti-Semitism, and the Holocaust* (Cork: Cork University Press, 1998), 19–25; Louis Hyman, *The Jews of Ireland from Earliest Times to the Year 1910* (Shannon: Irish University Press, 1972), 213; Glanz, *Jew and Irish*, 19–26. Gifts from Cork neighbors to Jewish refugees from the late-nineteenth-century pogroms in eastern Europe included a framed picture of Jesus, suggesting a genuine level of acceptance—and a profound ignorance of Judaism. See Cormac O'Grada, *Jewish Ireland in the Age of Joyce: A Socioeconomic History* (Princeton, N.J.: Princeton University Press, 2006), 14–16, 118, 179–81. *Within the Pale*, Davitt's 1903 report on pogroms in Russia, called for an independent Jewish homeland. See Hasia Diner, *The Jews of the United States, 1654–2000* (Berkeley: University of California Press, 2006), 92.

39. "'Ritual Murder' Protest Today," *Chicago Tribune*, October 18, 1913, 5; and "Irish Protest at Beilis Trial," *Chicago Tribune*, October 19, 1913, 5.

40. Louis Wirth, *The Ghetto* (Chicago: University of Chicago Press, 1928), 180–81; and Thrasher, *Gang*, 199–200. On the West Side Irish gangs in Chicago, see M. P. Carmichael, "Crimes and Criminals in Chicago, 1891," Burgess Papers, Box 129, Folder 3. On anti-Semitic attacks in the Irish part of the neighborhood near Holy Family parish, see "Arrest Boy Jew

Baiters," *Chicago Tribune*, February 10, 1906, 8. On the situation in an Irish South Philadelphia neighborhood bordering a Jewish community, see Foster, *Pages from a Worker's Life*, 16–17. See also John Higham, *Send These to Me: Jews and Other Immigrants in Urban America* (New York: Atheneum, 1975), 135.

41. Abraham Bisno, *Abraham Bisno, Union Pioneer* (Madison: University of Wisconsin Press, 1967), 54–55.

42. Tony Michels, *A Fire in Their Hearts: Yiddish Socialists in New York* (Cambridge, Mass.: Harvard University Press, 2005), 42–43.

43. Samors and Williams, *Old Chicago Neighborhood*, 51, 52. For similar problems in New York, see Harry Golden, *The Right Time: An Autobiography* (New York: Putnam, 1969), 49, 202–3; Nathan Glazer and Daniel Patrick Moynihan, *Beyond the Melting Pot: Irish, Jews, and Puerto Ricans in New York City* (Cambridge, Mass.: MIT Press, 1970), 230–38; and Thomas Kessner, *The Golden Door: Italian and Jewish Mobility in New York, 1880–1915* (New York: Oxford University Press, 1977), 144–45. See also Thomas Jesse Jones, *The Sociology of a New York Block* (New York: Columbia University Press, 1904), 99, 123.

44. Jones, *Sociology of a New York Block*, 12, 15.

45. John J. Appel, "*Betzemer*: A Nineteenth-Century Cognomen for the Irish," *American Speech* 38 (1963): 307–8. See also Glanz, *Jew and Irish*, 97–98.

46. Kisseloff, *You Must Remember This*, 435–36, 346; Robert A. Orsi, *The Madonna of 115th Street: Faith and Community in Harlem, 1880–1950* (New Haven, Conn.: Yale University Press, 1985), 16–17.

47. Samors and Williams, *Old Chicago Neighborhood*, 108.

48. Stephen Hardy, *How Boston Played: Sport, Race, and Community, 1865–1915* (Boston: Northeastern University, 1982), 137–38; and Steven A. Reiss, *City Games: The Evolution of American Urban Society and the Rise of Sports* (Urbana: University of Illinois Press, 1989), 16, 94, 104.

49. Carolyn A. Conley, *Melancholy Accidents: The Meaning of Violence in Post-Famine Ireland* (Lanham, Md.: Lexington Books, 1999); James S. Donnelly, "Factions in Prefamine Ireland," in Audrey Eyler and Robert Garratt, eds., *The Uses of the Past: Essays on Irish Culture* (Newark: University of Delaware Press, 1988), 113–30; Reiss, *City Games*, 15–21; Henry D. Inglis, *Ireland in 1834* (London: Whittaker, 1835), 1:129; Miller, *Emigrants and Exiles*, 60–61; Peter Way, "Evil Humors and Ardent Spirits: The Rough Culture of Canal Construction Laborers," *Journal of American History* 79 (March 1993): 1397–428.

50. Michael T. Isenberg, *John L. Sullivan and His America* (Urbana: University of Illinois, 1988); Elliot J. Gorn, *The Manly Art: Bare-Knuckle Prize Fighting in America* (Ithaca, N.Y.: Cornell University Press, 1986), 207–47, quote at 225; and Reiss, *City Games*, 15–21, 110.

51. Andrew J. Diamond, *Mean Streets: Chicago Youths and the Everyday Struggle for Empowerment in the Multiracial City, 1908–1969* (Berkeley: University of California Press, 2009), 38–41; and Gale Bederman, *Manliness and Civilization: A Cultural History of Gender and Race in the United States, 1880–1917* (Chicago: University of Chicago Press, 1995), 1–31.

52. Geoffrey C. Ward, *Unforgivable Blackness: The Rise and Fall of Jack Johnson* (London: Pimlico, 2006). See also Randy Roberts, *Papa Jack: Jack Johnson and the Era of White Hopes* (New York: Free Press, 1983). Although Bederman, *Manliness and Civilization*, analyzes Johnson's rise and fall as a critical moment in a middle-class masculinity crisis, the crisis was more keenly felt in working-class neighborhoods where a male youth culture was built largely

around fighting—in and out of the ring. See Diamond, *Mean Streets*, 36–38. On Boston, see Hardy, *How Boston Played*, 172–75.

53. Glanz, *Jew and Irish*, 98–103; Burton J. Hendrick, "The Jewish Invasion of America," *McClure's Magazine* 40 (March 1913), 144; Westbrook Pegler, "Jim Maloney Trains Mind, Forgets Wind," *Chicago Tribune*, May 6, 1927, 23; "Boxers Use Irish Names," *New York Times*, January 20, 1916, 7; Thrasher, *Gang*, 149; La Sorte, *La Merica*, 155.

54. James M. O'Kane, *The Crooked Ladder: Gangsters, Ethnicity, and the American Dream* (New Brunswick, N.J.: Transaction, 1992), 65–66, 71; Henderson, *Tammany Hall and New Immigrants*, 147; Howard Kimeldorf, *Reds or Rackets? The Making of Radical and Conservative Unions on the Waterfront* (Berkeley: University of California Press, 1988). On "Machine Gun" Jack McGurn, see J. H. Cohen, "Who's Who in Gangland," Burgess Papers, Box 129, Folder 9.

55. Emily Greene Balch, *Our Slavic Fellow Citizens* (New York: Charities Publication Committee, 1920), 412; Lilian Brandt, "A Transplanted Birthright: The Development of the Second Generation of the Italian in an American Environment," *Charities* 12 (May 7, 1904), 494.

56. Hardy, *How Boston Played*, 137–38; Reiss, *City Games*, 94–96. On the role of masculinity in city street gangs and ethnic territoriality, see Eric C. Schneider, *Vampires, Dragons, and Egyptian Kings: Youth Gangs in Postwar New York* (Princeton, N.J.: Princeton University Press, 1999), 23–26; and Diamond, *Mean Streets*, quote at 33. On the culturally constructed character of masculinity, see David D. Gilmore, *Manhood in the Making: Cultural Concepts of Masculinity* (New Haven, Conn.: Yale University Press, 1990). On the progression from street fighting to organized boxing on Manhattan's West Side, see Goldmark, *Boyhood and Lawlessness*, 31–36. On the Irish as models of urban masculinity for later immigrants, see Moses Rischin, *The Promised City: New York's Jews, 1870–1914* (New York: Harper & Row, 1962), 263–64.

57. David Gibson, "St. Brigid's Parish: A Pilgrim Church for an Immigrant People," in Terry Golway, ed., *Catholics in New York: Society, Culture, and Politics, 1808–1946* (New York: Fordham University Press, 2008), 65.

58. Reiss, *City Games*, 110.

59. On the strong territorial instinct in nineteenth-century rural Ireland, see William L. Jenkins, "In the Shadow of the Grain Elevator: A Portrait of an Irish Neighborhood in Buffalo, New York, in the Nineteenth and Twentieth Centuries," *Éire-Ireland* 37, no. 1 (Spring–Summer 2002): 14–37.

60. On Irish gangs and street fighting in antebellum cities, see Herbert Asbury, *The Gangs of New York: An Informal History of the Underworld* (New York: Capricorn Books, 1927), 21–45; Philip Rahv, "Crime among the Irish," June 10, 1938, File 4, Article 1, Federal Writers' Project, "The Irish in New York," New York City Municipal Archives, Microfilm, Reel 61; Bruce Laurie, "Fire Companies and Gangs in Southwark: The 1840s," in Allen F. Davis and Mark H. Haller, eds., *The Peoples of Philadelphia: A History of Ethnic Groups and Lower-Class Life, 1790–1940* (Philadelphia: Temple University Press, 1973), 71–88; Bernstein, *New York City Draft Riots*; Sante, *Low Life*, 197–207; Alvin F. Harlow, *Old Bowery Days* (New York: D. Appleton & Co., 1931), 185–201.

61. Ernest Harvier, "First Cathedral in New York City," *New York Times*, February 25, 1923, E12; Tyler Anbinder captures the essence of Irish resistance to neighborhood racial change in *Five Points*, 362–423.

62. Morgan S. Odell, "United Religious Survey of the Greater Grand Crossing Area," a report by the University of Chicago Divinity School, December 1929–January 1930, quoted in Thomas Lee Philpott, *The Slum and the Ghetto: Neighborhood Deterioration and Middle-Class Reform, Chicago, 1880–1930* (New York: Oxford University Press, 1978), 202. My thanks to Will Cooley for this reference.

63. Thomas J. Jablonsky, *Pride in the Jungle: Community and Everyday Life in Back of the Yards Chicago* (Baltimore, Md.: Johns Hopkins University Press, 1993), 106.

64. Robert Ford, interview by author, Chicago, 1979; Nasaw, *Children of the City*, 32; Jane Anne Evans, "Mexican Naturalization in Chicago" [1944], 30–31, Immigrant Protective League Papers, Daley Library, Special Collections, University of Illinois at Chicago, Box 2, Folder 83. See also Stella Nowicki [Vicky Starr], interview in *Union Maids*, New World Films, 1976.

65. Richard Schneirov, *Labor and Urban Politics: Class Conflict and Origins of Modern Liberalism in Chicago, 1864–1897* (Urbana: University of Illinois Press), 113.

66. For a survey of the sociological literature and an analysis of English acquisition based on the 1920 federal census, see Teresa G. Labov, "English Acquisition by Immigrants to the United States at the Beginning of the Twentieth Century," *American Speech* 73 (1998): 368–98. On the ethnically mixed character of immigrant neighborhoods, see Philpott, *Slum and the Ghetto;* and Kathleen Conzen, "Immigrants, Immigrant Neighborhoods, and Ethnic Identity: Historical Issues," *Journal of American History* 66 (December 1979): 603–15.

67. Labov, "English Acquisition by Immigrants," 369–70; Kenneth E. Nilson, "The Irish Language in New York, 1859–1900," in Bayor and Meagher, *New York Irish*, 252–74; Victor Walsh, "A Fanatic Heart: The Cause of Irish American Nationalism in Pittsburgh During the Gilded Age," *Journal of Social History* 15 (Winter 1981): 187–203; Quinn, *Looking for Jimmy*, 257–66.

68. Miller, *Emigrants and Exiles*, 518.

69. Daniel Cassidy, *How the Irish Invented Slang: The Secret Language of the Crossroads* (Oakland, Calif.: Counterpunch/A.K. Press, 2007), 2.

70. Ibid., 49–73, 6, 7, 24, 55–58. See also Howard Meroney, "Gaelic Loan-Words in American," *American Speech* 22 (December 1947): 289–91; Charles Vandersee, "Speakeasy," *American Speech* 59 (Autumn 1984): 268–69; and Peter Tamony, "The Origin of 'Phoney,'" *American Speech* 12 (April 1937): 108–10.

71. Cassidy, *How the Irish Invented Slang*, 7, 8; Irving Howe, *World of Our Fathers* (New York: Simon & Schuster, 1976), 558.

72. Quinn, *Looking for Jimmy*, 261, 262.

73. On the Irish content in American gambling terminology, see Cassidy, *How the Irish Invented Slang*, 39–53, and on the importance of Yiddish to American slang, Howe, *World of Our Fathers*, 226–27; Julius Rothenberg, "Some American Idioms from the Yiddish," *American Speech* 18 (February 1943): 43–45; and Allen, *City in Slang*.

74. Ann Douglas, *Terrible Honesty: Mongrel New York in the 1920s* (New York: Farrar, Straus & Giroux, 1995). See also Quinn, *Looking for Jimmy*, 262; Allen, *City in Slang*.

75. Cassidy, *How the Irish Invented Slang*, 59–73.

76. Margaretta Strid, untitled notes, n.d. [early 1930s], Sociology 269, Burgess Papers, Box 176, Folder 1. Although the notes do not clearly indicate this, it seems likely that the researcher changed the language to avoid explicit racial epithets. My thanks to Cate Wycoff for directing me to this source. Prejudice against Protestants, Jews, and others may be traced in rhymes recited by children on the streets of Irish cities. See Leslie Daiken, *Out She Goes:*

Dublin Street Rhymes: Collected with a Commentary (Chester Spring, Penn.: Dufour Editions, 1965).

77. David R. Roediger, *The Wages of Whiteness: Race and the Making of the American Working Class* (London: Verso, 1991), 120, quote at 135.

78. On the racialized character of urban parks and their function as centers for neighborhood identity and ethnic culture, see Robin F. Bachin, *Building the South Side: Urban Space and Civic Culture in Chicago, 1890–1917* (Chicago: University of Chicago Press, 2004), 160–65. On New York, see Roy Rosenzweig and Elizabeth Blackmar, *The Park and the People: A History of Central Park* (Ithaca, N.Y.: Cornell University Press, 1992), 373–411.

79. Jablonsky, *Pride in the Jungle*, 109–114; Sabine Haenni, *The Immigrant Scene: Ethnic Amusements in New York, 1880–1920* (Minneapolis: University of Minnesota Press, 2008), 50.

80. Goldmark, *Boyhood and Lawlessness*, 3–13, quotes at 8, 10, 11. See also Otho Cartwright, *The Middle West Side: A Historical Sketch: West Side Studies* (New York: Survey Associates, 1914).

81. Alfred E. Smith, *Up to Now: An Autobiography* (New York: Viking Press, 1929), 16–20. On the informal sports of young people in city streets and the ways in which they reflected and bridged ethnic and racial divisions, see Riess, *City Games*, 94–96.

82. "One Bath Tub to a Block But Oh! Such a Big Tub!" *Chicago Tribune*, September 21, 1913, G6.

83. Ibid.; Jeff Wiltse, *Contested Waters: A Social History of Swimming Pools in America* (Chapel Hill: University of North Carolina Press, 2007), 26, 32, 34, 48, 56–66. My thanks to Mark Leff for referring me to this source.

84. Samors and Williams, *Old Chicago Neighborhood*, 134, quote at 145.

85. Paul Cressey, "Report on Summer's Work with Juvenile Protective Association of Chicago" (1925), 3, Burgess Papers, Box 129, Folder 5; "Certain Relationships between Recreation and Juvenile Delinquency in Chicago," Folder 9 and other materials on recreation in Burgess Papers, Box 38; "Crime Board Tells How Boy Gangs Rise in New York Slums," *New York Times*, March 20, 1927, 1, 9; Ryan, *Beyond the Ballot Box*, 137; Wiltse, *Contested Waters*, 123–24; Tuttle, *Race Riot*; Samors and Williams, *Old Chicago Neighborhood*, 110.

86. James T. Farrell, *Studs Lonigan* (Urbana: University of Illinois Press, 1993), 18. See also Chicago Commission on Race Relations, *Negro in Chicago*.

87. Charles Fanning and Ellen Skerrett, "James T. Farrell and Washington Park," *Chicago History* 7 (1979), 87. Washington Park became a mecca for white and especially for African American radicals during the Great Depression. See Richard Wright, *Black Boy* (New York: Harper & Row, 1946); and St. Clair Drake and Horace Cayton, *Black Metropolis: A Study of Negro Life in a Northern City* (New York: Harcourt, Brace, & Co., 1945).

88. Samors and Williams, *Old Chicago Neighborhood*, 110. Continued discrimination in this neighborhood provided the subject for Lorraine Hansberry's 1959 play *A Raisin in the Sun* and the grievance in a famous Supreme Court case (*Hansberry vs. Lee*, 1940) brought by her father Carl. See Truman K. Gibson, Jr., "We Belong in Washington Park," *Chicago History* 34 (Fall 2006): 26–43.

89. Letter to the editor, *New York Times*, December 5, 1913, 10.

90. See New York governor Al Smith's recollections of growing up near the South Street port in Smith, *Up to Now*, 16–18.

91. Quoted in David Montgomery, *The Fall of the House of Labor: The Workplace, the State, and American Labor Activism, 1865–1925* (New York: Cambridge University Press, 1987), 100; Bruce Nelson, *Divided We Stand: American Workers and the Struggle for Black Equality* (Princeton, N.J.: Princeton University Press, 2001), 13–24. On defensive responses to "out-

siders" in New York Harbor and other settings, see also Kisseloff, *You Must Remember This*, 488; Eric Arnesen, *Waterfront Workers of New Orleans: Race, Class, and Politics, 1863–1923* (Urbana: University of Illinois Press, 1991); Arnesen, "Biracial Waterfront Unionism in the Age of Segregation," in Calvin Winslow, ed., *Waterfront Workers: New Perspectives on Race and Class* (Urbana: University of Illinois Press, 1998), 19–61; Winslow, "Men of the Lumber Camps Come to Town," ibid., 62–96; Colin J. Davis, "The Elusive Irishman: Ethnicity and the Postwar World of New York City and London Dockers," in Peter Alexander and Rick Halpern, eds., *Racializing Class, Classifying Race: Labour and Difference in Britain, the USA, and Africa* (New York: St. Martin's Press, 2000), 94–95; and James T. Fisher, *On the Irish Waterfront: The Crusader, the Movie, and the Soul of the Port of New York* (Ithaca, N.Y.: Cornell University Press, 2009), 23–25. For a similar mentality in a very different setting, see David M. Emmons, *The Butte Irish: Class and Ethnicity in an American Mining Town, 1875–1925* (Urbana: University of Illinois Press, 1989).

92. See John Logan, "The Ethnic Neighborhood, 1920–1970," Working Paper no. 113, Russell Sage Foundation, 1997; Dwyer quoted in Fisher, *On the Irish Waterfront*, 8.

93. Robert A. Woods, ed., *The City Wilderness: A Settlement Study* (Boston: Hougton Mifflin, 1898), 38–39.

94. Dominic A. Pacyga, "To Live Amongst Others: Poles and Their Neighbors in Industrial Chicago, 1865–1930," *Journal of American Ethnic History* 16 (Fall 1996), 56. See also Mike Royko, *Boss: Richard J. Daley of Chicago* (New York: Penguin, 1971), 30–32.

95. James T. Farrell, *Reflections at Fifty and Other Essays* (New York: Vanguard Press, 1954), 164, 166, quoted in Charles Fanning, "Introduction," *Studs Lonigan*, xi. See also Ellen Skerrett, "Catholic Dimension," in Lawrence J. McCaffrey et al., eds., *The Irish in Chicago* (Urbana: University of Illinois Press, 1987), 23.

96. When social historian Thomas Philpott asked an elderly respondent about her life in a particularly diverse Chicago neighborhood, she did not remember "anything but Irish." Philpott, *Slum and Ghetto*, 141–42. See also Pacyga, "To Live Amongst Others," 56; Philpott, *Slum and Ghetto*, 136–44, quote at 375n16; Roediger, *Working Toward Whiteness*, 165; Richard White, *Remembering Ahanagran: Storytelling in a Family's Past* (New York: Hill & Wang, 1998), 183. See also McFarland, *Inside Greenwich Village*, 217.

97. Whyte, "Race Conflicts in the North End of Boston," 626.

98. Glen E. Holt and Dominic A. Pacyga, *Chicago: A Historical Guide to the Neighborhoods* (Chicago: Chicago Historical Society, 1979), 116; Lawrence J. McCaffrey, "Overview: Forging Forward and Looking Back," in Bayor and Meagher, *New York Irish*, 229. On the theme of racial transformation in Catholic parishes, see John T. McGreevy, *Parish Boundaries: The Catholic Encounter with Race in the Twentieth Century North* (Chicago: University of Chicago Press, 1996).

99. Richard Alba and Nancy Denton, "Old and New Landscapes of Diversity: The Residential Patterns of Immigrant Minorities," in Nancy Foner and George Fredrickson, eds., *Not Just Black and White: Historical and Contemporary Perspectives on Immigration, Race, and Ethnicity in the United States* (New York: Russell Sage Foundation, 2004), 245–47; and Douglas Massey, "Ethnic Residential Segregation: A Theoretical Synthesis and Empirical Review," *Sociology and Social Research* 69 (April 1985): 315–50.

100. *Przebudzenie*, October 29, 1931, quoted in Pacyga, "To Live Amongst Others," 56.

101. Kisseloff, *You Must Remember This*, 577.

102. Ibid., 189.

103. "Riot Mars Funeral of Rabbi Joseph," *New York Times*, July 31, 1902, 1; "Mayor Low Starts

Riot Investigation," *New York Times,* August 1, 1902, 14; "Investigating the Rioting," *New York Times,* August 2, 1902, 2; Moses Rischin, *The Promised City: New York's Jews, 1870–1914* (Cambridge, Mass.: Harvard University Press, 1962), 91; Leonard Dinnerstein, "The Funeral of Rabbi Jacob Joseph," in David A. Gerber, ed., *Anti-Semitism in American History* (Urbana: University of Illinois Press, 1986), 275–77; Glanz, *Jew and Irish,* 91; Higham, *Send These to Me,* 135–36; Howe, *World of Our Fathers,* 123–24. Edward T. O'Donnell, "Hibernians Versus Hebrews?: A New Look at the 1902 Jacob Joseph Funeral Riot," *Journal of the Gilded Age and Progressive Era* 6, no. 2 (April 2007): 209–26, argues that Irish involvement was minimal. For a comparable attack in Brooklyn, see *Brooklyn Eagle,* July 31, 1902, 4. On Irish friction with Jews and Italians and fitful alliances among them in various New York neighborhoods, see Ware, *Greenwich Village,* 137–40; Bayor, *Neighbors in Conflict,* 1–56, 87–108. A second-generation Lithuanian-Polish person recalled similar alliances of Poles and Lithuanians against Irish in Bridgeport, Connecticut. See Stave and Sutherland with Salerno, *From the Old Country,* 80–81.

104. Asbury, *Gangs of New York,* 182–202, 226–46, 252–58; McFarland, *Inside Greenwich Village,* 166–69; Thrasher, *Gang,* 130.

105. Thrasher, *Gang,* first quote at 406; Chicago Commission on Race Relations, *Negro in Chicago,* 8. On Canaryville, see also Carl Sandburg, *The Chicago Race Riots* (New York: Harcourt, Brace, & Howe, 1919), 2–4; Thrasher, *Gang,* 409–51; "The Neighborhood" (1922), Burgess Papers, Addenda, Box 38, Folder 1. On the Irish roots of social athletic clubs in Boston, New York, and Chicago, see Hardy, *How Boston Played,* 137–38; Reiss, *City Games,* 16, 94–96.

106. John Landesco, untitled ms., Burgess Papers, Box 133, Folder 7; "Ragen Declares Ragen Colts' Record Good," *Chicago Tribune,* August 6, 1927, 14.

107. John Landesco, untitled ms., Burgess Papers, Box 133, Folder 7; "Two Wounded in Gun Duel of Ragen's Colts," *Chicago Tribune,* July 16, 1917, 9; "Stock Yards Club Members Who Sought to Lift Riot Lid," *Chicago Defender,* August 23, 1919, 3; "Sheldon Gang Member Shot at Ragen Colts," *Chicago Tribune,* February 1, 1927, 3; and "Danny Stantion Gangsters Due in Court Today," *Chicago Tribune,* October 31, 1928, 16.

108. "Trio Slugs Policeman; Caught After Chase," *Chicago Tribune,* May 11, 1923, 19; "Gunman Slays 2 Gangsters in Granada Café," *Chicago Tribune,* December 31, 1928, 1.

109. Nuala O'Faolain, *The Story of Chicago May* (New York: Riverhead, 2005), quote at 39. For May's own rather fanciful telling of her life story, see May Churchill Sharpe, *Chicago May, Her Story: A Human Document by the "Queen of the Crooks"* (New York: Macaulay, 1928); and on the Chicago underworld of which May was a part, see Herman Kogan and Lloyd Wendt, *Lords of the Levee: The Story of Bathhouse John and Hinky Dink* (Evanston, Ill.: Northwestern University Press, 2005), and Karen Abbott, *Sin in Chicago: Madams, Ministers, Playboys, and the Battle for America's Soul (New York: Random House, 2007).*

110. "Ragen Declares Colts Good Record," *Chicago Tribune,* August 6, 1927, 14.

111. "Giants vs. Ragens," *Chicago Defender,* October 6, 1917, 10; John Landesco, untitled ms., Burgess Papers, Box 133, Folder 7; Landesco, *Illinois Crime Survey,* 169.

112. Tuttle, *Race Riot,* 199; "Ragen Declares Colts Good Record," *Chicago Tribune,* August 6, 1927, 14.

113. Landesco, *Illinois Crime Survey,* 169.

114. Lizabeth Cohen, *Making a New Deal: Industrial Workers in Chicago, 1919–1939* (New York: Cambridge University Press, 1990), 145–46.

115. Chicago Commission on Racial Relations, *Negro in Chicago,* 12; "Chicago Police Gives Colored Man Up to Lynchers," *Chicago Defender,* August 27, 1910, 2; ibid., January 19, 1918,

1; "Riot Calls, Slugging Crew and Gun Play the Features," ibid., June 8, 1918, 1; "White Officers Beat Innocent Man," ibid., July 1, 1916, 3; "Irish Police Officer Becomes Too Officious," ibid., June 23, 1917, 7; "Woman Affronted at 35th Street Police Station," ibid., September 8, 1917, 1; "Capt. Fielden Beaten by Irish Officers," ibid., February 16, 1918, 5; "A Disgrace to the Police," *New York Times*, August 17, 1900, 6; "Prisoners Beg Recorder Goff for Mercy," ibid. July 13, 1901, 14; "Faces Murder Charge Now," ibid., December 29, 1904, 1; Gabriela F. Arredondo, *Mexican Chicago: Race, Identity, and Nation, 1916–1939* (Urbana: University of Illinois Press, 2008), 64–67. On common neighborhood connections between police and gangsters in Chicago, see J. H. Cohen, "Who's Who in Gangland," Burgess Papers, Box 129, Folder 9; and Philip Hauser, "Report on Funerals for Three of the Seven Members of the Moran Gang Killed in Valentine's Day Massacre," ibid., Box 132, Folder 2. For the similar phenomenon in early-twentieth-century New York involving trouble between Irish policemen, Jews, and African Americans, see William G. McAdoo, *Guarding a Great City* (New York: Harper & Bros., 1906), 260–61; Osofsky, *Harlem*, 48–49.

116. "5,000 Irish in British Flag Riot in 5th Av.," *New York Times*, November 26, 1920, 1.

117. David J. Talbot Memoir, Chicago History Museum.

118. Everett C. Hughes, "The Policeman as a Person," Burgess Papers, Box 132, Folder 4.

119. T. J. English, *Paddy Whacked: the Untold Story of the Irish American Gangster* (New York: HarperCollins, 2005), 74. On McDonald, see Asbury, *Gangs of Chicago*, 142–54.

120. Miller, *Emigrants and Exiles*, 522.

121. J. H. Cohen, "Who's Who in Gangland," Burgess Papers, Box 129, Folder 9.

122. On the fit between Irish labor bosses and Irish gangs, especially in the building trades, see William Z. Foster, *Misleaders of Labor* (Chicago: Trade Union Education League, 1927); Andrew W. Cohen, *The Racketeer's Progress: Chicago and the Struggle for the Modern American Economy, 1900–1940* (New York: Cambridge University Press, 2004); and Royal E. Montgomery, *Industrial Relations in the Chicago Building Trades* (Chicago: University of Chicago Press, 1927); and Nelson, *Divided We Stand*, 55–61. On the relationship between Tammany and the New York underworld, see George Kibbee Turner, "Tammany's Control of New York by Professional Criminals," *McClure's Magazine* 33 (June 1909): 117–36; and English, *Paddy Whacked*, 111, 232–39.

123. J. H. Cohen, "Who's Who in Gangland," Burgess Papers, Box 129, Folder 9; O'Kane, *Crooked Ladder*, 57–60; Asbury, *Gangs of New York*; Asbury, *Gangs of Chicago*; English, *Paddy Whacked*, 125–26, 170–75, 325–56.

124. O'Kane, *Crooked Ladder*, 70–75, English, *Paddy Whacked*, 175–93; Asbury, *Gangs of New York*; Humbert Nelli, *The Business of Crime: Italians and Syndicate Crime in the United States* (New York: Oxford University Press, 1976); Rich Cohen, *Tough Jews* (New York: Simon & Schuster, 1998); Albert Fried, *The Rise and Fall of the Jewish Gangster* (New York, Holt, Rinehart & Winston, 1980); Mark White, notes on the Parker Social Athletic Club, Everett C. Hughes Papers, Box 99, Folder 9, Special Collections, Regenstein Library, University of Chicago.

125. Barrett, *Work and Community in the Jungle*, 219–23; Diamond, *Mean Streets*, 19–26; Rick Halpern, "Race, Ethnicity and Union in the Chicago Stockyards, 1917–1922," *International Review of Social History* 37 (1992): 52–57; Dominic A. Pacyga, *Polish Immigrants and Industrial Chicago: Workers on the South Side, 1880–1922* (Columbus: Ohio State University Press, 1991), 219–27; Tuttle, *Race Riot: Chicago*, 32–33, 54–55, 102–3, 199–200. The Colts knew about blacking up, as they put on minstrel shows for the community.

126. Mary McDowell, "Prejudice," in Caroline Hill, ed., *Mary McDowell and Municipal House-keeping* (Chicago: Millar, 1938), 32–33. See also Thrasher, *Gang*, 50–51.

127. Pacyga, *Polish Immigrants in Industrial Chicago*, 219–20. See also David R. Roediger and James R. Barrett, "Making New Immigrants 'Inbetween': Irish Hosts and White Panethnicity, 1890–1930," in Nancy Foner and George M. Fredrickson, eds., *Not Just Black and White: Historical and Contemporary Perspectives on Immigration, Race, and Ethnicity in the United States* (New York: Russell Sage Foundation, 2004), 167–96. I am grateful to David Roediger for his insight on this point. For the case of an Irish American burglar going about his work in blackface masquerade, see "Black-Faced White Man Held by Police," *Amsterdam News*, December 28, 1927, 3.

128. "Murder at Club of Ragen Colts Arouses Fever," *Chicago Tribune*, March 9, 1926, 12; and "Ragen Colts Go on Spree; Murder Man," *Chicago Defender*, March 13, 1926.

129. Kenneth Jackson, *The Ku Klux Klan in the City, 1915–1930* (New York: Oxford University Press, 1967), 95; Tuttle, *Race Riot*, 257, 197–202; Thomas A. Guglielmo, *White on Arrival: Italians, Race, Color, and Power in Chicago, 1890–1945* (New York: Oxford University Press, 2004); and Humbert Nelli, *Italians in Chicago, 1880–1930: A Study in Ethnic Mobility* (New York: Oxford University Press, 1970), 229–30. In another case, Chicago gang members traveled to Oklahoma to help in a struggle there against the Klan. See Thrasher, *Gang*, 173.

130. *Dziennik Chicagoski*, August 5, 1919, quoted in Pacyga, *Polish Immigrants in Industrial Chicago*, 220–24, quote at 220; Barrett, *Work and Community in the Jungle*, 220–24; and Roediger, *Working Toward Whiteness*, 128. See also Thaddeus Radzialowski, "The Competition for Jobs and Racial Stereotypes: Poles and Blacks in Chicago," *Polish American Studies* 33 (Autumn 1976): 5–18; and Joseph Parot, "Ethnic Versus Black Metropolis: The Origins of Polish-Black Housing Tensions in Chicago," *Polish American Studies* 29 (Spring–Autumn 1972): 5–33. For the racialized discourse focusing on Poles and other "new immigrants," see James R. Barrett and David R. Roediger, "In Between Peoples: Race, Nationality and the 'New Immigrant' Working Class," *Journal of American Ethnic History* 16 (1997): 3–44.

131. Julia Goryl interview (GOR–120), Archives of the Oral History of Chicago Polonia, Chicago Historical Museum; Pacyga, *Polish Immigrants in Industrial Chicago*, 233.

132. Barrett and Roediger, "In Between Peoples"; Niles Carpenter, *Nationality, Color, and Economic Opportunity in the City of Buffalo* (Buffalo, N.Y.: Roswell Park Publication Fund, 1927).

133. Niles Carpenter and Daniel Katz, "A Study in the Acculturation of the Polish Group in Buffalo, 1926–1928," *University of Buffalo Studies* 7, no. 4 (June 1929): 129–30.

134. Arnold R. Hirsch, "Race and Housing: Violence and Communal Protest in Chicago, 1940–1960," in Peter d'Alory Jones and Melvin Holli, eds., *The Ethnic Frontier: Essays in the History of Group Survival in Chicago and Midwest* (Grand Rapids, Mich.: Eerdmans, 1977), 350–55; and Arnold R. Hirsch, *Making the Second Ghetto: Race and Housing in the United States, 1940–1960* (Chicago: University of Chicago Press, 1998), 68–99.

135. J. Adams Puffer, *The Boy and His Gang* (Boston: Houghton Mifflin, 1912), 27. See also Robert E. Park, Ernest Burgess, and Roderick D. McKenzie, *The City: Suggestions for Investigation of Human Behavior in the Urban Environment* (Chicago: University of Chicago Press, 1967), 112.

136. Pat Ireland, "Factors in the Americanization of a Second Generation Immigrant People," manuscript, University of Chicago, 1932, microfilm copy, Chicago History Museum, 66.

137. Thrasher, *Gang*, 215–17, quotes, 215. Thrasher is clearly using the term *races* to refer to ethnic

groups. See Victoria Hattam, "Ethnicity: An American Genealogy," in Foner and Fredrickson, *Not Just Black and White*, 42–60; and Roediger, *Working Toward Whiteness*, 10–34. On Harlem's ethnically mixed Commodore Social Athletic Club, sponsored by a black waiter with Jewish, Polish, Greek, African American, Italian, and Irish members, see "Where the Pot Is Boiling," *Amsterdam News*, February 15, 1928, 15.

138. Jacob A. Riis, *How the Other Half Lives: Studies Among the Tenements of New York* (New York: Charles Scribner's Sons, 1890), 218.

139. "A Study of Behavior Problems of Boys in the Lower North Community," Burgess Papers, Box 35, Folder 4; Diamond, *Mean Streets*, 71–73; Pacyga, *Polish Immigrants and Industrial Chicago*, 150.

140. Thrasher, *Gang*, 130–32; Jablonsky, *Pride in the Jungle*, 109. On the postwar panethnic white, black, and Latino gangs in Chicago and New York, see Diamond, *Mean Streets*, 152–92; and Schneider, *Vampires, Dragons, and Egyptian Kings*.

141. "Certain Relationships between Recreation and Juvenile Delinquency in Chicago," Burgess Papers, Box 38, Folder 9; and Donald Tricarico, *The Italians of Greenwich Village: The Social Structure and Transformation of an Ethnic Community* (New York: Center for Migration Studies, 1984).

142. Thrasher, *Gang*, 18, 62–65. See also Diamond, *Mean Streets*, 61–62; Roediger, *Working Toward Whiteness*, 126–28.

143. "The Melting Pot," n.d., Burgess Papers, Box 154, Folder 5; Florence Lyon Gaddis, "Conflict Between Mexicans and Poles" (1928), Burgess Papers, Box 142, Folder 3; and Diamond, *Mean Streets*, 63–64, 92–93. See also Arredondo, *Mexican Chicago*, 54–58, 73–75.

144. Kisseloff, *You Must Remember This*, 414.

145. Bachin, *Building the South Side*, 160.

146. Thrasher, *Gang*, 138–39, 194–95, 200–201, 215; Diamond, *Mean Streets*, 28; and James R. Grossman, *Land of Hope: Chicago, Black Southerners, and the Great Migration* (Chicago: University of Chicago Press, 1989), 178. Such gangs continued to enforce the segregated quality of "white ethnic" neighborhoods on Chicago's South Side until at least the 1990s.

147. Barrett and Roediger, "In Between Peoples"; Guglielmo, *White on Arrival*, emphasizes that the ascribed identity of Italians and more recent immigrants was "white" from the time of their arrival in the United States. Guglielmo agrees, however, that it often took considerable time for such immigrants to develop their own racial identities. Instead, they often clung first to local and regional identities, then eventually to a national identity, and only later to an image of themselves as "white."

148. Cohen, *Making a New Deal*, 120–47; Randy McBee, *Dance Hall Days: Intimacy and Leisure Among Working-Class Immigrants in the United States* (New York: New York University Press, 2000); Nasaw, *Children of the City*; David Nasaw, *Going Out: The Rise and Fall of Public Amusements* (New York: Basic Books, 1993), 48–51, quote at 45.

149. Paul G. Cressey, *The Taxi-Dance Hall; A Sociological Study in Commercialized Recreation and City Life* (Chicago: University of Chicago Press, 1932); Lewis Erenberg, *Steppin' Out: New York Night Life and the Transformation of American Culture* (Westport, Conn.: Greenwood Press, 1981); Nasaw, *Going Out*, 108, 116–18, quote at 117; George J. Sánchez, *Becoming Mexican American: Ethnicity, Culture, and Identity in Chicano Los Angeles, 1900–1945* (New York: Oxford University Press, 1993), 171–87; Diamond, *Mean Streets*, 73–74.

150. Nasaw, *Going Out*, 116–19; McBee, *Dance Hall Days*, 135.

151. Cressey, "A Study of Gaelic Park," 9, 22, 29, passim, Burgess Papers, Box 130, Folder 7. See also McBee, *Dance Hall Days*, 135, 142–43.

152. Paul Cressey, "Report on Summer's Work with the Juvenile Protective Association" (1925), 5, Burgess Papers, Box 129, Folder 5. On the dance hall culture and sources for ethnic tension within it, see also McBee, *Dance Hall Days*, 135, 145–46.

153. Cressey, *Taxi-Dance Hall*, 109–74.

154. Kevin J. Mumford, *Interzones: Black/White Sex Districts in Chicago and New York in the Early Twentieth Century* (New York: Columbia University Press, 1997), 23–35, especially 23–25; and Diamond, *Mean Streets*, 41–54. On the liminal location of and illicit activities in Chicago's "Bright Lights" district of the Black Belt, see Walter C. Reckless, *Vice in Chicago* (Chicago: University of Chicago Press, 1933).

155. On nineteenth-century anxiety and ambivalence, Roediger, *Wages of Whiteness*, 150–56; and Eric Lott, *Love and Theft: Blackface Minstrelsy and the American Working Class* (New York: Oxford University Press, 1993), 94–95. On the peculiar mix of hostility, curiosity, and desire among Irish American youth in the 1920s, see Mumford, *Interzones*, and Diamond, *Mean Streets*, 48–54.

156. Diamond, *Mean Streets*, 87; Ronald Edsforth, "Made in the USA: Mass Culture and the Americanization of Working-Class Ethnics in the Coolidge Era," in John Earl Haynes, ed., *Calvin Coolidge and the Calvin Coolidge Era* (Washington, D.C.: Library of Congress, 1998), 244–73; and David R. Roediger, *Towards the Abolition of Whiteness: Essays on Race, Politics, and Working-Class History* (London: Verso, 1994), 188–89.

157. Landesco, *Illinois Crime Survey*, 171.

CHAPTER 2: THE PARISH

1. "Old St. Patrick's Holds Centennial," *New York Times*, May 3, 1915, 7. See also "New St. Lucy's Dedicated," *New York Times*, November 8, 1915, 6.

2. John T. McGreevy, *Parish Boundaries: The Catholic Encounter with Race in the Twentieth-Century Urban North* (Chicago: University of Chicago Press, 1996), 4–5, 10, 15, 22.

3. Eileen Skerrett, "The Catholic Dimension," in Lawrence McCaffrey et al., eds., *The Irish in Chicago* (Urbana: University of Illinois Press, 1987), 40.

4. Jay P. Dolan, *In Search of American Catholicism: A History of Religion and Culture in Tension* (New York: Oxford University Press, 2002), 129–31, quotes at 130, 131. See also J. J. Lee, "Introduction: Interpreting Irish America," in J. J. Lee and Marion R. Casey, eds., *Making the Irish American: History and Heritage of the Irish in the United States* (New York: New York University, 2006), 27.

5. Skerrett, "Catholic Dimension," 40.

6. Evelyn Savidge Sterne, *Ballots and Bibles: Ethnic Politics and the Catholic Church in Providence* (Ithaca, N.Y.: Cornell University Press, 2003), quote at 36–37. On the significance of the ethnic working-class parish, see Leslie Woodcock Tentler, "Present at the Creation: Working-Class Catholics in the United States," in Rick Halpern and Jonathan Morris, eds., *American Exceptionalism? U.S. Working-Class Formation in an International Context* (New York: St. Martin's Press, 1997), 134–57.

7. Emmet Larkin, "The Devotional Revolution in Ireland, 1850–75," *American Historical Review* 77 (June 1972): 625–52; Mageean, "Making Sense and Providing Structure," 87; and Caitriona Clear, *Nuns in Nineteenth Century Ireland* (Dublin: Gill & Macmillan, 1987).

8. Hugh McLeod, "Catholicism and the New York Irish, 1890–1910," in Jim Obelkevich, Lyndal Roper, and Raphael Samuel, eds., *Disciplines of Faith: Studies in Religion, Politics and Patriarchy* (London: Routledge & Kegan Paul, 1987), 338; and Will Herberg, *Protestant,*

Catholic, Jew (Garden City, N.Y.: Doubleday & Co., 1960), 142n14, 163–64. Desmond Keenan diminishes the effects of the Famine and English suppression of popular Catholicism and argues that the Irish church was characterized by a kind of "modernism" even before the Famine. Whatever the timing of its rise, the Catholicism that the Irish brought with them was more formal, centralized, and "respectable" than that of the Italians and other new immigrants they encountered in the American city. Even Keenan notes a pervasive popular Catholicism among the Irish peasantry. See Desmond J. Keenan, *The Catholic Church in Nineteenth-Century Ireland: A Sociological Study* (Totowa, N.J.: Barnes & Noble, 1983), 89–113. For a black perspective on the effects of anti-Catholicism in enhancing the loyalty of the Irish and later immigrant groups, see also Herbert Adolphus Miller, "Race Pride and Race Prejudice," *Amsterdam News*, January 3, 1925, 9.

9. Colleen McDannell, "Catholic Domesticity, 1860–1960," in David G. Hackett, ed., *Religion and American Culture: A Reader* (New York: Routledge, 1995), 301.

10. Ibid. For admonishments by Boston clergy to decorate Irish American homes with religious imagery, see Dennis P. Ryan, *Beyond the Ballot Box: A Social History of the Boston Irish, 1845–1917* (Rutherford, N.J.: Fairleigh Dickinson University Press, 1983), 3.

11. McDannell, "Catholic Domesticity," 303.

12. Tentler, "Present at the Creation," 134–80.

13. David Noel Doyle, "Catholicism, Politics, and Irish America since 1890: Some Critical Considerations," in P. J. Drudy, ed., *The Irish in America: Emigration, Assimilation and Impact* (Cambridge, U.K.: Cambridge University Press, 1985), 191; and Harold J. Abramson, *Ethnic Diversity in Catholic America* (New York: John Wiley & Sons, 1973), 107–16.

14. Dolores Liptak, *Immigrants and Their Church* (New York: Macmillan, 1989), 11, 62; Jay P. Dolan, *The American Catholic Experience: A History from Colonial Times to the Present* (Notre Dame, Ind.: University of Notre Dame Press, 1992), quote at 303; McDannell, "Catholic Domesticity," 304. Thomas J. Shelley, "Twentieth Century American Catholicism and Irish Americans," in Lee and Casey, *Making the Irish American*, 578–80.

15. Robert E. Sullivan, "Beneficial Relations: Toward a Social History of the Diocesan Priests of Boston, 1875–1944," in Robert E. Sullivan and James M. O'Toole, eds., *Catholic Boston: Studies in Religion and Community, 1870–1970* (Boston: Roman Catholic Archbishop of Boston, 1985), 205, 206; Donna Merwick, *Boston Priests, 1848–1910: A Study of Social and Intellectual Change* (Cambridge, Mass.: Harvard University Press, 1973); James M. O'Toole, *Militant and Triumphant: William Henry O'Connell and the Catholic Church in Boston, 1859–1944* (Notre Dame, Ind.: Notre Dame University Press, 1992), 144–45; and Patrick J. McNamara, "A People Apart: The Church Grows in Brooklyn . . . and Queens," in Terry Golway, ed., *Catholics in New York: Society, Culture, and Politics, 1808–1946* (New York: Fordham University Press, 2008), 45.

16. Dolan, *American Catholic Experience*, 302. See also Henry B. Leonard, "Ethnic Tensions, Episcopal Leadership, and the Emergence of the Twentieth Century American Catholic Church: The Cleveland Experience," *Catholic Historical Review* 71, no. 3 (July 1985): 394–412.

17. Edward R. Kantowicz, *Corporation Sole: Cardinal Mundelein and Chicago Catholicism* (Notre Dame, Ind.: University of Notre Dame Press, 1983), 7; and David Noel Doyle, *Irish Americans, Native Rights, and National Empires: The Structure, Divisions, and Attitudes of the Catholic Minority in the Decade of Expansion* (New York: Arno Press, 1976), 15–16, 34n70.

18. For the Irish-German struggle in New York, see Michael Augustine Corrigan to Peter Paul Cahensly, New York, July 22, 1891, Series 1, Box 1, "Miscellaneous Correspondence

NOTES313

regarding Saint Raphaelverein," Center for Migration Studies, Italian Americans and Religion Collection, quoted in Mary Elizabeth Brown, *Churches, Communities, and Children: Italian Immigrants in the Archdiocese of New York, 1880–1945* (Staten Island, N.Y.: Center for Migration Studies, 1995), 34. On the struggle in Chicago, see "Irish vs. German Catholics," *Chicago Tribune*, June 4, 1891, 4; and "The Patriotic Catholic Clerical Union," ibid., June 25, 1891, 4. On the American Protective Association and the resurgence of anti-Catholicism, see John Higham, *Strangers in the Land: Patterns of American Nativism, 1860–1925* (New York: Athenaeum, 1963), 61, 77–87, 95, 108; and JoEllen McNergney Vinyard, *For Faith and Fortune: The Education of Catholic Immigrants in Detroit, 1805–1925* (Urbana: University of Illinois Press, 1998), 105–9.

19. Cardinal George Mundelein to President Theodore Roosevelt, June 5, 1916, quoted in Kantowicz, *Corporation Sole*, 25. See also John Tracy Ellis, *The Life of James Cardinal Gibbons, Archbishop of Baltimore, 1834–1921* (Milwaukee: Bruce, 1952), 1:373–74.

20. Shelley, "Twentieth Century American Catholicism and Irish Americans," 583. See also Thomas T. McAvoy, *The Americanist Heresy in Roman Catholicism, 1895–1900* (Notre Dame, Ind.: Notre Dame University Press, 1963).

21. See Dolan, *American Catholic Experience*, 236–37; on the Americanist controversy and on the Americanizing efforts of the church, 295–303. On the distinction between Irish American Catholic and Anglo-American theories of "Americanization," see Richard M. Linkh, *American Catholicism and European Immigrants, 1900–1924* (Staten Island, N.Y.: Center for Migration Studies, 1975), 22–28. See also Robert D. Cross, *The Emergence of Liberal Catholicism in America* (Cambridge, Mass.: Harvard University Press, 1958), and Rudolph Vecoli, "Prelates and Peasants: Italian Immigrants and the Catholic Church," *Journal of Social History* 2 (Spring 1969): 262–63.

22. Oscar Handlin, *The Uprooted* (New York: Grosset & Dunlap, 1951), 135, 138.

23. Shelley, "Twentieth-Century American Catholicism and Irish Americans," 578.

24. Liptak, *Immigrants and Their Church*, 61–89.

25. Henry J. Browne, "The Italian Problem and the Catholic Church of the United States, 1880–1900," *United States Catholic Historical Society: Historical Records and Studies* 35 (1946): 46–72; and Humbert S. Nelli, *The Italians in Chicago, 1880–1930: A Study in Ethnic Mobility* (New York: Oxford University Press, 1970), 187–94.

26. Vecoli, "Prelates and Peasants," 220–24, quotes at 222, 224; Nelli, *Italians in Chicago*, 188–91; Peter R. D'Agostino, *Rome in America: Transnational Catholic Ideology from the Risorgimento to Fascism* (Chapel Hill: University of North Carolina Press, 2004), 76–79; Harold J. Abramson, "Ethnic Diversity within Catholicism: A Comparative Analysis of Contemporary and Historical Religion," *Journal of Social History* 4 (Summer 1971): 359–83.

27. "Chicago Priests Live in Jeopardy," *Chicago Tribune*, February 26, 1908, 1; "Clerical Clash Given Pro and Con," ibid., March 1, 1908, 2; *La Tribuna Italiana*, August 20, 1904, Chicago Foreign Language Press Survey (CFLPS), University Library, University of Illinois at Urbana-Champaign, III-H; *Chicago Record-Herald*, March 1, 1908, CFLPS, II-D-6, I-B-4; Italian newspapers and Dunne quoted in Vecoli, "Prelates and Peasants," 225, 227; and Deborah A. Skok, *More Than Neighbors: Catholic Settlements and Day Nurseries in Chicago, 1893–1930* (DeKalb: Northern Illinois University Press, 2007), 75–82. Poor relations between the church, Italian anticlericals, and Hull House persisted: see D'Agostino, *Rome in America*, 71–74. Dunne, who was later elevated to bishop of Peoria, became a major spokesperson for the church's role as an "Americanizing" force among immigrants. See Edmund M. Dunne, "The Church and the Immigrant," in C. E. Maguire, ed., *Catholic Builders of the*

Nation (Boston, 1923), vol. 2. Dunne's *Memoirs of Zi Pre* (St. Louis: B. Herder, 1914) is a fictionalized account of his own experiences among West Side Italians.

28. Philip Cannistaro and Gerald Meyer, eds., *The Lost World of Italian-American Radicalism* (Westport, Conn.: Praeger, 2003); Victor R. Greene, *For God and Country: The Rise of Polish and Lithuanian Ethnic Consciousness in America, 1860–1910* (Madison: State Historical Society of Wisconsin, 1975), 144–56; and Bruce Nelson, *Beyond the Martyrs: A Social History of Chicago's Anarchists, 1870–1900* (New Brunswick, N.J.: Rutgers University Press, 1988).

29. A. Rakauskas, interview, January 26, 1925, Everett C. Hughes Papers, Box 99, Folder 9, Special Collections, Regenstein Library, University of Chicago.

30. Jacob Riis, "Feast Days in Little Italy," *Century Magazine* 57 (August 1899), 496–98, quoted in Anbinder, *Five Points*, 387; Ryan, *Beyond the Ballot Box*, 140–41; Vecoli, "Prelates and Peasants," passim; Salvatore Primeggia, "La Via Vecchia and Italian Folk Religiosity: The Peasants and Immigrants Speak," in Joseph Varacalli et al., eds., *Models and Images of Catholicism in Italian Americana: Academy and Society* (Stony Brook, N.Y.: Forum Italicum, 2004), 15–37.

31. A. J. Paulsen, "A Sociological Study of the Gimlet Gang," 33, Ernst Watson Burgess Papers, Box 181, Folder 7, Special Collections, Regenstein Library, University of Chicago. See also photos of the procession and children in the neighborhood.

32. On the centrality of the *festa* to Italian Catholics, see Robert A. Orsi, *The Madonna of 115th Street: Faith and Community in Harlem, 1880–1950* (New Haven, Conn.: Yale University Press, 1985), quote at 57. On the mixture in *campanilismo* of folk religious belief and ritual with magic, see Rudolph Vecoli, "Cult and Occult in Italian-American Culture: The Persistence of a Religious Heritage," in Randall M. Miller and Thomas D. Marzik, eds., *Immigrants and Religion in Urban America* (Philadelphia: Temple University Press, 1977), 25–47. On this aspect of the "Italian problem," see also Mary Elizabeth Brown, "'The Adoption of the Tactics of the Enemy': The Care of Italian Immigrant Youth in the Archdiocese of New York During the Progressive Era," in William Pencak, Selma Berrol, and Randall M. Miller, eds., *Immigration to New York* (Philadelphia: Balch Institute Press, 1991), 109–25; Ryan, *Beyond the Ballot Box*, 141–42, 154.

33. On the fusion of Polish American religious and national identity, see Matthew Frye Jacobson, *Special Sorrows: The Diasporic Imagination of Irish, Polish, and Jewish Immigrants* (Berkeley: University of California Press, 2002), 68–71; and Anthony J. Kuzniewski, "The Catholic Church in the Life of Polish Americans," in Frank Mocha, ed., *Poles in America: Bicentenial Essays* (Stevens Point, Wis.: Worzalla Publishing, 1978), 399–422; and John J. Bukowczyk, *And My Children Did Not Know Me: A History of Polish-Americans* (Bloomington: Indiana University Press, 1987), 44–45. See also Dominic A. Pacyga, *Polish Immigrants and Industrial Chicago: Workers on the South Side, 1880–1922* (Columbus: Ohio State University Press, 1991).

34. See Daniel S. Buczek, "Polish Americans and the Roman Catholic Church," *Polish Review* 21 (1976): 39–62, especially 48; Jacobson, *Special Sorrows*, 121–22, Dangiel quoted at 122. On Chicago, see Joseph Parot, *Polish Catholics in Chicago* (DeKalb: Northern Illinois University Press, 1981); and Victor R. Greene, *For God and Country: The Rise of Polish and Lithuanian Ethnic Consciousness in America, 1860–1910* (Madison: State Historical Society of Wisconsin, 1975).

35. Dolan, *American Catholic Experience,* 299–300. See also Dolan, *In Search of American Catholicism,* 138–41.

36. On the conflict in Detroit, see Leslie Tentler, "Who Is the Church? Conflict in a Polish

Immigrant Parish in Late Nineteenth-Century Detroit," *Comparative Studies in Society and History* 25, no. 2 (April 1983), 241–76; Thaddeus Radzialowski, "The View from a Polish Ghetto: Some Observations on the First One Hundred Years in Detroit," *Ethnicity* 1 (1974): 125–50; Vinyard, *For Faith and Fortune,* 101–5. On conflicts in New York City, see Alex Storozynski, "From Serfdom to Freedom," in Golway, *Catholics in New York,* 71, 73–74; and in Wisconsin, Anthony J. Kuzniewski, *Faith and Fatherland: The Polish Church War in Wisconsin, 1896–1918* (Notre Dame, Ind.: University of Notre Dame Press, 1980), 47–48, 62.

37. Hodur quoted in Jacobson, *Special Sorrows,* 69. On the Polish National Catholic Church, see Victor R. Greene, *For God and Country: The Rise of Polish and Lithuanian Ethnic Consciousness in America, 1860–1910* (Madison: State Historical Society of Wisconsin, 1975), 84, 96, 110, 112–14, 133; Pacyga, *Polish Immigrants in Industrial Chicago,* 145; Dominic A. Pacyga, "To Live Amongst Others: Poles and Their Neighbors in Industrial Chicago, 1865–1930," *Journal of American Ethnic History* 16 (Fall 1996): 56–57; Liptak, *Immigrants and Their Church,* 114–30; and McGreevy, *Parish Boundaries,* 31.

38. Daniel Buczek, *Immigrant Pastor: The Life of the Right Reverend Monsignor Lucyan Bojnowski of New Britain, Connecticut* (Waterbury, Conn.: Hemingway, 1974), 4. For a comparable observation regarding Italian Catholics, see Silvano Tomasi, *Piety and Power: The Role of Italian Parishes in the New York Metropolitan Area, 1880–1930* (Staten Island, N.Y.: Center for Migration Studies, 1975), 45.

39. George Cardinal Mundelein to Louis Bachand-Verefeuille, April 30, 1917, 1917B4, Madaj Collection, Archives of the Archdiocese of Chicago (AAC), quoted in Julie Satzik and Gregory A. Singleton, *Americanization in the Archdiocese of Chicago: George Cardinal Mundelein: A Pragmatic Americanizer* (Chicago: Northeastern Illinois University Press, 1994).

40. Letter in the name of the American hierarchy answering the memorial presented to the Holy See by the Polish legation in Rome regarding alleged discrimination by the American hierarchy, 1920, George Cardinal Mundelein Papers, June, 19, 1920/G/1, AAC. Although the letter was nominally a joint document, it is clear from an attached letter that the original draft was largely the work of Mundelein.

41. Ibid.

42. Mundelein, speech at dedication of St. Mary of the Angels, 1920, 1920M198, Madaj Collection, AAC, Chicago, quote at 41; Charles Shanabruch, *Chicago's Catholics: The Evolution of an American Identity* (Notre Dame, Ind.: Notre Dame University Press, 1981), 184, 204–8.

43. "Women and Children in Ireland are Hungry and Homeless," *Chicago Tribune,* April 8, 1921, 14. See also materials in Mundelein Papers.

44. "Poles Want a Bishop on the Cahensly Plan," *Chicago Tribune,* July 29, 1891, 10. See also Kantowicz, *Corporation Sole.*

45. Kantowicz, *Corporation Sole,* 72, 82–83, 151; Satzik and Singleton, *Americanization in Archdiocese of Chicago,* 24–25; Mundelein quoted in Dolan, *In Search of American Catholicism,* 139. On Mundelein's Americanization efforts—and the staunch Polish resistance—see also Lizabeth Cohen, *Making a New Deal: Industrial Workers in Chicago, 1919–1939* (New York: Cambridge University Press, 1990), 83–87.

46. Kantowicz, *Corporation Sole,* 85–98; Shanabruch, *Chicago's Catholics,* 187–88, 211–12.

47. "To Americanize the Schools," *New York Times,* May 12, 1916, 22; and "For Americanism," *Chicago Tribune,* July 26, 1916, 6.

48. Stazik, "Americanization in the Archdiocese of Chicago," 45–50.

49. Kantowicz, *Corporation Sole,* 74.

50. Letter in the name of the American hierarchy answering memorial presented to the Holy See by the Polish Legation, Mundelein Papers, June, 19, 1920/G/1, AAC.

51. Kantowicz, *Corporation Sole*, 25–26.

52. Brown, "'Adoption of the Tactics of the Enemy,'" 111. See also Vecoli, "Prelates and Peasants."

53. Quoted in Frederick M. Binder and David M. Reimers, *All the Nations Under Heaven: An Ethnic and Racial History of New York City* (New York: Columbia University Press, 1995), 146.

54. Bernard J. Lynch, "The Italians in New York," *Catholic World* 47 (April 1888), 68–70, quoted in Anbinder, *Five Points*, 379–80.

55. Vecoli, "Prelates and Peasants," quote at 233.

56. Orsi, *Madonna of 115th Street*, 199, quote at 56; Whyte, "Race Conflicts in the North End of Boston," 623–42.

57. Dolan, *In Search of American Catholicism*, 141–43, quote at 142. See also Anne M. Martinez, *Bordering on the Sacred: Religion, Nation, and U.S.-Mexican Relations, 1910–1929*, Ph.D. diss., University of Minnesota, 2003; and Brother Malachy Richard McCarthy, *Which Christ Came to Chicago: Catholic and Protestant Programs to Evangelize, Socialize, and Americanize the Mexican Immigrant, 1900–1940*, Ph.D. diss., Loyola University of Chicago, 2002).

58. Larkin, "Devotional Revolution," 639–45; Eric C. Schneider, *In the Web of Class: Delinquents and Reformers in Boston, 1810s–1930s* (New York: New York University Press, 1992), 123–24.

59. Dorothy M. Brown and Elizabeth McKeown, *The Poor Belong to Us: Catholic Charities and American Welfare* (Cambridge, Mass.: Harvard University Press, 1997); and Alfred E. Smith, *Up to Now: An Autobiography* (New York: Viking Press, 1929), 38–39.

60. James W. Sanders, *Education of an Urban Minority: Catholics in Chicago, 1833–1965* (New York: Oxford University Press, 1977).

61. Shanabruch, *Chicago's Catholics*, 1–30; Sanders, *Education of an Urban Minority*, 112–13, 200, 132; Suellen Hoy, *Good Hearts: Catholic Sisters in Chicago's Past* (Urbana: University of Illinois Press, 2006), 85–102, 47–70.

62. On the Irish background and the dispersion of Irish nuns to the United States, see Hoy, *Good Hearts*, 11–34. On their role in American cities, see Hasia R. Diner, *Erin's Daughters in America: Irish Immigrant Women in the Nineteenth Century* (Baltimore, Md.: Johns Hopkins University Press, 1983), 130–37.

63. Sarah Deutsch, *Women and the City: Gender, Space, and Power in Boston, 1870–1940* (New York: Oxford University Press, 2000), quote at 240.

64. Diner, *Erin's Daughters*, 28, 120–38.

65. Maureen Fitzgerald, *Habits of Compassion: Irish Catholic Nuns and the Origins of New York's Welfare System, 1830–1920* (Urbana: University of Illinois Press, 2006), 4.

66. Hoy, *Good Hearts*, 35–45.

67. Mageean, "Making Sense and Providing Structure," 242–43, 40; Carol K. Coburn and Martha Smith, *Spirited Lives: How Nuns Shaped Catholic Culture and American Life, 1836–1920* (Chapel Hill: University of North Carolina Press, 1999), 87, 221; and Eileen Brewer, *Nuns and the Education of American Women* (Chicago: University of Chicago Press, 1987), 18. On the disproportionate number of Irish women among Catholic nuns, see Diner, *Erin's Daughters*, 130–33. See also Deirdre Mageean, "Catholic Sisterhoods and the Immigrant Church," in Donna Gabaccia, ed., *Seeking Common Ground: Multidisciplinary*

Studies of Immigrant Women in the United States (Westport, Conn.: Greenwood Press, 1992), 89–100; Fitzgerald, *Habits of Compassion*; and Hoy, *Good Hearts*.

68. Hoy, *Good Hearts*, 86–124, 7. On work among African Americans in Boston, see Deutsch, *Women and the City*, 42.

69. Thomas Shelley, "Catholic Greenwich Village: Ethnic Geography and Religious Identity in New York City, 1880–1930," *Catholic Historical Review* 89, no. 1 (2003): 71–74; Nelson Callahan, "R. L. Burtsell: His Diary, His Life, His Times," *Working Paper No. 13*, Cushwa Center for the Study of American Catholicism, Notre Dame University, 1976, 2, 3.

70. *Irish World and Industrial Liberator*, August 11, 1883, 3; November 17, 1883, 3, December 8, 1883, 3; and April 14, 1917, 8; Jeffrey B. Perry, *Hubert Harrison: The Voice of Harlem Radicalism, 1883–1918* (New York: Columbia University Press, 2009), 70–73, especially 72.

71. Jean Carsello, interview, February 3, 1980, Italians in Chicago Project, 7, interview transcript copy, Special Collections, University of Illinois at Urbana-Champaign; Doyle, *Irish Americans, Native Rights*, 11; Deborah Skok, *More than Neighbors: Catholic Settlements and Day Nurseries in Chicago, 1893–1930* (DeKalb: Northern Illinois University Press, 2007), 71.

72. Mary Elizabeth Brown, "A Separate Feast: The Italian Influence on Catholic New York," in Golway, ed., *Catholics in New York*, 31, 34; McNamara, "People Apart," in *Catholics in New York City*, 48.

73. Edwin M. Fay to Cardinal Hayes, New York, January 1924 [1925] and Ida V. Collins to Cardinal Hayes, New York, January 1925, both in Archives of the Archdiocese of New York, Holy Rosary Folder, quoted in Brown, *Churches, Communities, and Children*, 68.

74. Rev. Julius DeVos, pastor of St. John Berchmans, to George Cardinal Mundelein, September 28, 1918, Mundelein Papers, M178, Archives of the Archdiocese of Chicago, Chicago.

75. O'Flynn to Corrigan, October 6, 1896, St. Joseph Parish file, Archives of the Archdiocese of New York (AANY), quoted in Shelley, "Catholic Greenwich Village," 71. For comparable conflicts in Boston, see Rev. Leonard Bacigalupo, "Some Religious Aspects Involving the Interaction of the Italians and the Irish," in Francis X. Femminella, ed., *Italians and Irish in America* (Staten Island, N.Y.: American Italian Historical Association, 1985), 120–24.

76. Brown, "Separate Feast," 37.

77. DiGiovanni, *Archbishop Corrigan*, 102–6; Charles S. Monahan to Monsignor Hoban, Chancery, 8, 1924, G 13, Archives of the Catholic Archdiocese of Chicago.

78. Thomas Lynch quoted by Bernard J. Lynch, "The Italians in New York," *Catholic World* 47 (1888): 67, 68, 70, 72; Stephen Michael DiGiovanni, *Archbishop Corrigan and the Italian Immigrants* (Huntington, Ind.: Our Sunday Visitor, 1994), 79–107. See also Mary Elizabeth Brown, *From Italian Villages to Greenwich Village: Our Lady of Pompeii, 1892–1992* (New York: Center for Migration Studies, 1992), 1–10.

79. "Italians Get Irish Church," *New York Times*, May 5, 1902, 5. On Italian protests, see Anbinder, *Five Points*, 380–82.

80. DiGiovanni, *Archbishop Corrigan*, 121–25; *Brooklyn Eagle*, August 17, 1902, 23.

81. "Minutes of the Meetings of the Archdiocesan Consultors," June 3, 1898, AANY, quoted in ibid., 71.

82. "Catholics Will Celebrate," *Chicago Tribune*, October 18, 1890, 3.

83. "No Place for KKK," *New York Times*, March 21, 1926, 20.

84. Vecoli, "Prelates and Peasants," 262; Vinyard, *For Faith and Fortune*, 165. On competition and frequent conflict between entrenched Irish clergy and Italian priests trying to make a place for themselves and their flocks in various locales, see Tomasi, *Piety and Power*,

44–47, 67–81; Browne, "Italian Problem and the Catholic Church"; Mary Elizabeth Brown, "The Making of Italian American Catholics," *Catholic Historical Review* 73 (1987), 200–202; Dolan, *American Catholic Experience*, 237; Richard A. Varbero, "Philadelphia's South Italians and the Irish Church: A History of Cultural Conflict," in Silvano M. Tomasi, ed., *The Religious Experience of Italian-Americans* (Staten Island, N.Y.: American Italian Historical Association, 1975), 50–51; Nelli, *Italians in Chicago*, 188–91; Judith E. Smith, *Family Connections: A History of Italian and Jewish Immigrant Lives in Providence, Rhode Island, 1900–1940* (Albany: State University of New York Press, 1985), 147.

85. Merwick, *Boston's Priests, 1848–1910*, 131; Kane, *Separatism and Subculture*.

86. On the role of settlement houses in conveying middle-class Protestant culture to the immigrant masses, see Allen F. Davis, *Spearheads for Reform: The Social Settlements and the Progressive Movement, 1890–1914* (New Brunswick, N.J.: Rutgers University Press, 1984), and *American Heroine: The Life and Legend of Jane Addams* (New York: Oxford University Press, 1973).

87. Shanabruch, *Chicago's Catholics*, 131–34; Eileen Skerrett, "The Irish of Chicago's Hull-House Neighborhood," in Charles Fanning, ed., *New Perspectives on the Irish Diaspora* (Carbondale: Southern Illinois University Press, 2000): 189–222; Deirdre M. Moloney, *American Catholic Lay Groups and Transatlantic Social Reform in the Progressive Era* (Chapel Hill: North Carolina University Press, 2002), 141–65.

88. *Philadelphia Standard and Times*, March 25, 1916, quoted in Richard N. Juliani, "The Interaction of Irish and Italians from Conflict and to Integration," in Femminella, *Italians and Irish in America*, 30.

89. Donald Tricarico, "Influence of the Irish on Italian Communal Adaptation in Greenwich Village," in Femminella, *Italians and Irish in America*, 55.

90. Smith, *Up to Now*, 41–46.

91. Shanabruch, *Chicago's Catholics*, 131–34; Skok, *More than Neighbors*, 4, 27–28, 20, 45, 65–66, 75, 46–47, 80–81, 96, quotes, 28, 96; Thomas Lee Philpott, *The Slum and the Ghetto: Neighborhood Deterioration and Middle-Class Reform, Chicago, 1880–1930* (New York: Oxford University Press, 1978), 82. On Boston, see Kane, *Separatism and Subculture*, and O'Toole, *Militant and Triumphant*, 153.

92. Although Protestant missions proselytized among New York's Italians and other immigrant groups, the Irish were likely also recalling Protestant efforts in their own communities in the wake of the Great Famine immigration. See Carroll Smith-Rosenberg, *Religion and the Rise of the American City: The New York City Mission Movement, 1812–1870* (Ithaca, N.Y.: Cornell University Press, 1971).

93. Brown, "'Adoption of the Tactics of the Enemy,'" 112–19. On Catholic social settlements in Chicago, see Skok, *More than Neighbors*. On the movement nationally, see Deirdre M. Maloney, *American Catholic Lay Groups*, 117–66.

94. Kane, *Separatism and Subculture*, 27; Dolan, *American Catholicism*, 329.

95. Brown, *Churches, Communities, and Children*, quote at 119. See also Caroline Ware, *Greenwich Village*, 311–18.

96. Gerald R. Gems, "Sport, Religion, and Americanization: Bishop Sheil and the Catholic Youth Organization," *International Journal of the History of Sport* 10, no. 2 (August 1993): 233–41; Timothy B. Neary, "'An Inalienable Right to Play': African American Participation in the Catholic Youth Organization," in Elliott J. Gorn, ed., *Sports in Chicago* (Urbana: University of Illinois Press, 2008), 184–96.

97. David Doyle, "Catholicism, Politics and Irish America, Since 1890: Some Critical Considerations," in P. J. Drudy, ed., *The Irish in America: Emigration, Assimilation, and Impact* (Cambridge, U.K.: Cambridge University Press, 1985), 202–209.

98. Gibbons quoted in *Irish World and American Industrial Liberator*, October 9, 1886, 4, emphasis in the original.

99. Higham, *Strangers in the Land*, 80–87.

100. J. E. Roohan, *American Catholics and the Social Question, 1865–1900* (New York: Arno Press, 1976), 371, quoted in Hugh McLeod, "Edward McGlynn: A Rebel Against the Archbishop of New York," in Stuart Mews, ed., *Modern Religious Rebels* (London: Epworth Press, 1993), 712; Robert Emmett Curran, "Prelude to 'Americanism': The New York Academia and Clerical Radicalism in the Late Nineteenth Century," *Church History* 47 (1978): 48–65.

101. McGlynn quoted in Stephen Bell, *Rebel, Priest and Prophet: A Biography of Dr. Edward McGlynn* (New York: Devin-Adair, 1937), 134, cited in Joseph A. McCartin, "*Ultraque Unum*: Finding a Way as a Catholic and a Historian," in Nick Salavatore, ed., *Faith and the Historian: Catholic Perspectives* (Urbana: University of Illinois Press, 2007), 172.

102. McGlynn quoted in *New York Tribune*, November 24, 1886, cited in Maurine Fitzgerald, *Habits of Compassion: Catholic Nuns and the Origins of New York's Welfare System, 1830–1920* (Urbana: University of Illinois Press, 2006), 154.

103. Bell, *Rebel, Priest and Prophet*; David Montgomery, "Racism, Immigrants, and Political Reform," *Journal of American History* 87, no. 4 (March 2001): 1267; and Elizabeth Gurley Flynn, *I Speak My Own Piece: The Autobiography of "The Rebel Girl"* (New York: Masses & Mainstream, 1955), 31. See also Edward T. O'Donnell, "Soggarth Aroon: The Rise and Fall of Rev. Edward McGlynn," in Terry Golway, ed., *Catholics in New York: Society, Culture, and Politics, 1808–1946* (New York: Fordham University Press, 2008), 147–61.

104. Fitzgerald, *Habits of Compassion*, 155–56.

105. Corrigan quoted in Fitzgerald, *Habits of Compassion*, 154–55.

106. José Martí, "El Cisma de los Catalicos de New York," in *Martí y Iglesia Catolica* (Havana, n.d.), 31, translated and quoted in Montgomery, "Racism, Immigrants, and Political Reform," 1267. The *Irish World and Industrial Liberator*, the largest-circulation Irish American paper in the United States and still strongly prolabor, carefully followed the controversy.

107. Quoted in Bell, *Rebel, Priest and Prophet*, 98.

108. Flynn, *I Speak My Own Piece*, 32. See also James T. McGreevy, *Catholicism and American Freedom: A History* (New York: W.W. Norton, 2004), 133–36, 158–59.

109. George quoted in *Irish World and American Industrial Liberator*, October 16, 1886, 5. On the interethnic quality of George's campaign, see Michels, *Fire in Their Hearts*, 44.

110. *Irish World and American Industrial Liberator*, October 23, 1886, 7. A similar Chicago movement was more narrowly based on the local Land League, but it marked a brief departure from the Democratic machine in the direction of independent labor politics. See Schneirov, *Labor and Urban Politics*, 132–35.

111. Montgomery, "Racism, Immigrants, and Political Reform," 1266; Louis F. Post, *The Prophet of San Francisco: Personal Memories and Interpretations of Henry George* (New York: Vanguard Press, 1930).

112. *Encyclical Letter of Our Holy Father by Divine Providence Pope Leo XIII: On the Condition of Labour: Official Translation* (London: Westminster Press, 1891).

113. On the development of the church's social teachings and social action, see Dolan, *American Catholic Experience*, 336–45; Joseph M. McShane, "*Sufficiently Radical*": Catholicism,

Progressivism, and the Bishops' Program of 1919 (Washington, D.C.: Catholic University of America Press, 1986); and Liptak, *Immigrants and Their Church*, 73–74.

114. Jay Dolan, *American Catholic Experience*, 336–45, Sinclair quoted 345, 401–5; John A. Ryan, *Social Doctrine in Action* (New York: Harper, 1941), 8–9; and Laura Murphy, "An 'Indestructible Right': John Ryan and the Catholic Origins of the U.S. Living Wage Movement, 1906–1938," *Labor: Studies in Working-Class History of the Americas* 6 (Spring 2009): 57–86. On Irish Catholic progressivism, see McShane, *"Sufficiently Radical"*; and Liptak, *Immigrants and Their Church*, 73–74.

115. John A. Ryan, *A Living Wage* (Washington, D.C.: Catholic University of America Press, 1906); David Montgomery, *The Fall of the House of Labor: The Workplace, the State, and American Labor Activism, 1865–1925* (New York: Cambridge University Press, 1987), 307–8, quote at 308; John A. Ryan, *The Church and Labor* (New York: Macmillan, 1924). On the gendered quality of the "family wage" as a working-class demand, see Martha May, "Bread Before Roses: American Workingmen, Labor Unions, and the Family Wage," in Ruth Milkman, ed., *Women, Work, and Protest: A Century of U.S. Women's Labor History* (Boston: Routledge & Kegan Paul, 1985), 1–21.

116. Leslie Woodcock Tentler, *Catholics and Contraception: An American History* (Ithaca, N.Y.: Cornell University Press, 2004), 40–41; and John A. Ryan, *Family Limitation, the Church and Birth Control* (New York: Paulist Press, 1916).

117. John A. Ryan, "Family Limitation, Church, and Birth Control," *Ecclesiastical Review* 54 (June 1916): 687, cited in Kathleen Tobin, "Catholicism and the Contraceptive Debate, 1914–1930," in Sally Barr Ebest and Ron Ebest, eds., *Reconciling Catholicism and Feminism? Personal Reflections on Tradition and Change* (Notre Dame, Ind.: Notre Dame University Press, 2003), 206. See also Kathleen A. Tobin, *The American Religious Debate over Birth Control, 1907–1937* (Jefferson, N.C.: McFarland, 2001).

118. Margaret Sanger, *My Fight for Birth Control* (New York: Farrar & Rinehart, 1931); Margaret Sanger, *An Autobiography* (New York: Norton, 1938).

119. Sanger, *Autobiography*, 5.

120. O'Neill, *Birth Control in America*, 74–75.

121. Ibid.; Leslie Regan, *When Abortion Was a Crime* (Berkeley: University of California Press, 1997), 23, 37, 137; Tentler, *Catholics and Contraception*, 68; and Ellen Chesler, *Woman of Valor: Margaret Sanger and the Birth Control Movement in America* (New York: Simon & Schuster, 1992), 294. See also David M. Kennedy, *Birth Control in America: The Career of Margaret Sanger* (New Haven, Conn.: Yale University Press, 1970).

122. Bruce Nelson, *Divided We Stand: American Workers and the Struggle for Black Equality* (Princeton, N.J.: Princeton University Press, 2001), 66–67; Steven Fraser, *Labor Will Rule: Sidney Hillman and the Rise of American Labor* (New York: Free Press, 1991), 355, 366, 367. On Ryan's opposition to Coughlin, see Broderick, *Right Reverend New Dealer*, 223–28; Kazin, *Populist Persuasion*, 126.

123. Richard Rovere, "Labor's Catholic Block," *Nation*, January 4, 1941; Douglas P. Seaton, *Catholics and Radicals: The Association of Catholic Trade Unionists and the American Labor Movement, from Depression to Cold War* (Lewisburg, Penn.: Bucknell University Press, 1981); Ronald Schatz, "American Labor and the Catholic Church, 1914–1950," *International Labor and Working Class History* 20 (Fall 1981): 46–53.

124. Meagher, *Inventing Irish America*, 370–71.

125. Robert D. Putnam, *Bowling Alone: The Collapse and Revival of American Community* (New

York: Simon & Schuster, 2000), 24; Elizabeth McKeown, *War and Welfare: American Catholics and World War I* (New York: Garland, 1988), 22.

126. Christopher J. Kauffman, *Faith and Fraternalism: The History of the Knights of Columbus, 1882–1982* (New York: Harper & Row, 1982), 121, quote, 93; Timothy Meagher, *The Columbia Guide to Irish American History* (New York: Columbia University Press, 2005), quote at 118. See also Douglas Brinkley and Julie M. Fenster, *Parish Priest: Michael McGivney and American Catholicism* (New York: William Morrow, 2006).

127. McKeown, *War and Welfare*, 23–29; Higham, *Strangers in the Land*, 179–86. The fact that the new onslaught played a key role in the anti-Semitic trial and lynching of Leo Frank (1914–15) likely encouraged the Catholic-Jewish cooperation that characterized the campaign against the Ku Klux Klan in the 1920s. On the persistence of anti-Catholicism well into the twentieth century, see Leonard Dinnerstein and David M. Reimers, *Ethnic Americans: A History of Immigration* (1988; reprint New York: Columbia University Press, 2009).

128. Cummings quoted in Kauffman, *Faith and Fraternalism*, 88. See also Philip R. McDevitt, *Records of the American Catholic Historical Society* 27 (1916), 181–90, as cited in Richard N. Juliani, "The Interaction of Irish and Italians: From Conflict and to Integration," in Femminella, *Italians and Irish in America*, 32.

129. *Przebudzenie*, October 29, 1931, quoted in Pacyga, "To Live Amongst Others," 56. On the push to systematize Catholic school curricula and enforce instruction in English in the interests of Americanization, see also Dolan, *American Catholic Experience*, 493–98, and Edward R. Kantowicz, *Corporation Sole: Cardinal Mundelein and Chicago Catholicism* (Notre Dame, Ind.: University of Notre Dame Press, 1983), 14–15, 85.

130. *Przebudzenie*, November 6, 1927, University of Illinois Urbana-Champaign, University Library Digital Collections, Chicago Foreign Language Press Survey, Polish 6, libsysdigi .library.uiuc.edu/OCA/Books2009-03/5423968/5423968_6/5423968_6_djvu.txt (accessed November 14, 2011). My thanks to Mark Leff for this reference.

131. Kauffman, *Faith and Fraternalism*, 7–8, 33, 121, 88–89, 139, 167–68, quotes 90, 167; Kathryn J. Oberdeck, *The Evangelist and the Impresari: Religion, Entertainment, and Cultural Politics in America, 1884–1914* (Baltimore, Md.: Johns Hopkins University Press, 1999), 190; Mark Carnes, *Secret Ritual and Manhood in Victorian America* (New Haven, Conn.: Yale University Press, 1989); Sterne, *Ballots and Bibles*, 141, 171; Dolan, *American Catholic Experience*, 141, 171–72; Timothy J. Meagher, *Inventing Irish America: Generation, Class, and Ethnic Identity in a New England City, 1880–1928* (Notre Dame, Ind.: University of Notre Dame Press, 2001), 338–39, 345–49, 351–55, 363; Miller, *Emigrants and Exiles*, 534.

132. "Calls on Hibernians to Fight the Ku Klux," *New York Times*, July 19, 1923, 17; Todd Tucker, "Notre Dame vs. the Klan," ibid., May 30, 1924, 1, and attached broadside; "A Kluxer" to President of Notre Dame, KKK materials, Box 1, Folder 3, University Archives, Special Collections, Hesburgh Library, Notre Dame University. See also Matthew J. Walsh Papers, Box 12, Folder 38, ibid. The Knights of Columbus also campaigned actively against the KKK; see Meagher, *Inventing Irish America*, 353–54.

133. Meagher, *Inventing Irish America*, 345.

134. Paula M. Kane, *Separatism and Subculture: Boston Catholicism, 1900–1920* (Chapel Hill: University of North Carolina Press, 2001), 39; Dennis Clark, *Hibernia America: The Irish and Regional Cultures* (Westport, Conn.: Greenwood Press, 1986), 128; *Catholic Messenger*, May 14, 1915, quoted in Meagher, *Inventing Irish America*, 345–46.

135. Ronald Bayor, *Neighbors in Conflict: The Irish, Germans, Jews, and Italians of New York City*,

1929–1941 (Baltimore, Md.: Johns Hopkins University Press, 1978), 4; Kauffman, *Faith and Fraternalism,* 262–63 and 269–73. See also Christopher J. Kauffman, *Columbianism and the Knights of Columbus* (New York: Simon & Schuster, 1992), 10, 23.

136. Giovanni E. Schiavo, *The Italians in Chicago: A Study in Americanization* (Chicago: Italian American Publishing Co., 1928), quote at 81; Vinyard, *For Faith and Fortune,* 188.

137. Nicholas John Russo, "Three Generations of Italians in New York City: Their Religious Acculturation," in Silvano M. Tomasi and Madeline H. Engel, eds., *The Italian Experience in the United States* (New York: Center for Migration Studies, 1970), 195–209; Louis Gesualdi, "A Comparison of the Attitudes and Practices of the Irish American and Italian American Catholics," in Varicalli et al., *Models and Images of Catholicism in Italian Americana,* 47–48. See also Francis X. Feminella, "The Impact of Italian Migration and American Catholicism," *American Catholic Sociological Review* 22 (Fall 1961): 233–41; and Brown, *Churches, Communities, and Children,* 117–77. For a similar argument regarding second- and third-generation Poles, see Bukowczyk, *And My Children Did Not Know Me,* 44–47.

138. Meaghan, *Inventing Irish America,* 343; Robert Orsi, *Thank You, St. Jude: Women's Devotion to the Patron of Lost Causes* (New Haven, Conn.: Yale University Press, 1996), 7–22; McDannell, "Catholic Domesticity," 309–11.

139. On the emergence of a "pan-Catholic" culture under Irish auspices, see Meagher, *Inventing Irish America,* 338–49, 370–71. The broader Catholic identity emerged by the 1940s not only in large cities but also in more isolated industrial communities. See Laurie Mercier, "'We Are Women Irish': Gender, Class, Religious, and Ethnic Identity in Anaconda, Montana," in Elizabeth Jameson and Susan Armitage, eds., *Writing the Range: Race, Class, and Culture in the Women's West* (Norman: University of Oklahoma Press, 1997), 325–26. For the ways in which this pan-Catholic identity could become racialized as a "white" Catholic identity, see McGreevy, *Parish Boundaries.*

140. Brown, *Churches, Communities, and Children,* 117–32.

141. Ibid., 132, 177. See also Orsi, *Madonna of 115th Street,* 160–61, 165–68.

142. William J. Walsh, address at Catechetical Conference, October 29, 1936, Folder 15, Box 2, Series II, John LaFarge Papers, Georgetown University Special Collections, quoted in McGreevy, *Parish Boundaries,* 34.

143. See Herberg, *Protestant, Catholic, Jew.*

144. Ruby Jo Reeves Kennedy, "Single or Triple Melting Pot? Intermarriage Trends in New Haven, 1870–1940," *American Journal of Sociology* 49, no. 4 (January 1944), 331–39; and Richard D. Alba, "Social Assimilation among American Catholic National-Origin Groups," *American Sociological Review* 41, no. 6 (December 1976): 1030–46; Abramson, *Ethnic Diversity in Catholic America,* especially 51–68. Both Alba and Abramson caution that interethnic marriage emerged slowly in the postwar era, and within the embrace of Catholicism.

145. See, for example, Paul Blanshard, *American Freedom and Catholic Power* (Boston: Beacon Press, 1949); and Paul Blanshard, *The Irish and Catholic Power: An American Interpretation* (Boston: Beacon Press, 1953).

146. Meagher, *Columbia Guide to Irish American History,* 142.

147. Richard D. Alba and Mitchell Chamlin, "A Preliminary Examination of Ethnic Identification among Whites," *American Sociological Review* 48, no. 2 (April 1983): 240–47.

148. Charles R. Morris, *American Catholics: The Saints and Sinners Who Built America's Most Powerful Church* (New York: Times Books, 1997), argues that the roots of the modern U.S. Catholic Church lay in nineteenth-century Ireland.

CHAPTER 3: THE WORKPLACE

1. John Keiser, *John Fitzpatrick and Progressive Labor*, Ph.D. diss., Northwestern University, 1965; David Brody, "John Fitzpatrick," in John A. Garraty, ed., *Dictionary of American Biography*, supp. 4 (New York: Scribner, 1974), 279–80; L. A. O'Donnell, *Irish Voice and Organized Labor in America: A Biographical Study* (Westport, Conn.: Greenwood Press, 1992), 143–61.

2. Fitzpatrick quoted in Mary McDowell, "Easter Day After the Decision," *Survey* 40 (April 13, 1918), 38. See also James R. Barrett, *Work and Community in the Jungle: Chicago's Packinghouse Workers, 1894–1922* (Urbana: University of Illinois Press, 1987), 191–202.

3. Barrett, *Work and Community in the Jungle*, 205–6; and Rick Halpern, *Down on the Killing Floor: Black and White Workers in Chicago's Packinghouses, 1904–1954* (Urbana: University of Illinois Press, 1997).

4. Bruce Nelson, *Divided We Stand: American Workers and the Struggle for Black Equality* (Princeton, N.J.: Princeton University Press, 2001), xxix, xxviii. See also David R. Roediger, *Working Toward Whiteness: How America's Immigrants Became White: The Strange Journey from Ellis Island to the Suburbs* (New York: Basic Books, 2006), 72–92; and James R. Barrett, "Americanization from the Bottom Up: Immigration and the Remaking of the Working Class in the United States, 1880–1930," *Journal of American History* 79 (December 1992): 996–1020.

5. Barrett, "Americanization from the Bottom Up."

6. David Montgomery, "The Irish and the American Labor Movement," in David Noel Doyle and Owen Dudley Edwards, eds., *America and Ireland, 1776–1976: The American Identity and the Irish Connection* (Westport, Conn.: Greenwood Press, 1980), 211. On the close relationship between Irish nationalism, land reform, and Irish influence in the Knights of Labor, see, for example, Kevin Kenny, *The American Irish: A History* (Harlow, U.K.: Pearson Education, 2000), 168, 175–79; Eric Foner, "Class, Ethnicity and Radicalism in the Gilded Age: The Land League and Irish America," *Marxist Perspectives* 1 (Summer 1978): 6–55; David Brundage, "Irish Land League and American Workers: Class and Ethnicity in Denver, Colorado," in Dirk Hoerder, ed., *"Struggle a Hard Battle": Essays on Working-Class Immigrants* (DeKalb: Northern Illinois University Press, 1986), 46–67; and Richard Schneirov, *Labor and Urban Politics: Class Conflict and Origins of Modern Liberalism in Chicago, 1864–1897* (Urbana: University of Illinois Press), 119–38.

7. Jacob Riis, *How the Other Half Lives* (New York: C. Scribner's Sons, 1890), 75; Kerby A. Miller, *Emigrants and Exiles: Ireland and the Irish Exodus to North America* (New York: Oxford University Press, 1985), 495; Reginald Byron, *Irish America* (Oxford: Clarendon Press, 1999), 71–72; and David N. Doyle, *Irish Americans, Native Rights, and National Empires: The Structure, Divisions and Attitudes of the Catholic Minority in the Decade of Expansion, 1890–1901* (New York: Arno Press, 1976), 46–47. On the relationship between region and social mobility, see Kenny, *American Irish*, 150; and James P. Walsh, "The Irish in the New America: 'Way Out West,'" in Doyle and Edwards, *America and Ireland*, 165–76. See also the introduction and several of the essays in Timothy J. Meagher, ed., *From Paddy to Studs: Irish-American Communities in the Turn of the Century Era, 1880 to 1920* (Westport, Conn.; Greenwood Press, 1986).

8. Miller, *Emigrants and Exiles*, 496; Doyle, *Irish Americans, Native Rights*, 38–76; Bayor and Meagher, "Conclusion," in Ronald H. Bayor and Timothy J. Meagher, eds., *The New York*

Irish (Baltimore, Md.: Johns Hopkins University Press, 1996), n3, 698–99; and Charles Shanabruch, *Chicago's Catholics: The Evolution of an American Identity* (Notre Dame, Ind.: Notre Dame University Press, 1981), 80–81. On the "lace curtain" terminology, see Timothy Meagher, *The Columbia Guide to Irish American History* (New York: Columbia University Press, 2005), 103.

9. Meagher, *Columbia Guide to Irish American History*, 97–98; Frederick M. Binder and David M. Reimers, *All the Nations Under Heaven: An Ethnic and Racial History of New York City* (New York: Columbia University Press, 1995), 154; William H. Williams, *"'Twas Only an Irishman's Dream": The Image of Ireland and the Irish in American Popular Song Lyrics, 1800–1920* (Urbana: University of Illinois Press, 1996), 178; U.S. Bureau of the Census, *Fifteenth Census of the United States: 1930*, vol. 3, part 2 (Washington, D.C.: GPO, 1933), 298–99, 302; and Miller, *Emigrants and Exiles*, 492–555.

10. On differential upward mobility and the tendency for many Irish to remain in the laboring ranks well into the twentieth century, see, for example, Stephan Thernstrom, *Poverty and Progress: Social Mobility in a Nineteenth-Century City* (Cambridge, Mass.: Harvard University Press, 1964); Stephan Thernstrom, *The Other Bostonians: Poverty and Progress in the American Metropolis, 1880–1970* (Cambridge, Mass.: Harvard University Press, 1973); Joel Perlmann, *Ethnic Differences: Schooling and Social Structure Among the Irish, Italians, Jews, and Blacks in an American City, 1880–1935* (New York: Cambridge University Press, 1988); Suzanne Model, "The Ethnic Niche and the Structure of Opportunity: Immigrants and Minorities in New York City," in Michael B. Katz, ed., *The "Underclass" Debate: Views from History* (Princeton, N.J.: Princeton University Press, 1993), 161–93; and Bruce Laurie, Theodore Hershberg, and George Alter, "Immigrants and Industry: The Philadelphia Story, 1850–1880," *Journal of Social History* 9, no. 2 (1975): 219–48.

11. Riis, *How the Other Half Lives*, 75, 74; Mary C. Kelly, *The Shamrock and the Lily: The New York Irish and the Creation of a Transatlantic Identity, 1845–1921* (New York: Peter Lang, 2005), 51; Ron Ebest, *Private Histories: The Writing of Irish Americans, 1900–1935* (Notre Dame, Ind.: University of Notre Dame Press, 2005), 24–25; Niles Carpenter, *Immigrants and Their Children* (1920; reprint New York: Arno Press, 1969), 203; Miller, *Emigrants and Exiles*, 506; Montgomery, "Irish and the American Labor Movement," 205–18. See also Thomas Kessner, *The Golden Door: Italian and Jewish Immigrant Mobility in New York City, 1880–1915* (New York: Oxford University Press, 1977), 5–6.

12. Doyle, *Irish Americans, Native Rights*, emphasizes the size and influence of the middle class at the turn of the century. See also William V. Shannon, *The American Irish* (New York: Macmillan, 1963); and Andrew M. Greeley, *The Irish Americans: The Rise to Money and Power* (New York: Harper & Row, 1981).

13. Thomas N. Brown, *Irish-American Nationalism, 1870–1890* (Philadelphia: Lippincott, 1966), 23, passim, stresses the American roots of the nationalism and frames much of his narrative around the personalities of Irish American elites. For the newer interpretation, see Eric Foner, "Class, Ethnicity, and Radicalism in the Gilded Age: The Land League and Irish America," in Foner, *Politics and Ideology in the Age of the Civil War* (New York: Oxford University Press, 1980), 150–200; Victor A. Walsh, "'Fanatic Heart': Cause of Irish American Nationalism in Pittsburgh During the Gilded Age," *Journal of Social History* 15 (December 1981): 187–204; David Brundage, "'In Times of Peace, Prepare for War': Key Themes in the Social Thought of New York's Irish Nationalists, 1890–1916," in Bayor and Meagher, *New York Irish*, 321–34; and Bruce Nelson, "Irish Americans, Irish Nationalism, and the Social Question, 1916–1923," *boundary 2* 31, no. 1 (2004): 147–78.

14. Miller, *Emigrants and Exiles*, 495–99, quotes at 493, 498, 499.

15. Quoted in Timothy Meagher, "Irish, American, Catholic: Irish-American Identity in Worcester, Massachusetts, 1880 to 1920," in Meagher, *From Paddy to Studs*, 79.

16. Kevin Kenny, *Making Sense of the Molly Maguires* (New York: Oxford University Press, 1998), 13–22; Kevin Kenny, "Labor and Labor Organizations," in J. J. Lee and Marion Casey, eds., *Making the Irish American* (New York: New York University Press, 2005), 357–60; Schneirov, *Labor and Urban Politics*, 109; and Michael A. Gordon, "The Labor Boycott in New York City, 1880–1886," *Labor History* 16 (Spring 1975): 184–229.

17. Leon Fink, *Workingmen's Democracy: The Knights of Labor and American Politics* (Urbana: University of Illinois Press, 1983).

18. Schneirov, *Labor and Urban Politics*, 123–25; Redpath and Parnell are quoted in Gordon, "Labor Boycott in New York City," 192.

19. Charles Barnes, *The Longshoremen* (New York: Survey Associates, 1915), 103–5.

20. Gordon, "Labor Boycott in New York City"; Kenny, *American Irish*, 155–56.

21. Nelson, *Divided We Stand*, xxxv. David Doyle rightly emphasizes the neglected but burgeoning Irish American lower middle class of the late nineteenth century; in his analysis of their occupations, they remained in close contact with working-class communities. He concludes that about two-thirds of the Irish American community remained in the working class, about 15 percent remaining in poverty. See Doyle, *Irish Americans, Native Rights, and National Empires*, 38–90, 64.

22. Kerby A. Miller, *Emigrants and Exiles: Ireland and the Irish Exodus to North America* (New York: Oxford University Press, 1985), 499–500, 503; Sarah Deutsch, *Women and the City: Gender, Space, and Power in Boston, 1870–1940* (New York: Oxford, University Press, 2000), 62; and Thomas Kessner, *The Golden Door: Italian and Jewish Mobility in New York, 1880–1915* (New York: Oxford University Press, 1977), 48–56.

23. Hasia R. Diner, *Erin's Daughters in America: Irish Immigrant Women in the Nineteenth Century* (Baltimore, Md.: Johns Hopkins University Press, 1983), 60–61; Barnes, *Longshoremen*, 129–53.

24. Such events occurred twice on New York building sites in the span of a month. See "Buried in Tunnel Cut," *New York Times*, October 19, 1907, 18; and "Killed in Central Cave-In," ibid., November 13, 1907, 9.

25. Dennis Clark, "The Irish Ethic and Spirit of Patronage," in Scott Cummings, ed., *Self-Help in Urban America: Patterns of Minority Business Enterprise* (Port Washington, N.Y.: Kennikat Press, 1980); Miller, *Emigrants and Exiles*, quote at 500–501; and Montgomery, "Irish and the American Labor Movement," 205–17, especially 211.

26. Steven P. Erie, *Rainbow's End: Irish-Americans and the Dilemmas of Urban Machine Politics, 1840–1945* (Berkeley: University of California Press, 1988), 59–61, 243.

27. Roediger, *Working Toward Whiteness*, 74–76; John T. Ridge, "Irish County Societies in New York, 1880–1914," in Bayor and Meagher, *New York Irish*, 280, 297; Miller, *Emigrants and Exiles*, 500.

28. Calvin Winslow, "Introduction," in Winslow, *Waterfront Workers: New Perspectives on Race and Class* (Urbana: University of Illinois Press, 1998), 5–6; Barnes, *Longshoremen*, 55–75; Nelson, *Divided We Stand*, xx–xxviii; Winslow, "Introduction," 7. On violent repercussions from the introduction of strikebreakers and the especially violent reactions to African American strikebreakers, see Eric Arnesen, "Biracial Waterfront Unionism in the Age of Segregation," in Winslow, *Waterfront Workers*, 22–23; Calvin Winslow, "'Men of the Lumber Camps Come to Town': New York Longshoremen in the Strike of 1907," in Winslow,

Waterfront Workers, 68–69, 83–84, 86–87, 90n; Calvin Winslow, "On the Waterfront: Black, Italian, and Irish Longshoremen in the New York Harbor Strike of 1919," in John Rule and Robert Malcolmson, eds., *Protest and Survival: Essays for E. P. Thompson* (London: Merlin Press, 1993), 389–90.

29. Nelson, *Divided We Stand*, 16, 19, first quote at xli; Eric Arnesen, *Waterfront Workers of New Orleans: Race, Class, and Politics, 1863–1923* (Urbana: University of Illinois Press, 1994), 19–20; Kenny, "Labor and Labor Organizations," 355; James T. Fisher, *On the Irish Waterfront: The Crusader, the Movie, and the Soul of the Port of New York* (Ithaca, N.Y.: Cornell University Press, 2009), 2–3, second quote at 6.

30. Earl F. Niehaus, *The Irish in New Orleans, 1800–1860* (Baton Rouge: Louisiana State University, 1965), 49–53, quote at 51; David Gleeson, *The Irish in the South, 1815–1877* (Chapel Hill: University of North Carolina Press, 2001), 55–73; Jay Rubin, "Black Nativism: The European Immigrant in Negro Thought, 1830–1860," *Phylon* 39, no. 3 (1978): 193–202; Barnes, *Longshoremen*, 5, 61.

31. David Montgomery, *The Fall of the House of Labor: The Workplace, the State, and American Labor Activism, 1865–1925* (New York: Cambridge University Press, 1987), 88–90; Barnes, *Longshoremen*, 28–54; Arnesen, *Waterfront Workers of New Orleans*, 38–41; and Peter Cole, *Wobblies on the Waterfront: Interracial Unionism in Progressive-Era Philadelphia* (Urbana: University of Illinois Press, 2007), 57. See also the testimony of Dennis Delaney and Timothy Carroll before the U.S. Commission on Industrial Relations, *Final Report and Testimony Submitted to Congress by the Commission on Industrial Relations*, 64th Cong., 1st sess., document 415 (Washington, D.C.: GPO, 1916), 3:2102–8 (Carroll), 2164–70 (Delaney).

32. Arnesen, *Waterfront Workers of New Orleans*; Eric Arnesen, "Biracial Waterfront Unionism in the Age of Segregation," in Winslow, *Waterfront Workers*, 29–61; Nelson, *Divided We Stand*, 48–50.

33. Nelson, *Divided We Stand*, 59, 64–65; Barnes, *Longshoremen*, 121–28.

34. Nelson, *Divided We Stand*, xli; Howard Kimeldorf, *Battling for American Labor: Wobblies, Craft Workers, and the Making of the Union Movement* (Berkeley: University of California Press, 1999), 24–26; Cole, *Wobblies on the Waterfront*, 24–26; Barnes, *Longshoremen*, 5–7. See also Lorenzo J. Greene and Carter G. Woodson, *The Negro Wage Earner* (New York: Russell & Russell, 1930), 113, 133.

35. Winslow, "On the Waterfront," 372.

36. E. Franklin Frazier, "The Negro Longshoremen" (1921), unpublished ms., Russell Sage Foundation, 27, quoted in Winslow, "On the Waterfront," 372, my emphasis. The distinction between white men—overwhelmingly Irish American here—and Italians suggests the stark distinctions drawn between ethnic groups whom we would today consider white.

37. *Brooklyn Eagle*, September 25, 1893, 4. See also Kessner, *Golden Door*, 57–58.

38. "Actual Work on the Big Tunnel Begun," *New York Times*, March 27, 1900, 14.

39. "Irishmen Fight Italians," *New York Times*, August 12, 1900, 12; and "Irish and Italian Laborers Engage in a Spirited Fight—Many Injured," *Chicago Tribune*, September 25, 1893, 3. For comparable confrontations in other cities, see Dennis P. Ryan, *Beyond the Ballot Box: A Social History of the Boston Irish, 1845–1917* (Rutherford, N.J.: Fairleigh Dickinson University Press, 1983), 142–43; Edwin Fenton, *Immigrants and Unions: A Case Study, Italians and American Labor, 1870–1920* (New York: Arno Press, 1975), 140–45; and "Strikers Attack the Workmen," *New York Times*, December 19, 1895, 9.

40. "Pitched Battle in Pit," *New York Times*, November 24, 1903, 1; and "Suspects a Labor

Feud," ibid., May 18, 1906, 2. The daily press for New York was full of reports of such violence.

41. Barnes, *Longshoremen*, 8–9; "Strikes Caused by Race Hatred," *Chicago Tribune*, September 19, 1903, 5; and *Brooklyn Eagle*, October 5, 1894, 6. For a large confrontation that was finally quelled by separating the Brooklyn construction site into two territories defined by nationality, see *Brooklyn Eagle*, June 18, 1894, 12.

42. Margaret F. Byington, *Homestead: The Households of a Mill Town* (1910; reprint, Pittsburgh: University Center for International Studies, 1974), 17–21; John Bodnar, *Immigration and Industrialization: Ethnicity in an American Mill Town, 1870–1940* (Pittsburgh: University of Pittsburgh Press, 1977), 6–7, 9, 57, 71–72.

43. Adam Walaszek, "'For in America Poles Are Like Cattle': Polish Peasant Immigrants and Work in America," in Marianne Debouzy, ed., *A l'ombre de la statue de la liberté: Immigrants et ouvriers dans la République américaine, 1880–1920* (Saint-Denis: Presses Universitaires de Vincennes, 1988), 95–105; Stephen Meyer, *The Five Dollar Day: Social Control in the Ford Motor Company, 1908–1921* (Albany: State University of New York Press, 1981), 56; "Negro Laborers on the Subway," *New York Times*, September 1, 1901, SM14; "Almost a Riot in Brooklyn," *New York Times*, November 5, 1891, 10; and "Success Story of an Italian Boy," *Chicago Tribune*, December 1, 1907, 1. See also Roediger, *Working Toward Whiteness*, 74–75; and Montgomery, *Fall of the House of Labor*, 92–93.

44. Diner, *Erin's Daughters*, 82–83; Deutsch, *Women and the City*, 30.

45. Maria Luddy, *Women and Philanthropy in Nineteenth-Century Ireland* (New York: Cambridge University Press, 1995), 11, 12; Mona Hearn, "Life for Domestic Servants in Dublin, 1880–1920," in Maria Luddy and Cliona Murphy, eds., *Women Surviving: Studies in Irish Women's History in the Nineteenth and Twentieth Centuries* (Dublin: Poolbeg Press, 1989), 148–79; and Mona Hearn, *Below Stairs: Domestic Service Remembered in Dublin and Beyond, 1880–1922* (Dublin: Lilliput Press, 1993).

46. John R. McGivigan and Thomas J. Robertson, "The Irish American Worker in Transition, 1877–1914," in Bayor and Meagher, *New York Irish*, 311; Kerby A. Miller, David N. Doyle, and Patricia Kelleher, "'For Love and Liberty': Irish Women, Migration and Domesticity in Ireland and America, 1815–1920," in Patrick O'Sullivan, ed., *Irish Women and Irish Migration*, vol. 4, *The Irish World Wide: History, Heritage, Identity* (Leicester, U.K.: Leicester University Press, 1995), 54; and Daniel E. Sutherland, *Americans and Their Servants: Domestic Service in the United States from 1800 to 1920* (Baton Rouge: Louisiana University Press, 1981), 50–53.

47. Christine Stansell, *City of Women: Sex and Class in New York, 1789–1860* (New York: Knopf, 1986), 156–61; David M. Katzman, *Seven Days a Week: Women and Domestic Service in Industrializing America* (New York: Oxford University Press, 1978), 49; Janet Nolan, *Ourselves Alone: Women's Emigration from Ireland, 1885–1920* (Lexington: University Press of Kentucky, 1989), 67–69; Diner, *Erin's Daughters*; and Bronwen Walter, *Outsiders, Inside: Whiteness, Place and Irish Women* (London: Routledge, 2001), 2.

48. Lillian Cavanaugh, interview by Paul E. Sigrist, Jr., n.d., Oral History Collection, Ellis Island Immigration Museum.

49. "The Servant Question—Is It to Be Eternal?" *New York Times*, October 20, 1907, SM9; "The Market for Domestics," ibid., September 12, 1909, 8; and "Why We Lack Servants," ibid., February 2, 1911, 8.

50. *Massachusetts Labor Bulletin* no. 8 (October 1898), 13, 22–26, cited in Ryan, *Beyond the Bal-*

lot Box, 43; Margaret Lynch-Brennan, "Ubiquitous Bridget: Irish Immigrant Women in Domestic Service in America, 1840–1930," in Lee and Casey, *Making the Irish American,* 337–39.

51. Henry Dana Ward, Diary, 1850–1857, entry for June 10, 1855, Manuscripts and Archives Division, New York Public Library, quoted in Sutherland, *Americans and Their Servants,* 40.

52. Quoted in Lynch-Brennan, "Ubiquitous Bridget," 335–36.

53. Lynch-Brennan, "Ubiquitous Bridget," 333n2, 347; Bertha Devlin, interview by Dana Gumb, September 19, 1985, Oral History Collection, Ellis Island Immigration Museum, 32; Ruth-Ann M. Harris, " 'Come All You Courageously': Irish Women in America Write Home," in Kevin Kenny, ed., *New Directions in Irish American History* (Madison: University of Wisconsin Press, 2003), 222–23.

54. Miller, Doyle, and Kelleher, " 'For Love and Liberty' "; and O'Sullivan, *Irish Women and Irish Migration,* 55. See also Faye E. Dudden, *Serving Women: Household Service in Nineteenth-Century America* (Middletown, Conn.: Wesleyan University Press, 1983), 228; and Diner, *Erin's Daughters,* quote at 94.

55. Janet Nolan, *Servants of the Poor: Teachers and Mobility in Ireland and America* (Notre Dame, Ind.: Notre Dame University Press, 2004), 83, 84.

56. Miller, Doyle, and Kelleher, " 'For Love and Liberty,' " 55. Diane M. Hotten-Somers, "Relinquishing and Reclaiming Independence: Irish Domestic Servants, American Middle-Class Mistresses, and Assimilation, 1850–1920," *Éire-Ireland* 36, no. 1–2 (Spring–Summer 2001): 185–201, argues, without benefit of much evidence, that Irish maids were thoroughly and successfully socialized by their middle-class mistresses.

57. Peter Quinn, *Looking for Jimmy: A Search for Irish America* (Woodstock, N.Y.: Overlook Press, 2007), 77.

58. Ronald Takaki, *A Different Mirror: A History of Multicultural America* (Boston: Little, Brown, 1993), 157.

59. Deutsch, *Women and the City,* 56–60; Dudden, *Serving Women,* 215–16.

60. Margaret Lynch-Brennan, *Ubiquitous Bridget: Irish Immigrant Women in Domestic Service in America, 1840–1930,* Ph.D. diss., State University of New York at Albany, 2002, 254; Lynch-Brennan, "Ubiquitous Bridget," 337.

61. On the low and declining level of prostitution in nineteenth-century Ireland, see Luddy, *Women and Philanthropy,* 97–148, especially 101; and Catriona Clear, *Social Change and Everyday Life in Ireland, 1850–1922* (Manchester, U.K.: Manchester University Press, 2008), 135–37.

62. Timothy J. Gilfoyle, *City of Eros: New York City, Prostitution, and the Commercialization of Sex, 1790–1920* (New York: W.W. Norton, 1992), 61–67; and Ruth Rosen, *The Lost Sisterhood: Prostitution in America, 1900–1918* (Baltimore, Md.: Johns Hopkins University, 1982), 139–42.

63. Diner, *Erin's Daughters,* 116–18; E. A. Ross, "The Celtic Tide," *Century* 87, no. 6 (1914): 952. In early-twentieth-century Chicago, Irish Americans ranked last among all ethnic groups for "crimes against chastity," while almost none of those women serving sentences in Massachusetts penal institutions in 1908–9 were there for sex-related crimes. See Diner, *Erin's Daughters,* 117; and O'Faolain, *Story of Chicago May,* 44.

64. Mary Condon, interview, November 2, 1980, no. 28, p. 9, New Yorkers at Work Oral History Project, Tamiment Institute Library, New York University. See also Helen Campbell, *Prisoners of Poverty: Women Wage-Earners, Their Trades, and Their Lives* (Boston: Little, Brown, 1900).

65. Quoted in Katzman, *Seven Days a Week*, 39.

66. Hotten-Somers, "Relinquishing and Reclaiming Independence," 198.

67. Quoted in Miller, Doyle, and Kelleher, "'For Love and Liberty,'" 56. See also Mary C. Kelly, *The Shamrock and the Lily: The New York Irish and the Creation of a Transatlantic Identity, 1845–1921* (New York: Peter Lang, 2005), 56.

68. *Irish World and Industrial Liberator,* July 17, 1886, 7; Levine, "Labor's True Woman"; Jonathan Garlock, *Knights of Labor Assemblies, 1879–1889* (Ann Arbor, Mich.: Inter-university Consortium for Political and Social Research, 1973).

69. Caroline White quoted in Walter, *Outsiders, Inside,* 64; her husband is quoted in Dudden, *Serving Women*, 59.

70. Robert L. Reid, ed., *Battleground: The Autobiography of Margaret A. Haley* (Urbana: University of Illinois Press, 1982), 9.

71. Nolan, *Servants of the Poor,* 20–22, 24.

72. Deirdre Mageean, "Making Sense and Providing Structure: Irish American Women in the Parish Neighborhood," in Christiane Harzig et al., eds., *Peasant Maids, City Women: From the European Countryside to Urban America* (Ithaca, N.Y.: Cornell University Press, 1997), 239.

73. Quoted in Nolan, *Ourselves Alone,* 26. See also Harris, "'Come All You Courageously,'" 223; Catherine Hannon English and Elizabeth Delaney Phillips, interviews, February 10, 1986, Oral History Collection, Ellis Island Immigration Museum. I often heard the phrase from my own mother.

74. Quoted in Campbell, *Prisoners of Poverty,* 226. See also Kelly, *Shamrock and Lily,* 56–57.

75. Mageean, "Making Sense and Providing Structure," 241; Pauline Jackson, "Women in Nineteenth Century Migration," *International Migration Review* 18, no. 4 (Winter 1984), 1008; Nolan, *Servants of the Poor,* 4.

76. Miller, Doyle, and Kelleher, "'For Love and Liberty,'" 56. See also Hotten-Somers, "Relinquishing and Reclaiming Independence," 199.

77. Quoted in Charles Fanning et al., *Nineteenth-Century Chicago Irish* (Chicago: Loyola University Press, 1980), 30.

78. Deutsch, *Women and the City,* 184–85; Diner, *Erin's Daughters,* 140–41.

79. Diner, *Erin's Daughters,* 97; Walter, *Outsiders, Inside,* 56; McKivigan and Roberts, "The Irish American Worker in Transition," in Bayor and Meagher, *New York Irish,* 313; Diner, *Erin's Daughters,* 98–99; Marjorie Murphy, *Blackboard Unions: The AFT and the NEA, 1900–1980* (Ithaca, N.Y.: Cornell University Press, 1990), 40; John F. Lyons, *Teachers and Reform: Chicago Public Education, 1920–1970* (Urbana: University of Illinois Press, 2008); 68; Ellen Skerrett, "The Catholic Dimension," in Lawrence J. McCaffrey, Ellen Skerrett, Michael F. Funchion, and Charles Fanning, eds., *The Irish in Chicago* (Urbana: University of Illinois Press, 1987), 46. On the proliferation of Irish Catholic teachers in a smaller industrial town, see Meagher, *Inventing Irish America,* 112–13.

80. James W. Sanders, "Catholics and the School Question in Boston: The Cardinal O'Connor Years," in Robert E. Sullivan and James M. O'Toole, eds., *Catholic Boston: Studies in Religion and Community, 1870–1970* (Boston: Roman Catholic Archbishop of Boston, 1995), 150–51, quote at 169; and Nolan, *Servants of the Poor,* 50, 59, 43–46, 75–77, 68, 92, 93, quote at 4. See also Diner, *Erin's Daughters,* 98–99; and Thomas H. O'Connor, *The Boston Irish: A Political History (Boston*: Northeastern University Press, 1995), 171–75.

81. Suellen Hoy, *Chasing Dirt: The American Pursuit of Cleanliness* (New York: Oxford University Press, 1995), 125; William Foote Whyte, *Street Corner Society: The Social Structure of an*

Italian Slum (Chicago: University of Chicago Press, 1943), 276, both quoted in Roediger, *Working Toward Whiteness*, 194, 195. See also Bruce M. Stave and John F. Sutherland, with Aldo Salerno, *From the Old Country: An Oral History of European Migration to America* (New York: Twayne, 1994), 181.

82. Myra Kelly, *Little Citizens: The Humors of School Life* (New York: McClure, Phillips, & Co., 1904), quote at 143; Obiturary, *New York Times*, April 1, 1920. See also Ebest, *Private Histories*, 214–21; Myra Kelly, *Little Aliens* (New York: Scribner's, 1910); and Myra Kelly, *Wards of Liberty* (New York: McClure Co., 1907).

83. Diner, *Erin's Daughters*, 97; Alvin F. Harlow, *Old Bowery Days* (New York: D. Appleton & Co., 1931), 487–88; Irving Howe, *World of Our Fathers* (New York: Simon & Schuster, 1976), 370. On allegations regarding teachers and political patronage, see also John Paul Bocock, "The Irish Conquest," *Forum* (1894): 186–95; and Herbert N. Casson, "The Irish in America," *Munsey's* (1906): 94.

84. Quoted in E. A. Ross, *The Old World in the New* (New York: Century, 1913), 41. See also Nolan, *Servants of the Poor*, 52–53.

85. Fitzgerald, *Habits of Compassion*, 10; Nolan, *Servants of the Poor*, 1.

86. Diner, *Erin's Daughters*, 95; E. P. Hutchinson, *Immigrants and Their Children, 1850–1950* (New York: Russell and Russell, 1956), 88; see also Susan M. Reverby, *Ordered to Care: The Dilemma of American Nursing, 1850–1945* (New York: Cambridge University Press, 1987).

87. Deutsch, *Women and the City*, 192; Rhetta Child Dore and William Hard, "The Women's Invasion," *Everybody's* 20 (1909): 82; Diner, *Erin's Daughters*, 95.

88. Deutsch, *Women and the City*, 192, 184–85.

89. Diner, *Erin's Daughters*, 68.

90. Barrett, *Work and Community in the Jungle*, 119–31; Howard B. Myers, *The Policing of Labor Disputes in Chicago*, Ph.D. diss., University of Chicago, 1929, chap. 3; Richard Schneirov, "Chicago's Great Upheaval of 1877," *Chicago History* 9 (Spring 1977): 3–17; Schneirov, *Labor and Urban Politics*, 100–10.

91. E. J. Hobsbawm, "The Machine Breakers," *Past and Present* 1 (1952): 57–70. See also E. P. Thompson, "The Moral Economy of the English Crowd in the Eighteenth Century," *Past and Present* 50 (1971): 76–136. For the application of this concept to immigrant working-class communities in the United States, see Herbert Gutman, *Work, Culture, and Society in Industrializing America: Essays in Working-Class and Social History* (New York: Vintage Books, 1976), 3–78.

92. David Montgomery, "Strikes in Nineteenth Century America," *Social Science History* 4 (February 1980): 81–104; Schneirov, *Labor and Urban Politics*, 102; Barrett, *Work and Community in the Jungle*. 119–31.

93. John R. Commons, "The Teamsters of Chicago," in John R. Commons, ed., *Trade Unionism and Labor Problems* (Boston: Ginn & Co. 1905); David Witwer, *Corruption and Reform in the Teamsters Union* (Urbana: University of Illinois Press, 2003), 16–19, 26–33 and Ernest Poole, "How a Labor Machine Held Up Chicago and How the Teamsters' Union Smashed the Machine," *World's Work* (July 1904): 896–905; Steven Sapolsky, "Between Class Conscious Belligerents: The Teamsters and the Class Struggle in Chicago, 1901–1905," unpublished seminar paper, University of Pittsburgh, 1974, in author's possession; Georg Leidenberger, " 'The Public Is the Labor Union': Working-Class Progressivism in Turn-of-the-Century Chicago," *Labor History* 36 (Spring 1995): 187–210.

94. On black strikebreakers, see Sterling Spero and Abram Harris, *The Black Worker: A Study*

of the Negro and the Labor Movement (New York: Columbia University Press, 1931), 132. On racial violence and strike's legacy of racism in the Chicago labor movement, see William Tuttle, *Race Riot: Chicago in the Red Summer of 1919* (New York: Atheneum, 1970), 121–22; and Matthew Filter, "Blacks, Blockades, and Brutality: Race, Class, and Labor in Chicago during the 1905 Teamsters' Strike," senior honors thesis, University of Illinois at Urbana-Champaign, 2007. For a treatment by an Irish teamster who stresses labor solidarity across racial lines, see "The Chicago Strike: A Teamster," in David M. Katzman and William M. Tuttle, eds., *Plain Folk: The Life Stories of Undistinguished Americans* (Urbana: University of Illinois Press, 1982), 119–23.

95. Graham Taylor, *Chicago Commons Through Forty Years* (Chicago: Chicago Commons Association, 1936), 118. See also Jane Addams, *Twenty Years at Hull House, with Autobiographical Notes* (New York: Macmillan, 1910), 229.

96. On efforts to organize Chicago's black and immigrant workers, successive stockyard strikes, and their effects on race relations, see Barrett, *Work and Community in the Jungle*, 119–31, 165–81, 191–239; Tuttle, *Race Riot*; and Halpern, *Down on the Killing Floor*.

97. "Chicago Strike," 116–17; Tuttle, *Race Riot*, 120–23; and Murphy, *Blackboard Unions*, 7–11. A generation later, Slavic and Italian students employed the labor tactic to protest the racial integration of their high schools. See Andrew J. Diamond, *Mean Streets: Chicago Youths and the Everyday Struggle for Empowerment in the Multiracial City, 1908–1969* (Berkeley: University of California Press, 2009), 129, 135; Roediger, *Working Toward Whiteness*, 239; and Thomas A. Guglielmo, *White on Arrival: Italians, Race, Color, and Power in Chicago, 1890–1945* (New York: Oxford University Press, 2003), 191.

98. "Strikers Prevent Refuse Collection," *New York Times*, November 10, 1911, 1; and William Z. Foster, *Pages from a Worker's Life* (New York: International Publishers, 1939), 18. See also Schneirov, *Labor and Urban Politics*, 102. New York's street cleaning department was a major site of conflict between Irish and Italians in the 1890s, so the interethnic strike represented a breakthrough of sorts. See "Riot at Street Cleaning Department," *Chicago Inter Ocean*, February 4, 1892.

99. Winslow, "'Men of the Lumber Camps Come to Town,'" 80–81, 86–87, quote at 81.

100. Nelson, *Divided We Stand*, 63. On the long heritage of conflict between African and Irish Americans on the New York waterfront, see Joe Doyle, "Striking for Ireland on the New York Docks," in Bayor and Meagher, *New York Irish*, 366–67.

101. Quoted in Spero and Harris, *Black Worker*, 199–200.

102. Deutsch, *Women and the City*, 206, 211–12, 214, 217–18; and Stephen Norwood, *Labor's Flaming Youth: Telephone Operators and Labor Militancy, 1878–1923* (Urbana: University of Illinois Press, 1990), 169–98.

103. Norwood, *Labor's Flaming Youth*, 269–94. On the fraternization of Irish American policemen with strikers in early-twentieth-century Chicago, see Howard B. Meyer, *The Policing of Labor Disputes in Chicago: A Study*, Ph.D. diss., University of Chicago, 1929. On the Boston police strike and its aftermath, see Francis Russell, *A City in Terror: 1919, the Boston Police Strike* (New York: Viking Press, 1975).

104. On the relatively low Irish electoral support for the Socialist Party, see Gary Marks and Matthew Burbank, "Immigrant Support for the American Socialist Party, 1912 and 1920," *Social Science History* 14 (Summer 1990), 175–202; Charles Leinenweber, "The Class and Ethnic Bases of New York City Socialism, 1904–1915," *Labor History* 22 (1981): 31–56; and Melvyn Dubofsky, "Success and Failure of Socialism in New York City, 1900–1918: A Case Study," *Labor History* 9, no. 4 (Fall 1968): 361–75. On their opposition to the socialism in

the AFL, see Marc Karson, *American Labor Unions and Politics* (Carbondale: Southern Illinois University Press, 1958). On aspects of the Irish American radical tradition (which remains largely unexplored), see L. A. O'Donnell, *Irish Voice and Organized Labor: A Biographical Study* (Westport, Conn.: Greenwood Press, 1997), 117–41. On Flynn and Foster's Irish nationalist family backgrounds, see Elizabeth Gurley Flynn, "How I Became a Rebel," *Labor Herald,* July 1922, 23–24; Flynn, *I Speak My Own Piece,* 13–21; and James R. Barrett, *William Z. Foster and the Tragedy of American Radicalism* (Urbana: University of Illinois Press, 1999), 10.

105. *Irish World and Industrial Liberator,* December 18, 1886, 3; Susan Levine, "Labor's True Woman: Domesticity and Equal Rights in the Knights of Labor," *Journal of American History* 70 (September 1983): 323–39; and Meredith Tax, *The Rising of the Women: Feminist Solidarity and Class Conflict, 1880–1917* (New York: Monthly Review Press, 1980), 42–47. Leonora Barry, another important Knights leader, shared a similar background.

106. On women's activism in Ireland, see Margaret Ward, *Unmanageable Revolutionaries: Women and Irish Nationalism* (London: Pluto Press, 1983); and Beth McKillen, "Irish Feminism and National Separatism," *Éire-Ireland* 17 (1982): 72–90. On their activism in New York, see Kelly, *Shamrock and Lily,* 63–72.

107. Margaret Dreier Robins quoted in Nelson, "Irish Americans, Irish Nationalism, and the Social Question," 171.

108. Mary J. Bularzik, "The Bonds of Belonging: Leonora O'Reilly and Social Reform," *Labor History* 24 (Winter 1983): 60–83; Mari Jo Buhle, *Women and American Socialism, 1870–1920* (Urbana: University of Illinois Press, 1981), 199–200; and Nancy Schrom Dye, *As Equals and As Sisters: Feminism, the Labor Movement, and the Women's Trade Union League of New York* (Columbia: University of Missouri Press, 1980), 34–35.

109. Dye, *As Equals and As Sisters,* 45–47, 52–56, 120, quote at 60.

110. Elizabeth Anne Payne, *Reform, Labor, and Feminism: Margaret Dreier Robins and the Women's Trade Union League* (Urbana: University of Illinois Press, 1988), 48, 60–64, quote at 67. For similar tensions in Boston, see Deutsch, *Women and the City,* 248.

111. Doyle, "Striking for Ireland on the New York Docks," 360, 363.

112. Mary Kenney O'Sullivan, autobiography ms., Schlesinger Library, Radcliffe College, Cambridge, Mass., in Edward T. James, ed., *Papers of the Women's Trade Union League and Its Principal Leaders,* microfilm ed. (Woodbridge, Conn.: Research Publications, 1979); Robert L. Reid, ed., *Battleground: The Autobiography of Margaret A. Haley* (Urbana: University of Illinois Press, 1982); Agnes Nestor, *Woman's Labor Leader: An Autobiography* (Rockford, Ill.: Bellevue Books, 1954); and Nolan, *Servants of the Poor,* 69. On the connections between Irish women's organizing and the WTUL in Chicago and New York, see Payne, *Reform, Labor, and Feminism*; Dye, *As Equals and as Sisters*; Buhle, *Women and American Socialism,* 189–200; Kathleen Banks Nutter, *The Necessity of Organization: Mary Kenney O'Sullivan and Trade Unionism for Women, 1892–1912* (New York: Garland, 2000); and Patricia Lamoureux, "Irish Catholic Women and the Labor Movement," *U.S. Catholic Historian* 16 (Summer 1998): 24–44.

113. See Dorothy Richardson, "Trade Unions in Petticoats," *Leslie's Monthly Magazine* 57 (March 1904): 489–500; and Norwood, *Labor's Flaming Youth,* 91–122.

114. C. Desmond Greaves, *The Life and Times of James Connolly* (New York: International Publishers, 1971); James Connolly, "Labor, Nationality, and Religion," in P. Berresford-Ellis, ed., *James Connolly: Selected Writings* (Harmondsworth, U.K.: Penguin, 1973), 57–118; and Joseph Lee, *The Modernisation of Irish Society, 1848–1918* (Dublin: Gill & Macmillan, 1989),

140–41, 149–52. On the Irish Socialist Federation, see Flynn, *I Speak My Own Piece*, 65–66, quote at 66.

115. David Howell, *A Lost Left: Three Studies in Socialism and Nationalism* (Manchester, U.K.: Manchester University Press, 1986), 53–74.

116. Larkin quoted in Emmett O'Connor, "James Larkin in the United States, 1914–23," *Journal of Contemporary History* 37, no. 2 (2002): 194. See also Emmet O'Connor, *James Larkin: Irish Labour Leader* (Cambridge, Mass.: MIT Press, 1965).

117. Flynn, *I Speak My Own Piece*, 32–33.

118. Ibid. On the fit between militant republicanism and socialism among Irish immigrant workers in the 1930s, see Joshua B. Freeman, "Catholics, Communists, and Republicans: Irish Workers and the Organization of the Transit Workers Union," in Michael H. Frisch and Daniel J. Walkowitz, eds., *Working-Class America: Essays on Labor, Community, and American Society* (Urbana: University of Illinois Press, 1983).

119. William Z. Foster, *The Twilight of World Capitalism* (New York: International Publishers, 1949), 158–59. When Irish Catholic radicals like Foster, William F. Dunne, Elizabeth Gurley Flynn, Margaret Sanger, and others broke with the church, their attitude toward the institution tended to be rather intolerant. The Irish American Communist and founder of the American Trotskyist movement, James Cannon, experienced a trajectory very similar to Foster's. See Bryan Palmer, *James P. Cannon and the Origins of the American Revolutionary Left, 1890–1928* (Urbana: University of Illinois Press, 2007), 31–32.

120. William Z. Foster, *From Bryan to Stalin* (New York: International Publishers, 1937); and Edward P. Johanningsmeier, *Forging American Communism: The Life of William Z. Foster* (Princeton, N.J.: Princeton University Press, 1994), 353.

121. Barrett, "Americanization from the Bottom Up," 1000–1002; Nick Salvatore, "Some Thoughts on Class and Citizenship," and Catherine Collomp, "Les organizations ouvrières et la restriction de l'immigration aux États-Unis à la fin du dix-neuvième siècle," both in Debouzy, *A l'ombre de la statue de la liberté*, 215–30, 231–46; Gwendolyn Mink, *Old Labor and New Immigrants in American Political Development: Union, Party, and State, 1875–1920* (Ithaca, N.Y.: Cornell University Press, 1986), 228–35; A. T. Lane, "American Unions, Mass Immigration, and the Literacy Test, 1900–1917," *Labor History* 25 (Winter 1984): 5–25; and Roediger, *Working Toward Whiteness*, 78–92.

122. "Letter from Jere Sullivan" and "Interview with J. E. Roach," both in David J. Saposs Papers, Wisconsin State Historical Society, Madison.

123. Robert Asher, "Union Nativism and the Immigrant Response," *Labor History* 23, no. 3 (Summer 1982), 334–35; Roediger, *Working Toward Whiteness*, 81–82; and Mink, *Old Labor and New Immigrants*.

124. On the immigrant upsurge between 1909 and the early 1920s, see Montgomery, *Fall of the House of Labor*, 294, 335–47; Montgomery, *Workers' Control in America: Studies in the History of Work, Technology, and Labor Struggles* (New York: Cambridge University Press, 1979), 91–112; and James Barrett, "Unity and Fragmentation: Class, Race, and Ethnicity on Chicago's South Side, 1900–1922," *Journal of Social History* 18 (Fall 1984): 37–56. Capraro is quoted in Thomas Mackaman, *The Foreign Element: New Immigrants and American Industry, 1914–1924*, Ph.D. diss., University of Illinois at Urbana-Champaign, 2009, chap. 4, p. 9. On the tension between Irish clergy and the immigrant strikers at Lawrence in 1912 and 1919, see also James M. O'Toole, *Militant and Triumphant: William Henry O'Connell and the Catholic Church in Boston, 1859–1944* (Notre Dame, Ind.: Notre Dame University Press, 1992), 160–62.

125. Montgomery, "Irish and the American Labor Movement," 206; and David Noel Doyle, "The Irish and American Labor, 1880–1920," *Saothar: Journal of the Irish Labour History Society* 1 (1975): 44. On the political influence of the Irish at the national level of the AFL, see also Karson, *American Labor Unions and Politics,* 221–24.

126. Ryan, *Beyond the Ballot Box,* 147n24.

127. Royal Montgomery, *Industrial Relations in the Chicago Building Trades* (Chicago: University of Chicago Press, 1927), 209–29; William Haber, *Industrial Relations in the Building Industry* (Cambridge, Mass.: Harvard University Press, 1930), 321–22, 352–58; John R. Commons. "The New York Building Trades," in Commons, *Trade Unionism and Labor Problems,* 65–86; John Hutchinson, *The Imperfect Union: A History of Corruption in American Trade Unions* (New York: Dutton 1970), 53–61, quote at 33–34; and William Z. Foster, *Misleaders of Labor* (Chicago: Trade Union Educational League, 1927), 129–30.

128. David Montgomery, "Strikes in the Nineteenth Century," *Social Science History* 3–4 (1980): 81–104.

129. Stephen Norwood, *Strikebreaking and Intimidation: Mercenaries and Masculinity in Twentieth-century America* (Chapel Hill: University of North Carolina Press, 2002); Edward Levinson, *"I Break Strikes!": The Technique of Pearl L. Bergoff* (New York: R. M. McBride & Co., 1935); and Hutchinson, *Imperfect Union,* 60–61.

130. Henry J. Browne, "Comment," in John H. M. Laslett and Seymour Martin Lipset, eds., *Failure of a Dream? Essays in the History of American Socialism* (Berkeley: University of California Press, 1984), 103–12; and Shanabruch, *Chicago's Catholics,* 142–52.

131. Cardinal O'Connell, "Pastoral Letter on the Laborer's Rights," in National Catholic Welfare Conference, *The Church and Labor* (New York: Macmillan, 1920), 177–86, quoted in Karson, *American Labor Unions and Politics,* 226; *America* 2, no. 13 (January) 1910, 352, quoted in Karson, *American Labor Unions and Politics,* 227.

132. Karson, *American Labor Unions and Politics,* 225–26; Shanabruch, *Chicago's Catholics,* 142–53; and Damien Murray, " 'Go Forth as a Missionary to Fight It': Catholic Antisocialism and Irish American Nationalism in Post–World War I Boston," *Journal of American Ethnic History* 28 (Summer 2009): 1.

133. David J. Saposs, "The Catholic Church and the Labor Movement," *Modern Quarterly* 7 (June 1933): 294–98; Karson, *American Labor Unions and Politics,* 243–55; Montgomery, *Fall of the House of Labor,* 306–10, quote at 307; and Shanabruch, *Chicago's Catholics,* 152–54.

134. John H. M. Laslett, *Labor and the Left: A Study of Socialist and Radical Influences in the American Labor Movement, 1881–1924* (New York: Basic Books, 1970), 145–55; Aaron Ignatius Abell, *American Catholicism and Social Action: A Search for Social Justice, 1865–1950* (Garden City, N.Y.: Hanover House, 1960), 136–53; and Montgomery, *Workers' Control in America,* 77.

135. Quoted in David Steven Cohen, ed., *America, the Dream of My Life: Selections from the Federal Writers' Project's New Jersey Ethnic Survey* (New Brunswick, N.J.: Rutgers University Press, 1990), 45.

136. Howard E. Wilson, *Mary McDowell, Neighbor* (Chicago: University of Chicago Press, 1928): 95–97; Barrett, *Work and Community in the Jungle,* 135–36; Suellen Hoy, "The Irish Girls' Rising: The Stockyard Strike of 1900 and the Origins of the Chicago Women's Trade Union League," unpublished manuscript. My thanks to Suellen Hoy for allowing me to read this work. Maude Gonne had recently spoken before huge crowds in Chicago under the auspices of nationalist groups. See "Received by the 98 Club," *Chicago Tribune,*

March 4, 1900, 8. See also Maud Gonne, *Servant of the Queen: Reminiscences* (London: Victor Gollancz, 1938); Greaves, *James Connolly*, 81, 88–9, 116; and Nancy Cardozo, *Lucky Eyes and a High Heart: The Biography of Maud Gonne* (Indianapolis, Ind.: Bobbs-Merrill, 1978), 127–30. For a similar fusion of class and nationalist politics among young Irish American telephone operators, see Norwood, *Labor's Flaming Youth*, 18, 218–19.

137. Barrett, *Work and Community in the Jungle*, 136; Hoy, "Irish Girls' Rising"; Wilson, *Mary McDowell*, 95–97; Dominic A. Pacyga, *Polish Immigrants and Industrial Chicago: Workers on the South Side, 1880–1922* (Columbus: Ohio State University Press, 1991), 172–74; Commons, "Labor Conditions in Slaughtering and Meat Packing," in John R. Commons, ed., *Trade Unionism and Labor Problems* (Boston: Ginn & Co., 1905) 239–40.

138. McDowell quoted in Wilson, *Mary McDowell*, 58. See also Alice Henry, *The Trade Union Woman* (New York: D. Appleton & Co., 1915), 52–58.

139. Quoted in Asher, "Union Nativism," 345.

140. Quoted ibid.

141. Amalgamated Meat Cutters and Butcher Workmen of North America, Official Journal 5 (September 1904) 7. See also *Official Journal* 1 (March 1901), 1. For other examples of Irish American activists advocating for new immigrant workers, see Asher, "Union Nativism," 333.

142. Barrett, "Americanization from the Bottom Up," 1008–11.

143. Ethelbert Stewart, "The Influence of Trade Unions on Immigrants," U.S. Bureau of Labor Statistics, *Bulletin* no. 56 (Washington, D.C.: GPO, 1905), in Robert LaFollette, ed., *The Making of America*, vol. 3, *Labor* (1905; reprint New York: Arno Press, 1969), 230; Peter Roberts, *The New Immigration* (1912; reprint New York: Arno Press, 1970), 195; and Howard E. Wilson, *Mary McDowell, Neighbor* (Chicago: University of Chicago Press, 1928), quote at 99. See also Winthrop Talbot, ed., *Americanization* (New York: H. W. Wilson Co., 1917), 305, 307, 177–78; and Roediger, *Working Toward Whiteness*, 83–85.

144. Barrett, *Work and Community in the Jungle*, 139–42, Commons quoted at 164–65. See also Michael Kazin, *Barons of Labor: The San Francisco Building Trades and Labor Power in the Progressive Era* (Urbana: University of Illinois Press, 1987); and Julie Greene, *Pure and Simple Politics: The American Federation of Labor and Political Mobilization, 1881–1917* (New York: Cambridge University Press, 1998).

145. Barrett, *Work and Community in the Jungle*, 132.

146. Antanas Kaztauskis, "From Lithuania to the Chicago Stockyards—An Autobiography," *Independent* 57 (August 4, 1904): 241–48, reprinted in Katzman and Tuttle, *Plain Folk*, 112–13. Rather than the autobiography of one worker, this piece was a composite based on extensive interviews with immigrants during the journalist Ernest Poole's six weeks of research in the Chicago stockyards. See Ernest Poole, *The Bridge: My Own Story* (New York: Macmillan, 1940), 95.

147. Mackaman, *Foreign Element*; Barrett, *Work and Community in the Jungle*, 202–24.

CHAPTER 4: THE STAGE

1. "Hissed Off the Stage by Angry Irishmen," *New York Times*, January 25, 1907, 3; "Egg Russell Brothers in a Brooklyn Theatre," *New York Times*, February 1, 1907, 1; and M. Alison Kibler, "The Stage Irishwoman," *Journal of American Ethnic History* 24 (Spring 2005): 5–7. See also Geraldine Maschio, "Ethnic Humor and the Decline of the Russell Brothers,"

Journal of Popular Culture 26 (Summer 1992): 81–92; and Kathryn J. Oberdeck, *The Evangelist and the Impresario: Religion, Entertainment, and Cultural Politics in America, 1884–1914* (Baltimore, Md.: Johns Hopkins University Press, 1999), 201.

2. John Kuo Wei Tchen, "Quimbo Appo's Fear of Fenians: Chinese-Irish-Anglo Relations in New York City," in Ronald H. Bayor and Timothy J. Meagher, eds., *The New York Irish* (Baltimore, Md.: Johns Hopkins University Press, 1996), 143–45.

3. On the British tradition, see G. C. Duggan, *The Stage Irishman: A History of the Irish Play and Stage Characters from the Earliest Times* (London: Longmans Green, 1937); Declan Kiberd, "The Fall of the Stage Irishman," *Genre: A Quarterly Devoted to Generic Criticism* 12 (Winter 1979): 451–54; and Kathleen Donovan, "Good Old Pat: An Irish American Stereotype in Decline," *Éire-Ireland* 15, no. 3 (1980): 6–14. On derogatory comic caricatures of the Irish in nineteenth-century British print culture, see L. Perry Curtis, *Apes and Angels: The Irishman in Victorian Caricature*, rev. ed. (Washington, D.C.: Smithsonian Press, 1997).

4. Tyler Anbinder, *Five Points: The Nineteenth Century New York City Neighborhood That Invented Tap Dance, Stole Elections, and Became the World's Most Notorious Slum* (New York: Free Press, 2001), 172–75, quotes at 175; William H. A. Williams, *"'Twas Only an Irishman's Dream: The Image of Ireland and the Irish in American Popular Song Lyrics, 1800–1920* (Urbana: University of Illinois Press, 1996), 122. One hundred and fifty years later, the Irish immigrant rock musician Larry Kirwan consciously invoked this African-Irish fusion in creating the band Black 47, which reimagined Irish history and politics with reggae and rap beats. See Larry Kirwan, "Forgetting to Remember," in Andrew Higgins Wyndham, ed., *Re-Imagining Ireland* (Charlottesville: University of Virginia Press, 2006), 43–46.

5. Graham Hodges, "Desirable Companions and Lovers: Irish and African Americans in the Sixth Ward, 1830–1970," in Bayor and Meagher, *New York Irish*, 107–24; David R. Roediger, *The Wages of Whiteness: Race and the Making of the American Working Class* (London: Verso, 1991), 150–56; Eric Lott, *Love and Theft: Blackface Minstrelsy and the American Working Class* (New York: Oxford University Press, 1993).

6. On blackface minstrelsy on the Irish stage in the era of the Great Famine, see Douglas Riach, "Blacks and Blackface on the Irish Stage, 1830–1860," *Journal of American Studies* 7 (1973): 231–41.

7. Mick Moloney, "Irish-American Popular Music," in J. J. Lee and Marion Casey, eds., *Making the Irish American* (New York: New York University Press, 2005), 382, 383. See also Roediger, *Wages of Whiteness*, 118–19.

8. Roediger, *Wages of Whitness*, 133–63; Lott, *Love and Theft*; Michael Rogin, *Blackface, White Noise: Jewish Immigrants in the Hollywood Melting Pot* (Berkeley: University of California Press, 1996), 56–58; Moloney, "Irish-American Popular Music," 383.

9. David R. Roediger, *Working Toward Whiteness: How America's Immigrants Became White: The Strange Journey from Ellis Island to the Suburbs* (New York: Basic Books, 2005), 169; and Mary Elizabeth Brown, *From Italian Villages to Greenwich Village: Our Lady of Pompeii, 1892–1992* (New York: Center for Migration Studies, 1992), 31. See also Rogin, *Blackface, White Noise*.

10. On the nineteenth-century American stage Irishman, see Dale T. Knobel, "A Vocabulary of Ethnic Perception: Content Analysis of the American Stage Irishman, 1820–1860," *Journal of American Studies* 15 (1981): 45–71; and Patricia L. Ireland, *Blarney Streets: The Staging of Ireland and Irish–America by the Chicago Manuscript Company*, Ph.D. diss., Southern Illinois University, 1998, 201 and passim.

11. Lauren Onkey, *Blackness and the Transatlantic Irish Identity* (New York: Routledge, 2010), 32–61.

12. "Mr. Harrigan as Actor and Maker of 'Documents,'" *New York Times*, September 3, 1893, 16; Harley Erdman, *Staging the Jew: The Performance of an American Ethnicity, 1860–1920* (New Brunswick, N.J.: Rutgers University Press, 1997), 89.

13. Moloney, "Irish-American Popular Music," 389; Harrigan quoted in "American Playwrights on the American Drama," *Harper's Weekly*, February 2, 1889, 98; William Dean Howells, *Selected Literary Criticsm*, vol. 2, *1886–1897*, ed. David J. Nordloh (Bloomington: Indiana University Press, 1993), 25, both quoted in Jon W. Finson, "Realism in the Late Nineteenth-Century American Musical Theatre: The Songs of Edward Harrigan and David Braham," in Jon W. Finson, ed., *Collected Songs: Edward Harrigan and David Braham*, Music of the United States of America (Madison: University of Wisconsin Press, 1977), xxvii. Finerty quoted in Charles Fanning, *Finley Peter Dunne and Mr. Dooley: The Chicago Years* (Lexington: University Press of Kentucky, 1978), 158. For a sketch of Five Points in the era of Harrigan's greatest popularity, see "Not for Open Saloons," *New York Times*, January 25, 1895, 9.

14. Krystyn R. Moon, *Yellowface: Creating the Chinese in American Popular Music and Performance, 1850s–1920s* (New Brunswick, N.J.: Rutgers University Press, 2005), 53. See also James H. Dormon, "Ethnic Cultures of the Mind: The Harrigan–Hart Mosaic," *American Studies* 33 (Summer 1992), passim.

15. Excerpted in Moloney, "Irish–American Popular Music," 389.

16. Quoted in E. J. Kahn, Jr., *The Merry Partners: The Age and Stage of Harrigan and Hart* (New York: Random House, 1955), 69.

17. Tchen, "Quimbo Appo's Fear of Fenians," quote at 144; David Braham and Edward Harrigan, *Mulligan's Silver Wedding* (1881), cited in Dormon, "Ethnic Cultures of the Mind," 35.

18. Mixed race Irish-Chinese marriages remained popular in early-twentieth-century plays like *Patsy O'Wang, An Irish Farce with a Chinese Mix-Up*. See Robert G. Lee, *Orientals: Asian Americans in Popular Culture* (Philadelphia: Temple University Press, 1999), 78–81.

19. Harrigan's play and the street tune are both quoted in Moon, *Yellowface*, 50. On the rise of the Chinese hand laundry, see Mary Tin Yi Lui, *The Chinatown Trunk Mystery: Murder, Miscegenation, and Other Dangerous Encounters in Turn-of-the-Century New York City* (Princeton, N.J.: Princeton University Press, 2005), 55–58. On the laundryman's perceived femininity, see Ronald Takaki, *Strangers from a Different Shore: A History of Asian Americans* (New York: Penguin Books, 1989), 92–93.

20. *Irish World and Industrial Liberator*, July 12, 1879, 5. On the working-class base of the anti-Chinese movement, see Alexander Saxton, *Indispensable Enemy: Labor and the Anti-Chinese Movement in California* (Berkeley: University of California Press, 1971), and on the conflict between Chinese men and Irish women, see Moon, *Yellowface*, 49–51.

21. On "*The Mulligan Guard Ball*," see also Onkey, *Blackness and Tranatlantic Irish Identity*, 71–76; and Catherine Eagan, "*I Did Imagine . . . We Had Ceased to Be White-Washed Negroes*": The Racial Formation of Irish Identity in Ireland and America, Ph.D. diss., Boston College, 2000. On musical renderings of Chinese-Irish intermarriage, see Moon, *Yellowface*, 51–52. On the affinity between Irish and African Americans in Harrigan's plays, see Robert Toll, *Blacking Up: The Minstrel Show in Nineteenth-Century America* (New York: Oxford University Press, 1974), 247, 249. Thanks to Dennis McNulty for his observations regarding race and class anxieties in *The Mulligan Guard Ball*. See Dennis McNulty,

"Blackface as Irish Mask? Liminality and Resistance in Irish Blackface Performance," unpublished seminar paper, 2005.

22. Joyce Flynn, "Melting Plots: Patterns of Racial and Ethnic Amalgamation in American Drama Before Eugene O'Neill," *American Quarterly* 38 (1986): 430.

23. Robert W. Snyder, "The Irish and Vaudeville," in Lee and Casey, *Making the Irish American*, 406.

24. Alexander Saxton, "Blackface Minstrelsy and Jacksonian Ideology," *American Quarterly* 27 (1975): 14–15; Roediger, *Wages of Whiteness*, 119; Lott, *Love and Theft*, 190–91.

25. Robert W. Snyder, "Big Time, Small Time, All Around the Town: New York Vaudeville in the Early Twentieth Century," in Richard Butsch, ed., *For Fun and Profit: The Transformation of Leisure into Consumption* (Philadelphia: Temple University Press, 1990), 119. For a careful delineation of various kinds of theaters in the neighborhoods of New York, see Michael Davis, *The Exploitation of Pleasure* (New York: Russell Sage Foundation, 1910).

26. Davis, *Exploitation of Pleasure*, table 8, 30. See also David Nasaw, *Going Out: The Rise and Fall of Public Amusements* (New York: Basic Books, 1993), 23–32.

27. Richard Butsch, *The Making of American Audiences, From Stage to Television* (New York: Cambridge University Press, 2000), 141–46; Davis, *Exploitation of Pleasure*, 30; Nasaw, *Going Out*, 168–71, 186–204.

28. Snyder, "Big Time, Small Time," 120.

29. Snyder, "Irish and Vaudeville," 406.

30. Gavin Roger Jones, *Strange Talk: The Politics of Dialect Literature in Gilded Age America* (Berkeley: University of California Press, 1999), 173–77; Moloney, "Irish American Popular Music," 387.

31. Ibid.; Flynn, "Melting Plots," 426, quote at 429; "Dramatic and Musical," *New York Times*, November 13, 1900, 6; Paul Antoine Distler, "Ethnic Comedy in Vaudeville and Burlesque," in Myron Matlaw, ed., *American Popular Entertainment* (Westport, Conn.: Greenwood Press, 1979), 38; Rogin, *Blackface, White Noise*, 53.

32. Moon, *Yellowface*, 114.

33. Moon, *Yellowface*, 140–42; Lee, *Orientals*, 34–35, 61–65; Lott, *Love and Theft*, 48.

34. On foreign-language ethnic theater in Irish, Italian, German, Yiddish, and other communities, see James H. Dormon, "European Immigrant/Ethnic Theatre in Gilded Age New York: Reflections and Projections of Mentalities," in William Pencak, Selma Berrol, and Randall M. Miller, eds., *Immigration to New York* (Philadelphia: Balch Institute Press, 1991), 148–55; Maxine Schwartz Seller, *Ethnic Theatre in the United States* (Westport, Conn.: Greenwood Press, 1983); Matthew Frye Jacobson, *Special Sorrows: The Diasporic Imagination of Irish, Polish, and Jewish Immigrants* (Berkeley: University of California Press, 2002), 82–93; and Butsch, *Making of American Audiences*, 133–35.

35. *New York Dramatic Mirror*, October 16, 1899; and "Hebrews Have Been Chosen to Succeed Coons in Vaudeville," *New York Telegraph*, August 28, 1899, both quoted in Dormon, "European Immigrant/Ethnic Theatre," 161, 160.

36. Dormon, "European Immigrant/Ethnic Theatre," 156–66; Moses Rischin, *The Promised City: New York's Jews, 1870–1914* (New York: Harper & Row, 1962), 265–66.

37. Gunther Barth, *City People: The Rise of Modern City Culture in Nineteenth-Century America* (New York: Oxford University Press, 1980), 193. See also Thomas J. Schlereth, *Victorian America: Transformations in Everyday Life, 1876–1915* (New York: HarperPerennial, 1991), 232–33.

38. Hartley Davis, "In Vaudeville," *Everyone's* 24 (August 1905): 238, quoted in Dormon, "European Immigrant/Ethnic Theatre," 165.

39. Snyder, "Irish and Vaudeville," 407; Paul Antoine Distler, "Ethnic Comedy in Vaudeville and Burlesque," in Myron Matlaw, ed., *American Popular Entertainment* (Westport, Conn.: Greenwood Press, 1979), 36; Sabine Haenni, *The Immigrant Scene: Ethnic Amusements in New York, 1880–1920* (Minneapolis: University of Minnesota Press, 2008), 14–16.

40. Kazin is quoted in Stephen Whitfield, *In Search of American Jewish Culture* (Waltham, Mass.: Brandeis University Press, 1999), 51. On the increasing diversity of vaudeville audiences, see Snyder, "Big Time, Small Time," 125; and M. Alison Kibler, *Rank Ladies: Gender and Hierarchy in American Vaudeville* (Chapel Hill: University of North Carolina Press, 1999), 25. On racial segregation policies, see Kibler, *Rank Ladies*, 34–36; and Mary Carbine, "The Finest Outside the Loop: Motion Picture Exhibition in Chicago's Black Metropolis, 1905–1925," *Camera Obscura* 23 (1990): 9–41. On the balance among slapstick, nostalgia, and urban realism in vaudeville sketches, see Oberdeck, *Evangelist and Impresario*, 91–108. On Irish performers integrating contemporary social and political issues into their acts, see ibid., 97–98.

41. Nasaw, *Going Out*, 52–53.

42. Armond Fields and L. Marc Fields, *From the Bowery to Broadway: Lew Fields and the Roots of American Popular Theatre* (New York: Oxford University Press, 1993), 32–33, 85; George Peter Murdock, ed., *Studies in the Science of Society* (Freeport, N.Y.: Books for Libraries Press, 1969), 21. See also Moon, *Yellowface*, 148–50.

43. Rogin, *Blackface, White Noise*, 56–58, quote at 56.

44. Roediger, *Working Toward Whiteness*, 125n75, 186–87; and Robert W. Snyder, *Voice of the City: Vaudeville and Popular Culture in New York* (Lanham, Md.: Ivan R. Dee, 2000), 120.

45. Kathleen Donovan, "Good Old Pat: An Irish-American Stereotype in Decline," *Éire-Ireland* 15 (1980): 6–14; Oberdeck, *Evangelist and Impresario*, 198–204; and Kibler, *Rank Ladies*, 60–69.

46. Snyder, "Irish and Vaudeville," 406–9; Kibler, *Rank Ladies*, 55–57, 63–64, 71–74; Charles Fanning, *The Irish Voice in America: 250 Years of Irish American Fiction* (Lexington: University Press of Kentucky, 2000), 179–82; and Carl Wittke, "The Immigrant Theme on the American Stage," *Mississippi Valley Historical Review* 39 (September 1952): 222–23. The comic pretensions of the upwardly mobile Irish was a constant refrain in Finley Peter Dunne's popular "Mr. Dooley" columns and books.

47. Quoted in Deborah Skok, *More than Neighbors: Catholic Settlements and Day Nurseries in Chicago, 1893–1930* (DeKalb: Northern Illinois University Press, 2007), 33.

48. Patricia Ireland, *Blarney Streets: The Staging of Ireland and Irish-Americans by the Chicago Manuscript Company*, Ph.D. diss., Southern Illinois University, 1998, 197–98; *New York Tribune*, March 28, 1903, 1; and Managers' Report Book, p. 252, Boston, April 27, 1903, Keith/Albee Collection, Special Collections, University of Iowa Library. My thanks to M. Alison Kibler for this reference.

49. "Irish Comedian Must Go," *Chicago Tribune*, May, 1902, 1; M. Alison Kibler, "Pigs, Green Whiskers, and Drunken Widows: Irish Nationalists and the 'Practical Censorship' of McFadden's Row of Flats in 1902 and 1903," *Journal of American Studies* 42 (December) 2008: 489–514; and Donovan, "Good Old Pat," 13. The United Irish Societies quote is in Oberdeck, *Evangelist and Impresario*, 201. See also Nasaw, *Going Out*, 167.

50. Oberdeck, *Evangelist and Impresario*, 343–49; Report Book 8, 124, Keith/Albee Collection, quoted in Kibler, *Rank Ladies*, 56.

51. On the Synge boycott and riots, see "Riot in Theatre Over an Irish Play," *New York Times*, November 28, 1911, 1, 3; "More Theatre Riots Greet 'The Playboy,'" ibid., January 17, 1912, 2; and Adele Dalsimer, "Players in the Western World: The Abbey Theatre's American Tours," *Éire-Ireland* 16 (1981): 75–93. The protests against *Playboy of the Western World* were transnational, beginning in Dublin and spreading through the Irish diaspora communities. See Kiberd, "Fall of the Stage Irishman," 458–59.

52. "McKee Wants City to Censor Movies," *New York Times,* October 12, 1927, 1; and "Film Men Absent at Censor Hearing," *New York Times,* October 15, 1927, 21. As late as 1928, the AOH and Knights of Columbus launched a boycott of the film *The Callahans and the Murphys* because they felt its depiction of drinking and fighting, and its crude slapstick comedy, was a degrading portrayal of Irish American family life. See Timothy Meagher, *The Columbia Guide to Irish American History* (New York: Columbia University Press, 2005), 137; and Joseph Curran, *Hibernian Green on the Silver Screen: The Irish and American Movies* (New York: Greenwood Press, 1989), 34–35.

53. Fanning, *Irish Voice in America*, 219.

54. The theme of Irish defensiveness producing an obsession with respectability is developed and documented most effectively in Miller, *Emigrants and Exiles*, 497–99, quote at 498. See also Thomas Rowland, "Irish Americans and the Quest for Respectability in the Coming of the Great War, 1900–1917," *Journal of American Ethnic History* 15 (Winter 1996): 3–31. On the changing composition of the audience in Harrigan's plays and other musical theater by 1900, see James H. Dormon, "Ethnic Cultures of the Mind: The Harrigan-Hart Mosaic," *American Studies* 33 (Summer 1992): 37.

55. Fanning, *Irish Voice in America*, 153–76; and Chris McNickle, "When New York Was Irish, and After," in Bayor and Meagher, *New York Irish*, 345–46.

56. Kibler, "The Stage Irishwoman," 5–30; and Kibler, "Pigs, Green Whiskers, and Drunken Widows," 11–14. The characterization of "belligerent masculinity" is from Meagher, *Making of Irish America*, 243. On the working-class character of the AOH, see Miller, *Emigrant and Exiles*, 534–35. Identities of those arrested at the *Playboy* protests and in earlier New York theater riots show that the movement was a mixture of skilled and unskilled workers with a few small merchants and white-collar workers. See "Riot in Theatre Over an Irish Play," *New York Times*, November 28, 1911, 1, 3; and "Egg Riot at Theatre; Irishmen in a Rage," *New York Tribune*, March 28, 1903, 1.

57. Timothy Meagher, "Introduction," in Timothy Meagher, ed., *From Paddy to Studs: Irish American Communities in Turn of the Century Era, 1880–1920* (Westport, Conn.: Greenwood Press, 1986), 2.

58. Managers' Report Book, page 297, Boston, April 27, 1903, Keith/Albee Collection. My thanks to M. Alison Kibler for this reference.

59. Kibler, *Rank Ladies*, 34–36; Nasaw, *Going Out*, 53–56, 167–68.

60. "All Races to War on Play Ridicule," *Chicago Tribune*, April 25, 1913, 5; quote in "Anti-Defamation Move Becomes Nationwide," November 14, 1913, 14; and "To Boycott the State Jew," *New York Times*, April 25, 1913, 3.

61. "Irish Cheer General Miles," *Chicago Tribune*, September 21, 1903, 4; and Kibler, *Rank Ladies*, 56. See also Matthew Frye Jacobson, *Whiteness of a Different Color: European Immigrants and the Alchemy of Race* (Cambridge, Mass.: Harvard University Press, 1998), 183. On Jewish protests, see Nasaw, *Going Out*, 53.

62. Oberdeck, *Evangelist and Impresario*, 341–49; and "Stage Folk Dispute Virtues of Make-Up," *New York Times*, July 15, 1923, E6.

63. Meaghan Dwyer-Ryan, "'Yankee Doodle Paddy': Themes of Patriotism in *Yankee Doodle Dandy*," *Journal of American Ethnic History* 30 (Summer 2011): 57–62; Daniel Patrick Moynihan, "The Irish," in Lee and Casey, *Making the Irish American*, 492.

64. Quoted in Quinn, *Looking for Jimmy*, 26.

65. Snyder, "Irish and Vaudeville," 408–10; and Kibler, *Rank Ladies*, 171–98. The deep class divide in the community persisted as the industry matured. In 1916–17, Casey helped to blacklist Broadway actors trying to gain a union shop in New York theater. In conflicts between impresarios and organizers for the White Rats Actors' Union, Irish Americans were prominent on both sides.

66. Snyder, "Irish and Vaudeville," 408–10; and Daniel Czitrom, "Underworlds and Underdogs: Big Tim Sullivan and Metropolitan Politics in New York, 1889–1913," *Journal of American History* 78, no. 2 (September 1991): 551–52.

67. Lyrics in Mick Moloney, *Far from the Shamrock Shore: The Story of Irish-American Immigration Through Song* (New York: Crown, 2002), 34.

68. Williams, "'*Twas Only an Irishman's Dream*," 192–94. "I've Got Rings on My Fingers; or, Mumbo Jumbo Jijjiboo J. O'Shea," words by Weston and Barnes, music by Maurice Scott (New York: Francis, Day & Hunter, 1909). My thanks to Jeff Magee for directing me to this sheet music.

69. Williams, "'*Twas Only an Irishman's Dream*," 190.

70. Rogin, *Blackface, White Noise*, 57–58.

71. Song by William Jerome (Flannery) and Jean Schwartz. This and the previous paragraph draw on Williams, "'*Twas Only an Irishman's Dream*," 194–99, song lyrics quoted at 196. See also Moloney, "Irish-American Popular Music," 393–96; and Moloney, *Far from the Shamrock Shore*, 36–37. For a broader sampling of songs featuring Jewish-Irish relations, see Mick Moloney, *The Irish and the Jews* (Nashville, Tenn.: Compass Records, 2009).

72. "Comedies for All," *New York Times*, August 29, 1926, X1; Anne Nichols, *Abie's Irish Rose: A Novel* (New York: Grosset & Dunlap, 1927), 75–79, 95–98, 101–6; Riv-Ellen Prell, *Fighting to Become Americans: Jews, Gender, and the Anxiety of Assimilation* (Boston: Beacon Press, 1999), 72–77; Rudolf Glanz, *Jew and Irish: Historic Group Relations and Immigration* (New York: Waldon Press, 1966), 105–6; Curran, *Hibernian Green*, 36; Ted Merwin, "The Performance of Jewish Identity in Anne Nichols's 'Abie's Irish Rose,'" *Journal of American Ethnic History* 20 (Winter 2001): 3–37; and Rogin, *Blackface, White Noise*, 104. See also Lester D. Friedman, *Unspeakable Images: Ethnicity and the American Cinema* (Urbana: University of Illinois Press, 1991), 58–60; Mari Kathleen Fielder, "Fatal Attraction: Irish-Jewish Romance in Early Film and Drama," *Éire: A Journal of Irish Studies* 20, no. 3 (Fall 1985): 6–18; and Eric Goldstein, *The Price of Whiteness: Jews, Race and American Identity* (Princeton, N.J.: Princeton Univeristy Press, 2006), 134, 135.

73. Edward T. O'Donnell, "Abie's Irish Rose," *Irish Echo*, May 19, 2004; *Irish Echo*, November 4–10, 2009, 18; "Moe and Jawn Practice Their 'Abie's Irish Rose' Jokes," *Chicago Tribune*, April 15, 1928, A3; Erdman, *Staging the Jew*, 120; "Abie Sings an Irish Song" (1913), words and music by Irving Berlin, in Charles Hamm, ed., *Irving Berlin: Early Songs* (Madison, Wis.: A-R Editions, 1994); and Mick Moloney, *If It Wasn't for the Irish and the Jews*, CD, Compass Records, 2009. My thanks to Ed O'Donnell, Jo Kibbee, and Jeff Magee for their suggestions regarding the Irish and the Jews. On Berlin's early career, see Michael Freeland, *Irving Berlin* (New York: Stein & Day, 1974). On the affinity of the Irish and Jews and its relationship to American popular culture, see also Rogin, *Blackface, White Noise*, 58; Whitfield, *In Search of American Jewish Culture*; and Williams, "'*Twas Only an Irishman's Dream*," 198–99.

74. Timothy J. Meagher, "Abie's Irish Enemy: Irish and Jews, Social and Political Realities and Media Representations," in Ruth Barton, ed., *Screening Irish America: Representing Irish American in Film and Television* (Dublin: Irish Academic Press, 2009), 45–58.

75. Prell, *Fighting to Become Americans*, 67-77, quote at 77. On intermarriage in the third generation and beyond, and along religious lines, see Will Herberg, *Protestant, Catholic, Jew: An Essay on American Religious Sociology* (Chicago: University of California Press, 1955); Harold Abramson, *Ethnic Diversity in Catholic America* (New York: Wiley, 1973), 51–99; Joel Perlmann, "The Romance of Assimilation? Studying the Demographic Outcomes of Ethnic Intermarriage in American History," Working Paper no. 230 (Jerome Levy Economics Institute, Bard College, 1988), especially table 9; Perlmann, "Demographic Outcomes of Ethnic Intermarriage in American History: Italian Americans Through Four Generations," Working Paper no. 372 (Levy Institute, 2000), especially table 13; Julius Drachsler, *Intermarriage in New York City: A Statistical Survey of the Amalgamation of European Peoples*, Ph.D. diss., Columbia University, 1921, 56; and Stephen Steinberg, *The Ethnic Myth: Race, Ethnicity and Class in America* (Boston: Beacon Press, 1989), 68.

76. Fielder, "Fatal Attraction," 9, 11.

77. For the experiences of an Irish Catholic woman who married her Jewish employer and the struggles of their son in a Catholic school, see "The Experiences of a Jew's Wife," *American Magazine* 78 (December 1914), 49–53, 83–86. My thanks to Edward T. O'Donnell for directing me to this source.

78. Bruce M. Stave and John F. Sutherland with Aldo Salerno, eds., *From the Old Country: An Oral History of European Migration to America* (New York: Twayne, 1994), 185–87, 190; Fielder, "Fatal Attraction," 12, 13. The question of whether mixed marriages involving the Irish led to more Irish-identified offspring has yielded differing answers. See Richard Alba, *Ethnic Identity: The Transformation of White America* (New Haven, Conn.: Yale University Press, 1990), 59–61. For the view that Irish identity claims approximated "actual" ancestry, see Michael Hout and Joshua R. Goldstein, "How 4.5 Million Irish Immigrants Became 40 Million Irish Americans: Demographic and Subject Aspects of the Ethnic Composition of White Americans," *American Sociological Review* 59 (February 1994), 64–82. Thanks to Gillian Stevens for this citation.

79. Anbinder, *Five Points*, 389–90, 314, 320, 263; Graham Hodges, " 'Desirable Companions and Lovers': Irish and African Americans in the Sixth Ward, 1830–1870," in Bayor and Meagher, *New York Irish*, 107–24; Sarah Deutsch, *Women and the City: Gender, Space, and Power in Boston, 1870–1940* (New York: Oxford University Press, 2000), 86–89; Tchen, "Quimbo Appo's Fear of Fenians," 128–30; and Lui, *Chinatown Trunk Mystery*, 154–60.

80. Julius Drachsler, *Intermarriage in New York City: A Statistical Survey of the Amalgamation of European Peoples*, Ph.D. diss., Columbia University, 1921, passim and especially 56; Bronwen Walter, *Outsiders Inside: Whiteness, Place, and Irish Women* (New York: Routledge, 2000), 34–35; Thomas J. Archdeacon, *Becoming American: An Ethnic History* (New York: Free Press, 1983), 139–40; Hasia R. Diner, *Erin's Daughters in America: Irish Immigrant Women in the Nineteenth Century* (Baltimore, Md.: Johns Hopkins University Press, 1983), 8–9, 30–34, 51; William Z. Ripley, "Races in the United States," *Atlantic Monthly* 102 (December 1908), 745–59; Herberg, *Protestant, Catholic, Jew*; Harold Abramson, *Ethnic Diversity in Catholic America* (New York: Wiley, 1973), 51–99; Perlmann, "The Romance of Assimilation?" especially table 9; and Perlmann, "Demographic Outcomes of Ethnic Intermarriage," especially table 13. See also R. J. R. Kennedy, "Single or Triple Melting Pot? Intermarriage Trends in New Haven, 1870–1940," *American Journal of Sociology* 49, no. 4

(January 1944): 331–39, and, for the persistence of these trends, Kennedy, "Single or Triple Melting Pot? Intermarriage in New Haven, 1870–1950," *American Journal of Sociology* 58, no. 1 (July 1952): 56–59.

81. Steven J. Ross, *Working-Class Hollywood: Silent Films and the Shaping of Class in America* (Princeton, N.J.: Princeton University Press, 1999), 4, 5, 16–19, passim. See also Butsch, *Making of American Audiences*, 165–66.

82. "Presentation of Research Problem in Class on Family Research," May 9, 1934, Ernst Watson Burgess Papers, Box 132, Folder 3, Special Collections, Regenstein Library, University of Chicago. See also Lizabeth Cohen, *Making a New Deal: Industrial Workers in Chicago, 1919–1939* (New York: Cambridge University Press, 1990), 124–29, 143–47.

83. Bruce Nelson, *Divided We Stand: American Workers and the Struggle for Black Equality* (Princeton, N.J.: Princeton University Press, 2001), xxxiv. See also Rogin, *Blackface, White Noise*; Larry May, *The Big Tomorrow: Hollywood and the Politics of the American Way* (Chicago: University of Chicago Press, 2000), 55–100; and Lawrence J. McCaffrey, "*Going My Way* and Irish American Catholicism: Myth and Reality," *New Hibernia Review* 4 (2000): 119–27. See also Christopher Shannon, *Bowery to Broadway: The American Irish in Classic Hollywood Cinema* (Scranton, Penn.: Scranton University Press, 2010).

84. Curran, *Hibernian Green on the Silver Screen*, 17–26.

85. Jay P. Dolan, *The Irish Americans: A History* (New York: Bloomsbury Press, 2008), 231–32; Curran, *Hibernian Green on the Silver Screen*, 52–58; Lawrence J. McCaffrey, *Textures of Irish America* (Syracuse, N.Y.: Syracuse University Press, 1992), 39, 40.

86. Ibid., 39–48; Anthony Burke Smith, "The Mick Turns Federal Agent: James Cagney, G-Men, and Ethnic Masculinity," in Barton, *Screening Irish America*, 113–34; and Christopher Shannon, "Public Enemies, Local Heroes: The Irish American Gangster Film in Classical Hollywood Cinema," *New Hibernia Review* 9, no. 4 (Winter 2005): 48–64. Jewish American actors like George Raft, Edward G. Robinson, and John Garfield were also important models, as were Jewish gangsters, particularly for second-generation Jewish immigrant youth. On the Jewish American gangsters on screen and in the streets, see Rich Cohen, *Tough Jews* (New York: Simon & Schuster, 1998); and Jenna Weisman Joselit, *Our Gang: Jewish Crime and the New York Jewish Community, 1900–1940* (Bloomington: Indiana University Press, 1993).

87. Andrew J. Diamond, *Mean Streets: Chicago Youths and the Everyday Struggle for Empowerment in the Multiracial City, 1908–1969* (Berkeley: University of California Press, 2009), 113–17; McCaffrey, *Textures of Irish America*, 246–47; and Nathan Glazer and Daniel Patrick Moynihan, *Beyond the Melting Pot: Irish, Jews, and Puerto Ricans in New York City* (Cambridge, Mass.: MIT Press, 1970), 246–47.

88. Frank Walsh, *Sin and Censorship: The Catholic Church and the Motion Picture Industry* (New Haven, Conn.: Yale University Press, 1996); Curran, *Hibernian Green on the Silver Screen*, 49.

89. Charles Morris, *American Catholics: The Saints and Sinners Who Built America's Most Powerful Church* (New York: Vintage Books, 1998), 196–209; and Curran, *Hibernian Green on the Silver Screen*, 48–52. See also Thomas Doherty, *Hollywood's Censor: Joseph I. Breen and the Production Code Administration* (New York: Columbia University Press, 2009), 56–60.

90. Lawrence J. McCaffrey, "Diaspora Comparisons and Irish-American Uniqueness," in Charles Fanning, ed., *New Perspectives on the Irish Diaspora* (Carbondale: Southern Illinois University Press, 2000), 22.

91. Luc Sante, *Low Life: Lures and Snares of Old New York* (New York: Farrar, Strauss & Gir-

oux, 1991), 125–32; Tchen, "Quimbo Appo's Fear of Fenians," 143–47; John Kuo Wei Tchen, *New York Before Chinatown* (New York: New York University Press, 1999); and Lui, *Chinatown Trunk Mystery*. On the surge of interest in foreign objects and people at the turn of the century, see Matthew Frye Jacobson, *Barbarian Virtues: The United States Encounters Foreign Peoples at Home and Abroad, 1876–1917* (New York: Hill & Wang, 2000); and Kristin Hoganson, *Consumers' Imperium: The Global Production of American Domesticity, 1865–1920* (Chapel Hill: University of North Carolina Press, 2007). On the middle-class fascination with and voyages to immigrant slums, see Haenni, *Immigrant Scene*, 40–44; Catherine Cocks, *Doing the Town: The Rise of Urban Tourism in the United States, 1850–1915* (Berkeley: University of California Press, 2001); and Robert M. Dowling, *Slumming New York: From the Waterfront to Mythic Harlem* (Urbana: University of Illinois Press, 2007).

92. Tchen, "Quimbo Appo's Fear of Fenians," 147.

93. Madelon Power, *Faces Along the Bar: Lore and Order in the Workingman's Saloon, 1870–1920* (Chicago: University of Chicago Press, 1998); and Thomas J. Schlereth, *Victorian America: Transformations in Everyday Life, 1876–1915* (New York: HarperPerennial, 1991), 225–26.

94. On women running *shebeens* in Ireland, see James R. Barrett, "Why 'Paddy' Drank: The Social Significance of Whiskey in Pre-Famine Ireland," *Journal of Popular Culture* 11 (1977): 17–28. On the same phenomenon in Chicago and Boston, see Deirdre Mageean, "Making Sense and Providing Structure: Irish-American Women in the Parish Neighborhood," in Christiane Harzig et al., eds., *Peasant Maids, City Women: From the European Countryside to Urban America* (Ithaca, N.Y.: Cornell University Press, 1997), 227–28; and Deutsch, *Women and the City*, 85.

95. Perry Duis, *The Saloon: Public Drinking in Chicago and Boston, 1880–1920* (Urbana: University of Illinois Press, 1983); E. C. Moore, "The Social Value of the Saloon," *American Journal of Sociology* 3 (July 1897): 1–12; Roy Rosenzweig, *Eight Hours for What We Will: Workers and Leisure in an Industrial City, 1870–1920* (New York: Cambridge University Press, 1983), 49, 188–89, 57–64; and Madelon Powers, *Faces Along the Bar: Lore and Order in the Workingman's Saloon, 1870–1920* (Chicago: University of Chicago Press, 1998).

96. Quoted in Barbara Scharf, *Mr. Dooley's Chicago* (Garden City, N.Y.: Anchor Press/Doubleday, 1977), 21.

97. Charles Fanning, *Finley Peter Dunne and the Chicago Irish: Autobiography of an American Ethnic Group* (Lexington: University of Kentucky Press, 1987), 24.

98. Dunne quoted in Fanning, *Irish Voice in America*, 218; Charles Fanning, *Finley Peter Dunne and Mr. Dooley: The Chicago Years* (Lexington: University Press of Kentucky, 1978), 225–32, quotes at 226, 231.

99. Scharf, *Mr. Dooley's Chicago*, 18–22; Fanning, *Irish Voice in America*, quotes, 214; Finley Peter Dunne, *Mr. Dooley in Peace and in War* (Boston: Small, Maynard & Co., 1899). See also Charles Fanning, "Mr. Dooley Reconsidered: Community, Memory, Journalism, and the Oral Tradition," in Ellen Skerrett, ed., *At the Crossroads: Old Saint Patrick's and the Chicago Irish* (Chicago: Wild Onion Books, 1997), 69–83.

100. Fanning, *Finley Peter Dunne and Mr. Dooley*, 157–59; and Ron Ebest, *Private Histories: The Writing of Irish Americans, 1900–1935* (Notre Dame, Ind.: University of Notre Dame Press, 2005), 66–70, 75. Patrick Ford's *Irish World*, in its respectable new Republican form, refused to accept advertising for Dunne's Mr. Dooley books, apparently because Dunne's use of Irish dialect. See Dunne to Herbert Small, November 7, 1899, Finley Peter Dunne Letters, Chicago History Museum. On persistent skepticism about the pursuit of wealth and advancement and an antipathy toward those who sought to distance themselves from the

community, see Meagher, "Introduction," 10; Paul R. Messbarger, *Fiction with a Parochial Purpose: Social Use of American Catholic Literature, 1884–1900* (Brookline, Mass.: Boston University Press, 1971); and David Noel Doyle, *Irish Americans, Native Rights, and National Empires: The Structure, Divisions, and Attitudes of the Catholic Minority in the Decade of Expansion* (New York: Arno Press, 1976), 55.

101. Quoted in Charles Fanning, "The Literary Dimension," in McCaffrey et al., *Irish in Chicago*, 108–9.

102. On Nast's caricatures, see Joshua Brown, *Beyond the Lines: Pictorial Reporting, Everyday Life, and the Crisis of Gilded Age America* (Berkeley: University of California Press, 2002).

103. Kerry Soper, "From Swarthy Ape to Sympathetic Everyman and Subversive Trickster: The Development of Irish Caricature in American Comic Strips Between 1890 and 1920," *Journal of American Studies* 39 (2005): 257–86.

104. Ibid., 286–95, quotes at 290, 291. On the highly gendered discourse on Irish American upward mobility and the symbol of the striving Irish wife in Irish American popular culture, see Harrigan's plays generally and especially *Cordelia's Aspirations* (1883); Meagher, *Columbia Guide to Irish American History*, 180; and Diner, *Erin's Daughters*, 66. For the trials and tribulations of upwardly mobile families in Mr. Dooley's Bridgeport, see "The Piano in the Parlor" and "The Denehy Boy Back from Notre Dame" in Charles Fanning, ed., *Mr. Dooley and the Chicago Irish* (New York: Arno Press, 1976), 207–9, 220–22.

105. George McManus, "McManus Points Road to Comic Art Success," twentieth anniversary of *Bringing Up Father*, newspaper supplement, King Features Syndicate, 1932, 4, quoted in Soper, "From Swarthy Ape," 289.

106. Soper, "From Swarthy Ape," quotes at 293, 292–93.

107. J. W. Sullivan, *Tenement Tales of New York* (New York: Henry Holt & Co., 1895), 91–113; and Ebest, *Private Histories*, 203–10. Sullivan's book was published in a pocket-size popular fiction series that appears to be aimed at a working-class audience. For another satire of bourgeois literary circles, see Katherine E. Conway, *The Way of the World and Other Ways: A Story of Our Set* (Boston: Pilot, 1900).

108. Fanning, *Irish Voice in America*, 178–97, contains a rare sketch of Sullivan and his work, locates him among early Irish American urban realists, and draws the analogy between Sullivan's writing and James T. Farrell's. For other Irish American writers who confronted the theme of anti-Semitism, see Ebest, *Private Histories*, 203–10. On the romantic nationalist tradition, see also Jacobson, *Special Sorrows*, 123–35.

109. Charles Fanning and Ellen Skerrett, "James T. Farrell and Washington Park," *Chicago History* 7 (1979), 87. On the black migration, see James R. Grossman, *Land of Hope: Chicago, Black Southerners, and the Great Migration* (Chicago: University of Chicago Press, 1989); and Chicago Commission on Race Relations, *The Negro in Chicago: A Study of Race Relations and a Race Riot* (Chicago: University of Chicago Press, 1922). Washington Park itself became a mecca for white and especially African American radicals during the Great Depression. See Richard Wright, *Black Boy* (New York: Harper & Row, 1946**)**, and St. Clair Drake and Horace Cayton, *Black Metropolis: A Study of Negro Life in a Northern City* (New York: Harcourt, Brace, & Co., 1945).

110. Farrell, *Studs Lonigan*, 18. See also Chicago Commission on Race Relations, *Negro in Chicago*.

111. Farrell, *Studs Lonigan*, 375–76, 455–58, 560; Lauren Onkey, "James Farrell's *Studs Lonigan* Trilogy and the Anxieties of Race," *Éire-Ireland* 40 (Fall–Winter 2005): 105; and John McGreevy, *Parish Boundaries: The Catholic Encounter with Race in the Twentieth Century*

North (Chicago: University of Chicago Press, 1996), passim. Anxieties about the encroachment of new immigrants were also characteristic of the earlier popular novelist and journalist Maurice Egan, who deplored the fact that the immigrant Irish were "fading away before the swarm of newcomers . . . the outcasts of old nations." See Fanning, *Irish Voice in America*, 205.

112. On the real-life context for Farrell's story, see Edgar M. Branch, *Studs Lonigan's Neighborhood and the Making of James T. Farrell* (Newton, Mass.: Arts End Books, 1996), 15–16; Ellen Skerrett, "The Catholic Dimension," in Lawrence McCaffrey, Ellen Skerrett, Michael Funchion, and Charles Fanning, eds., *The Irish in Chicago* (Urbana: University of Illinois Press, 1987), 52; and Fanning, "Literary Dimension," 128–29.

113. William V. Shannon, *The American Irish: A Social and Political Portrait* (New York: Collier Books, 1963), 252.

114. Farrell, *Studs Lonigan*, 79.

115. Ibid., 80.

116. Ibid.

117. Ibid., 402.

118. Robert K. Landers, *An Honest Writer: The Life and Times of James T. Farrell* (San Francisco: Encounter Books, 2004), 35; and Onkey, "Farrell's *Studs Lonigan* Trilogy," 112–13.

119. Farrell, *Studs Lonigan*, 454, 455.

120. On the Chicago School of Sociology, see Martin Bulmer, *The Chicago School of Sociology: Institutionalization, Diversity, and the Rise of Sociological Research* (Chicago: University of Chicago Press, 1984). On its "race relations cycle," see Stow Persons, *Ethnic Studies at Chicago, 1905–45* (Urbana: University of Illinois Press, 1987), 62–75. For Farrell's time at the University of Chicago, see Robert K. Landers, *An Honest Writer: The Life and Times of James T. Farrell* (San Francisco: Encounter Books, 2004), 52–70. On the influence of the Chicago sociologists, see Carla Cappetti, *Writing Chicago: Modernism, Ethnography, and the Novel* (New York: Columbia University Press, 1993), 112–25.

121. Whitfield, *In Search of American Jewish Culture*, 6.

122. Farrell, *Studs Lonigan*, 408.

123. In a speech before the First American Writers' Conference in 1935, just as he was finishing his *Studs Lonigan* trilogy, Farrell said that he had been particularly influenced by Langston Hughes and Richard Wright, both of whom shared his temporary connection with the Communist Party. He emphasized the sorts of stereotypes against which both Irish and African Americans struggled. See Onkey, "Farrell's *Studs Lonigan* Trilogy," 107. On Farrell's early political commitments, see Alan M. Wald, *James T. Farrell: The Revolutionary Socialist Years* (New York: New York University Press, 1978).

124. Meagher, *Columbia Guide to Irish American History*, 108.

CHAPTER 5: THE MACHINE

1. "Class Lines Vanish at Sullivan Burial," *New York Times*, September 16, 1913, 5; *New York Sun*, September 16, 1913, 4, quoted in Daniel Czitrom, "Underworlds and Underdogs: Big Tim Sullivan and Metropolitan Politics in New York, 1889–1913," *Journal of American History* 78, no. 2 (September 1991): 558.

2. "Thousands Mourn at 'Big Tim's' Bier," *New York Times*, September 15, 1913, 9; Richard F. Welch, *King of the Bowery: Big Tim Sullivan, Tammany Hall, and New York City from the*

Gilded Age to the Progressive Era (Madison, N.J.: Fairleigh Dickinson University Press, 2008), 183–85.

3. Czitrom, "Underworlds and Underdogs," 536–58; Welch, *King of the Bowery,* passim.

4. William V. Shannon, *The American Irish* (New York: Macmillan, 1963), 139–40.

5. Terry Golway, *So Others Might Live: A History of New York's Bravest, the NYFD from 1700 to the Present* (New York: Basic Books, 2002), 78.

6. Gary Gerstle and John Mollenkopf, "The Political Incorporation of Immigrants, Then and Now," in Gary Gerstle and John Mollenkopf, eds., *E Pluribus Unum? Contemporary and Historical Perspectives on Immigrant Political Incorporation* (New York: Russell Sage Foundation, 2001), 1.

7. John Paul Bocock, "The Irish Conquest," *Forum,* April 1894, quote, 186; Steven P. Erie, *Rainbow's End: Irish-Americans and the Dilemmas of Urban Machine Politics, 1840–1945* (Berkeley: University of California Press, 1988), 2.

8. Erie, *Rainbow's End,* 101; and David Hammack, *Power and Society: Greater New York at the Turn of the Century* (New York: Russell Sage Foundation, 1982), 89. On Sullivan, see Czitrom, "Underworlds and Underdogs," 536–58.

9. Michael F. Funchion, "The Political and Nationalist Dimensions," in Lawrence J. McCaffrey, Ellen Skerrett, Michael F. Funchion, and Charles Fanning, eds., *The Irish in Chicago* (Urbana: University of Illinois Press, 1987), 72, 81, 96; and Thomas M. Henderson, *Tammany Hall and the New Immigrants: The Old World in the New Progressive Years* (New York: Arno Press, 1976), 47, 90.

10. Avinere Toigo, interview by Cullom Davis, 1972–73, interview T573, transcript, Illinois State Oral History Collection, University of Illinois at Springfield. My thanks to Tom Mackaman for this reference.

11. Henry Childs Merwin, "The Irish in American Life," *Atlantic Monthly,* March 1896, 294–95, quoted in Matthew Frye Jacobson, *Whiteness of a Different Color: European Immigrants and the Alchemy of Race* (Cambridge, Mass.: Harvard University Press, 1999), 49.

12. E. A. Ross, *Old World in the New* (New York: Century, 1913), 275.

13. Nathan Glazer and Daniel Patrick Moynihan, eds., *Beyond the Melting Pot: The Negroes, Puerto Ricans, Jews, Italians, and Irish of New York City* (Cambridge, Mass.: MIT Press, 1970).

14. Jane Addams, "Why the Ward Boss Rules," *Outlook* 58 (April 2, 1898), 879–89, reprinted in Christopher Lasch, *The Social Thought of Jane Addams* (Indianapolis: Bobbs-Merrill, 1965), 124–33.

15. Chris McNickle, *To Be Mayor of New York: Ethnic Politics in the City* (New York: Columbia University Press, 1993), 8.

16. Edward M. Levine, *The Irish and Irish Politicians: A Study in Cultural and Social Alienation* (Notre Dame, Ind.: University of Notre Dame Press, 1966); Glazer and Moynihan, *Beyond the Melting Pot*; and David Noel Doyle, *Irish Americans, Native Rights, and National Empires: The Structure, Divisions, and Attitudes of the Catholic Minority in the Decade of Expansion* (New York: Arno Press, 1976), 57.

17. John Bodnar, *The Transplanted: A History of Immigrants in Urban America* (Bloomington: Indiana University Press, 1987), 204; Henderson, *Tammany Hall and New Immigrants,* 73–75; Jeff Kisseloff, *You Must Remember This: An Oral History of Manhattan from the 1890s to World War II* (San Diego, Calif.: Harcourt Brace Jovanovich, 1989), quote at 414.

18. John Paul Bocock, "The Irish Conquest," *Forum,* April 1894, 186; McCaffrey et al., *Irish in*

Chicago, map and table, 160–61; Henderson, *Tammany Hall and New Immigrants*, 73–77; Ronald Bayor and Timothy Meagher, eds., *The New York Irish* (Baltimore, Md.: Johns Hopkins University Press, 1996), table A.6, 558–59, map, 571.

19. Charles Edward Merriam and Harold Foote Gosnell, *Nonvoting: Causes and Methods of Control* (Chicago: University of Chicago Press, 1924), 90–96; and Ewa Morawska, "Immigrants, Transnationalism, and Ethnicization: A Comparison of This Great Wave and the Last," in Gerstle and Mollenkopf, *E Pluribus Unum?*, 175–212. Evelyn Savidge Sterne has provided the fullest analysis of this process, but her observations apply to larger cities; see her *Ballots and Bibles: Ethnic Politics and the Catholic Church in Providence* (Ithaca, N.Y.: Cornell University Press, 2003). See also Sterne, "Beyond the Boss: Immigration and Political Culture from 1880 to 1940," in Gerstle and Mollenkopf, *E Pluribus Unum?*, 33–66, quote at 57; Sterne, "Bringing Religion into Working Class History: Parish, Public, and Politics in Providence, 1890–1930," *Social Science History* 24, no. 1 (2000): 149–82.

20. Martin Shefter, "Electoral Foundations of the Political Machine: New York City, 1884–1897," in Joel Silbey, Allen G. Bogue, and William H. Flanigan, eds., *The History of American Electoral Behavior* (Princeton, N.J.: Princeton University Press, 1978), 263–98.

21. Richard Wade, "Urbanization," in C. Vann Woodward, ed., *The Comparative Approach to American History* (New York: Basic Books, 1968), quoted in Shefter, "Electoral Foundations," 272. See also Erie, *Rainbow's End*, 28, 71.

22. On the political functions of the saloon, see Perry Duis, *The Saloon: Public Drinking in Chicago and Boston, 1880–1920* (Urbana: University of Illinois Press, 1983); Kingsdale, "The Best Poor Man's Club: Social Functions of the Urban Working-class Saloon," *American Quarterly* 24, no. 4 (October 1973): 472–89; Madelon Powers, *Faces Along the Bar: Lore and Order in the Workingman's Saloon, 1870–1920* (Chicago: University of Chicago Press, 1998); and Roy Rosenzweig, *Eight Hours for What We Will: Workers and Leisure in an Industrial City* (New York: Cambridge University Press, 1983), 171–90.

23. Paul Michael Green, "Irish Chicago: The Multiethnic Road to Machine Success," in Melvin G. Holli and Peter d'Alory Jones, eds., *Ethnic Chicago: A Multicultural Portrait*, 4th ed. (Grand Rapids, Mich.: Eerdmans, 1995), 223.

24. Jane Addams, "Why the Ward Boss Rules"; and Nancy Joan Weiss, *Charles Francis Murphy, 1858–1924: Respectability and Responsibility in Tammany Politics* (Northampton, Mass.: Smith College, 1968). On Sullivan, see Czitrom, "Underworlds and Underdogs," 536–58.

25. Alfred E. Smith, *Up to Now: An Autobiography* (New York: Viking Press, 1929), 30–33; Shefter, "Electoral Foundations," 290–91; Czitrom, "Underworlds and Underdogs," 543–44.

26. Green, "Irish Chicago," 223–25; Herman Kogan and Lloyd Wendt, *Lords of the Levee: The Story of Bathhouse John and Hinky Dink* (Evanston, Ill.: Northwestern University Press, 2005), 9–33.

27. T. J. English, *Paddy Whacked: The Untold Story of the Irish American Gangster* (New York: HarperCollins, 2005), 106.

28. *Chicago Herald and Examiner*, June 5, 1924, quoted in Green, "Irish Chicago," 223.

29. Hammack, *Power and Society*, 137–39, 315; Shannon, *American Irish*, 74–76.

30. Shannon, *American Irish*, 199.

31. Jack Beatty, *The Rascal King: The Life and Times of James Michael Curley, 1874–1958* (Reading, Mass.: Addison-Wesley, 1992).

32. Carl Sandburg, *The Chicago Race Riots, July 1919* (1919; reprint Boston: Houghton Mifflin Harcourt, 1969), 2; and Frederic M. Thrasher, *The Gang: A Study of 1,313 Gangs in Chicago*

(Chicago: University of Chicago Press, 1927), 452–86. On the black Republican machine, see also Harold Gosnell, *Negro Politicians: The Rise of Negro Politics in Chicago* (Chicago: University of Chicago Press, 1967), 37–62. On "Big Bill" Thompson's reputation among the Irish for anti-Catholicism, see William Tuttle, *Race Riot: Chicago in the Red Summer of 1919* (Urbana: University of Illinois Press, 1996).

33. "Bearded Rabbis and Erin's Sons Acclaim J. Ham," *Chicago Tribune*, November 1, 1920, 6.

34. Michael J. Funchion, "The Political and National Dimension," in McCaffrey et al., *Irish in Chicago*, 64; and Lawrence J. McCaffrey, "Forging Ahead and Looking Back," in Bayor and Meagher, *New York Irish*, 222–43.

35. Bodnar, *Transplanted*, 204; Oliver Simmons, "Passing of the Sullivan Dynasty," *Muncey's Magazine* 50 (December 1913), 408, quoted in Henderson, *Tammany Hall and New Immigrants*, 10. See also Kevin Kenny, *The American Irish: A History* (Harlow, U.K.: Pearson Education, 2000), 161.

36. "West Wise Foreign Know-Nothings," *Chicago Tribune*, March 27, 1890, 4; and "Long and Short Terms, In the New Wards, the Candidates Must be Designated," March 15, 1890, 2. See also "Hordes of Ignorant New Voters," *Chicago Tribune*, March 17, 1891, 5.

37. Reed Ueda, "Naturalization and Citizenship," in *Harvard Encyclopedia of American Ethnic Groups* (Cambridge, Mass.: Harvard University Press, 1980), 747; Humbert S. Nelli, *The Italians in Chicago, 1880–1930: A Study in Ethnic Mobility* (New York: Oxford University Press, 1970), 48–49; Mark Wyman, *Round-Trip to America: The Immigrants Return to Europe, 1880–1930* (Ithaca, N.Y.: Cornell University Press, 1993), 10–12; Erie, *Rainbow's End*, 85–106; and Alexander Keyssar, *The Right to Vote: The Contested History of Democracy in the United States*, rev. ed. (New York: Basic Books, 2009), 127.

38. Philip L. Seman, "Citizenship Survey," ms. (1914), 4; and Charles E. Merriam, "The Unnaturalized," ms. (1924), 14, 16, both in Charles E. Merriam Papers, Box 114, Folder 1, Special Collections, Regenstein Library, University of Chicago; Kristi Anderson, *The Creation of a Democratic Majority, 1928–1936* (Chicago: University of Chicago Press, 1979), 39–41, 88–89; and James J. Connolly, *The Triumph of Ethnic Progressivism: Urban Political Culture in Boston, 1900–1925* (Cambridge, Mass.: Harvard University Press, 1998), 55–60.

39. Donald Tricarico, "Influence of the Irish on Italian Communal Adaptation in Greenwich Village," in Francis Femminella, ed., *Italians and Irish in America: Proceedings of the Sixteenth Annual Conference of the American Italian Historical Association* (Staten Island, N.Y.: American Italian Historical Association, 1985), 57.

40. Thomas Lee Philpott, *The Slum and the Ghetto: Neighborhood Deterioration and Middle-Class Reform, Chicago, 1880–1930* (New York: Oxford University Press, 1978), 86.

41. "Many Heads Broken," *Chicago Tribune*, March 16, 1893, 3.

42. Erie, *Rainbow's End*, 11. On the problem in Chicago during the early 1900s, see Bertha Gray, "Election Frauds [Chicago], 1919–1930," n.d., Harold F. Gosnell Papers, Box 18, Folder 5, Special Collections, Regenstein Library, University of Chicago.

43. Tricarico, "Influence of the Irish," 57; Erie, *Rainbow's End*, 105; and Harold Gosnell, *Machine Politics: Chicago Model*, 2nd ed. (Chicago: University of Chicago Press, 1968), 30–32, 44–45, 64–66.

44. Gosnell, *Machine Politics*, 30–32, 44–45, 64–66.

45. Wendt and Kogan, *Lords of the Levee*; Czitrom, "Underworlds and Underdogs," 545; Henderson, *Tammany Hall and New Immigrants*, 1–10.

46. Henderson, *Tammany Hall and New Immigrants*, 43–46.

47. John Kelley, "D'Andrea 'Vivas' Loud; Johnny De Pow 'Veevas,' Too," *Chicago Tribune*, January 28, 1921, 9; "Political Bomb Injures 17," ibid., February 12, 1921, 1; "Assassin Band Kills 2," ibid., March 9, 1921, 1; and "Nineteenth Ward Killers Get 13th Victim," ibid., August 15, 1921, 1. See also Nelli, *Italians in Chicago,* 88–112. For a description of the ward in transition from Irish to Italian, and the strength of the old machine there, see "Nineteenth Ward's Crowning Glory," *Chicago Tribune*, October 10, 1897, 25; and "What Is the Nineteenth Ward?" ibid., February 13, 1898, 25.

48. "Riot Mars Funeral of Rabbi Joseph," *New York Times*, July 31, 1902, p. 1; Moses Rischin, *The Promised City: New York's Jews, 1870–1914* (Cambridge, Mass.: Harvard University Press, 1962), 91; Rudolf Glanz, *Jew and Irish: Historic Group Relations and Immigration* (New York: Waldon Press, 1966); and Tony Michels, *A Fire in their Hearts: Yiddish Socialists in New York* (Cambridge, Mass.: Harvard University Press, 2005), 44. On Tammany's growing intolerance of anti-Semitism among its minions, see Chris McNickle, *To Be Mayor of New York: Ethnic Politics in the City* (New York: Columbia University Press, 1993), 13–17; Welch, *King of the Bowery*, 48.

49. Quoted in Rischin, *Promised City,* 266.

50. Erie, *Rainbow's End,* 102–3; William L. Riordan, *Plunkitt of Tammany Hall: A Series of Very Plain Talks on Very Practical Subjects,* ed. Terrence J. McDonald (Boston: Bedford Books, 1994), 75; and Louis Eisenstein and Elliot Rosenberg, *A Stripe of Tammany's Tiger* (New York: Robert Speller & Sons, 1966), 10–17.

51. Eisenstein and Rosenberg, *Stripe of Tammany's Tiger,* quote at 30.

52. Hammack, *Power and Society,* 170.

53. Weiss, *Charles Francis Murphy;* Eisenstein and Rosenberg, *Stripe of Tammany's Tiger,* 21; and "Back from Tammany Hall to Good Ground," *New York Tribune*, August 24, 1919, 4.

54. Chris McNickle, "When New York Was Irish, and After," in Bayor and Meagher, *New York Irish,* 339–40; Hammack, *Power and Society,* 170–71.

55. Henderson, *Tammany Hall and New Immigrants,* 211–16, 227, 231–34.

56. Funchion, "Political and Nationalist Dimensions," 65–67; Richard Allen Morton, *Justice and Humanity: Edward F. Dunne, Illinois Progressive* (Carbondale: Southern Illinois University, 1997); and Thomas R. Pegram, *Partisans and Progressives: Private Interest and Public Policy in Illinois, 1870–1922* (Urbana: University of Illinois Press, 1992), 190–96. On numerous other Irish American urban progressives, see John Buenker, *Urban Liberalism and Progressive Reform* (New York: Scribner's, 1973). On the cross-class political alliance Dunne created in Chicago, see Georg Leidenberger, *Chicago's Progressive Alliance: Labor and the Bid for Public Streetcars* (DeKalb: Northern Illinois University Press, 2006).

57. Ed Flynn, *You're the Boss: The Practice of American Politics* (New York:, Collier Books, 1962), 53, quoted in Weiss, *Murphy,* 87. See also Robert F. Wesser, *A Response to Progressivism: The Democratic Party and New York Politics, 1902–1918* (New York: New York University Press, 1986).

58. Weiss, *Murphy,* 82–91; Hammack, *Power and Society,* 168, 180.

59. "Smith and the Newer Americans," *Chicago Tribune*, August 5, 1928, F1, quoted in Robert A. Slayton, *Empire Statesman: The Rise and Redemption of Alfred E. Smith* (New York: Free Press, 2001), 35.

60. Eddie Cantor, *Take My Life* (Garden City, N.Y.: Doubleday, 1957), 187–88, quoted in Slayton, *Empire Statesman,* 63.

61. McNickle, *To Be Mayor of New York,* 12–19, 30; Erie, *Rainbow's End,* 103–5; Slayton, *Empire Statesman,* 76, 81–100. On the relationship between labor movements and machine sup-

port for social and economic reform, see Buenker, *Urban Liberalism and Progressive Reform*; David Montgomery, *The Fall of the House of Labor: The Workplace, the State, and Labor Activism, 1865–1925* (New York: Cambridge University Press, 1987), 303.

62. McNickle, *To Be Mayor of New York*, 20–32; Matthew Josephson and Hannah Josephson, *Al Smith: Hero of the Cities* (Boston: Houghton Mifflin, 1969), 141, 232; Shannon, *American Irish*, 160–75.

63. Aileen Kraditor, *The Ideas of the Woman Suffrage Movement, 1890–1920* (New York: Columbia University Press, 1965); James J. Kenneally, "Catholicism and Woman's Suffrage in Massachusetts," *Catholic Historical Review* 53 (April 1967): 43–57; Barbara Solomon, *Ancestors and Immigrants, a Changing New England Tradition* (Cambridge, Mass.: Harvard University Press, 1956), 54, quoted in Buenker, *Urban Liberalism and Progressive Reform*, 158; and John D. Buenker, "The Urban Political Machine and Woman Suffrage," *Historian* 33 (February 1971): 264–79.

64. Diner, *Erin's Daughters in America*, 147–52; Kraditor, *Woman Suffrage Movement*, 123–62.

65. On Molly Donahue, a recognizable character in the Irish American community, see Deirdre Mageean, "Making Sense and Providing Structure: Irish-American Women in the Parish Neighborhood," in Christiane Harzig et al., eds., *Peasant Maids, City Women: From the European Countryside to Urban America* (Ithaca, N.Y.: Cornell University Press, 1997), 253–55, and the columns, "Molly Donahue and the Divided Skirt," "Molly Tries to Vote," "The New Woman," and "The Woman's Bible," all reproduced in Charles Fanning, ed., *Mr. Dooley and the Chicago Irish: An Anthology* (New York: Arno Press, 1976), 201–15.

66. Nancy Schrom Dye, *As Equals and as Sisters: Feminism, the Labor Movement, and the Women's Trade Union League of New York* (Columbia: University of Missouri Press, 1980); Agnes Nestor, *Woman's Labor Leader* (Rockford, Ill.: Bellevue Books, 1954), 87–104; and Maureen A. Flanagan, *Seeing with Their Hearts: Chicago Women and the Vision of the Good Society, 1871–1933* (Princeton, N.J.: Princeton University Press, 2002), 77–83.

67. Dye, *As Equals and as Sisters*, quote at 125. On Boston, see Sarah Deutsch, *Women and the City: Gender, Space, and Power in Boston, 1870–1940* (New York: Oxford University Press, 2000), 258.

68. "Women Win Votes of Longshoremen," *New York Times*, July 13, 1915, 11; "Subway's Diggers Cheer Suffragists," ibid., June 30, 1915, 11, quote; and "Margaret Hinchey Tells of Wilson," *New York Times*, February 5, 1914, 9. See also Meredith Tax, *The Rising of the Women: Feminist Solidarity and Class Conflict, 1880–1917* (New York: Monthly Review Press, 1980), 174–78.

69. Deutsch, *Women and the City*, 222–23, quote at 223.

70 Foley to Mrs. Bagley, July 29, 1918, Foley Papers, Carton 1, Folder 7, Schlesinger Library, Radcliffe College, Cambridge, Mass., quoted in Deutsch, *Women and the City*, 227. See also Dennis P. Ryan, *Beyond the Ballot Box: A Social History of the Boston Irish, 1845–1917* (Rutherford, N.J.: Fairleigh Dickinson University Press, 1983), 51–52.

71. Deutsch, *Women and the City*, 222–28, quote at 228.

72. Kraditor, *Woman Suffrage Movement*, 147–62; Kenneally, "Catholicism and Woman's Suffrage," 51–52; Stephen Norwood, *Labor's Flaming Youth: Telephone Operators and Labor Militancy, 1878–1923* (Urbana: University of Illinois Press, 1990), 143–45; Flanagan, *Seeing with Their Hearts*, 109–14; John Keiser, *John Fitzpatrick and Progressive Unionism, 1915–1925*, Ph.D. diss., Northwestern University, 1965. On the shift of many urban machine politicians from opposition to support of suffrage, see Buenker, *Urban Liberalism and Progressive Reform*, 156–62; and Buenker, "Urban Political Machine and Woman Suffrage," 264–79.

73. McNickle, *To Be Mayor of New York*, 9. For the Dooley sketch, see Fanning, *Mr. Dooley and Chicago Irish*, 176–78.

74. *Dziennik Chicagoski*, February 4, 1922, Chicago Foreign Language Survey, quoted in Dominic A. Pacyga, *Polish Immigrants and Industrial Chicago: Workers on the South Side, 1880–1922* (Columbus: Ohio State University Press, 1991), 198.

75. Erie, *Rainbow's End*, 13; McNickle, *To Be Mayor of New York*, quote at 8–9.

76. John R. McKivigan and Thomas J. Robertson, "The Irish American Worker in Transition, 1877–1914: New York City as a Test Case," in Bayor and Meagher, *New York Irish*, estimate the proportion of Irish in city jobs in 1930 at one-third (313); Erie, *Rainbow's End*, at just under one-fourth (59, table 7, 60). In either case, the Irish share was grossly disproportionate. On Chicago, see Funchion, "Political and Nationalist Dimensions," 69–70.

77. Erie, *Rainbow's End*, 11, 96–98, 103–13, 69–71, 80, and 102–6; and Ronald H. Bayor, *Neighbors in Conflict: The Irish, Germans, Jews, and Italians of New York City, 1929–1941* (Baltimore, Md.: Johns Hopkins University Press, 1978), 30–56.

78. Erie, *Rainbow's End*, 103–13, 69–71, 80, and 102–6; and McGivigan and Robertson, "Irish American Worker," 313–16.

79. On bridging and bonding social capital in this context, see David R. Roediger and James R. Barrett, "Making New Immigrants 'Inbetween': Irish Hosts and White Panethnicity, 1890–1930," in Nancy Foner and George Frederickson, eds., *Not Just Black and White: Historical and Contemporary Perspectives on Immigration, Race, and Ethnicity in the United States.* (New York: Russell Sage Foundation Press, 2004), 178–79. David Roediger and Mark Leff helped me to clarify my thinking on this point.

80. Erie, *End of the Rainbow*, 105; *L'Italia*, October 29, 1892, Chicago Foreign Language Press Survey, I-F-1. On the New Orleans lynchings, see John S. Kendall, "Who Killa de Chief?" *Louisiana Historical Quarterly* 22 (April 1939): 492–530; Nelli, *Italians in Chicago*, 130–31; "Chief Hennesy Avenged," *New York Times*, March 15, 1891, 1; and Jacobson, *Whiteness of Different Color*, 56–61.

81. "Seek a Unity G.O.P. Meeting for New York," *Chicago Tribune*, July 1, 1918, 11; " 'Johnny De Pow' Faces 'Burial' By Undertaker," ibid., February 10, 1919, 11; and John Allswang, *A House for all Peoples* (Lexington: University of Kentucky Press, 1971).

82. Bayor, *Neighbors in Conflict*, 30, 33–35; Alfred Connable and Edward Silberfarb, *Tigers of Tammany* (New York: Holt, Rinehart & Winston, 1967), 316–17.

83. Donald Tricarico, *The Italians of Greenwich Village: The Social Structure and Transformation of an Ethnic Community* (New York: Center for Migration Studies, 1984), 59–62.

84. Daniel Patrick Moynihan, "The Irish," in Glazer and Moynihan, *Beyond the Melting Pot*; Kenny, *Irish in America*, 217; McNickle, *To Be Mayor of New York*, 33–37; McNickle, "When New York Was Irish, and After," 339; Allswang, *House for All Peoples*, 103–8; Funchion, "Political and Nationalist Dimension," 80–91; Green, "Irish Chicago." See also Erie, *Rainbow's End*, 107–39.

85. Walker quoted in Bayor and Meagher, "Conclusion," in Bayor and Meagher, *New York Irish*, 536; Eisenstein and Rosenberg, *Stripe of Tammany's Tiger*, 43, 176.

86. Erie, *End of the Rainbow*, 107–8, 111–18. On Depression conditions in New York, see Irving Bernstein, *The Lean Years: A Social History of the American Worker, 1920–1933* (Boston: Houghton Mufflin, 1960), 291–96.

87. Erie, *End of the Rainbow*, 118; Anderson, *Creation of a Democratic Majority*, 37–38; Bayor and Meagher, "Conclusion," 536.

88. White and Mouzen quoted in Slayton, *Empire Statesman*, x. See also Alan J. Lichtman,

Prejudice and the Old Politics: The Presidential Election of 1928 (Chapel Hill: University of North Carolina Press, 1969).

89. Thomas N. Brown, "The Political Irish: Politicians and Rebels," in David Noel Doyle and Owen Dudley Edwards, eds., *America and Ireland, 1776–1976: The American Identity and the Irish Connection* (Westport, Conn.: Greenwood Press, 1980), 145.

90. McNickle, *To Be Mayor of New York*, 34.

91. Quoted in Thomas Kessner, *Fiorello H. La Guardia and the Making of Modern New York* (New York: McGraw-Hill, 1989), 161.

92. Ibid., 253; Arthur Mann, *La Guardia Comes to Power: 1933* (Philadelphia: Lippincott, 1965); and Jay P. Dolan, *The Irish Americans: A History* (New York: Bloomsbury Press, 2008), quote at 255.

93. Henderson, *Tammany Hall and New Immigrants*, 43–46, quotes at 45, 46; Erie, *Rainbow's End*, 85–91, 118–33; Glazer and Moynihan, *Beyond the Melting Pot*, 221–29; and Bayor, *Neighbors in Conflict*, 37. Where the Labor Party made inroads among the Irish, it tended to be with Irish American candidates in heavily Irish neighborhoods in Brooklyn and the Bronx. See L. Jordan, "Irish and the American Labor Party," August 24, 1938, File 7, Article 3, Federal Writers Project, *The Irish in New York*, New York City Municipal Archives, Microfilm, Reel 58.

94. Kessner, *La Guardia*, 290.

95. Ibid., 288–90.

96. Erie, *End of the Rainbow*, 90, 122; Bayor, *Neighbors in Conflict*, 106–7, 98–99, 104; Kessner, *La Guardia*, 288–90; McNickle, "When New York Was Irish, and After," 354; Ruth Jacknow Markowitz, *My Daughter, the Teacher: Jewish Teachers in the New York City Schools* (New Brunswick, N.J.: Rutgers University Press, 1993), 2, 33, 154–55, 162–63; Marjorie Murphy, *Blackboard Unions: The AFT and the NEA, 1900–1980* (Ithaca, N.Y.: Cornell University Press, 1990); Hasia R. Diner and Beryl L. Benderly, *Her Works Praise Her: A History of Jewish Women in America from Colonial Times to the Present* (N.Y.: Basic Books, 2003), 223; and John Higham, *Send These to Me: Jews and Other Immigrants in Urban America* (New York: Atheneum, 1975), 190–91. On the international issues, see John F. Stack, Jr., *International Conflict in an American City: Boston's Irish, Italians, and Jews, 1935–1944* (Westport, Conn.: Greenwood Press, 1979); and Leonard Dinnerstein, *Antisemitism in America* (New York: Oxford University Press, 1994), 113–14.

97. Quoted in Bayor, *Neighbors in Conflict*, 6.

98. Dolan, *Irish Americans*, 235–36; and Bruce Nelson, *Divided We Stand: American Workers and the Struggle for Black Equality* (Princeton, N.J.: Princeton University Press, 2001), 70. See also Bayor, *Neighbors in Conflict*, 87–108; Dinnerstein, *Antisemitism in America*, 113–23.

99. Stack, *International Conflict in an American City*, 22–23, 55–56, 134–39, 92, 94, 130, 151; Bayor, *Neighbors in Conflict*, 152–56; and Dinnerstein, *Antisemitism in America*, 132–33. See also Stephen H. Norwood, "Marauding Youth and the Christian Front: Antisemitic Violence in Boston and New York During World War II," *Jewish American History* 91 (2003): 233–67.

100. Steven Fraser, "The 'Labor Question,'" in Steven Fraser and Gary Gerstle, eds., *The Rise and Fall of the New Deal Order, 1930–1980* (Princeton, N.J.: Princeton University Press, 1989), 72–74; and Steven Fraser, *Labor Will Rule: Sidney Hillman and the Rise of American Labor* (New York: Free Press, 1991), 356, 366, 417.

101. Joshua B. Freeman, *Working-Class New York: Life and Labor Since World War II* (New York: New Press, 2000), 72–75, 83–84.

102. Joshua M. Zeitz, *White Ethnic New York: Jews, Catholics, and the Shaping of Postwar Politics* (Chapel Hill: University of North Carolina Press, 2007), 117–25; Freeman, *Working-Class New York*, 83–84; and Matt J. O'Brien, "After the Flood," in Ruth Barton, ed., *Screening Irish America: Representing Irish American in Film and Television* (Dublin: Irish Academic Press, 2009). See also John Wayne's 1952 film *Big Jim McLain*.

103. On Catholic opposition to Coughlin, see Alan Brinkley, *Voices of Protest: Huey Long, Father Coughlin, and the Great Depression* (New York: Knopf, 1982), 156–58; and Fraser, *Labor Will Rule*, 338, 367, 424. On left-wing influence in some Irish American labor circles, see Joshua B. Freeman, "Catholics, Communists, and Republicans: Irish Workers and the Organization of the Transit Workers Union," in Michael H. Frisch and Daniel J. Walkowitz, eds., *Working-Class America: Essays on Labor, Community, and American Society* (Urbana: University of Illinois Press, 1983), 256–83.

104. Bayor, *Neighbors in Conflict*, 39–40; and George Q. Flynn, *American Catholics and the Roosevelt Presidency* (Lexington: University of Kentucky Press, 1968). On the persistence of Irish political power in Brooklyn, see Jerome Krase, "The Missed Step: Italian-Americans and Brooklyn Politics," and Charles LaCerra, "Irish Politics, the Madison Club of Brooklyn, and John H. McCooey," both in Femminella, *Italians and Irish in America*, 191–92, 225–39. On Albany and Jersey City, see Dolan, *Irish Americans*, 254–55; and Erie, *Rainbow's End*, 132–33.

105. Lizabeth Cohen, *Making a New Deal: Industrial Workers in Chicago, 1919–1939* (New York: Cambridge University Press, 1990), 213–49; Bernstein, *Lean Years*, 296–98; and Stanley Lieberson, *A Piece of the Pie: Blacks and White Immigrants Since 1880* (Berkeley: University of California Press, 1980), 242–43.

106. "Form Bar Permit Party," *Chicago Tribune*, May 31, 1906, 5; Alex Gottfried, *Boss Cermak of Chicago: A Study of Political Leadership* (Seattle: University of Washington Press, 1962), 9–11, 367, 106; Anderson, *Creation of Democratic Majority*, 89–91; and Douglas Bukowski, *Big Bill Thompson, Chicago, and the Politics of Image* (Champaign: University of Illinois Press, 1998), 233. On the referenda strategy, see Gosnell, *Machine Politics*, 144–49.

107. Bukowski, *Big Bill Thompson*, 16, 29; and Carl Sandburg, *The Chicago Race Riots* (New York: Harcourt, Brace, & Howe, 1919), 2, quoted in William J. Tuttle, *Race Riot: Chicago in the Red Summer of 1919* (New York: Atheneum, 1972), 184.

108. Thomas A. Guglielmo, *White on Arrival: Italians, Race, Color, and Power in Chicago, 1890–1945* (New York: Oxford University Press, 2003), 100–101; *Chicago Tribune*, March 1, 1927, 1; ibid., April 4, 1927, 2; and *Chicago Herald Examiner*, March 27, 1927, 1, all quoted in Guglielmo, *White on Arrival*, 99, 98.

109. Allswang, *House for All Peoples*, 53, table III–1, 42; Guglielmo, *White on Arrival*, 104.

110. Gottfried, *Boss Cermak*, 177–80, 195.

111. Edward R. Kantowicz, *Polish-American Politics in Chicago, 1880–1940* (Chicago: University of Chicago Press, 1975), 209.

112. Allswang, *House for All Peoples*, 52–53, 224; Bukowski, *Big Bill Thompson*, 232; and *Dziennik Chicagoski*, April 3, 1931, 4, quoted in Kantowicz, *Polish-American Politics*, 152.

113. Allswang, *House for All Peoples*, 48, 51–52; and Anderson, *Creation of Democratic Majority*, 92. Cohen, *Making a New Deal,* stresses class issues and an ideological turn toward a "moral capitalism" in the New Deal. The industrial union drives undoubtedly facilitated the shift of immigrant industrial workers into the New Deal camp—and the construction of the city's new, interethnic coalition. On Chicago's huge proportion of first- and second-generation new immigrants, see Lieberson, *Piece of the Pie,* 58–9.

114. Allswang, *House for All Peoples*, 161, 106.
115. *Chicago Defender*, April 11, 1931, 1, quoted ibid., 162.
116. Harold F. Gosnell, *Negro Politicians: The Rise of Negro Politics in Chicago*, 2nd ed. (Chicago: University of Chicago Press, 1935), 133–34; Funchion, "Political and Nationalist Dimensions," 85–86; Bukowski, *Big Bill Thompson*, 250.
117. Erie, *Rainbow's End*, 126; and Roger Biles, *Big City Boss in Depression and War: Mayor Edward J. Kelly of Chicago* (DeKalb: Northern Illinois University Press, 1984), 135–37.
118. Allswang, *House for All Peoples*, 76–90; Erie, *Rainbow's End*, 126, 133–34, 137–38; and Gosnell, *Machine Politics*, 74–75.
119. Kantowicz, *Polish-American Politics*, 154–55.
120. Funchion, "Political and Nationalist Dimensions," 90; Dennis Clark, *Hibernia America: The Irish and Regional Cultures* (Westport, Conn.: Greenwood Press, 1986), 128.
121. David Carroll Cochran, "Ethnic Diversity and Democratic Stability: The Case of Irish Americans," *Political Science Quarterly* 110 (Winter 1995–96): 587–604.
122. Andrew M. Greeley, "Political Participation Among Ethnic Groups in the United States: A Preliminary Reconnaissance," *American Journal of Sociology* 80, no. 1 (1974): 170–204.
123. Moynihan, "Irish," 475.

CHAPTER 6: THE NATION

1. "Hours of Oration for Irish Freedom," *New York Times*, March 6, 1916, 4.
2. Garvey quoted in Colin Grant, *Negro with a Hat: The Rise and Fall of Marcus Garvey* (New York: Oxford University Press, 2008), 246.
3. "Cheering Negroes Hail Black Nation," *New York Times*, August 3, 1920, 7.
4. For the connections between Irish and African American nationalism, and an indication that some saw a common enemy in the British Empire, see Matthew Pratt Guterl, *The Color of Race in America, 1900–1940* (Cambridge, Mass.: Harvard University Press, 2001), 88–91.
5. Thomas N. Brown, *Irish-American Nationalism, 1870–1890* (Philadelphia: Lippincott Co., 1966), 21. See also Lawrence McCaffrey, ed., *Irish Nationalism and the American Contribution* (New York: Arno Press, 1976); Matthew Frye Jacobson, *Special Sorrows: The Diasporic Imagination of Irish, Polish, and Jewish Immigrants* (Berkeley: University of California Press, 2002), 28; and Declan Kiberd, *Inventing Ireland*. (London, 1995), 2, quoted in Alan O'Day, "Imagined Irish Communities Networks of Social Communication of the Irish Diaspora in the United States and Britain in the Late Nineteenth and Early Twentieth Centuries," *Immigrants and Minorities* 23 (July–November. 2005): 402. On the accentuation of Irish nationalist sentiment in American ethnic enclaves and the connection between old-world religious and new-world class grievances, see Brown, *Irish-American Nationalism*, 20, 63.
6. Patrick Ford to Michael Davitt, January 19, 1899, Trinity College Dublin, Davitt Papers, MS 9483/6741, quoted in O'Day, "Imagined Irish Communities," 401.
7. O'Day, "Imagined Irish Communities," 403–6; Kerby A. Miller, *Emigrants and Exiles: Ireland and the Irish Exodus to North America* (New York: Oxford University Press, 1985), 554; Timothy J. Meagher, *Inventing Irish America: Generation, Class, and Ethnic Identity in a New England City, 1880–1928* (Notre Dame, Ind.: University of Notre Dame Press, 2001), 271–73, 359; and David M. Emmons, *The Butte Irish: Class and Ethnicity in an American Mining Town, 1875–1925* (Urbana: University of Illinois Press, 1989), 317–28.
8. Howard Ralph Weisz, *Irish-American and Italian-American Educational Views and Activi-*

ties, 1870–1900: A Comparison (New York: Arno Press, 1976), 329–32; and Miller, *Emigrants and Exiles*, 534.

9. Miller, *Emigrants and Exiles*, 551–55; Kevin Kenny, *The American Irish: A History* (Harlow, U.K.: Longman, 2000), 176–79.

10. Finley Peter Dunne, "On the Philippines," in *Mr. Dooley in Peace and War* (Boston: Small, Maynard, 1899), 43, quoted in Jacobson, *Special Sorrows*, 178.

11. *Liberator*, December 6, 1839, quoted in Bruce Nelson, "'Come Out of Such a Land, You Irishmen': Daniel O'Connell, American Slavery, and the Making of the Irish Race," *Éire-Ireland* 42 (Spring–Summer 2007): 74. On the anti-imperial tradition in Irish history and Irish sympathy for colonial peoples, see Kerby A. Miller, "Re-Imagining Irish Revisionism," in Andrew Higgins Wyndham, ed., *Re-Imagining Ireland* (Charlottesville: University of Virginia Press, 2006), 234–40; Kerby A. Miller, "Epilogue: Re-Imagining Irish and Irish Migration History," in Kerby A. Miller, ed., *Ireland and Irish America: Culture, Class, and Transatlantic Migration* (Dublin: Field Day, 2008); Kevin Kenny, "Historiography," in Kevin Kenny, ed., *Ireland and the British Empire* (New York: Oxford University Press, 2004); and the essays in *Éire-Ireland* 42, nos. 1–2, (Spring–Summer 2007). My thanks to Kerby Miller for directing my attention to these sources.

12. Elizabeth Gurley Flynn, *The Rebel Girl: An Autobiography* (New York: International Publishers, 1973), 35.

13. David Noel Doyle, *Irish Americans, Native Rights, and National Empires: The Structure, Divisions, and Attitudes of the Catholic Minority in the Decade of Expansion* (New York: Arno Press, 1976), 271; Jacobson, *Special Sorrows*, 93.

14. Niall Whelehan, "Skirmishing, the *Irish World*, and Empire, 1876–86," *Éire-Ireland* 42, nos. 1–2 (Spring–Summer 2007): 180–200.

15. Doyle, *Irish Americans, Native Rights*, 271; Jacobson, *Special Sorrows*, 149, 154–55, 164–66, 171–72, 180, 214. See also Michael F. Funchion, "Irish Chicago: Church, Homeland, Politics, and Class—1870 to 1900," in Melvin G. Holli and Peter d'Alory Jones, eds., *Ethnic Chicago: A Multicultural Portrait*, 4th ed. (Grand Rapids, Mich.: Eerdmans, 1995), 89–90. On Roosevelt's notion of the army as a crucible for a new American race, see Gary Gerstle, *American Crucible: Race and Nation in the Twentieth Century* (Princeton, N.J.: Princeton University Press, 2001), 16–17, 27–28, 33–38, 44–50.

16. Jacobson, *Special Sorrows*, 142; Cockran quoted in Doyle, *Irish Americans, Native Rights*, 285; Flynn, *I Speak My Own Piece*, 22–24.

17. David Doyle, "Catholicism, Politics and Irish America, Since 1890: Some Critical Considerations," in P. J. Drudy, ed., *The Irish in America: Emigration, Assimilation, and Impact* (Cambridge, U.K.: Cambridge University Press, 1985), 209. See also Jacobson, *Special Sorrows*, passim.

18. Quoted in Jacobson, *Special Sorrows*, 179.

19. Quoted ibid., 205. On sympathy among black troops, often referred to as "Smoked Yankees," for the Filipino insurgents, see Willard Gatewood, *Black Americans and the White Man's Burden* (Urbana: University of Illinois Press, 1975), 180–221, especially 181–83. While the Irish reaction took its own distinctive form, Jacobson's work shows widespread opposition to imperialism among several immigrant communities.

20. John Higham, *Strangers in the Land: Patterns of American Nativism, 1860–1925* (New York: Atheneum, 1963), 80–87. On Anglo-Saxonism as the ideological basis for American imperialism, see Thomas F. Gossett, *Race: The History of an Idea in America* (Dallas: Southern Methodist University Press, 1963), 310–38.

21. Guterl, *Color of Race*, 79–80; and Matthew Frye Jacobson, *Barbarian Virtues: The United States Encounters Foreign People at Home and Abroad, 1876–1917* (New York: Hill & Wang, 2000), 191–93, 158–59, 259.

22. Guterl, *Color of Race*, 76.

23. See also Matthew Frye Jacobson, *Whiteness of a Different Color: European Immigrants and the Alchemy of Race* (Cambridge, Mass.: Harvard University Press, 1998), 208–9.

24. *Boston Pilot*, October 1, 1898, 4, quoted in Jacobson, *Whiteness of a Different Color*, 208.

25. Jacobson, *Special Sorrows*, 182–200, quote at 189.

26. Ibid., quote at 185.

27. Doyle, *Irish Americans, Native Rights*, 287–88.

28. *Boston Pilot*, March 21, 1898, 4, quoted in Jacobson, *Special Sorrows*, 192.

29. "Irish for the Boer Army," *Chicago Tribune*, January 1, 1900; "Denounce the Boer War," ibid., January 1, 1900; "Heard About Town," *New York Times*, January 31, 1900, 7; "Politics Around Chicago," ibid., February 25, 1900, 15; and Una Ni Bhromeil, "The South African War, Empire, and the *Irish World*, 1899–1902," in Simon J. Potter, ed., *Newspapers and Empire in Ireland and Britain: Reporting the Empire, 1857–1921* (Dublin: Four Courts, 2004), 195–216.

30. Jacobson, *Special Sorrows*, 182–85; Doyle, *Irish Americans, Native Rights*, 290–94, Desmond quoted at 290; and Jacobson, *Barbarian Virtues*, 256. Doyle notes that Desmond's views, liberal on many other subjects, evolved over time. He eventually supported some measure of Filipino rights and also antilynching legislation.

31. *Irish World and Industrial Liberator*, October 9, 1880, quoted in Eric Foner, "Class, Ethnicity, and Radicalism in the Gilded Age: The Land League and Irish-America," in Eric Foner, *Politics and Ideology in the Age of the Civil War* (New York: Oxford University Press, 1980), 160; and James Paul Rodechko, *Patrick Ford and His Search for America: A Case Study of Irish-American Journalism, 1870–1913* (New York: Arno Press, 1976), 27–37, 48–49.

32. Foner, "Land League and Irish-America," 168–77, quote at 176.

33. Ibid., quotes at 178–79; David Montgomery, "Racism, Immigrants, and Political Reform," *Journal of American History* 87 (March 2001): 1253–74; David Brundage, "Irish Land and American Workers: Class and Ethnicity in Denver Colorado," in Dirk Hoerder, ed., "*Struggle a Hard Battle*": Essays on Working-Class Immigrants (DeKalb: Northern Illinois University Press, 1986); David Brundage, *The Making of Western Radicalism: Denver's Organized Workers, 1878–1905* (Urbana: University of Illinois Press, 1994); and Emmons, *Butte Irish*.

34. Quoted in Foner, "Land League and Irish-America," 167.

35. *Irish Nation*, March 4, 11, 1882, quoted in Foner, "Land League and Irish-America," 167.

36. Rodechko, *Patrick Ford*, 156–82. See also Kenny, *American Irish*, 193.

37. David Brundage, "'In Time of Peace, Prepare for War': Key Themes in the Social Thought of New York's Irish Nationalists, 1890–1916," in Ronald H. Bayor and Timothy J. Meagher, eds., *The New York Irish* (Baltimore, Md.: Johns Hopkins University Press, 1996), 329.

38. Rodechko, *Patrick Ford*, 89–121, 156–82, 242, 263–65; Jacobson, *Special Sorrows*, 189; Whelehan, "Skirmishing, *The Irish World*, and Empire"; Ni Bhromeil, "South African War, Empire, and *The Irish World*."

39. Miller, *Emigrants and Exiles*, 448–50; Brundage, "'In Time of Peace, Prepare for War,'" 321–34.

40. Kevin Kenny, "American-Irish Nationalism," in J. J. Lee and Marion Casey, eds., *Making the Irish American* (New York: New York University Press, 2005), 289–293.

41. Brundage, "'In Time of Peace, Prepare for War,'" 328–32; Thomas N. Brown, "The Origins

and Character of Irish-American Nationalism," *Review of Politics* 18 (July 1956), quote at 337.

42. Guterl, *Color of Race*, 71, 73; "Hours of Oration for Irish Freedom," *New York Times*, March 6, 1916, 4.

43. "Dix Names Cohalan for Supreme Court," *New York Times*, May 19, 1911, 4; Michael Doorley, *Irish-American Diaspora Nationalism: The Friends of Irish Freedom, 1916–1935* (Dublin: Four Courts Press, 2005), 26–27; Guterl, *Color of Race*, 7, 71; Terry Golway, *Irish Rebel: John Devoy and America's Fight for Irish Freedom* (New York: St. Martin's Press, 1998), quote at 201.

44. Miller, *Emigrants and Exiles*, 448–50; Brundage, "'In Time of Peace, Prepare for War,'" 321–34; Golway, *Irish Rebel*.

45. *Irish World*, March 16, 1916; Doorley, *Irish-American Diaspora Nationalism*.

46. On the shift in Irish American opinion, see Joseph Edward Cuddy, *Irish-America and National Isolationism, 1914–1920* (New York: Arno Press, 1976), 107–11, Spring-Rice quoted at 111.

47. Kenny, "Irish Nationalism," 293–94; Miller, *Emigrants and Exiles*, 451–52, 458–59; Brundage, "'In Time of Peace, Prepare for War,'" 321; Kenny, *American Irish*, 193–96; Doorley, *Irish-American Diaspora Nationalism* 90, table 8, 188.

48. Elizabeth McKillen, *Chicago Labor and the Quest for a Democratic Diplomacy, 1914–1924* (Ithaca, N.Y.: Cornell University Press, 1995), 140–45; and Elizabeth McKillen, "American Labor, the Irish Revolution, and the Campaign for a Boycott of British Goods: 1916–1924," *Radical History Review* 61 (1995): 35–61. On the movement for a boycott of British goods in the United States and its connections to the Indian movement, see Michael E. Chapman, "'How to Smash the British Empire': John Forest Kelly's *Irish World* and the Boycott of 1920–1921," *Éire-Ireland* 43 (Fall–Winter) 2008: 217–52; Guterl, *Color of Race*, 35, 37, 68–99.

49. Madison Grant, *The Passing of the Great Race: Or, the Racial Basis of European History* (New York: Charles Scribner's Sons, 1916); Gossett, *Race*, 360–61; *Proceedings of the Irish Race Convention Which Met in Dublin* (Dublin: Irish National Federation, 1896); "The Convention of the Irish Race," *Times*, London, September 2, 1896, 7; and "For a Union Irish Party," *New York Times*, September 2, 1896, 4. For the shift in racist thinking regarding the Irish, see Guterl, *Color of Race*, 35, 37, 68–99.

50. Jacobson, *Whiteness of a Different Color*, 51–52.

51. Luke Gibbons, "Race Against Time: Racial Discourse and Irish History," in Luke Gibbons, *Transformations in Irish Culture* (Notre Dame, Ind.: Notre Dame University Press, 1996), 149–63, quote at 15.

52. Guterl, *Color of Race*, 84–86; Jason Kinrick, "The Dominion of Ireland: The Anglo-Irish Treaty in an Imperial Context," *Éire-Ireland* 42, no. 1–2 (Spring–Summer 2007), 241.

53. "Report, Freedom for India March, March 1–13, 1920," 29, "Miscellaneous," 88, *U.S. Military Intelligence Reports: Surveillance of Radicals in the United States, 1917–1941*, microfilm ed. (Frederick, Md.: University Publications of America, 1984), Reel 16; Guterl, *Color of Race*, 94–95; Éamon de Valera, *India and Ireland* (New York: Friends of Freedom for India, 1920).

54. Brundage, "'In Time of Peace, Prepare for War,'" 325–26; and Kenny, *American Irish*, 192–99. On the importance of ethnic nationalism in eastern European working-class communities, see Victor Greene, *For God and Country: The Rise of Polish and Lithuanian Ethnic Consciousness in America, 1860–1910* (Madison: University of Wisconsin Press, 1975), chaps.

7–9; Doorley, *Friends of Irish Freedom*, 170–73; David Montgomery, "Nationalism, American Patriotism, and Class Consciousness Among Immigrant Workers in the United States in the Epoch of World War One," in Hoerder, "*Struggle a Hard Battle,*" 327–51; and Jacobson, *Special Sorrows*, passim. On black nationalism in these years, see Minkah Makalani, *For the Liberation of Black People Everywhere: The African Blood Brotherhood, Black Radicalism, and Pan-African Liberation in the New Negro Movement*, Ph.D. diss., University of Illinois at Urbana-Champaign, 2004; Grant, *Negro with a Hat;* and Judith Stein, *The World of Marcus Garvey: Race and Class in Modern Society* (Baton Rouge: Louisiana State University Press, 1986). On comparisons and contacts between Irish, African, Polish, and other American ethnic nationalists, see Joe Doyle, "Striking for Ireland on the New York Docks," in Bayor and Meagher, *New York Irish*, 357–73; Guterl, *Color of Race*, passim, 88–91; McKillen, *Chicago Labor and the Quest for a Democratic Diplomacy*, 19–55; and Jacobson, *Shared Sorrows*, 66–68, 78–82, 205–7, 221–32.

55. Bruce Nelson, "Irish Americans, Irish Nationalism, and the 'Social' Question, 1916–1923," *boundary 2* , no. 1 (2004): 151–52; Conor Kostick, *Revolution in Ireland: Popular Militancy, 1917–1923* (London: Pluto Press, 1997), 149, 163, 179, 182; and J. J. Lee, *Ireland, 1912–1985: A Social and Political History* (Cambridge, U.K.: Cambridge University Press, 1989), 38–41. On the transnational character of wartime Irish American nationalism, see McKillen, "American Labor, the Irish Revolution," 35–61; and McKillen, "Ethnicity, Class, and Wilsonian Internationalism Reconsidered: The Mexican-American and Irish-American Immigrant Left and U.S. Foreign Relations: 1914–1924," *Diplomatic History* 25 (2001): 553–87.

56. Cuddy, *Irish-America and National Isolationism*, 40–41, 54–56, quote at 41; Russell A. Kazal, *Becoming Old Stock: The Paradox of German-American Identity* (Princeton, N.J.: Princeton University Press, 2004), 160; and Doorley, *Irish-American Diaspora Nationalism*, 34–36. On meetings of German and Irish American communities in opposition to American entry, see *Irish World,* February 10, 1917, 2; ibid., February 17, 1917, 3; Francis M. Carroll, *American Opinion and the Irish Question, 1910–1923: A Study in Opinion and Policy* (Dublin: Gill & Macmillan, 1978), 94–95; and McKillen, *Chicago Labor and the Quest for a Democratic Diplomacy*, 27–32.

57. Robert Lansing, *The Peace Negotiations: A Personal Perspective* (Boston: Houghton Mifflin, 1921), 98, quoted in Cuddy, *Irish-America and National Isolationism*, 169.

58. Francis M. Carroll, "Irish Progressive League," in Michael Funchion, ed., *Irish American Voluntary Organizations* (Westport, Conn.: Greenwood Press, 1983), 207–10.

59. Carroll, "Irish Progressive League"; Nelson, "Irish Americans, Irish Nationalism, and the Social Question," quote at 164; Doorley, *Irish-American Diaspora Nationalism*, 71–72.

60. C. Desmond Greaves, *Liam Mellows and the Irish Revolution* (London: Lawrence & Wishart, 1971), 131–32, 150. For similar Socialist Party results in fourteen other cities, see McKillen, *Chicago Labor and the Quest for a Democratic Diplomacy*, 11.

61. On Mitchel's downfall, see John F. McClymer, "Of 'Mornin' Glories' and 'Fine Old Oaks': John Purroy Mitchel, Al Smith, and Reform as an Expression of Irish-American Aspiration," in Bayor and Meagher, *New York Irish*, 374–94.

62. "Irish Here Address Appeal to Wilson," *New York Times,* May 19, 1918, 19; and Greaves, *Liam Mellows*, passim.

63. Cuddy, *Irish-America and National Isolationism*, 144–46; McKeown, *War and Welfare*, passim, quote at 49.

64. Thomas J. Shelley, "Twentieth Century American Catholicism and Irish Americans," in Lee and Casey, eds., *Making the Irish American*, 585; Thomas J. Rowland, "Irish American

Catholics and the Quest for Respectability in the Coming of the Great War, 1900–1917,"
Journal of American Ethnic History 15, no. 2 (Winter 1996): 3–32; and Nancy Gentile Ford,
Americans All! Foreign-born Soldiers in World War I (College Station: Texas A&M Press,
2001), 20–22.

65. John Patrick Buckley, *The New York Irish: Their View of American Foreign Policy, 1914–1921,*
Ph.D. diss., New York University, 1974, 161; Greaves, *Liam Mellows*, 159–60.

66. Greaves, *Liam Mellows*, 160, 162; Buckley, "New York Irish," 149, 163, 179, 182; Gerstle,
American Crucible, 93; Report of Agent R. R. Evans, "Re: Cornelius Lehane, Socialist and
Labor Agitator, New Haven, CT, March 21, 1918"; "Re: Cornelius Lehane, Socialist Activ-
ity, Ansonia, CT, March 23, 1918"; and Edmund Leigh, U.S. Military Intelligence, to Chief,
U.S. Military Intelligence, March 28, 1918, *U.S. Military Intelligence Reports*, Reel 9. My
thanks to Tom Mackaman for this reference.

67. Richard Slotkin, *Lost Battalions: The Great War and the Crisis of American Nationality* (New
York: Henry Holt & Co., 2005), 7; Julius Adler, *History of the Seventy-seventh Division*
(New York: W. H. Cranfer Co. for the Seventy-seventh Division Assoc., 1919), quote at 8.

68. David M. Kennedy, *Over Here: The First World War and American Society* (New York: Oxford University Press, 1980), 158; Roosevelt quoted in Gerstle, *American Crucible*, 84

69. Anne Nichols, *Abie's Irish Rose: A Novel* (New York: Grosset & Dunlap, 1927), 103, 47. On
the theme of ethnic integration in the war films, see Slotkin, *Lost Battalions*.

70. Jennifer D. Keene, *Doughboys, the Great War, and the Remaking of America* (Baltimore, Md.:
Johns Hopkins University Press, 2001), quote at 94; and Arthur E. Barbeau and Florette
Henri, *The Unknown Soldiers* (Philadelphia: Temple University Press, 1974), 41.

71. Slotkin, *Lost Battalions*, 105, 553.

72. Cuddy, *Irish-America and National Isolationism*, 144. For contrasting impressions of relations between Irish and Jewish soldiers, see Francis P. Duffy, *Father Duffy's Story* (New
York: George H. Doran, 1919), 106, 379; and Slotkin, *Lost Battalions*, 104–6. Blaustein might
well have been a prototype for the lone Jewish soldier in the film *The Fighting 69th* who
becomes accepted by passing for the quintessential American soldier—that is, an Irishman.

73. Jonathan H. Ebel, *Faith in the Fight: Religion and the American Soldier in the Great War*
(Princeton, N.J.: Princeton University Press, 2010), 5, 23.

74. James J. Cooke, *The Rainbow Division in the Great War, 1917–1919* (Westport, Conn.: Praeger, 1994), 15; Albert M. Ettinger and A. Churchill Ettinger, *A Doughboy with the Fighting Sixty-ninth: A Remembrance of World War I* (Shippensburg, Penn.: White Main,
1992), 7–8, 254–55, quote at 7. On the history of the Fifteenth New York and its troubles in
South Carolina, see Ettinger, *Doughboy with the Fighting Sixty-ninth*, 240–41. On the
situation of black troops generally, see Florette Henri, *Bitter Victory: A History of Black
Soldiers in World War I* (Garden City, N.Y.: Doubleday, 1970); and Kennedy, *Over Here*,
158–62.

75. John J. Pershing, *My Experiences in the World War* (New York, Frederick A. Stokes Co.,
1931), 1:316, quoted in Cooke, *Rainbow Division*, 41.

76. Philip S. Foner, *History of the Labor Movement in the United States*, vol. 3: *The Policies
and Practices of the American Federation of Labor, 1900–1909* (New York: International Pub-
lishers, 1973), 161–73; Eric Hirsch, *Urban Revolt: Ethnic Politics in the Nineteenth-Century
Chicago Labor Movement* (Berkeley: University of California Press, 1990); Bruce C. Nelson,
Beyond the Martyrs: A Social History of Chicago's Anarchists, 1870–1900 (New Brunswick,
N.J.: Rutgers University Press, 1988); and James Green, *Death in the Haymarket: A Story of*

Chicago, the First Labor Movement and the Bombing That Divided Gilded Age America (New York: Pantheon Books, 2006).

77. Hutchins Hapgood, *The Spirit of Labor* (1907; reprint Urbana: University of Illinois Press, 2004), 293–322, 403–7.

78. John Keiser, *John Fitzpatrick and Progressive Unionism, 1915–1925*, Ph.D. diss., Northwestern University, 1965, 30–32.

79. McKillen, *Chicago Labor and the Quest for a Democratic Diplomacy*, 4.

80. Frank Walsh to John Fitzpatrick, February 11, 1921; "Suppression of Free Speech on the South Side in Chicago" (1920?); Milton Webster to John Fitzpatrick, January 26, 1928; and other materials in Box 25, John Fitzpatrick Papers, Chicago History Museum.

81. David Montgomery, *Workers' Control in America: Studies in the History of Work, Technology, and Labor Struggles* (Cambridge, U.K.: Cambridge University Press, 1979), 93–101; David Montgomery, "Immigrants, Industrial Unions, and Social Reconstruction in the United States, 1916–1923," *Labour/Le Travail* 13 (Spring 1984): 104–9; and Thomas Mackaman, *The Foreign Element: New Immigrants and American Industry, 1914–1924*, Ph.D. diss., University of Illinois at Urbana-Champaign, 2009. On the movement in meatpacking, see James R. Barrett, *Work and Community in the Jungle: Chicago's Packinghouse Workers, 1894–1922* (Urbana: University of Illinois Press, 1987); and Rick Halpern, *Down on the Killing Floor: Black and White Workers in Chicago's Packinghouses, 1904–1954* (Urbana: University of Illinois Press, 1997).

82. David Brody, *Steelworkers in America, the Non-Union Era* (New York: Harper Torchbooks, 1969), 214–78; William Z. Foster, *The Great Steel Strike* (New York: B. W. Huebsch, 1920); James R. Barrett, *William Z. Foster and the Tragedy of American Radicalism* (Urbana: University of Illinois Press, 2000), 81–101; and Mackaman, *Foreign Element.*

83. McKillen, *Chicago Labor and the Quest for a Democratic Diplomacy*, 130–36; James R. Barrett, "Ethnic and Racial Fragmentation: Toward a Reinterpretation of a Local Labor Movement," in Joe W. Trotter, Earl Lewis, and Tera Hunter, eds., *The African American Urban Experience: Perspectives from the Colonial Period to the Present* (New York: Palgrave, 2004), 294–300; Keiser, *John Fitzpatrick*, 143–61; and Andrew Strouthous, *U.S. Labor and Political Action, 1918–1924* (New York: St. Martin's Press, 2000).

84. L. A. O'Donnell, *Irish Voice and Organized Labor: A Biographical Study* (Westport, Conn.: Greenwood Press, 1997), 143–61; McKillen, *Chicago Labor and the Quest for a Democratic Diplomacy*, 140–46, 162, 214; and Elizabeth McKillen, "Hybrid Visions: Working-Class Internationalism in the Mexican Borderlands, Seattle, and Chicago, 1910–1920," *Labor: Studies in Working-Class History of the Americas* 2 (1995): 77–107, especially 91–92, 101.

85. Emmons, *Butte Irish;* and David M. Emmons, "Faction Fights: The Irish Worlds of Butte, Montana, 1875–1917," in Patrick O'Sullivan, ed., *The Irish in the New Communities* (Leicester, U.K.: Leicester University Press, 1992), 2:82–98, quote at 87.

86. Emmons, *Butte Irish*, 340–97.

87. Emmons, "Faction Fights," 2:88–98, quote at 88.

88. Stephen Norwood, *Labor's Flaming Youth: Telephone Operators and Labor Militancy, 1878–1923* (Urbana: University of Illinois Press, 1990), 243; and Emmet Larkin, *James Larkin: Irish Labour Leader, 1876–1947* (Cambridge, Mass.: MIT Press, 1965), 244.

89. Damien Murray, "'Go Forth as a Missionary to Fight it': Catholic Antisocialism and Irish American Nationalism in Post–World War I Boston," *Journal of American Ethnic History* 28 (Summer 2009): 1–23.

90. *New York Sun*, August 28, 1920, 1, quoted in Bruce Nelson, *Divided We Stand: American Workers and the Struggle for Black Equality* (Princeton, N.J.: Princeton University Press, 2001), 71; Chapman, "'How to Smash the British Empire,'" 235–37.

91. Joe Doyle, "Striking for Ireland on the New York Docks," in Bayor and Meagher, *New York Irish*, 357–73; Nelson, *Divided We Stand*, 30–45, quotes at 37–38; Nelson, "Irish Americans, Irish Nationalism," 171–75; "Are You a Friend of Ireland? Mayor MacSwiney is Dead" (1920), Chicago Friends of Irish Freedom, broadside, Chicago History Museum. The following year Irish American labor activists failed to persuade the 1921 AFL convention to call a boycott against all British goods in protest of Birish violence and abuse of political prisoners during the Irish War of Independence. See Sam Evans to Walsh, "Supplemental Report on the Trip to Forty-First Annual Convention of the AFL," Denver, Colo., June 12–25, 1921; "Resolution on the Irish Question Adopted by the 41st Annual Convention of the AF of L on June 22, 1921"; Thomas J. O'Flaherty, Irish American Labor League (NYC), to Frank Walsh, June 24, 1921; all in Box 26, Frank Walsh Papers, New York Public Library.

92. Cyril V. Briggs, "Heroic Ireland," *Crusader* 4 (February 1921): 5, quoted in Nelson, "Irish Americans, Irish Nationalism," 149.

93. See Guterl, *Color of Race*, 91–95. On the Irish influence on Garvey, see Jeffrey B. Perry, *Hubert Harrison: The Voice of Harlem Radicalism, 1883–1918* (New York: Columbia University Press, 2009), 338, 489n30; and Grant, *Negro with a Hat*, 173–74, 197–98. It is possible to overstate the significance of these connections. African Blood Brotherhood leaders held up the Irish Republican Brotherhood as a kind of model, but there is no evidence that the latter shaped the political program of the former, which emphasized social class as well as racial oppression and soon entered the Workers' (Communist) Party. Some on the left wing of the Irish nationalist movement sustained a similar political trajectory. See Makalani, *For the Liberation of Black People Everywhere*, 104–5.

94. Perry, *Hubert Harrison*, 266, 312, 487–88n16, 286, 325, 298; Harrison quoted at 287. See also Harrison's writings: "The Drift in Politics," *Voice*, July 25, 1917; "The New Policies for the New Negro," *Voice*, September 4, 1917; "Declaration of Principles [of the Liberty League]," *Voice*, September 1, 1917; "Race First, a Negro for President," *Negro World* 8 (June 1920); "The Cracker in the Caribbean" (c. 1920); all reproduced in Jeffrey B. Perry, ed., *A Hubert Harrison Reader* (Middletown, Conn.: Wesleyan University Press, 2001), 90, 92, 139, 140, 148, 237.

95. Guterl, *Color of Race*, 94.

96. Sean O'Casey joined a long queue of Irish literary exiles and ended his days in London. On the Irish Renaissance, see Richard Falls, *The Irish Renaissance* (Syracuse, N.Y.: Syracuse University Press, 1977); and Tracy Mishkin, *The Harlem and Irish Renaissances: Language, Identity, and Representation* (Gainesville: University of Florida Press, 1998). The Irish Renaissance had a considerable impact on Irish American writers between the 1890s and the 1920s. See Charles Fanning, *The Irish Voice in America: 250 Years of Irish American Fiction* (Lexington: University Press of Kentucky, 2000), 167–76.

97. Guterl, *Color of Race*, n. 48, 208; and Mishkin, *Harlem and Irish Renaissances*, 12–20.

98. Alain Locke, "The New Negro," in Alain Locke, ed, *The New Negro: An Interpretation* (New York: Albert & Charles Boni, 1925), 7.

99. Ernest Gellner, *Nations and Nationalism* (Ithaca, N.Y.: Cornell University Press, 1983), 57.

100. Mishkin, *Harlem and Irish Renaissances*, 90–101. For the use of dialect for similar aesthetic and political purposes and for a discussion of similarities between certain Irish and Afri-

can American dialects, see Brian Gallagher, "About Us, For Us, Near Us: The Irish and Harlem Renaissances," *Éire-Ireland* 16, no. 4 (Winter 1981): 15–26.

101. Quoted in Herbert Aptheker, "Introduction," in W. E. B. DuBois, *The Gift of Black Folk: The Negroes in the Making of America* (1924; reprint Millwood, N.Y.: Kraus-Thomson, 1975), 5.

102. Guterl, *Color of Race*, 97.

103. W. E. B. DuBois to D. J. Bustin, March 30, 1921, W. E. B. DuBois Papers, University of Massachusetts Library, Amherst; Cyril Briggs, "Our Lone Monopoly," *Crusader* (March 1920), 8; both quoted in Guterl, *Color of Race*, 97, 98.

104. Higham, *Strangers in the Land*, 123–24; and Thomas F. Gossett, *Race: The History of an Idea in America* (New York: Oxford University Press, 1997), 442. On the Klan's anti-Catholicism and the church's opposition in the context of 1920s intolerance, see Jay P. Dolan, *In Search of American Catholicism: A History of Religion and Culture in Tension* (New York: Oxford University Press, 2002), 134–36. On the use of the immigration restriction issue to mobilize immigrant support, see James J. Connolly, *The Triumph of Ethnic Progressivism: Urban Political Culture in Boston, 1900–1925* (Cambridge, Mass.: Harvard University Press, 1998), 141, 174, 175; Jack Beatty, *The Rascal King: The Life and Times of James Michael Curley, 1874–1958* (Reading, Mass.: Addison-Wesley, 1992), 132–36, 143–44; and Funchion, "Irish Chicago," 88.

105. Kenneth Jackson, *The Ku Klux Klan in the City, 1915–1930* (New York: Oxford University Press, 1967), 175–80. On the rise of the Klan nationally, see Higham, *Strangers in the Land*, 286–99. On its efforts in smaller industrial towns with large Catholic populations, see Meagher, *Inventing Irish America*, 306–13; and William D. Jenkins, *Steel Valley Klan: The Ku Klux Klan in Ohio's Mahoning Valley* (Kent, Ohio: Kent State University Press, 1990).

106. Jackson, *Klan in the City*, 93–102, 108, 117, 125–26, quote at 93; David Craine, "The Klan Moves North," *Chicago History* 34, no. 3 (Fall 2006): 4–25; "Here's a Close Up on the Ku Klux Klan," *Chicago Tribune*, August 20, 1922, 1, 3; "Supposed K.K.K. Move in Schools Brings Inquiry," ibid., November 26, 1922, 3. See also Thomas Lee Philpott, *The Slum and the Ghetto: Neighborhood Deterioration and Middle-Class Reform, Chicago, 1880–1930* (New York: Oxford University Press, 1978), 188–89.

107. Jackson, *Klan in the City*, 102–7, 117, quote at 104; *Dawn*, May 12, 1923, quoted in Jackson, *Klan in the City*, 104; and Philpott, *Slum and Ghetto*, 190.

108. "Dunne Out to Pull Teeth of Ku Klux Klan," *Chicago Tribune*, September 15, 1921, 1; ibid., December 5, 1921, 1; ibid., January 22, 1923, 1; "Aid for Ku Klux Firemen Traced to Ald. Garner," ibid., January 6, 1923, 5; "Bills Aimed at Klansmen Who Hold State Jobs," ibid., January 18, 1923, 7; "Busch Orders 2 'Klan' Firemen Be Reinstated," ibid., May 4, 1923, 13.

109. Jackson, *Klan in the City*, 107–26; "All But Two Lundin Aldermen Put into Discard," *Chicago Daily Tribune*, April 4, 1923, 1. On Boston, see Beatty, *Rascal King*, 241–45.

110. Philpott, *Slum and Ghetto*, 190.

111. Higham, *Strangers in the Land*, 123–24.

112. Sharon Leon, "Our Immigration Problem: U.S. Catholic Response to U.S. Immigration Restriction, 1915–1930," unpublished paper, University of Minnesota, 1998. My thanks to Dr. Leon for sharing her work.

113. Gerstle, *American Crucible*, 95.

114. Rt. Rev. Edmund F. Gibbons, D.D., "Review of the Work of the N.C.W.C. Legal Depart-

ment," *N.C.W.C. Bulletin* (October 1926): 15, quoted in Leon, "Our Immigration Problem," 18.

115. Arthur Sears Henning, "Aliens Demand Entry; Senate Says 'Come In!'" *Chicago Tribune,* February 7, 1921, 5.

116. Desmond King, *Making Americans: Immigration, Race, and the Origins of the Diverse Democracy* (Cambridge, Mass.: Harvard University Press, 2000), 210–11, 219–23; Roger Daniels, *Guarding the Golden Door: American Immigration Policy and Immigrants Since 1882* (New York: Hill & Wang, 2004), 48–58; and Mae M. Ngai, *Impossible Subjects: Illegal Aliens and the Making of Modern America* (Princeton, N.J.: Princeton University Press, 2004), 21–29. On opposition to the act and the resulting emergence of a broader immigrant identity, see Emily Pope-Obeda, unpublished seminar paper, University of Illinois at Urbana-Champaign, 2010.

117. *Congressional Register,* April 5, 1924, 5627, quoted in Gerstle, *American Crucible,* at 117.

118. On civic identity, see Rogers M. Smith, *Civic Ideals: Conflicting Visions of Citizenship in U.S. History* (New Haven, Conn.: Yale University Press, 1997).

119. Connolly, *Triumph of Ethnic Progressivism,* 133–60.

120. Christopher J. Kauffman, *Patriotism and Fraternalism in the Knights of Columbus: A History of the Fourth Degree* (New York: Crossroad Publishing, 2001), 3.

121. Christopher J. Kauffman, *Faith and Fraternalism: The History of the Knights of Columbus, 1882–1982* (New York: Harper & Row, 1982), 262–67, 273–78; Aptheker, "Introduction," 7–9. Besides the DuBois volume, the series included Frederick Franklin Schrader, *The Germans in the Making of America* (Boston: Stratford Co., 1924), and George Cohen, *The Jews in the Making of America* (Boston: Stratford Co., 1924). McSweeney's introduction, "The Racial Contributions to the United States," appeared in each volume. On McSweeney's attack on Anglo-Saxonism and the Knights' notion of equality of all racial and ethnic groups, see Knights of Columbus Historical Commission, *Bulletin Number One* (New York, 1921); Christopher J. Kauffman, "Edward McSweeney, the Knights of Columbus, and the Irish-American Response to Anglo-Saxonism, 1900–1925," *American Catholic Studies* 114, no. 4 (2003): 51–65.

122. Michael Kazin, *The Populist Persuasion: An American History* (New York: Basic Books, 1995), 112. See John T. McGreevy, "Thinking on One's Own: Catholicism in the American Intellectual Imagination, 1928–1960," *Journal of American History* 84 (June 1997): 97–131.

123. James McGurrin, *Bourke Cockran: A Free Lance in American Politics* (New York: Arno Press, 1972). On Cockran's close contact with his Manhattan constituents and Tammany, see for example, Cockran to Charles F. Murphy, July 20, 1904, regarding help for Mr. O'Brien; and Thomas F. Smith to Cockran, June 27, 1921; on his advocacy of church interests, see D. Falconio, Apostolic Delegate, to Cockran, February 21, 1908; Archbishop Corrigan of New York to Cockran, May 21, 1921, all in Box 4, Congressional Correspondence, 1908–1924, William Bourke Cockran Papers, Special Collections, New York Public Library. For his opposition to U.S. policy in the Philippines and Cuba, see his correspondence with the Anti-Imperialist League and Patrick Ford in Box 1. On his support for free and open immigration; his campaign for recognition of the Armenian genocide; his support of the Boer cause, Irish independence, and woman suffrage; and his frequent objections to socialism, see his speeches in Boxes 11 and 12. When the Illinois politician Adlai E. Stevenson asked Winston Churchill on whom he had based his own oratorical style, he was surprised when Churchill said it was Cockran.

EPILOGUE

1. Chris McNickle, *To Be Mayor of New York: Ethnic Politics in the City* (New York: Columbia University Press, 1993), 53–57, 61–67, 82–84; and George Walsh, *Public Enemies: The Mayor, the Mob, and the Crime that Was* (New York: Norton, 1980).

2. McNickle, *To Be Mayor of New York*; and Paul O'Dwyer, *Counsel for the Defense: The Autobiography of Paul O'Dwyer* (New York: Simon & Schuster, 1979). On the Catholic Left, see Charles A. Meconis, *With Clumsy Grace: The American Catholic Left, 1961–1975* (New York: Seabury Press, 1979).

3. John Field, *Social Capital* (New York: Routledge, 2003), 1.

4. Bourdieu, "Forms of Capital," in John G. Richardson, ed., *Handbook of Theory and Research for the Sociology of Education* (New York: Greenwood Press, 1986), 249.

5. On Bourdieu's use of the concept to explain elite power and influence, see ibid., 251–52. See also Pierre Bordieu, *Distinction: A Social Critique of the Judgment of Taste*, trans. Richard Nice (Cambridge, Mass.: Harvard University Press, 1984); and J. R. Fedderke, R. de Kadt, and J. Luiz, "Economic Growth and Social Capital: A Critical Reflection," *Theory and Society* 28 (2001): 709–45. On the significance of networks in the migration process, see Charles Tilly, "Transplanted Networks," in Virginia Yans-McLaughlin, ed., *Immigration Reconsidered: History, Sociology, and Politics* (New York: Oxford University Press, 1990), 79–95.

6. On "bonding social capital," see Robert D. Putnam, *Bowling Alone: The Collapse and Revival of American Community* (New York: Simon & Schuster, 2000), 22–24 and passim; Jan Nederveen Pieterse, "Social Capital and Migration: Beyond Ethnic Economies," in Sarah A. Radcliffe, ed., *Culture and Development in a Globalizing World: Geographies, Actors and Paradigms* (London: Routledge, 2006), 126–49; and Dennis Clark, "The Irish Ethic and Spirit of Patronage," in Scott Cummings, ed., *Self-Help in Urban America: Patterns of Minority Business Enterprise* (Port Washington, N.Y.: Kennikat Press, 1980).

7. Quoted in Rudolf Glanz, *Jew and Irish: Historic Group Relations and Immigration* (New York: Waldon Press, 1966), 92.

8. Nelson Algren, *Never Come Morning* (New York: Four Walls Eight Windows, 1987), 127–28. Thanks to Dave Roediger for this quote.

9. Such networks and the institutions that grew from them were of great significance throughout the Irish Catholic diaspora. See Enda Delaney and Donald M. MacRaild, "Irish Immigration, Networks and Ethnic Identities Since 1750: An Introduction," *Immigrants and Minorities* 23, nos. 2–3 (July–November 2005): 127–42; and the other studies on Irish immigrants and social networks in Wales, England, Australia, New Zealand, Canada, Spain, and the northern and southern United States in this special issue of the journal.

10. Field, *Social Capital*, 3; Alejandro Portes, "The Dark Side of Social Capital," *American Prospect* 26 (1996): 18–21, 94.

11. Gary Gerstle, *American Crucible: Race and Nation in the Twentieth Century* (Princeton, N.J.: Princeton University Press, 2001). See also Rogers M. Smith, *Civic Ideals: Conflicting Visions of Citizenship in U.S. History* (New Haven, Conn.: Yale University Press, 1997).

12. Obituary, *New York Times*, June 25, 1998.

13. On "bridging social capital," see Putnam, *Bowling Alone*, and Pieterse, "Social Capital and Migration."

14. Bronwen Walter, *Outsiders Inside: Whiteness, Place, and Irish Women* (New York: Routledge, 2000). On the low status of many new immigrant groups in the racial hierarchy, see Mat-

thew Guterl, *The Color of Race in America, 1900–1940* (Cambridge, Mass.: Harvard University Press, 2001); Matthew Jacobson, *Whiteness of a Different Color: European Immigrants and the Alchemy of Race* (Cambridge, Mass.: Harvard University Press, 1998); James R. Barrett and David R. Roediger, "In Between Peoples: Race, Nationality, and the 'New Immigrant' Working Class," *Journal of American Ethnic History* 16 (1997): 3–44; and David R. Roediger, *Working Toward Whiteness: How America's Immigrants Became White: The Strange Journey from Ellis Island to the Suburbs* (New York: Basic Books, 2005). On the questionable racial status of the Irish in the nineteenth century, see David R. Roediger, *The Wages of Whiteness: Race and the Making of the American Working Class* (London: Verso, 1991).

15. Philip Kasinitz, "Race, Assimilation, and the 'Second Generations,' Past and Present," in Nancy Foner and George Fredrickson, eds., *Not Just Black and White: Historical and Contemporary Perspectives on Immigration, Race, and Ethnicity in the United States* (New York: Russell Sage Foundation, 2004), 281.

16. Nathan Glazer and Daniel Patrick Moynihan, *Beyond the Melting Pot: Irish, Jews, and Puerto Ricans in New York City* (Cambridge, Mass.: MIT Press, 1970), v.

17. Andrew M. Greeley, *The Irish Americans: The Rise to Money and Power* (New York: Harper & Row, 1981), 111. See also Marjorie R. Fallows, *Irish Americans: Identity and Assimilation* (Edgewood, New Jersey: Prentice Hall, 1979), 103–106.

LIST OF ILLUSTRATIONS

INDEX

Page numbers in *italics* refer to llustration captions.